THE LOST VILLAGES OF ENGLAND

THE LOST VILLAGES OF ENGLAND

MAURICE BERESFORD

ALAN SUTTON
1983

Alan Sutton Publishing Limited
17a Brunswick Road
Gloucester GL1 1HG

First published by Lutterworth Press 1954
This edition published 1983

ISBN 0-86299-108-0

Printed and bound in Great Britain

TO MY FRIENDS
WHO HAVE WALKED
AND DUG WITH ME

Author's Preface and Acknowledgements

The genesis of this book and the progress of the investigation are described in Chapter Eight and its general scope summarised in the Introduction. Decisions about presentation cannot hope to please all readers, and an author can only explain what advantages his own particular method seemed to him to carry with it.

The first Part of the book is descriptive of lost village sites as seen by the author in his field-work, by contemporaries while the desertions were still novel and by royal investigators while the State inquiries were in progress. In the second Part the chronology, causes and distribution of lost sites are arbitrarily separated into three chapters of an analytical character, but the narrative returns to the first person in Part Three with an impressionistic account of some of the sites visited in the course of the investigation. The last Part begins with a long account of the documentary sources useful in such inquiries with frequent quotation from unprinted manuscripts. The final chapter is in the form of a county gazetteer of the principal sites which have been noted, very brief notes on the history of the individual sites and a map reference if the site is known or suspected.

Readers who are not concerned with the detailed historical argument will probably find that Chapters Four and Nine can be omitted at first reading. Chapters Nine and Ten are designed to help those who wish to carry forward further local inquiries in their own counties.

I have ventured to segregate the notes at the end of the book (pp. 419–32) together with some of the statistical tables and the longer quotations from documents. A short bibliography of the principal printed works used is given, but those who wish for a full bibliography will find it supplied by the notes and the account of documentary sources which occupies all Chapter Nine. Except for odd phrases, I have translated all Latin quotations. Spelling has been modernised in all quotations from printed works: in quotations from unpublished documents the original spelling has been preserved except in cases of repetition and instances where the old spelling would confuse a reader.

I have expressed my principal obligation in my dedication, and I should like to rescue from that collective anonymity two friends who shared many explorations: Peter Ransom in the Midlands and Keith Allison in the North; and three other friends who cheerfully acted as chauffeur: Mrs. E.H. Rudkin, Philip Sheard and Clive Semple. The early stages of the work were much expedited by the example and encouragement of Dr. W.G. Hoskins and by discussions with Professor Postan, Mr. John Saltmarsh and Dr. Steensberg. The later stages profited from discussions with Professor Carus-Wilson and Mr. Lawrence Stone. In Germany Professor Mortensen of Göttingen introduced me to the continental type of site and in England Mr. John Hurst, an Assistant Inspector of Ancient Monuments, introduced me to the discipline of archaeological digging. Work that has lain so much in local archives and libraries has placed me much in debt with their officers, particularly at the Public Record Office and the Royal Air Force Print Library. The care and skill of successive cartographers of the Ordnance Survey have produced a set of maps indispensable in this branch of study, and the Archaeological Officer, Mr. C.W. Phillips, kindly afforded me facilities to work through sets of 6-inch maps inaccessible in northern libraries. The tolerance of landowners in allowing excavation will be apparent all through the first three chapters, but I may particularly thank the Rt. Hon. Lord Middleton of Birdsall for his toleration of our annual occupation of Wharram Percy where I hope he has not seen the last of us.

The credit for realising that a book on this subject could be written must go to Miss Margaret Stewart, through whom it was commissioned in June 1949. She has been a patient advocate of the reader's cause, making many useful suggestions for improvement of form and clarity. Where imperfections remain, my stubbornness must be blamed. Miss Gladys Scott Thomson performed a service of which she may not yet be fully aware.

Acknowledgement is made to the following for permission to reproduce maps and photographs: Air Ministry for Plates 1*b*, 3,

5*b*, 6, 7*a*, 11, 12, 13 and 15. The Librarian, All Souls College, Oxford, for Plates 2, 4 and 5*a*. Mr. E.J. Lawton for Plate 8. Dr. O.G.S. Crawford and the Society of Antiquaries of London for Plate 10. The Trustees of the British Museum for Plate 9. The Public Record Office, London, for Plate 14. The Director-General of the Ordnance Survey for permission to use Ordnance Survey maps as the base for Plates 1*a* and 11*b* and Figs. 1, 3, and 9–15. H. Frederick Low, A.R.P.S., and the Norwich and Norfolk Aero Club for Plate 7*b*. The *Manchester Guardian* for Plate 16*b*.

Fig. 2 was drawn by Mr. Peter Ransom and Fig. 11 is taken from maps drawn by the cartographers of the Royal Geographical Society. The author is indebted to the Society for the loan of this and other blocks, originally published in the *Geographical Journal*.

The indexes have been made by Mr. A.B. Craven, Leeds City Reference Librarian.

Introduction to the 1983 Reprint

The first suggestion that a book might be made out of this subject came in a letter from the Lutterworth Press of 30 June 1949. At that time I had no book to my name although I was at work on a commissioned history of the Leeds Chamber of Commerce for their centenary in 1951; my first article on agrarian history had been published in the *Economic History Review* in 1943. Between 1942 and 1948 I was warden of a community centre for adults, The Percival Guild house, Rugby, with responsibilities for organising classes and a range of social activities as well as giving some courses of lectures on history and literature myself. The terrain around Rugby, the classic Midlands of nucleated villages and much old grassland, gave me an interest in seeking visible remains of past landscapes but initially only that of field systems. A close examination of the fields of the parish of Bittesby on the Warwickshire-Leicestershire border drew my attention to earthworks which were different from anything so far encountered, and Dr Levi Fox informed me of the work that William Hoskins had been pursuing on the deserted sites of Leicestershire. I set out to visit as many as possible of the Warwickshire sites, much aided by the observation which Dugdale had incorporated in his county history (1656) and then by access to the library of RAF vertical air photographs housed at Medmenham.

My first published account of these researches was in the *Birmingham Post* for 26 March 1947 and in a printed catalogue of an exhibition, *The Hedge and the Plough*, mounted at Rugby Public Library in November of that year. A paper, subsequently published as 'The Deserted Villages of Warwickshire' was read to the Birmingham and Midland Archaeological Society on 10 December 1947. By that time, in an endeavour to prove that an earthwork at Stretton Baskerville (Warws.) covered the foundations of the former parish church I had become an amateur archaeologist but I left the Midlands for the University of Leeds in April 1948. In March 1948 I had published a short note on 'Lost Villages' (*Ashridge Quarterly*, iii, 112–3) and on 15 October 1948 an illustrated article, 'Tracing Lost Villages', in *Country Life*. This article was noticed by the late Margaret Stewart, Book Editor for the Lutterworth Press leading to their proposition in June 1949 that I might extend my researches to the whole country.

Work to enlarge the area of study began at once but I was not confident enough to sign a contract until 14 November 1951 by which time I was also committed to the collaborative work with Kenneth St Joseph which eventually resulted in *Medieval England: an aerial survey* (1958). The excavations which have since continued each July at Wharram Percy began in June 1950. *Lost Villages* went to press in the spring of 1953 and was published in March 1954. It was later to be supplemented by Maurice Beresford and John G. Hurst, eds., *Deserted Medieval Villages: Studies* (Lutterworth Press 1973) bringing together historical and archaeological work in the period since 1954, together with a more complete gazetteer.

List of Abbreviations

and works frequently cited in the notes. Works only cited once have been given a full bibliographical reference in the note.

A.A.S.R.P.	Reports and Papers of the Associated Architectural and Archaeological Societies.
A.J.	Antiquaries Journal.
A.N.L.	*Archaeological News Letter.*
Arch.J.	Archaeological Journal.
B.B.T.	A. E. Bland, P. A. Brown and R. H. Tawney, *English Economic History, Select Documents* (1914).
Beresford, Warwickshire	M. W. Beresford, *The Deserted Villages of Warwickshire* (Transactions of the Birmingham Archaeological Society, lxvi (1945–46) pp. 49–106).
Beresford, Yorkshire	M. W. Beresford, *The Lost Villages of Yorkshire* (Yorkshire Archaeological Journal, 1951–54 (in course of publication in parts)).
B.M.	British Museum.
Bodl.	Bodleian Library, Oxford.
Bradley	Harriet Bradley, *Enclosures in England* (1914).
C	References consisting of *C* followed by a number represent documents in the various Chancery classes at the P.R.O.
Cal. Ch. Rolls	*Calendar of Charter Rolls.*
Cal. Inq. Misc.	*Calendar of Inquisitions, Miscellaneous.*
Cal. Pat. Rolls	*Calendar of Patent Rolls.*
C.L.	*Country Life.*
Clapham	Sir J. H. Clapham, *Concise Economic History of Great Britain* (1949).
CPE	References consisting of CPE followed by letters or numbers represent air photographs at the R.A.F. Print Library.
C.S.P.D.	*Calendar of State Papers, Domestic.*
D.I.	*Domesday of Inclosures* ed. I. S. Leadam (1897) 2 vols., with continuous pagination.
Discourse	E. Lamond, ed., *A Discourse of the Commonweal of this Realm of England* (1893).
D.N.B.	*Dictionary of National Biography.*
D.R.O.(Y)	Diocesan Record Office, York.
Dugdale	W. Dugdale, *History of Warwickshire* (1730 ed.).
E	References consisting of E followed by a number represent documents in the various Exchequer classes at the P.R.O.
Ec.H.R.	Economic History Review.
E.E.T.S.	Early English Text Society.

E.H.R.	English Historical Review.
E.J.	Economic Journal.
E.P.N.S.	English Place Name Society. The reference P.N. followed by a county name or abbreviation represents the county volume, *The Place Names of . . .*
F.A.	*Feudal Aids, Inquisitions and Assessments relating to* (6 vols, 1891-1920).
Foster	C. W. Foster and T. Longley, *Lincolnshire Domesday* (L.R.S., xix (1924)).
Gay 1517	E. F. Gay, *Quarterly Journal of Economics*, xvii (1903).
Gay 1607	E. F. Gay, *Transactions of the Royal Historical Society, new series*, xviii (1904).
G.J.	Geographical Journal.
Homans	G. C. Homans, *English Villagers in the Thirteenth Century* (1941).
Hoskins	W. G. Hoskins, *Essays in Leicestershire History* (Liverpool, 1951).
K.B.	References of this form represent documents in the class, King's Bench at the P.R.O.
L.A.C.	Lincolnshire Archives Committee MSS, at present at Exchequer Gate, Lincoln.
Lipson	E. Lipson, *The Economic History of England* (ed. 1947). 3 vols.
L.P.H.	*Calendar of Letters and Papers of Henry VIII*, ed. S. R. Gairdner and J. S. Brewer.
L.R.	References of this form represent documents in the class, Land Revenue at the P.R.O.
L.R.S.	Lincolnshire Record Society.
LS.	Lay Subsidy.
N.C.H.	*History of Northumberland*, (14 vols. 1890–1940).
Non. Inq.	*Nonarum Inquisitiones* (Record Commission, 1807).
O.H.S.	*Oxford Historical Society.*
Orwin	C. S. and C. S. Orwin, *The Open Fields* (1938)
O.S.	Ordnance Survey.
Oxon.	Oxoniensia.
P.C.A.S.	Proceedings of the Cambridgeshire Antiquarian Society.
P.N.	See *E.P.N.S.*
Postan	M. Postan, *Some Economic Consequences of a Declining Population*, Economic History Review, 2nd series, ii, pp. 221–47.
Power	Eileen Power, *The Wool Trade in English Medieval History* (1941).
P.R.O.	Public Record Office, London.
PT.	Poll tax.
Putnam	Bertha Putnam, *The Enforcement of the Statutes of Labourers* (New York, 1908).
Q.J.E.	Quarterly Journal of Economics.
R.C.H.M.	Royal Commission on Historical Monuments, county *Inventories.*
Requests	This reference followed by a number represents documents in the files of the Court of Requests, P.R.O.

R.H.	*Rotuli Hundredorum* (Record Commission, 2 vols, 1812–18).
Rous	John Rous, *Historia Regum Angliae* (ed. T. Hearne) 2nd ed. 1745.
R.P.	*Rotuli Parliamentorum* (1771–83).
S.A.C.	Sussex Archaeological Collections.
S.C.	This reference followed by a number represents documents in the class, Special Collections at the P.R.O.
S.P.(D).	These two references are to documents in the class, State Papers at the P.R.O.
St. Ch.	This reference followed by a number is to the class, Star Chamber at the P.R.O.
Surt. Soc.	Surtees Society.
Tawney	R. H. Tawney, *The Agrarian Problem in the Sixteenth Century* (1912).
Tax. Ecc.	*Taxatio Ecclesiastica* (Record Commission, 1802).
T.B.G.A.S.	Transactions of the Bristol and Gloucestershire Archaeological Society.
T.E.R.A.S.	Transactions of the East Riding Archaeological Society.
T.L.A.S.	Transactions of the Leicestershire Archaeological Society.
T.P.	R. H. Tawney and Eileen Power, *Tudor Economic Documents*, 3 vols. (1937).
T.R.H.S.	Transactions of the Royal Historical Society.
T.S.R.S.	Thoroton Society, Record Series.
Val. Ecc.	*Valor Ecclesiasticus* (Record Commission, 1810–34).
VCH.	*Victoria County History* (followed by county name).
Willard	J. E. Willard, *Parliamentary Taxes on Personal Property* (Camb., Mass., 1934).
Willard and Johnson	J. E. Willard and H. C. Johnson, *Surrey Taxation Returns* (Surrey Record Society, xi (1932)).
Y.A.J.	Yorkshire Archaeological Journal.
Y.A.S.	Yorkshire Archaeological Society, manuscripts.
Y.A.S., R.S.	Yorkshire Archaeological Society, Record Series.
123456	Six figure references to the Grid of 1″ O.S. maps.

The conventional abbreviations for English counties have been freely used.

The manuscript sources are fully described in Chapters Four and Nine.

The contemporary printed sources are described in Chapter Three.

Contents

List of Illustrations and Tables

PLATES

LINE DRAWINGS IN THE TEXT

LIST OF TABLES IN THE TEXT

LIST OF TABLES IN THE APPENDIX

Introduction

I

OUR first task must be to describe and define our objective, the "lost village".

There are many villages still alive whose changes of fortunes in the last few centuries have meant that more people might be found in the Poll Tax lists of 1377 than in the Census of 1951. These shrunken villages are another story, and we must resist the temptation to turn our attention to them or to include them in our definition of depopulation. It may be that forces similar to those described in this book assisted in their shrinkage, but the crucial fact is that they did not result in the total destruction of human settlements, and our care is with those settlements which were destroyed.

We shall therefore confine ourselves to those villages where we have clear evidence of their existence as communities in the Middle Ages: but where we now have no more than (at most) a manor house and a farm and a church. In many villages in our case-histories we shall have only one of these three buildings surviving; and in quite a number of cases, not even these. The only latitude from this strict delimitation is this: to include a village which we know was deserted (or brought down to our minimum of three buildings), but subsequently repopulated. It would be a pity to disqualify Hilderthorpe simply because the accident of the growth of a watering-place at Bridlington has spread suburbia over its once deserted fields. It would be a pity to exclude Cottam because its fields were replanted with Nissen huts or Weddington because a housing estate from Nuneaton has grown up in the deserted fields around the church.

We shall see that contemporary opinion was well aware of the destruction of villages and that some sections of opinion were loud in protests. We shall have to study what action the Tudor government took, and whether the virtual cessation of the movement in the mid-sixteenth century had any connection with State action against the depopulator.

If contemporaries were well aware that the English landscape had its deserted villages, we have also to explain why it is that their rediscovery in the last twenty years has something of the air of novelty: why, for example, it was possible for the *Victoria County History* to have village histories with so little attention to the villages which were not there; why it was possible for Sir John Clapham to write in 1946,

> deserted villages are singularly rare

—and Sir John was a man who knew the face of England well, and whose writing of economic history had great feeling for landscape and locale.

We must also show how the existence of a lost village site can be traced and its history investigated. Here we shall be in a field of research where the traditional methods of searching in archives are reinforced by the aerial survey and by field-work. We shall examine in detail the retreat of settlement from a few selected areas, but for the remainder of the country no more than samples can be taken.

In every inquiry there comes the point where two opposing calls have to be reconciled: the call to pursue the subject to finality, and the call to consolidate a study in print while the volume of material is still of manageable compass. To follow the first call would mean a full county-by-county survey of the lost village sites. I have partly served that call in a parish-by-parish study of Warwickshire and the three Ridings of Yorkshire, and a slightly less detailed study of three other counties. Dr. Hoskins' study of Leicestershire and Canon Foster's work on Lincolnshire are also available in print to supplement mine.

Further detailed county and parish studies will be necessary, but it does seem that the proper place for such studies, or the more strictly provincial and parochial aspects of them, is in the pages of the local archaeological Journals. It also seems likely that the best results will be obtained by those who are living in or near these other counties; by those who can visit every site; by those who can draw upon local archives and local family papers—almost every one of which will have something relevant to the inquiry—and upon local tradition and local historians. This book might encourage professional excavators to excavate sites, and it might encourage local historians to investigate their local lost village sites further. They will be exceptionally unlucky if they find the pages of their local archaeological *Journal* or *Transactions* not wide open to them. If it is any encouragement to further local searches for the lost villages of this county or that, I will gladly pass on any notes which I have collected.

2

The study of the lost village impinges upon a number of academic disciplines, and there are a number of points from which the depopulation can be viewed. In the discipline of geography the abandonment of these sites marks more than a retreat of settlement after a period of rapid expansion, for it indicates that any consideration of the early medieval pattern of village settlement upon the landscape must in future take into account not only those survivors which appear as villages on the map today, but also those others whose life as communities ceased in the fifteenth and sixteenth centuries. Only when these are added have we a true map of the extent of settlement in centuries before the fourteenth.

In the discipline of economic history the deserted village is the sign of men changing their view of the most profitable use to which land could be put. In social history it is the sign of a class of men who were able to pursue their own advantage to the point of the annihilation of communities. In the history of land use it marks the end of the primacy which the plough had enjoyed in the Midlands and the northern plains. In the study of village morphology it affords an opportunity of seeing a medieval village plan without any of the accretions of later building. In the study of the form of the medieval domestic house it offers by excavation an opportunity of adding to our meagre knowledge of the ground plan of the peasant house before the Great

Rebuilding of the sixteenth and seventeenth centuries gave us the cottages of the picturesque "Old English" village.

In some of these disciplines, notably village morphology and domestic architecture, this book will not hope to do more than touch on the results of inquiries and pass them on for further study by the specialists. If the study of the deserted village helps them to push their studies further, I shall have offered something in exchange for the eavesdropping which I have inflicted upon them.

PART ONE

In this Part we must describe the lost village. After a description of a typical site we shall examine the earthworks which make up a village and its fields and interpret them in the light of our knowledge of the medieval village in the days of its full activity. A chapter is devoted to the impact of the destruction on the contemporary imagination, and another to the investigations carried out by the Government in the sixteenth century and the legislation seeking to forbid depopulation.

Chapter One

THE LANDSCAPE OF THE LOST VILLAGE

It retayneth the name of the township thowgh at this daye ther doe remayne but onlie one howse wherein the sayde (tenant) dwelleth, a compotent howse for a gent.

Survey of East Lilling, 1625
(*B.M. Harl. MSS. 6288*)

I

NO traveller comes easily to a lost village. Such empty sites are not well served by public transport and many lack even the convenience of a metalled road along which to approach them. You must be friend to mud, to green lanes and unused footpaths, to rotting footbridges and broken stiles, to brambles and to barbed wire. It is a landscape which has forgotten that human beings may want access, and it may be pardoned for its forgetfulness. It is so long since anyone wanted to come this way.

In fact it is some four hundred years since these empty green fields were part of a network of human activity: since these fields saw the labour of men and women, the building of houses, the visits of neighbours or officials, the welcome to a new priest or the burial of an old lord. These mounds in the field were houses; those hollows in the grass were roads; that broken piece of squared stone once cornered a room; this bank of earth dammed the fishpond; that bank of earth bounded the orchards and gardens of the husbandmen; the fields around were cultivated by them. It was to create these fields out of forest that the villagers had first come together as a community, and the slow expansion of fields and the slow retreat of woodland had marked the stages in their growing ambitions and in their growing numbers.

It is now some four hundred years since the villagers left

the village and the fields were put to other uses. Animals began to graze where there had been corn crops. The rough cottages of timber and mud fell down. The stonework of the church was valuable and was seized upon as a ready-made quarry by neighbouring villages. The dust blew along the street and the rain washed down the earth. Weeds and grass grew among the houses and eventually over them. The square corners and sharp sides of stonework have been blurred with a covering of soil and turf. Only with the excavators' spades or in the air photograph is clarity restored and coherence brought to the intermingled mounds, depressions, hollows and bumps.

In the course of the narrative we shall visit a number of these sites, sometimes on foot, sometimes with the aid of the air camera—sometimes in the company of documents. So far, the spade has contributed less to clarification than has the air photograph or the document. Indeed, if this book persuades archaeologists to dig some of the lost village sites in their own district it will have achieved something.

The narrative will show that most of these villages have disappeared for a very simple but unspectacular reason. They had grown up as communities of husbandmen, whose lives were wholly or partly centred on the growing of cereal crops. In the century from 1450 to 1550 the owners of the fields wished to put their property to another farming use, a more profitable use, bringing them not only more money but smaller labour-costs than in corn-growing. These men wished to become graziers of sheep or cattle.

Such a transformation of cornfields into pastures was more than a transformation of scenery. It took away the need for the services of most of the villagers—all, perhaps, except the shepherd and his family who turn up so often in contemporary documents. The villagers left or were evicted. The pastures would be watched over by the shepherd, and his cottage was the only house in the parish; or from the profits of wool the lord of the manor might build himself a new manor house on the site or enlarge his old house. Around it would stretch the parkland that was both attractive to the eye and useful to the pocket: in it roamed the deer for ornament and the sheep for income. Many a lost village stands in the shadow of the Great House.

2

To describe any lost village site as "typical" is a dangerous general statement, since lost village sites have quite as much variety as living villages. If we do begin with the description of a certain site it is not with the intention of raising it to the position of a model. We shall try and remedy any such dangers as we describe features from many other deserted sites in the course of the book. Here we shall describe one site as the observer may see it. We shall do that first in words, supplemented by photographs taken on the ground. We shall then take up a point of advantage in the air above a site and call in the aid of the air photograph.

The air photograph is not a solemn mystery. It does not confine the investigation of villages to those who have aeroplanes or to those who have access to the R.A.F. Library of air photographs. The air photographs may clarify or record the earthworks of the sites, but these cannot conceal themselves when you walk into their field. The man who has once walked over a site will not have difficulty in recognising another when he comes to it.

The fields which we shall first describe will be those of East Lilling, in the North Riding of Yorkshire. East Lilling will always rank among my favourite lost village sites. It was the first which I found on coming north from the Midlands, and it gave me confidence that the factors which had brought about the destruction of Midland villages had also operated in the northern counties, and that the visible remains of such villages were as clear on the Yorkshire turf as they were in Warwickshire or Leicestershire.

I came across the evidence for Lilling quite by accident. I was in London for a meeting and I had an unexpected hour or so to wait for the train. I went along to the manuscript room at the British Museum to have a look at any early Yorkshire maps which they might have. I found nothing in the catalogue before 1650, but I was attracted by a volume in the Harleian catalogue (MS 6288) which was a survey of Crown lands in Yorkshire.[1] It was mainly a survey in words and figures, giving tenants' names with the size and value of their holdings. The information was collected in 1625, a time when the Crown was selling or preparing to sell lands to fill the empty royal purse, and this survey was part of the procedure in the sale. I noticed a little plan of Sheriff Hutton park on folio 2, and this was followed by a long list of the holders of the 46 oxgangs of land, "totally tenantes by lease". At the end of the rental a new name caught my eye.

The jurors had come to the southern boundary of the Park and were telling the surveyor what land this was:

> East Lillinge it is called and retayneth the name of East Lilling township thowgh at this daye ther doe remayne but onlie one howse wherein the sayde Mistres Hall now tenant dwelleth, a compotent howse for a gent.

This seemed promising, and I tried to recall whether I had seen the name of Lilling on any of the new Yorkshire Ordnance Survey maps which had just come to my shelves. I read on to see if any further guidance was given:

> But by tradition and by apparent anceint buyldinges and wayes for horse and carte visiblie descerned leadinge unto the place where the towne stoode within Sheriffe Hutton park, it hath been a hamlet of some capacitie, though now utterlie demolished, and the place where it stood dismembered from the present territories of East Lillinge and is now made a part of and impayled to the parke of Sheriffe Hutton, how long since doth not appeare.

The document then went on to details of West Lilling, the adjacent village, which is still a flourishing settlement.

When I returned to Yorkshire I took up the map impatiently. As soon as I saw it I knew that I ought to have been suspicious from the first, for in its clear italic capitals the Ordnance Survey had printed the parish name—Lillings Ambo—"Both Lillings", as the parish name, but only West Lilling was to be seen as a village. There was another clue on the map, the word "moats" at a point to the south of Sheriff Hutton Park. I had already found in the Midlands that where the Ordnance Survey could recognise only moats there might in fact be a village.

When I was able to walk to East Lilling all doubts were settled: it was as clear a site as could be wished. The site lies just off the road from Flaxton station to West Lilling, on ground slightly sloping up from the flat level of the reclaimed marshlands to the south. Just as the 1625 survey had said, the site was

> dismembered from the present territories of East Lillinge and is now made a part of and impayled to the parke of Sheriffe Hutton.

The site is wholly in Sheriff Hutton parish, its southern edge being the bounds of Lillings parish (44/664645). It is all grass land and has clearly been once part of the Park. But the southern part of the Park has had two farms cut from it and the Park pale runs to the north of the old village site, leaving the grassy streets to form part of Lodge Farm.

I was fortunate in finding that the owner of Lodge Farm, Mr. W. Thompson of York, was willing to allow excavations of the site to take place; and also in that Mrs. Egerton of Sheriff Hutton Park was a keen local historian who did not mind us trespassing over into the parkland in search of "the wayes for horse and carte visiblie descerned".

Lillings Ambo—"Both Lillings"—stood on the edge of the Foss valley, marshlands drained only in the seventeenth century. The parish boundary of Sheriff Hutton follows the marsh edge (even into a sharp "creek"). To its south are now the flat, rectangular fields of the drained marsh. Inside the boundary to the north are the more irregular hedged fields of the sloping land.

The present line of the Flaxton–West Lilling road is a nineteenth-century one, probably straightened at the opening of the railway station. The older road ran through the centre of East Lilling village, and it can be seen swinging away from the present line of the road just before the village site is reached. Like many roads at deserted village sites, it is sunken to a depth of more than 2 feet below the level of the surrounding fields, and this depression continues through the village centre, becoming wider and shallower near the eastern pond in what may (from the absence of houses) have been the central green.

These sunken roadways are the most immediately visible features of village sites. The depth to which the road has sunk may at first sight surprise a visitor. It is less surprising when one has looked critically at the streets of existing villages. It is common for streets to lie lower than the doorsteps of cottages and gardens.

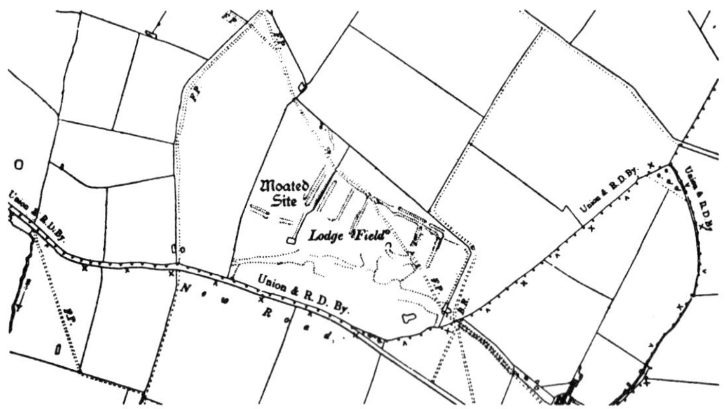

(Fig. 1). EAST LILLING, YORKS. N.R.

Ground plan of streets shown as earthworks on the six-inch O.S. map: scale here, approx. 4 inches to the mile.

Now that surfaces are metalled it is unlikely that further lowering of level will take place, but before a durable surface there were a number of occasions of everyday life in which erosion of the street surface could take place. The passage of men, animals and carts stirred the dust in hot weather and the mud in winter. Wind soon blows dust, and the wheel and the boot carry the mud away. In rainy weather any street with a positive slope will carry a stream with its further scouring action. Such cumulative erosion will have partial compensation in earth washed down from houses and gardens, but once a solid retaining wall had been built this compensation would be small in volume. In none of the lost village sites which we have excavated were paved street surfaces found.

It is more than three centuries since the party of villagers from Sheriff Hutton accompanied a royal surveyor into the fields where the site of East Lilling lies. The village had already been depopulated so long that the neighbouring village was vague about the point in time: but the tradition of a former village had survived, and in support of his memory the jurors showed the surveyor the deeply etched roads and the marks of the foundations of houses. They saw the roads leaving the village centre and making away across the fields for West Lilling and Sheriff Hutton. We have already said that the West Lilling road is very clearly delineated at the western edge of the village, but there is little left of the old Sheriff Hutton road after the first hundred yards or so of its course. The air photograph does show part of its course across what is now Sheriff Hutton Park, but the road would have had little or no use after the emparking in the fifteenth century. The West Lilling road, on the other hand, was in use less than a century ago for through traffic to Flaxton. At the eastern edge of the village there is a raised embankment which carried the road over the wetter ground of the marsh "creek". This embankment has now been ploughed out, leaving only a 30-yard stretch undisturbed at the village edge.

Running from this central road are a number of tributary depressions. They are less depressed than the central thoroughfare by about a foot. They leave the thoroughfare at about ninety degrees and thus divide the site by parallel lines (north–south). They are not evenly spaced, and there is no impression of a formal plan. Other smaller depressions run from point to point parallel to the main road, giving marked crossroads with the tributary depressions.

The sides of these roads are now sloping where soil has been washed down and any vertical face obscured. Sections were cut into them and no stone facing of any quantity was found. In some places a single course of faced stone was found to top the built-up earth sides. It is always possible that other courses of stone have been pillaged. Excavation at Wilstrop and Steeton (Yorks., W.R.) and Stretton Baskerville (Warws.) also failed to yield any stone facing to street-sides.

These three sites are linked with East Lilling in that all four stood on clay, some distance from accessible stone. This factor, with the limitations of transport, helps to explain why so little stonework was found in the domestic buildings on these four sites: the peasant houses would have had to be mainly of wood. Buildings with timber frames and mud-and-wattle walling were not well-equipped to weather the four centuries after their decay, nor has the clay soil been the efficient preserver of house-plans that we found the chalk of Wharram Percy to be when we came to excavate there.

In chalk country, easily-quarried and easily-squared stone lay near the surface—there is a modern quarry within sight of Wharram. Chalk stonework might tumble and be trampled over by animals, but its squared face was rarely lost, and the mass of tumbled and trampled stones surrounded the lower courses of walling and helped to protect them. For this reason the precision of saying "that must be a house corner, and there is the opposite corner" was easily afforded us at Wharram and rarely at East Lilling.

The sites of houses at East Lilling are marked in a more general way. The outer boundary of the garden and house-yard (earth walls with wooden fencing) is not difficult to see. This enclosed area has one side facing the street, and a generally rectangular plan with the short side at the street. At the street, the door or gate-opening is represented by a marked fall in the level of the grass for a yard or so. Here again fallen soil and the grassy cover obliterate a precise right angle. Once inside the enclosure, inner walls show as narrow ridges in the grass. Where animals have been treading, exposed pebble or stone walling may be seen. In dry weather the grass which grows above stonework has obstructions to its roots, and a line of walling may be seen in a line of parched grass. In buttercup time the comparatively moist soil below and outside a wall offers hospitality to the flowers and the pattern of boundaries is for a few weeks sketched out in yellow.

East Lilling has two ponds. One lies at the eastern end of the village where the central thoroughfare widens into a "green". Excavation proved that at least two of its sides were faced with large stones and the mud yielded plenty of broken pottery. The western pond has had its dam strengthened in modern times but here again the mud and surrounds yielded much pottery.

A landmark in the East Lilling fields is a central mound which stands near a crossroads. This mound, about four feet high, had a circular plan and we hoped that it might prove to be a small windmill. A sectional trench did no more, however, than establish that it was constructed of packed earth but without any evidence of wooden or stone superstructure. I suspect it may have carried a dovecote, which we know was there in 1388 alongside the Manor House and the six messuages and ten tofts of the lord's estate in the village.

The other remarkable feature of East Lilling is the boundary ditches on the west, north and east sides. The size of these caught the attention of the Ordnance Surveyor and they are in fact the outer "Moats" of the 1-inch map. It is unlikely that they were ever moats, unless water could be persuaded to run uphill. They resemble in accentuated form the mound and ditch which we shall see marking the perimeter of many village areas, encasing the houses and gardens in an almost rectangular shell. Immediately beyond them the first furlongs of the open fields began.

Excavation did not discover more than isolated stones in the bank which lay on the village side of the ditch. The vertical distance from ditch bottom to bank top at Lilling is in places 8–9 feet and the slope of the banks has harboured seeds and protected young scrub until they are now lined with hawthorns and blackberries. These thorns follow the perimeter of the village, and at a distance give the false impression of a hedge. The thorn-grown depression is a common feature in hollow-ways of other sites.

East Lilling did not have a church, so that no characteristic earthworks of the churchyard appear here. On other sites the east–west line of former building can be seen, and at Stretton Baskerville we found the church floor only a sod's depth, with the fallen slates from the roof lying over the tiles, chipped and cracked where animals had kicked them in the days when the church was a byre.

East Lilling is a good example of a site whose clarity on the ground is not matched by clarity in any existing air photograph in the R.A.F. Library. Village sites, like any other earthwork, will only show on air photographs under favourable conditions, and these were not present when Lilling was flown over. The air photograph which is to be clear and unambiguous needs a good clear day without cloud obstruction; good lighting from an oblique sun so that shadows will emphasise relief; and a season when subterranean obstructions can show themselves in differences of growth in a young crop or of colour in a ripening crop. None of these were present when the Lilling photograph was taken, and it shows little more than the bounds of the earthworks and the deeper roadways. This disappointment is a salutary lesson that the air photograph is not a substitute for investigation in the field. In this book air photographs have been used for illustration because they have the advantage of showing the whole area of sites in one view, and (despite distortions towards the edge of pictures) with something of the scale of a map, so that air photographs and Ordnance maps can be set side by side for comparison and orientation. As well as seeing a site whole, the air photograph makes intelligible a pattern of shadows and crop colourations which the eye of the ground observer finds confusing or meaningless.

An enlarged photograph of a second site, Wharram Percy (Yorks., E.R.), appears in Plate 1. The very favourable conditions under which it was taken have produced a photograph of exceptional clarity and interest. Since this was a site whose earthworks were noticed and drawn by the surveyor of the 1st edition of the O.S. 6-inch map we could set the photograph and the map side by side for comparison. The clarity of the photograph was such that when excavation began in 1950 we were able to begin our excavation of walls and corners with confidence which experience confirmed.

In the photograph of Wharram Percy, as in our ground

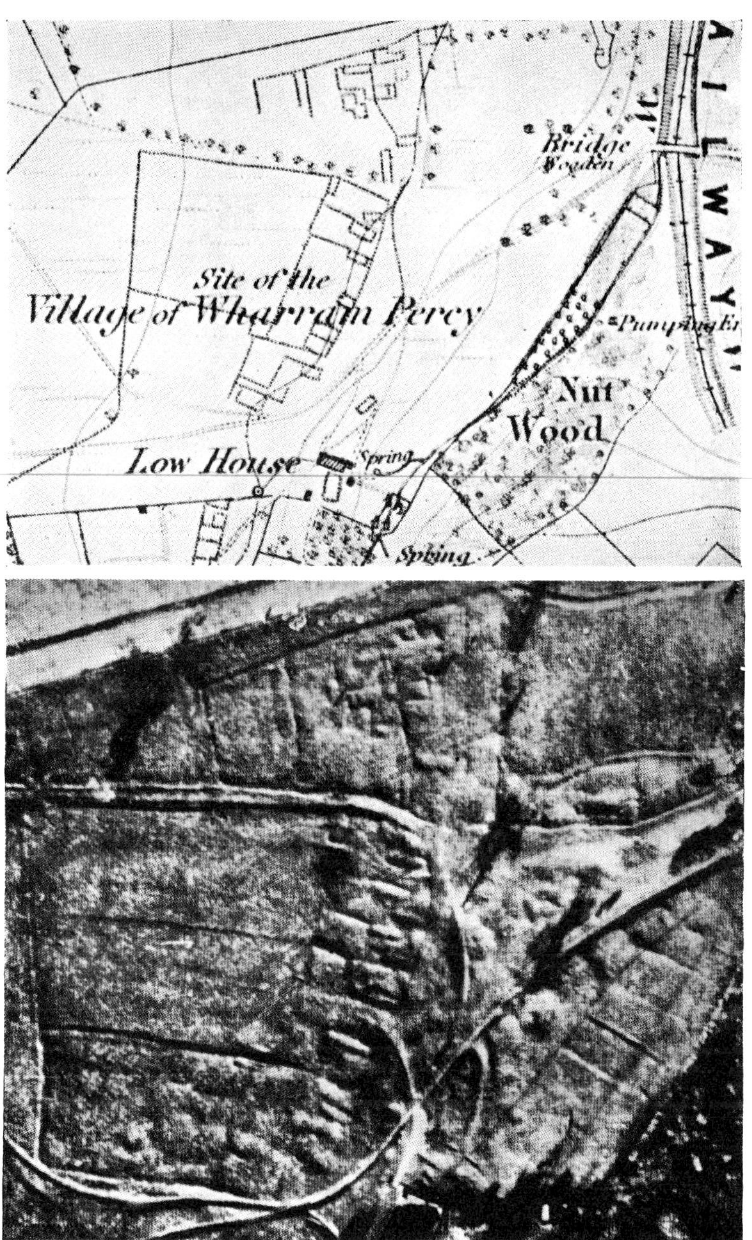

(1) WHARRAM PERCY, YORKS., E.R.

(Above). Part of the site, surveyed in 1850–1 for the first edition of the six-inch Ordnance Survey map. Scale here: c. 12 inches to a mile.

(Below). The site from the air. Note the complex of rooms and buildings at the top of the plate, separated by a deeply-worn road from the row of long, narrow house enclosures (centre). Cp. Plates 8 and 16.

viewpoint at East Lilling, the depressions of the road system are the first details to spring to the eye as shadows from the bank side are thrown on to the road floor. One such road runs along the lip of the plateau on which the village stands, to turn back along the edge of the house gardens, forming their boundary. Another road runs up from the valley, slowly climbing the scarp edge. It then cuts between one group of houses and the next, making a line parallel to the other road and marking off a rectangular area of crofts or enclosed gardens. Both these roads disappear out into the fields.

When you look at those smaller earthworks which have rectilinear shape you see that they are of two distinct forms. At the upper end of the photograph the earthworks are compact, almost continuous. The rectangular areas which they bound are small, small enough to be rooms and passages. At the very top of the photograph they merge with the boundary earthwork of the village. We christened this group of earthworks the "Manor" since it seemed to be separate from the village houses, divided off by the road. It seemed to bear the interpretation of a number of small rooms. Only the spade could confirm.

The other earthworks—which from the photograph we christened "houses"—lie on the other side of the road which separates them from the Manor. They are separate from each other; they have few visible internal divisions; and they lie along a coherent frontage facing the stream over the scarp edge and backing on to the long, thin rectangles of the crofts. Those nearest to the Manor (nine in all) have their short sides in the same direction. Once over the second road, the houses continue to be placed along the scarp edge but with a less regular alinement. The total distance from top to bottom of the site is 600 yards and from the stream up to the end of the crofts is 380 yards.

As at East Lilling, the whole site has firmly delineated boundaries on three of its sides. On one side is the firm line of earthwork where the crofts end and the fields begin. This runs down the left-hand side of the photograph. At the extremities of the site this boundary takes right-angled turns.

We investigated the nature of the earthwork at the point where it ran by the Manor, and at this point the Manor walls and the boundary mound were identical. The mound was made up of earth retained behind stone walling which had a step-like face on the outside. But beyond the Manor the boundary mound appeared to consist only of thrown-up soil. As at Lilling, it has not yet been possible to discover whether the depression between this mound and the fields was a defensive ditch or the line of a roadway, or both.

We shall describe the results of excavation at Wharram Percy in a later chapter, and here we have done no more than to indicate the present appearance of a grassy site as it appears to the visitor or to the air camera. Many of the details of the physical appearance of such a village will be more clear when we have examined the physical features of medieval villages in general.

Chapter Two

THE FABRIC OF THE VILLAGE

He hath often seen the plain marks and indications of divers frontsteads and the foundation of divers houses. . . .

Evidence of William Wilkinson, 1689.
York Diocesan Registry MS. R. VII. H. 4202.

I

IN this chapter we shall be linking together the physical remains of the lost villages with what is known of the physical appearance of medieval villages and their fields. From our knowledge of the appearance of medieval villages we shall be able to elucidate the meaning of earthworks on a deserted site: and, conversely, the lost sites may repay some of the debt by reinforcing our knowledge of the lay-out of medieval villages, which, so far, has had to rely mainly on scattered documentary references, and on inferences from maps drawn no earlier than the end of the sixteenth century.

The lay-out of the modern village probably represents the same general plan as the medieval village on the same site, but the detail of houses and crofts has been obscured by the re-building of the Tudor and Victorian periods. In the nature of things, there has not been much excavation beneath the floors of modern cottages to find the medieval hearths; village streets have not been systematically excavated for cobbled medieval surfaces; village gardens have not had the cabbage-patch trenched for signs of the medieval out-buildings. But in the lost village site we have nothing to disturb with the spade except grass, and we may hope to retrieve its houses very much in the state in which they were abandoned, perhaps a century before the first English village-plan was drawn.

The physical appearance of the medieval village was intimately related to the purposes of living there. Our description will have most to say about the homes and fields of corn-growing husbandmen, since it is to the displacement of the corn-crop by the grass-crop that many of our depopulations must be traced. When we come in a later chapter to treat of causation and chronology in this depopulating movement we shall return again to the living medieval village as described in the following pages. We shall return to it on that occasion, not with the eye which seeks to explain its form and purpose, but with the eye that tries to see what elements in its life made it an easy victim for the encloser; what position in the living village was occupied by the devouring sheep or the would-be encloser in the generations before the final expulsion.

Our description here will also be invoked again when we come to discuss the extent of depopulation in the different counties and regions of England. If we find an area with few depopulated villages we may have to explain it, not in terms of an unusually merciful landlord or an unusually resistant peasantry, but in terms of a form of village life initially different from the corn-growing villages, and so inoculated against the chance of catching their mortal infection. The best inoculation against many diseases is a mild injection of the infecting virus, and there were many villages which were not dislocated by the conversion to grass for the very reason that they were already largely devoted to pastoral pursuits.

The pastoral villages of the western hills, the Peak District, the Pennines, or the Lake District knew some arable fields—even open fields—but the small area of corn grown was dominated by the larger area under grass and the preoccupation of the villagers with the grazing of animals and the cultivation of grass. In the country-wide agrarian changes of the late fifteenth and early sixteenth century the pastoral villages did not remain undisturbed by the ambitions of landlords. Many landowners succeeded in enlarging their estate at the expense of the common pastures. Their villagers were among those in the Pilgrimage of Grace in 1536 who asked[1] that

> all enclosures and intakes since 1488 be pulled down.

Such villages would know some decay of houses, but they

were inoculated against the worst shocks of total depopulation which came elsewhere whenever a parish of arable fields was converted to grass. The Dales of the north have few lost villages from this period.

In the same way we shall find that lost villages are few in areas where forest occupations provided an alternative to work in the medieval fields. This is well illustrated in Warwickshire. The absence of lost villages in "Forest" Warwickshire (Arden) is a feature of Fig. 11(2), p. 228, and the contrast with "Field" Warwickshire, with its scatter of depopulated settlements, is marked. Like the pastoral villages, the forest villages were in their own way inoculated against the ill effects of enclosure. The open fields had played little part in their life. The terrain had not been attractive to plough-carrying settlers and it had alternative uses even in a time of land-hunger. It was valued by the King and the nobility for other virtues than corn crops: as a hunting preserve. Its products of timber, fruit, honey, fuel and charcoal were not to be despised as sources of income and livelihood. But these occupations were the occupations of the single wood-cutter, the scattered groups of charcoal-burners, the isolated hunting lodges of the forest servants. Land was cleared for corn near such settlements, but it was a small area, individually cleared and cropped. No fellow-villagers were needed to help with the small-scale clearing and the maintenance of the plough in its war with encroaching scrub. The fields did not need to be either extensive or open or communally worked. The villagers did not depend solely on the plough; and they did not fall with it.

The result is that we can claim exemption from giving an account of the economy and appearance of the pastoral or the forest village, interesting as these are. Our concern will be with the villages where the peasant spent a considerable proportion of his time at the plough, since these were the villages most likely to fall with the fall of the plough. The landscape of the ploughman was the landscape of the open fields. Where was this to be found?

To the claims of the pastoral and forest areas for exemption we must now add the areas of early enclosure: that is, of open fields which passed into hedged fields and individual occupation before the end of the fourteenth century. We should not expect such villages to be the victims of the enclosing depopulators of the next two centuries. Kent, Surrey, Sussex, Essex, Devon, Cornwall, Herefordshire, Shropshire, Cheshire and Lancashire have reasonable claims to be placed in this group.

These three classes of exemption leave us with a core of counties in the Midlands, the lowlands of the south and south-west, and the plains of the north. Two maps[2] of suggested open-field distribution have been published. One was by H. L. Gray; the more recent, that of the Orwins, is much too conservative in its estimate.

It will be these Open Counties whose villages we must now describe. They are the villages of "champion" England, to use G. C. Homans' phrase.[3] A variant of the word in the Oxford Dictionary is *champine* and that form, more closely linked with "fields", will be used here. It is also a form of spelling which avoids the ambiguities which might arise in a reader's mind from the modern sense of "champion".

2

Every English village—whether lost or surviving—represented a community organised for work.[4] In the champine country the village was organised principally for the work of raising arable crops, whether for the immediate consumption of lord and village or for the sale of a marketable surplus. In the first generations of settlement the purpose would have been principally that of keeping alive. It seems likely that the clearing of the land, which was a necessary preliminary to any cultivation, had been a communal task, and that the communal rights and duties of the medieval village were a continuation of that communal effort. On occasions in the Middle Ages the pressure of hungry mouths or the pursuit of profit pushed the fields out in to the surrounding woods and scrub. On other occasions a contraction of population or of demand—or of both—reversed this advance, and the plough retreated before the returning scrub or grass.

There is evidence that some of this later colonisation was the work of individuals as well as of the group, but very few champine villages in the English lowlands had completely abandoned the open-field organisation by 1500, although in each, from the earliest time, some land individually owned and farmed would have been seen, either as crofts and gardens near the houses or as hedged fields away from the village. In each there would be pasture and meadow where grass and not corn was grown.

The communal character of the clearing away of woodland and the slow piecemeal nature of the advance and retreat help to explain the characteristic phenomena of the strips and the furlongs. These sub-divisions of the arable area are those which first catch the eye when an open-field map is examined, and they must have given the villager a view very different from the modern chequerboard of hedges as he looked out from his church tower towards the parish boundary.

An open-field map of a village in the heart of champine England is reproduced as Plate 2. The first large-scale plans of villages and fields were not surveyed before the sixteenth century. In some counties this was too late to catch the appearance of the fields before the conquest by the hedge. In others the surveyor was in time, and in Northamptonshire we have the excellent draughtsmanship of the parish map of Weston and Weedon commissioned by All Souls' College, Oxford, in 1593.

There are dangers in using an Elizabethan map to illustrate a description of a typical fourteenth-century village. But the recent changes at Weston had been in tenure rather than in the topography of the fields. The villeins had been replaced by peasant proprietors and customary tenants, and these changes are shown in the names written on each strip on the map. But there is no reason to think that the shape and sizes of fields had materially changed, and the description of an open-field village which follows is a description of Weston—which was mapped—in terms which could be true of many hundreds of other villages which did not have the fortune to be mapped or whose maps did not have the fortune to survive. The description will emphasise only those features relevant to the subject of this book.

The original map consists of a single sheet covering the whole parish, with its two townships, and a number of sectional maps giving detail on a larger scale. Plates 2 and 4 are taken from the north-western section. (Another section of the map was reproduced[5] in A. L. Rowse's *England of Elizabeth.*)

On the right of the map, from which Plate 4 is taken, are the village houses; on the left, Plate 2, the multiplicity of arable strips among which the villagers moved in the farming year. The eye passes from the hundreds of strips to the bundles within which they were gathered. These bundles were called "furlongs" at Weston (and many other villages) and each was distinctively named: thus we have "*Ducke furlonge*", "*Gartridge furlonge*" and "*Grenewaye hedge furlonge*". The furlong was a furrow-long, and gave its name to a unit of measurement: in the same way that a "foot" was taken to name a standard length of twelve inches.

C. S. and C. S. Orwin first suggested how the strip and the furlong patterns might be explained. No village could have cleared all the parish area in one season or in one generation. The Anglo-Saxon settlers cleared as much as they needed to ensure survival, but continued with further clearing and addition of cleared land to the fields only when need grew. The furlongs may reasonably be supposed to be the units of clearing. Each of these bundles is different from its neighbour. The difference which strikes the eye is caused by a change in direction or by a change in one of the dimensions of the unit strips. The strips of one furlong may be running north to south, then the next from east to west (see *Grenewaye Hedge furlonge* (N.–S.) and *Gartridge furlong* (E.–W.)). The strips of one bundle may be 200 yards long and those of the next, 240 yards. The number of strips in each furlong also varies, although in some of the very large furlongs it is not possible in all cases to judge whether they include a number of adjacent furlongs—with strips of the same size and direction—thrown together. This is the case with *Barfootes Corner furlong*.

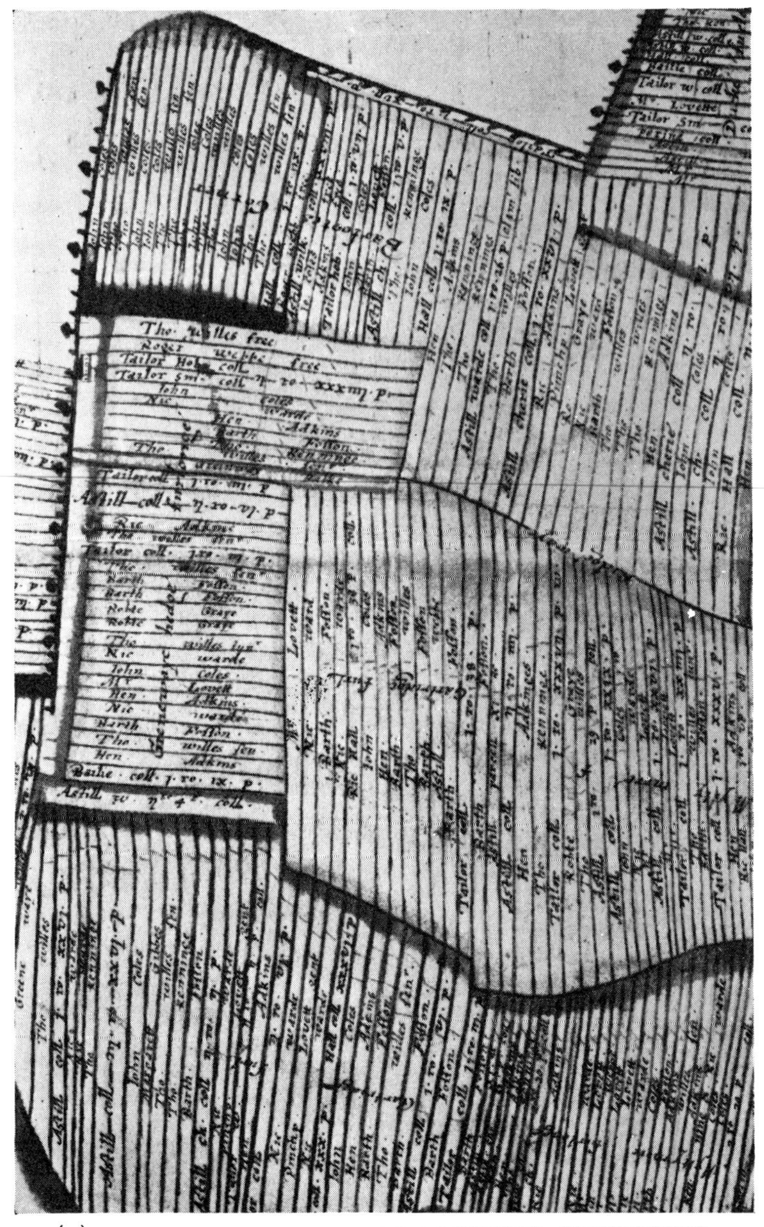

(2) FIELDS SOUTH OF WESTON PINKNEY, NORTHANTS., IN 1593

Part of the open fields surveyed in 1593, showing strips, furlongs and a balk. Compare Plate 3. Scale: c. 15 inches to a mile.

Each bundle has a unity (in direction and, often, size of strips) which would seem to show that it is a single act of creation, different in these details from its neighbours. It is reasonable to suppose that this unity arises from the single furlong bundle being the result of one year's clearing and ploughing at some unknown point in the colonisation of the parish. This land, cleared and ploughed, was shared among the villagers who had participated in the work of preparing the soil for its first crop. The strip—we may suppose—was the individual share.

At a later point in time the same villagers or their descendants would clear other land. A new furlong would be ploughed and allocated. Some of the villagers would already possess strips in other furlongs, so that their land would now be one strip here and one strip there. With more clearing, with more new furlongs and new strips the individual holding of land would begin to take on that characteristic medieval pattern of a strip in this furlong, a strip in that . . . and so on, across the fields. This pattern still persists in the 1593 map, although much distorted by the sale and exchange of strips in the fifteenth and sixteenth century land market . . . John Coles and Thomas Willes have each acquired two adjacent strips in *Barfootes Corner furlong*.

Some differences between one furlong and the next may also be explained in terms of the different circumstances prevailing at the time of clearing. One difference lies in the number of strips in the furlong. Now the number of participants would affect both the area they could clear and the number of shares into which the new land was divided. It would have been possible to make all new furlongs the same size, perhaps, and give bigger strips when there were fewer claimants, but the strip size does not vary greatly and it would seem that a fairly regular standard-sized strip was preferred, and any variations confined to the number of strips in a furlong.

Furlongs also differ from their neighbours in the directions in which their strips run. In the furlongs first cleared this direction could have been at the villagers' discretion if no slope or some other natural feature had pre-determined it.

The early settlers had migrated from other countries where they had had experience of similar clearing and ploughing, and doubtless they had learned the utility of a slope to carry away surplus water down the plough furrows. In such cases the long side of the strips would run down-slope.

But as more and more of the parish was converted to fields any new furlongs would have to be cut out of any remaining pieces of uncleared land, and the question of direction would then become less and less a matter of free choice and more a matter of fitting in to any gaps, and adjusting sizes and shapes to major obstacles like streams, rock outcrops or steep slopes.

The creation of strips and furlongs—even of the most recent—has not been well documented, and much of it took place in the centuries before extant written records. The description which has been given cannot, therefore, claim to be more than an intelligent attempt at explaining the scenes in open-field maps in terms of the simple emotions and thoughts of early settlers. From other countries, where the open fields in their most primitive pattern of strip-scattering remained undisturbed longer than in England, I find some consolation and confirmation. The map of 1593 has lost any signs of a regular scatter of a given individual's lands throughout all the furlongs, although there is English evidence of an older regularity elsewhere. This would seem to buttress the suggestion which has been made of a deliberate allocation of strips at each first ploughing, or of a wholesale re-allocation at some later point when the tenurial relationships were simple enough to allow this to be done—"when I turn, you all turn". Such a re-allocation was often said to have taken place regularly in the open-field village, but no documentary evidence which I have seen has yet convinced me that this did occur. Many so-called evidences of re-allocation of arable turn out on inspection to be re-allocation of meadowland. This was often done by lot or by rota. But to have a general post of strip-occupiers once the furlongs were numerous, land different in quality and tenurial obstacles firmly planted would have been very difficult, and we cannot yet say that it did take place. (In the simpler conditions of Denmark[6] the Crown did organise something

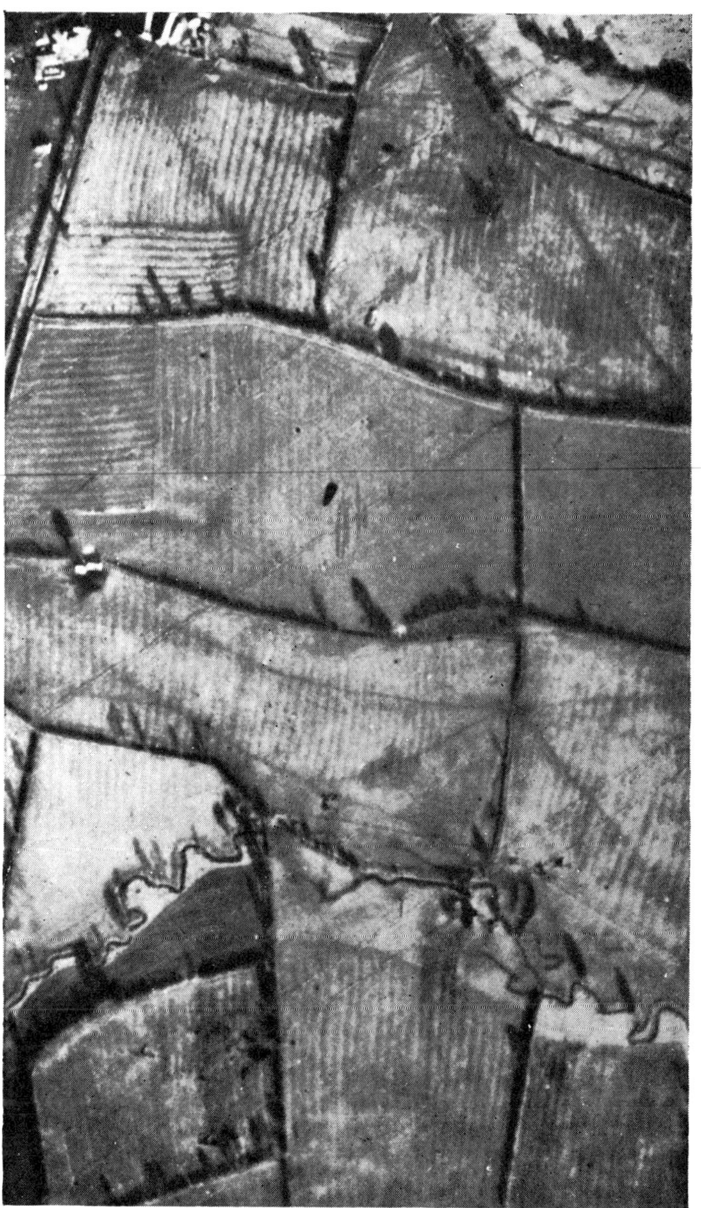

(3) FIELDS SOUTH OF WESTON PINKNEY, FROM THE AIR

The open fields seen from the air as ridge-and-furrow. A good point to begin the comparison of ridge-and-furrow with the strips in the map of 1593 is the top left-hand corner. Here the "across" pattern of Grenewaye Hedge *furlong abuts on to the "up and down" pattern of* Barfootes Corner. *The air photograph extends further south than the map. The stream is the boundary of Weston and Helmdon parishes. Scale: c. 10 inches to a mile.*

very similar as late as the eighteenth century.) The map of 1593 may fairly be said to mirror the topography of 1293 if not of 993 and 693. . . .

The map of Weston is a map designed to show ownership rather than the land-use of the year when it was surveyed. No crops are indicated on the strips, and there is no indication of the three Fields of the village. These Fields were the units by which the land was rested in fallow every two, three or four years. The Field was a unit of administration and agricultural routine rather than a distinct physical division easily recognisable at sight. In the medieval village, the Fields would have been recognised by the fact that a half, a third or a quarter of the cultivated land was not under an arable crop at any one time. The boundaries of the Fields do not seem to have varied once the final clearing of land had been achieved. But it was not necessary for the boundary to follow any very marked line of division. Many did follow a stream or a road, but others wound their way among the furlongs, turning and twisting with the furlong boundaries. This means that we shall not find in lost villages any distinctive earthwork surviving as a sign that Field boundaries ran that way. The most we can hope for is a particularly thick hedge growth or narrow belt of spinney on the no-man's-land between Fields, but this is by no means common.

The area devoted to permanent grass crops is marked on the map by the absence of strips. This area of meadow and pasture provided the valuable fodder and grazing for the animal stock of the village. The balance between this area and the arable area need not have been permanent. There is a suggestion in another part of the map that some pasture had recently been ploughed again. The number of plough marks which survive on grass-enclosures near villages suggest that these individually owned plots had at one time been ploughed: and probably in open field. The balance between corn and grass could also be changed by having grass as one of the crops in the open fields. Sixteenth and seventeenth-century "terriers" (that is, land-surveys) often list the individual's strips as "Arable in the (North) Field" and "Grass ground in the (North) Field".

Meadowland lying by the side of streams or rivers was usually permanent and unploughed. In air photographs its smooth surface contrasts with the corrugations of ploughing. In villages where a pre-enclosure map of the Weston type can be compared with the appearance of the ground today it will be found that the medieval junction of arable and meadow (which the map marks by the limit of strips) is delineated in the modern field by the visible end of ridge and furrow, followed by a smooth grassy surface of the land between that boundary and the water edge.[7] Even where, as at Ilmington (Warws.), the meadow was away from running water, its boundary on the pre-enclosure map can be seen to correspond with the end of ridging and the beginning of smoothness.

The map shows another feature of the open field landscape which will survive among the fields of the deserted village. This is the access-lane to inner furlongs which lay away from a road. One such is marked as *Greneway balke* on the map. It enabled the ploughman to reach *Gartridge furlong* and the *Ridge Waye*, and from the Laxton experience the Orwins suggested that such lanes were put to use as rough grazing for tethered animals.

Since this lane formed an edge to the ploughed area on either side of it, soil was ploughed away at each ploughing; with rain and with trampling at reaping time the gap would never be large, but it has produced a slight fall in level from lane to ploughland in the field. This leaves something like a causeway running across the fields, and unless these fields have been extensively ploughed in the last century the causeway will be visible as you look across the fields today.

3

We have come to the first suggestion (apart from the boundary of meadow and ploughland mentioned above) that any trace of the medieval field pattern can be expected to survive on the surface of modern fields. In the pursuit of a lost village such a survival would be a useful tool. As we sought among the fields of the parish for the site of the village-

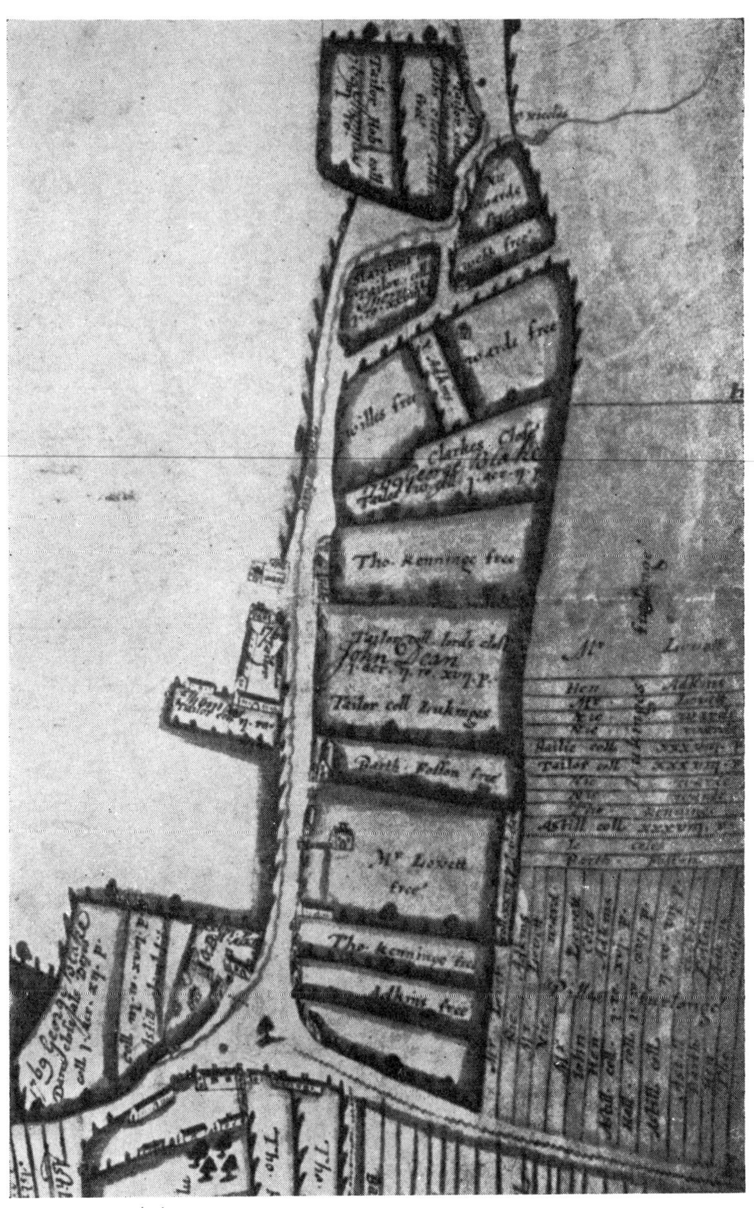

(4) WESTON PINKNEY VILLAGE IN 1593

The crofts, houses, streets and fields of an Elizabethan village surveyed in 1593. These features in a village which was not destroyed can be compared with similar features in the earthworks of the air photographs of depopulated villages. Scale: c. 17 inches to a mile.

centre we could eliminate fields which indicated that they had been part of the medieval fields or grass-lands. Slowly working over these, we should eventually come to fields which had not borne crops, but houses, streets and gardens.

This was the technique of elimination which was followed in a journey to the first lost village site which I ever saw. This was Bittesby in Leicestershire. The course of that journey is shown in Figure 2. In this small Leicestershire parish, where the village was destroyed[8] in 1494, I began at the north-west corner where the Watling Street makes the parish boundary. I then began to trace the physical signs of the medieval ploughlands. These waves or corrugations are usually known as ridge-and-furrow. These (like the ploughlands on the Weston map) did not continue always in the same direction, and my map marked these changes in direction. It was not long before my map began to have a strip and furlong pattern similar in general form to the Weston map. Among these furlongs there were the "causeways" like the access-lanes at Weston which have just been described.

Then the plough-marks finished. In their place were earthworks of a very different type: the earthworks of short lengths, straight sides, right-angled turns, hollow interiors, hollow ways—in short the earthworks of the deserted village.

The Leicester–Rugby railway crossed the village site on an embankment, bisecting the village earthworks, obliterating some, but providing in compensation a ready-made grandstand for the better observation of the fields. To the east of the village the fields resumed their ridged surface.

The assumption which lay behind the journey to Bittesby was one which must now be made explicit. It was that the strips and furlongs of the open fields can survive as ridge-and-furrow in modern fields, so that a plan drawn from ridge-and-furrow is a plan of strips and furlongs. It will be seen that the plan of the fields which surrounded the site of Bittesby village does have the same general characteristics as the strips and furlongs of an open-field map such as that of Weston: near-rectangular blocks of strips with frequent changes of direction. This in itself would be only indirect evidence that our assumption was permissible. But the air photographs of Weston (Plate 3) enable us to place the map of 1593 side by side with the ridge-and-furrow, and show that the furlongs and strips of Weston are in fact represented by the pattern of ridge-and-furrow in the fields there today; and this cannot be coincidence. Nor can it be the result of

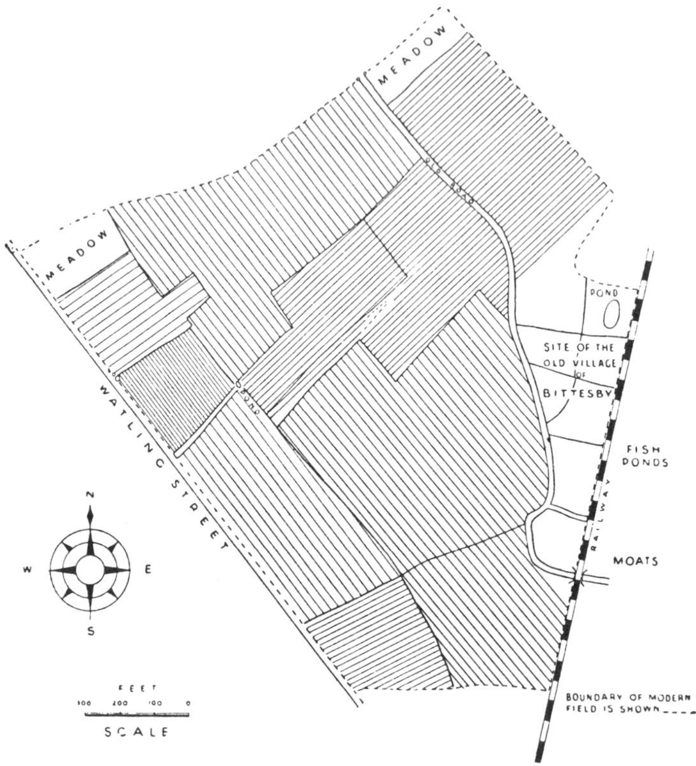

(Fig. 2). BITTESBY, LEICS.

The site of the former village as an island among the ridges of old ploughlands.

medieval and modern ploughmen adopting the same line along which to drive the furrow: for the modern fields—staked out at enclosure—differ in size and position from the open-field furlongs of the 1593 map. Modern hedges cut across furlong boundaries just as the air photograph shows the hedge cutting across the ridges and furrows. Inside the modern fields the ridge-and-furrow obeys the twists and turns of the medieval strips, changing direction where they changed direction, stopping where they stopped at the

(Fig. 3). WIVERTON, NOTTS.

The visible earthworks of the former village together with the ridge-and-furrow added to the six-inch O.S. map (scale here: approx. 3 inches to the mile).

meadow edge. Indeed some fields already enclosed in 1593 have ridging on them, indicating that they, too, had once formed part of an open-field ploughland. Such are the closes near the east end of the village street.

If the identity of strips and ridge-and-furrow at Weston were our sole example it might be explained away as a freak of coincidence comparable to Aldous Huxley's conceit that an army of monkeys on a battery of typewriters might one day by chance produce *Hamlet*. Other open-field maps in Leicestershire, Warwickshire, Buckinghamshire, Derbyshire, the East and West Ridings of Yorkshire, Northamptonshire and Oxfordshire have been compared with the ridge-and-furrow in the fields without damage to the identity which has been suggested.[9]

Open-field maps of deserted villages are few. Many had been depopulated before large-scale maps were known. Nor was the deserted village likely to be surveyed by contemporary surveyors. The motives of early open-field map making were generally those of property-owners wanting a sure record of the complications of intermingled ownership of small areas. No such problem faced the proprietor of a whole parish converted into a small number of large pasture fields.

It is the more fortunate, therefore, that one deserted village and its open fields were surveyed and mapped in the sixteenth century. This village was Whatborough, surveyed for All Souls College in 1586. The village had been depopulated in 1495, but when the surveyor came to make his map he was aided by a local jury from neighbouring villages. For the detail of his map he must have drawn partly on this body of folk-memory, for no amount of observation in the fields would have given him the names of furlongs. No doubt he also had access to the deeds and rentals still preserved among the All Souls' muniments. (It is not likely that an earlier open-field map existed to help him. If there had been, it would have been about the earliest English map of a whole parish on a large scale. Certainly no such map now survives.)

The surveyor's map nevertheless does show the pattern of strip and furlong and it indicates one way in which this pattern might have been drawn. In three of the closes at the south-east of the map are written:

These grounds have likewise been arable
These grounds do appear to have been arable also
These grounds do likewise lie ridge and furrow.

That is, the surveyor and the jury accepted the identity of ridge-and-furrow with former open-field arable. It is an identity which still holds. The air photographs of Whatborough show that the ridge-and-furrow of 1946 exactly mirrored the furlongs drawn by the surveyor of 1586. These two pieces of evidence can be seen in Plate 5.

(5) WHATBOROUGH, LEICS.

(Above). The survey of 1586, with the single shepherd's house on the village site. The strips and furlongs of the abandoned open fields were indicated. Three streams rose in the village.

(Below). The air photograph shows the confused earthworks of streets and houses. The boundary between field-land and crofts is marked by a low perimeter bank. Note the double-headed stream at the foot of the plate, uniting just outside the village as in the map of 1586.

The identity of ridge-and-furrow which has been suggested here has been recently challenged, principally on the grounds that ploughing in the last two centuries might have produced similar patterns.[10] This seems to me to overestimate the ability or the knowledge of the ploughmen of the last two centuries to etch an open-field pattern between and through the modern hedges. That general defence can, in the case of the parishes with deserted villages, be buttressed by a particular argument: in the nature of things, a deserted village is not likely to have seen much of any plough between its depopulation and the ploughing-up campaign of 1940. Depopulation had been as much an eviction of the plough as an eviction of ploughmen.

For these reasons we shall assume in describing lost villages and their surrounding fields, and in interpreting the air photographs of these areas that the equation is true which links ridge-and-furrow with the open fields. This was the assumption which led through the chequer-board of furlongs to the earthworks of Bittesby, and it will be the assumption in explaining why, in almost every lost village photograph which we have, the ridge-and-furrow pattern begins where the back-gardens of the village end. Fig. 3 shows such a conjunction at the lost Wiverton.

4

By developing this argument we have already said as much as we need about the physical remains of the former plough-lands of the lost village. Enclosure took the plough from them, and they fell back to grass. They were then encompassed by widely-flung hedges. The pastures of the lost village are markedly larger than the enclosed fields of later and less revolutionary enclosure. Where there has not been recent sub-division of these fields, the Ordnance map shows the difference in size quite clearly. There is also often a difference in shape. Early enclosers were not concerned that a pasture field should be of an exact size: it did not represent an exchange for an equivalent area of open-field strips. Such an exchange was the essence of later enclosure by agreement or Act of Parliament, and it was the surveyors' task to stake out fields which would represent the exchange. Where they could, they made fields with right-angled corners and parallel sides. They created the hedged landscape of the rectangle, the square and the rhombus. The hedged landscape of the lost village is cast much more in the form of the circle or the sweeping arc. The great sweeping fields of the early enclosures have sometimes survived without any modern sub-division by straight hedges: something of their size can be gauged from the great Town Field at Bittesby (Fig. 2) or Cestersover (Plate 15).

While the biggest area of a depopulated parish is taken up with the remains of medieval fields and grassland, our major interest must be in that smaller area which represents the site of the houses and streets, together with the enclosed crofts or gardens which abutted on to the houses.

We have already described the deep depressions which are the remains of streets. Had Weston been depopulated, these depressions would have had their principal junction at the end of the main street where the road from Weedon entered. The street plan of Weston was simple, and there does not seem to have been any back lane. Such a lane is still known in compact villages of the English lowlands. It runs parallel to the main street behind the houses. If the houses are on both sides of the main street there will be two back lanes, each turning back into the main street at the village-end, forming an envelope inside which the houses, the church, the manor, the green and the gardens lay. The air photograph of Sunderlandwick (Yorks., E.R.) in Plate 6 shows such a lane very clearly, and I suspect one at East Lilling. If the village houses lay at all regularly along a street-front, and the gardens had a uniform length, then the back lane would be exactly parallel to the main street and the whole plan possess a simple symmetry.

In villages where the plan was more irregular, streets turned off from the main street and ran between houses and gardens to other houses and gardens. We have seen one such street separating houses and Manor House at Wharram Percy. The air photograph of Cottam in Plate 6 shows two

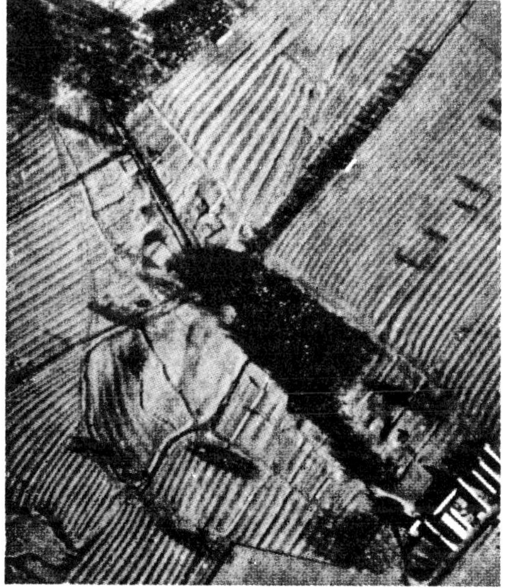

(6)
COTTAM, YORKS., E.R.

(*left*) OLD SUNDERLANDWICK YORKS., E.R.

Cottam has a deeply-incised road with clear earthworks where the narrow crofts of the village have been. On the right there are square enclosures with circular buildings within. The farm and plantations cover further earthworks. Sunderlandwick lay on both sides of a road which is still a green way. The perimeter of the crofts is marked by the beginning of ridges.

such streets forking from the main street at the pond. East Lilling had several minor crossroads within its inhabited area. At Quarrendon (Bucks) the side streets are marked enough to be easily confused with the seventeenth-century fortifications.

In deserted village sites the sides of the streets rise from the street floor. The ground beyond is sometimes lower than the crown of this rise, representing an inner yard or fore-court. Medieval houses did not necessarily abut straight on to the street. It will be seen in the Weston map that they stand irregularly. The same irregularity shows in the village plans of Padbury and Laxton.[11] In such cases as these, the houses would stand within their surrounding enclosure, and the street frontage would be no more than a bank with a fence. Where the houses stood more regularly along a street frontage, the house wall was also the boundary wall with the street.

The earthworks of the deserted villages are frequently indented, as if with doorways or gates leading from street to house or to court. The wearing down of the road level has left the sill of these doors above road level, and from the very few houses excavated it would seem that the floor level of the house or the inner yard was lower than the sill of the entrance. Fallen walling has raised this level somewhat, so that on the present grassy surface the step down may be very small.

It is the exterior wall of the house and its garden which shows so clearly on many air photographs. The area embraced by this boundary is that of house, yards and croft. The usual shape of this enclosure is a long rectangle with its short side at the street frontage, most of the rectangle being a single small field, the croft or garden individually owned, fenced off from the open fields so that animals could not stray to damage growing crops. The earthworks will be the earth mounds on which the protective fences stood. At the street end of the rectangle is a more complicated pattern of interior earthworks, the buildings for the peasant and his animals. What little has been learned of houses from excavation of deserted sites is described below.

The house and its croft are a unity in the air photograph. All the houses and crofts taken together form another unity—the village—whose physical separation from the fields was often marked by a surrounding ditch and mound. As we have seen, the ditch could also be the back lane. It would be easy to assume that this earthwork had a defensive origin, but it would have been a large perimeter to defend and not very effective as a barrier. The natural defensive point would be the manor or the church. It is more likely that the circumference earthwork was used as a barrier to animals: to keep domestic animals in the crofts away from the field crops, and to keep wild animals from the domestic animals sleeping by the houses. Whatever their purpose, these striking earthworks marked the point where the individually-owned crofts finished and the open fields began. At Weston, as the map shows, they marked where Luckinges Furlonge and Pilles Furlonge ended and the hedges of Mr. Lovett and Thomas Kenninge and Bartholomew Fosson began. These boundaries still face the walker who dips and tosses across the footpath from Plumpton Church, for the footpath has to climb the ridges and dip into the furrows of Pilles Furlonge.

Of all the buildings in the depopulated villages, the manor house had the greatest chance of survival. Many sheep-masters retained the manor house as their own residence, and many enlarged it or rebuilt it with the profits of grazing. At Wormleighton,[12] Warws., the enclosing landlord defended himself by the claim that he had replaced a sorry house by a fine manor (which can still be seen to bear out his words).

The manor house standing alone in the fields is as much the sign of a New Order as the courtiers' houses which stand beside the ruins of the monasteries, built from monastic stone and financed from the former monastic estates, the Halls at Fountains, Jervaulx, Bolton Priory or Whitby.

The manor house might in its turn be replaced later by a larger great house, a Compton Wyniates or a Compton Verney, with the former villages buried beneath the chestnuts or drowned in the great lake; or the manor house might move downwards in the social scale and become the farm-house which is the sole occupant of so many lost village sites.

Indeed this house among the pastures is the classical landscape of the lost village.

Village houses and cottages were less substantial in construction than manors. In the excavated sites we found no sign of burning, but cottages would easily fall down or be pushed down if anyone thought that worth the trouble. Any good timber or stone would quickly be put to other uses by the grazier or by neighbours. We know that a village near Scarborough provided timber for neighbours' buildings after it had been depopulated, and there is a similar tradition at Newton by Biggin (Warws.).[13]

There is little enough in contemporary statements about the fate of houses. The Returns of 1517–18 often speak of the village as "cast down" and the fields "enclosed with ditches and banks", but there are not many detailed records of pulling down and putting up. The rooms of houses at Wharram Percy choked with fallen walling are silent witnesses of decay. The skeleton of Plate 8 may have been a tramp from the days when the walls still offered rough shelter. He lay on the house floor covered with rubble and masonry. It would be attractive to cast him in the role of the Last Villager.

The rectory of a medieval village might be no more than a peasant house. At Lillingstone Dayrell it had disappeared with the glebe when the village was depopulated, as we know from the report of an aggrieved parson to his archdeacon in 1601. At Calceby in Lincolnshire, where there were only eighteen parishioners in 1563, the vicarage house stood long enough for it to be described in the 1602 terrier, or land-survey. There were two parlours and a hall; a kitchen, buttery, milk-house and stable. There were no upstairs rooms: it was one of the simple one-storey houses with the added luxury of domestic offices built on at the rear or side. An acre of glebe ran up to the churchyard, and had the Queen's highway on the other side. In 1952 the highway, again a Queen's, was widened and the old graveyard yielded its bones to the bulldozer. Of Parson Dennis' house nothing remains but the square-sided mounds in the pasture, while sheep and heifers shelter in the ruined church. When Parson

Dennis died in May, 1621, his cheeses were three times as valuable as his books. Among his inventory we read "thirtie and three ould sheepe and ten lambs". Only the ruins of his chancel arch tower over the motorists who speed along Bluestone Heath road to the Lincolnshire coast; the widening of the road has scattered the verge with fragments of medieval pottery.

In 1517, among the very few Returns from the Herefordshire juries we have a description of the decayed Rectory at Little Cowarne:

> There was a certain house in Little Cowarne . . . called the Rectory of Little Cowarne, with 54 acres of arable belonging to it. This house has been uninhabited for a long time, and there used to be a ploughteam of six oxen there. Sometime within the last twenty years Richard Hulles lived there with his wife and family and worked with six oxen yoked to one plough, and now the hall, kitchen and chamber of the house are fallen and ruinous. The timbers and walls have been carried off and the inhabitants have been forced to leave, and there is no dwelling left except a shed for grain and a cow-house called a "shyppen" which are in the possession of John Bole the parson of Ullingswick and Little Cowarne. In the latter village there are not more than four people dwelling.

Here again, it will be noticed, the timber was found useful and removed. At Cestersover, Warws., the manse stood by the chapel in 1221, but the chapel is now part of a farm-building.[14]

The medieval village would have other buildings than houses. The windmill, the water-mill, the dovecote appear on our earliest maps. If the village were depopulated the water-mill and dovecote might still be used by the occupier of the manor. The ruined dovecote at Barforth on Tees once housed the doves which were the pride of the Pudsays, but it now shares the deserted site above the Tees meadows with the ruins of the chapel of St. Margaret where generations of Pudsays worshipped. Windmill mounds are represented in the air photographs by the circular ditch from which the central mound was thrown up. One such appears as a crop-mark in an air photograph[15] of Burton Constable, with the former road leading to it through the park landscape of Capability Brown.

The water-mill reveals its presence not so much from the survival of buildings as from the survival of the distinctive earthwork of the mill-race, the artificial channel which held back a conduit of water until it had sufficient head to drive a wheel before rejoining the stream.

Another earthwork, more common than those of the mills, is that of the fishponds. These consisted of an elaboration of a stream-course by means of a retaining dam. The pool which was created was then stocked with fish. At Stretton Baskerville the King sent the lord some bream from the pool at Kenilworth Castle to stock his fishponds; the dam has now been breached so that the small stream flows straight through the dried-up ponds. At Stretton, as at many other sites, the primary pond was supplemented by a system of smaller ponds fed by culverts, with overflow channels back to the main stream.

Such systems of interlinked pools have occasionally been marked on the Ordnance map with the "antiquities" sign in gothic type as "fish ponds". Others have been interpreted as "moats". In the search for a village site within the fields of a parish the earthworks of the fishponds have proved an informative guide. In general, the "moats" of the Ordnance map have proved to be fishponds or streets rather than the defensive waterwork of a house or whole settlement. But in those parts of the country where the medieval manor house was defended with a small moat the deserted site will include both types of earthwork. At Steeton (Yorks., W.R.) the stream was dammed to create three or four fishponds, and the Fairfaxes' Manor was also moated. At this site, after the depopulation there stretched from the Manor gardens a park where the village houses had once stood. Then in 1525 the Fairfaxes obtained a licence to build a great ornamental pond, *magnum stagnum*, and this 4-foot-deep dried-out depression is the most striking earthwork of the site, dwarfing the medieval fishponds further up the stream. In making this ornamental pool much of the ground which had borne houses was removed, but the outer ends of the crofts are still to be seen on the edge of the pool.

The new Manor House of Sir Guy Fairfax, Justice of the King's Bench, was granted its chapel, part of which still stands, in 1491. The judge had bought the estate in 1478. By 1514 Gabriel Fairfax of Steeton was leaving money in his will to the poor of Bilbrough, Colton and Tadcaster. But there was no mention of the poor of Steeton, probably because there had been no Steeton since 1478. In 1377 there had been thirty people to pay the Poll Tax.

In a recital which forms part of a deed of partition in 1568 we have the transformed landscape, the perfect Tudor parkland:

> the Manor House with its dovecote, all the other buildings, the orchards, gardens and an enclosed pasture called *le little Old Parke*; along with the *grete stank sive Stange* with all the pools and waters running into it; a piece of pasture lying on the other side of the pool on the east side of the great *Stange* called *a pece of the same little park*; pasture called *Laive More* with a close there called *Jordans Close* lying alongside *le Howe*; a close called *Moor Field* with an enclosed piece of the park belonging to it; then in the tenure of Leonard Foster; a close called *High Moor;* a close called *Lawfull Londes*, half inside the *New Park* and half outside; a close called *Horse Mill close*; a close called *Hannous* lying by Colton Field; a close called Thornton; another called *Brughs*; a close called *Withill*; and another called *alongst le Cawsey*.
>
> [This last may have been the line of the York–Tadcaster road which ran at the edge of Steeton fields in 1255 when a diversion to the line of the Roman Road was in question.]

We may guess at the use to which the Fairfaxes were putting their New Park and Lawfull Londes by the inventory of the goods of Sir William Fairfax who died in 1558. The Manor House of 1491 had become

> a hall; a parlour; nine bedrooms; the low and high study; the buttery; the chapel; the brew-house; the kitchen.

Among the stock were:

> 78 cows; 2 oxen; 26 calves; 6 bulls; 66 wethers; 6 tups; 72 ewes; 100 lambs; 16 swine; 100 sheep; 15 horses and 9 foals.

When we dug trial trenches in the pond-banks the floor levels of the houses could be traced by burned material. In the centre of the pond is a circular mound. The purpose of this is not clear: it may have carried some ornamental feature on an island created by building up earth within the stone retaining course which we found on excavation; or it may simply be a circular area of the original village level left undisturbed when the pond was cut. Its shape gave rise to suggestions that it carried a windmill, but there does not seem any good reason why it should have been continued as an island.[16]

A similar earthwork—the island in a deep pond—can be seen at Knaptoft (Leics.) among the earthworks which flank the ruined church and a manor house turned farm-house. Other villages whose cottage-sites fringe new ornamental ponds or lie submerged beneath them are Wotton Underwood (an eighteenth-century depopulation) and Compton Verney (a fifteenth-century depopulation). In the engraving of Compton Verney for the 1721 edition of Dugdale's *Warwickshire* the artist marked the "Town Elms" in the park at the water's edge.

5

The most substantial building in the medieval village was likely to be its church. In many villages it would have been the only stone building, and in all villages it would have been the tallest. With prosperity had come extension of the fabric and with pious gifts the endowments of chantries in the side-chapels. Only a castle could have been more impressive as a token of wealth, power and building skill.

The destruction of the church at depopulation was an event which impressed itself on the imagination of contemporaries. If this building could be thrown down and its purpose put to naught, then how easy to override the obstacle of smaller buildings and to evict husbandmen whose status and office were unlinked to an organisation of administrative supervision like that of the Church. And if churches can tumble to the earthworks of trivial grassy mounds it is not surprising that the peasant houses should leave remains so few and slight.

It is true that there were many depopulations (like those at Wharram Percy and Lillingstone Dayrell) which stopped short at the destruction of the church. In these villages the church is isolated among the pastures, and acts as a finger-post to the deserted village site. We do not know exactly why the depopulator held back in these cases, and from the number of profaned churches we know that many who wanted to shake off restraint could succeed in their ambition. Some graziers no doubt wanted to continue to use the church as a private place of worship and interment. Others might have had religious awe to restrain them. Others might fear that public opinion would be aroused. There is something of this attitude of guilt in Willington's protests that the church of Barcheston (Warws.) was well built and well equipped, when the accusation against him had said nothing about the church.[17]

We know from a contemporary survey that Robert Delaval depopulated Hartley, Northumberland, just after 1573:

> Hartley being a great husbandry town . . . the said Robert at several times purchased all the said free holders' lands and tenements, defaced their tenements, converted their tillage to pasture being 720 acres of arable ground . . . and made one demesne.[18]

It is significant that a letter to the Duke of Northumberland written in 1598 says that Delaval had continued to pay the tithes after the depopulation in order to avoid a lawsuit. He was paying the full amount to the incumbent

> as when the town was in full tillage.

It is from the diocesan officials that restraint might be expected to have come. They had continuity of knowledge. The bishops' registers would have had the record of past institutions of clergy. Even if the lord were the owner of the advowson and even if the incumbent quietly and uncomplainingly received an income from his invisible church, there were still church officers who had a concern and a knowledge. In Chapter Nine we shall illustrate this point from sixteenth-century visitations. These inquiries were not specifically intended to hunt out the depopulated village, but routine questions by an archdeacon about the state of the fabric of the churches could hardly avoid recording a fabric which was reduced to broken walls. But these inquiries came too late to restore the ruined fabric, and it does not seem that the Church was able to restrain the determined depopulator.

The ruined church continued to occur as a theme in popular complaint against enclosure, in pamphlets and sermons. It also occurred in the first general statute against the pulling down of villages, 4 Henry VII, c. 19.

This Act of 1489 had spoken of "the service of God prophaned" and the depopulation was said in the same preamble to be as offensive to God as to the King. The juries of 1517 made much of profaned churches in their evidence: at Stretton Baskerville they reported animals wandering among the graves and sheltering in the aisle. Dugdale, riding by on the Watling Street more than a century later, was indignant to see this church made a byre. In 1633 Bishop Wright of Lichfield and Coventry sent to his archbishop[19]

> A Brief of such depopulated lordshippes within the diocese of Coventrie and Lichfeild the Inhabitants whereof goe to other Churches as I have founde by inquirie in my Visitation.

He had visited Stretton Baskerville where he found an absentee incumbent with an income of £13 6*s*. 8*d*. per annum "dwellinge neare London". He had investigated the local tradition, and had been told

> ther hath beene a Towne with in this lordshipp but burnt downe about two hundred yeares since and never reedified.

This was, in fact, a neat rationalisation in folk memory, which had preserved the recollection of the village and added a likely explanation. There is still a folk myth in the villages near Stretton, as we found when we excavated the church floor, but it is more sophisticated. Bosworth Field lies within riding distance, so Stretton Baskerville had been destroyed after the battle by the victorious Henry Tudor in revenge on the local landowner who had refused to supply a contingent against Richard Crookback. Unfortunately for either of these romantic explanations, the jurors of 1517 were very explicit.

In 1489 Thomas Twyford had destroyed seven dwelling houses when he enclosed 160 acres of open-field land. He then sold his lands to Henry Smith, gentleman. The jurors continued:

> There were twelve houses each with a garden and closes and four other cottages (in 1494). There were 640 acres under the plough as far back as human memory went. Smith built ditches and banks to enclose the fields and make his sheep-run. He wilfully allowed the houses to fall to ruin and turned the fields from cultivation to be a feeding place for brute animals. Eighty people who worked here went away sorrowfully to idleness; to drag out a miserable life, and—truthfully—so to die in misery.
>
> What was even more grievous, the parish church of Stretton has fallen to ruin and still is so. Christian men who would wish to come here for the holy services cannot, and the worship of God is almost at an end. Animals shelter in the church from storms and feed among the graves of Christian men in the churchyard, so that it and the church are desecrated and prophaned. It is an evil example to other men who might be inclined to act in the same way.[20]

There were others who acted in precisely the same way. In Warwickshire Bishop Wright visited four comparably desecrated churches. Five years after his letter which we have quoted, Nathaniel Hulhed, a clergyman, sent a petition to Archbishop Laud on the same subject. It is preserved among the State Papers with the notes[21] of Laud and Sir John Lambe: they had found these churches "altogether demolished".

Interest in the demolished church had been lively in the early sixteenth century, apart from the preambles to statutes. As a symbol of depopulation it was much in use: it was something of an Awful Warning. It occurs in More's *Utopia* as the church made a sheep-house. In the ballad of *Nowadays* listeners heard how

> The townes goe downe, the land decayes
> Of cornefeldes playne leyes,
> Gret men makithe now a dayes
> A shepecote in the Church.

and in Joseph Hall's *Virgedemiarum* a more sophisticated poet had the same theme:

> Would it not vexe thee where thy syres did keepe
> To see the dunged foldes of dag-tayled sheepe
> And Ruined house where holy things were said?

A few hours' walk from Stretton Baskerville one can see the walls of St. Peter's church at Smite—chancel, nave and south aisle—made into the farm of Peter House; another few miles and there is Cestersover where the former chapel of Monks Kirby forms part of the farm. In 1776 Stukeley rode by and saw the chapel a barn.

At the end of the sixteenth century the authors of *Pericles* made their avaricious whales

> never leave gaping till theyve swallowed the whole parish, church, steeple, bells and all.

This image of the buried church is not dead: like the myth of the buried gold at deserted village sites, it lingers in the tales of countryfolk. You can hear the bells on Hallowe'en, they will tell you. Or, the Devil has moved it, they say.

We know that church stone was often taken away for local building. At Stretton Baskerville I saw some of it unmistakably in the walling of a sunken tennis court at the Manor House, and learned that it had been collected from decaying barns. But only at Kiplingcotes on the Yorkshire Wolds do we know what was the fate of the bells. In 1689 there was a dispute[22] over tithes, and the plaintiff was concerned to prove that there never had been a village, a church, an incumbent nor a penny of tithes paid. The questions put to witnesses by his opponent sought to establish the village among the upland pastures to which they saw the drovers from the village taking their flocks each spring.

> do you know or have you heard and do you believe that in ancient time there was a Town called Kiplingcotes, and that within the parish of Middleton cum Kiplingcotes?
>
> item, is mention made in ancient deeds and writings of "Middleton cum Kiplingcotes"?
>
> item, do you know part of Kiplingcotes which for all your time has been called Kiplingcotes Garth? and a hole there called Town Well?

and from the well to the steeple—

> was one of the bells in Middleton church steeple brought thither from Kiplingcotes chapel? how long is it since the said town and chapel of Kiplingcotes were demolished as you have heard and believe?

Four witnesses agreed that there had been a village. One other answered:

> nor have I sufficient inducement to believe that there was ever any such town.

But the sixth and last witness, William Wilkinson, yeoman, was not so sceptical.

> He had heard divers ancient people say and affirm that in old time there was a Town within the parish of Middleton called Kiplingcotes. That he hath often seen the plain marks and indication of divers frontsteads and the foundations of divers houses, and also a large hole where there was a well for the use of the inhabitants of Kiplingcotes. There was a chapel, and the lesser of the two bells in Middleton church was brought thither when the town was demolished.

The tradition of a lost Kiplingcotes has survived locally into the twentieth century, but the incumbent of Middleton-on-the-Wolds tells me that nothing is known about the Kiplingcotes bell among his peal, although his churchyard is said to have Kiplingcotes tombstones. But the air camera still discerns by the side of the main road

> the plain marks and indication of divers frontsteads and the foundations of divers houses.

(7) PUDDING NORTON, NORFOLK

(Above). Vertical air photograph.

(Below). Oblique air photograph. The site is surrounded by fields which are now under the plough again. The tower of the ruined church is to the right of the buildings of Norton Hall, near the hedge. A double-moated site can be seen above the farm buildings, probably the Manor House.

It is not uncommon, where the tradition of a former church in the fields has survived, for open-air services to be held annually by a neighbouring incumbent. Indeed, the name of the village may be preserved in the second of the two names of a conjoint modern parish. Some ruined churches have their occasional services also.

Surviving churches in empty parishes pose a difficult problem. In these days they are most likely to be linked to another living. The income of the joint livings and the funds for maintaining two churches are usually small, and a difficult problem of maintaining the fabric is posed. To maintain one country church adequately is enough of a problem for the church officers: what of the case (as at Wharram le Street with Wharram Percy) where they have a second to maintain, a mile from the nearest road, in a virtually empty parish? The walls of Wharram Percy church show where the two aisles were pulled down when the congregation was shrinking, probably in the fifteenth century. In the baptisms of the 1580's and 1590's it is the children of Thixendale who are being brought to the font.[23] Thixendale, which still flourishes, was another village within the parish; Towthorpe, Raisthorpe and Burdale were former hamlets, but now depopulated. Now Thixendale is detached, and the modern churchwardens of Wharram-Percy-with-Wharram-le-Street have open to them no such easy way of adapting their fabric to a tiny population.

6

In my own researches on the lost villages the role played by excavation has been small. My time and efforts have been concentrated on the investigation through documents, field work and air photographs. With the assistance of friends I have been able to do a little exploratory digging, but the time and skill of professionally trained archaeologists is necessary if the medieval village is to be thoroughly explored with the spade. The historian's main task, as I see it, is to provide the archaeologists with as much information as possible about the location of sites and their dating, and then sit back: or better still, offer his services as an unskilled labourer or trainee.

The amount of attention devoted to medieval settlements by professional archaeologists has been small until recent years. This has been partly due to their need to allot their small resources among many competing claims on their time and money. Partly, no doubt, it is because they have received the impression that historians know all about the Middle Ages from documents and have no need of assistance from archaeology. Meanwhile, in Denmark Dr. Axel Steensberg has been pioneering in the layer by layer examination of deserted farmsteads.

When I myself began to dig at Stretton Baskerville in Warwickshire in the winter of 1947 I knew of one other site whose excavation had been reported in print, that of Seacourt, Berkshire, which Mr. Bruce-Mitford had dug in 1938–39. In fact, as I later discovered, other explorations on various scales had taken place, some of them unreported. A list which Mr. John Hurst compiled for me appears in the Appendix.

The site at Hullasey, Glos., which W. St. Clair Baddelely[24] dug in 1910 is poorly documented and the date of the depopulation can only be deduced from the evidence of pottery petering out in the fifteenth century. Bruce-Mitford made preliminary excavations at Seacourt before the War, as a first attempt to fill what Christopher Hawkes had called[25] in 1937

> a gap of full four centuries (of medieval history) which is a standing reproach to the good name of British excavators.

This site was better documented: the cure of souls ceased in 1439 when the church, already collapsed, ministered to only two parishioners. The church-site was found, and (as at Stretton) all the stonework above ground had been pillaged. Neighbours in search of ready-worked stone had removed some of the foundation stones also. The photographs printed by Bruce-Mitford show church walls which seem as solid as those which we found in the Manor House at Wharram Percy when we began to excavate there in 1949. The houses at Seacourt had walling rather flimsier than ours, but the Berkshire village can boast a good road surface which was uncovered and photographed.

Bruce-Mitford's report is illustrated by an oblique air photograph which is kind to the detail of roads, but uninformative about house plans or the church foundations. A sketch-plan is given, relating the photographs to the trenches. Had the war not intervened, Seacourt might have become the first medieval village to be completely excavated.

In the winter of 1947–48, with the assistance of Mr. Owen and some boys from Hinckley Grammar School, I made a number of trial excavations at the site of Stretton Baskerville. At the traditional site of the church a longitudinal trench soon reached the level of significant rubble. Roofing slates, with holes for nails, lay sometimes whole, sometimes broken. Some had the nails twisted with rust, but still in position. There was no sign of timber or burned wood. Ridge-tiles, with a lip made by the tile-maker's thumb, were common. There was a little glass, and one H-shaped piece of lead into which glass could have fitted. This was found at the east end of the church.

To the north of the site was found a worked copper clasp with a hinge, of the size that might have fitted a book. Holes had been bored through it for rivets, and the holes continued as a simple geometrical pattern. Many broken pieces of pottery, glazed and unglazed, were found.

In our limited time and in poor weather we were not able to follow all the walls along to their ends, but it did seem that other buildings had either joined or lain very contiguous to the church. A rough flooring of tiles, some broken by the impact of falling tiles or trampling cattle, was found at some points within the church. Much worked stone of good quality was lying away from the site down by the (now-breached) fishponds, and more of it lines the walls of the sunken tennis-court at Stretton House. Colonel Atkins, to whom we were indebted for permission to deface his fields, told me that this had been recovered from the bottom and sides of the ponds.

Our attempts to find any walls within the mounds which

we interpreted as "houses" were unsuccessful, and the hollow-way which runs through the village parallel to the Watling Street yielded no paved surface. It is interesting to note that Stretton must have continued the common practice of the Anglo-Saxon settlements along the line of the Watling Street, being staggered from it by anything from half a mile to a mile. There is no medieval village on its course for the fifty miles from Towcester to Atherstone, although the reasons for this aloofness can only be conjectured.

In the spring of 1948 I left Warwickshire and the site at Stretton was closed up. That summer Dr. Hoskins and some Leicestershire archaeologists began to dig at Hamilton, a site near Leicester which had been marked on the Ordnance map by the traditional name "Town of Hamilton". In 1948 and 1949 the Rugby branch of the Historical Association mapped the visible street lay-out of the former hamlet of Onley by Barby, Northamptonshire, but no buildings of any substance have been found there. Mr. Franey tells me that excavation of Holme (or Biggin) by Newton has been disappointing.

The first site which I was able to obtain permission to excavate in the North was East Lilling, which has been already mentioned in Chapter One. Mr. W. Thompson, the owner, allowed us to dig trial trenches and to excavate the ponds, in the spring and summer of 1948–49. In 1949 I was also allowed to dig a few trenches at Wilstrop, whose history will be summarised on page 301.

Both these sites were in heavy clay, and in both we found the same disappointment. Roads were etched deeply into the soil; the former line of earth-banks and field-boundaries was very clear: but when it came to any solid stone walling, the results were very meagre. The only worked stonework which we found was scattered, probably where it had fallen. That is, at Stretton, at Onley, at Lilling, at Wilstrop (and, I believe, at Hamilton) the detail of house walling was poor.

The next site which I was able to dig (by permission of Lord Middleton and his tenant, Mr. Midgeley) was at Wharram Percy. Our experience here was so different and

(8) WHARRAM PERCY, YORKS., E.R.

(Above). Skeleton found just inside one of the abandoned houses at the former floor level.
(Below). A face of the wall of the "Manor House" (cp. Plate 1).

so rewarding that I am inclined to think that an explanation must lie in the nature of the terrain. In the clay villages where we had first dug, good easily-worked building stone did not lie at hand: at Wharram there was a natural chalk quarry in the valley, and indeed a large modern quarry only a few hundred yards from it. Chalk was plentiful elsewhere, and the incentive to pillage from the deserted site would be small. Neighbours would not want to transport chalk stone five or ten miles when it could be quarried for less effort near their own village. In the clay plain at Lilling, Wilstrop and Stretton worked stone would be at a premium.

In the physical conditions of these three villages it is not likely that a great deal of worked stone would have been used for houses in any case. There was sufficient of it found in or near Stretton to make it likely that part, if not all, of the church was of stone. At Wilstrop and Lilling there were no medieval churches, and any stone that had been used in the medieval manors would have been re-used in the Tudor Halls which succeeded them, and in which the graziers lived. The houses of Hullasey were made of local oolite, undressed, but Hullasey stands on or near good stone. The fabric of the churches at Wharram Percy and at Wharram le Street is not of local chalk but of sandstone and limestone brought from a distance. Small numbers of such alien stones were found among the rough chalk building stones of the houses which we were able to excavate at Wharram, the majority of them at points which suggested a door or window place.

The preservation of the lower courses of walling at Wharram has been so good that we were able to uncover four houses and some walls of the Manor in 1950–53. Lord Middleton has fenced these off from animals and it is possible that he may allow them to be left open for visitors to see.

The lower courses have been preserved below the modern ground level. The surface of the ground before excavation usually showed a rise of 6 or 9 inches over the spot where the wall proved to lie. On removal of the sods a mass of rubble was found, most of it consisting of broken pieces of the same roughly worked stone that was to appear in the walls. When this was removed with pick and shovel a regular course of walling appeared, and further removal of rubble and fallen walling stones enabled us to move down to the bottom course and then to follow the walls along to their corners, and eventually to clear the whole outer walling of the house along its interior face. No floor was found: under the broken rubble and fallen stones was natural "soft" chalk of the type normally found at that depth locally. The bottom courses were continuous, but the third and higher courses had interruptions which we attributed to doors or window spaces.

At the level of the bottom course we were anything from 12 to 18 inches below the general level of the grass today. Even allowing something for accretions of soil since the sixteenth century, it is clear that many houses at Wharram had their floor level sunken below the level of the lane or croft behind the house. Dr. Singleton, who measured the building for me, cast an architect's eye on these levels and suggested that they arose out of the natural conditions of the site. It will be seen from the air photograph that the houses are perched on the lip of a steep scarp, and that they are themselves lower than the crofts and fields at their rear. Any level floor-surface would necessitate either building up soil to equalise the slope or excavating at the higher end and using that soil to raise the level of the lower end. This suggestion seemed plausible, although such a practice must have had the added convenience which our excavations brought out: only the *interior* face of the outer walls was level and properly made up. The exterior surfaces were both rough and shapeless. They had every appearance of being packed in to fill a space between the front courses already laid in position and the earth face of the trench which had been excavated by the builders.

The Wharram houses were of the long, narrow type, roughly 15 feet by 50 feet. On the analogy of farm-houses in Saxony, the animals occupied one end and the family the other. Apart from pottery,[26] the successive families who lived in the house had left us only a few scraps of metal and some charcoal. Elsewhere in the village we added a bone needle, a door-hinge and a door-hasp. The skeleton of Plate

8 was found just inside one of the houses excavated in 1951, with rubble and fallen masonry covering him. We shall never know whether he was the last of the villagers or a stray vagabond who wandered in while the walls were still standing, the body being buried as they tottered and fell.

In the two week-ends which we spent at the site in 1952 it became clear that the floor level of the house which we were exploring itself concealed an older and deeper building whose walls lay beneath it and at a totally different alinement. Preliminary tests suggested that at least three consecutive houses may have stood on this spot.

The air photographs give a tolerable account of the shape and position of these domestic houses which line the lip of the scarp at Wharram. At the far end of the village the earthworks assume a much more complex pattern, one suggesting a number of small rooms or buildings gathered together. This we dubbed, The Manor. We were not able to do more than sample the walling of this complex, but what we did uncover was strikingly different from the walling of the ordinary house. The walling was thicker, the stones larger, the face smooth and the corners carefully worked. Packing and mortaring had been carefully executed, and both faces of the wall were regular and straight. The exterior wall had its bottom course underset, as if it had been built in a trench and the wider second course laid over it. These walls will be seen in Plate 8, contrasted with the house walls of the smaller dwellings. Time was not sufficient to explore the interior of this building. Near the wall there occurred much pottery, the usual animal bones and a fine bone needle seven inches long.

These details are not very impressive by professional archaeological standards, but they are sufficient to show that local initiative in excavating any sites of this category would be well rewarded. In stone country the labour of pick and shovel on heavy rubble is likely to be rewarded by neat walling beneath; in clay country the resistance to the spade will be less, and further excavation by others may prove that the poor results at Wilstrop, Stretton and Lilling were bad luck if not bad judgment. But our knowledge of the simpler medieval house is so meagre and so few examples have survived the Great Rebuilding that any further examples would be a significant increment to knowledge. Nor is there any reason to believe that medieval houses had a national uniformity, so that Wharram House A, B, C and D will never be elevated to the dignity of a Type. In June, 1953, while this book was in proof, the Deserted Medieval Village Research Group began excavations at Wharram under the direction of Mr. J. Golson and Mr. J. G. Hurst.

7

Buildings leave earthworks behind them and can be excavated. The villagers from the lost villages have left little record of their fate. No villager achieved later fame and wrote an autobiography. If any evicted husbandman turned pamphleteer he failed to record any personal experiences. Few villagers, as we shall see in Chapter Four, recorded their grievances in petitions to Authority.

The nearest thing we have to personal experiences is evidence given to the Inquiry of 1517. The day and month of the final eviction were given to the Commission with a statement of the number of people evicted. This statement was sometimes followed by a phrase or phrases describing the fate of the evicted.[27] At Stretton Baskerville the eighty persons evicted

> were compelled to go from thence unwilling and lamenting; and they have remained in idleness since that day and lead unhappy lives and truly have died in such a pitiful state.

Across the north edge of the parish of Stretton ran the Watling Street, and no doubt it was to this vagrants' highway that the villagers betook themselves.

At Wretchwick (Oxon.) the evicted were reported in 1517 as having left to seek bread elsewhere. The evicted of some farms at Castor near Peterborough

> earned their living in cultivating the enclosed lands, and by reason of the destruction of the houses they have left and are now unemployed.

In Peterborough itself the eviction of eighty-three persons had sent them into "idleness and misery". From Carswell in Northamptonshire twenty-four people "left weeping". At Papley the fate of fifty-four villagers was "idleness and poverty". At Kirby in Woodend 108 persons were "compelled to leave and go wandering". At Thorpe by Norton the dispossessed totalled a hundred, and these on May 4, 1488,

> left their houses weeping and became unemployed and finally, as we suppose, died in poverty and so ended their days.

At Apethorpe the evicted left "to look for work". At Barford "almost the whole village has been destroyed".

These quotations from the Returns of 1517 tell the same story of vagabondage in search of work as the well-known passage in the Sheep Pamphlets:[28]

> now these . . . persons had need to have living: whither shall they go? into Northamptonshire? and there also is the living of twelve score persons lost: whither shall they go?—forth from shire to shire and to be scattered thus abroad within the King's majesty's realm where it shall please Almighty God and for lack of masters by compulsion driven some of them to beg and some to steal.

At the end of the century a speaker in the Commons described the double fate of the evicted:[29]

> if the poor being thrust out of their houses go to dwell with others, straight we catch them with the Statute of Inmates; if they wander abroad they are within danger of the Statute of the Poor to be whipped.

These statutory terrors were not abroad in 1517, but the terrors of hunger and idleness were no strangers to the evicted. Thomas Bastard was to write:[30]

> The grass grows green where little Troy did stand
> The forlorn father hanging down his head
> His outcast company drawn up and down
> The pining labourer doth beg his bread
> The plow-swain seeks his dinner from the town.

Certain towns could have been a refuge for those evicted from the countryside. The vagrants of the highways were on the move from town to town seeking work. If a town prospered, its craftsmen and tradesmen would welcome unskilled labour; in time of depression their presence would be resented. After such an experience in a town would come another period on the roads in search of seasonal labour in the fields as casual employment. In 1597 the Dean of Durham, writing to Cecil, complained that the evicted countryman was a burden on the borough rates, and in another letter of the same year he said that Northumberland people were being driven to the "poor port towns". These northern evictions were not exactly parallel with the earlier depopulations, but the urban opportunities for the evicted husbandman in 1597 must have been better if anything than in 1497, and a Dean of Lincoln or Lichfield in 1497 would have had harder words to write.

We shall see later that the social dangers were not lost on the Crown. The Act of 1489 spoke of idleness as "ground and beginning of all mischief". A proclamation at the time of the provincial troubles of 1548 said:[31]

> by the enclosing of lands and arable grounds in divers and sundry places of this Realm many have been driven to extreme poverty and compelled to leave the places where they were born and to seek them livings in other Counties with great misery and poverty.

Notes among the Cecil MSS. for a debate in 1597 (the year of the Act for the Maintenance of Husbandry and Tillage) included the following head for argument:[32]

> Swarms of poor loose and wandering people bred by these decays miserable to themselves, dangerous to the State.

and Bacon had made the same point in his *Of Seditions*:

> poverty in the body politic is the great occasion of riots and tumults.

Few of the agrarian disturbances of the sixteenth century were free from an element recruited from indignation at enclosure and the total or partial depopulation of villages. In the Midland riots of 1607 the rioters said that they knew of 300 places depopulated. It is likely that they were repeating a tale then in currency rather than speaking of what they knew at first hand; the number of Midland villages destroyed in their own life-time was small. Their perspective of time was crude: to them the past was all one undifferentiated past, and somewhere in it lay the events which men still spoke of. Among the rioters would be descendants of the evicted: from fathers and grandfathers the story of how the graziers cast down the towns had been handed on. Nottinghamshire J.P.'s expressed the same fear of the past when in 1631 they wrote to the King's Council[33]

> by reason of the great de-populacions that, as we fear, have beane and nowe are in committinge in diverse our neighbours' counties, the inhabitants if they be supplanted there will in likelyhood seek habitacon amongst us.

Chapter Three

TRAVELLERS TO THE LOST VILLAGE

Ut vidi sic dico . . .
John Rous on the depopulation of Warwickshire, in his Historia (c. 1485).

I

THE empty village site, the pillaged church, the tumbled houses and the disused roads would not have retained for very long the appearance of a scar. Grass is a quick-growing shroud, easily created by blown seed and quickly making its own humus. Soft soil from the crofts would be washed through the houses and down the banks to the streets in every rainstorm. Other soil would be windblown, and (as retaining walls collapsed) earth would slip down into hollows and across streets, rounding off the sharp corners and the straight sides. Grazing animals have hooves which easily level a low falling wall and scatter rubble across the grass.

In this chapter we shall try to assess how much accurate knowledge of deserted village sites was current among informed Tudor opinion, leaving for later treatment the information which was deliberately collected at that time by the Crown as part of its action against enclosures. We shall then show how little recollection of depopulation was preserved in historical and topographical writing of the seventeenth, eighteenth and nineteenth centuries, and how this limited knowledge gave sceptical colour to the treatment of the subject by modern historians.

When we examine Tudor writing on depopulation we find that it rather resembles the appearance of a lost village site today. There is sufficient visible evidence of a general kind that there have once been streets and buildings, just as it is clear that the Tudors had a general apprehension of the problem and its extent. But just as a grass-covered site is not precisely informative about detail beneath it, so Tudor writing on this topic is totally (and sometimes wildly) generalised. Round numbers are used in illustrations; districts or county names are the only clues to locations; particular villages or the fates of particular villagers are not used in illustration. There is plenty of evidence that all levels of opinion knew about the phenomenon, and, indeed, that an exaggerated fear of its continuance remained for some time after depopulating enclosure had diminished.

Such vague and indiscriminate writing helps to explain why contemporary statements have been received sceptically by recent historians, especially when they are in a position to discount the Tudor fears of a diminished *total* population. Tudor writers had used the empty villages to back their fears of an emptying England, and having proved this fear to be unfounded it was only a small step for historians to regard the dispeopled village as an exaggeration. E. F. Gay[1] styled it

> hysterical and rhetorical—its very exaggeration condemns it.

Armstrong had written of 400 Midland villages lost in sixty years, but Gay thought a tenth of this number nearer the mark

> Search reveals only a round two dozen, full half in Northamptonshire,

and Miss Bradley[2] comforted herself with the thought that

> it is to the credit of landowners that there are so few authentic cases of depopulation.

Writing far from England she might be pardoned her scepticism. It was not easy for her to see the landscape of the deserted village in the grassy shires. It is more surprising that Sir John Clapham[3] allowed himself to write:

> deserted villages are singularly rare in England

and:

> there is very little evidence of [emptied villages] in Britain.

Clapham was writing before 1946, without the advantage of seeing Dr. Hoskins' work in print, but Canon Foster's work on Lincolnshire had been in print for twenty years and more.[4] Clapham was an economic historian who had walked the face of his countryside. When he was Professor at Leeds he lived less than 15 miles from four or five deserted sites; and when he lived at Linton he must often have handled the 1-inch Ordnance map which shows the empty parishes of Cambridgeshire. As it was, it remained for Mr. John Saltmarsh, preparing Clapham's manuscript for the press, to add a footnote:

> recent work suggests that there has been more abandonment of medieval village sites than Sir John Clapham believed at the time when he wrote this chapter. But the subject awaits fuller investigation.

Lipson's *Economic History* shows caution:[5]

> another writer tells us that sheep farming had destroyed four or five hundred villages in the Midland counties. Fortunately we have a more trustworthy source of evidence in the returns of the two Commissions held in 1517 and 1607 . . . [but] we need not charge [contemporaries] with wilful misrepresentation.

Professor R. H. Tawney was aware of the extent of the problem but cautious about accepting contemporary figures.[6]

> These isolated instances are worthless as a basis for generalisation

he wrote, and further:

> though we cannot say such depopulation was general we can say that it was not unknown . . . on the whole our quantitative measurement must be a negative one.

Tawney had indeed printed a transcription of the Whatborough map which succeeded in distorting some of the figures and script on its face—and in bringing despair to my first attempt to find the site of Whatborough by using it. But there is no indication that he visited Whatborough, despite that traditional injunction of his to economic historians to take to their boots.

There was one contemporary writer against whom charges of generality and vagueness cannot be levelled. He was a chantry priest of Warwick, John Rous. He left behind him at his death in 1491 a general History of England, the *Historia Regum Angliae.* This remained unprinted until 1716 when it was edited from Oxford by the antiquary, Thomas Hearne. A second edition appeared in 1745. At least three manuscript copies of the *History* have survived.[7]

The *History* is undistinguished in its general narrative. But it breaks away from conventional narration when the author's indignation at depopulating enclosure burst through. He was describing the harrying of the provinces by the victorious William the Conqueror. Rous thought that this would merit punishment, but, he continues:

> What shall be said of the modern destruction of villages which brings Dearth to the commonwealth? The root of this evil is greed. The plague of avarice infects these times and it blinds men. They are not sons of God, but of Mammon.

He then quotes a number of scriptural texts approving those who build and condemning those who destroy.

> As Christ wept over Jerusalem so do we over the destruction of our own times. There are men who rejoice: and Christ's sorrow is their pleasure. The Church suffers also and our land looks as if an enemy had passed over it. How many outrageous things do men perform!
>
> They enclose the area of a village with mounds and surround it with ditches. In such places the King's highway is blocked and poor people cannot pass through. Where villages decay, there also do tithes. The word of God to Noah is mocked: Grow, multiply and fill the earth.
>
> If such destruction as that in Warwickshire took place in other parts of the country it would be a national danger. Yet not all my list is of Warwickshire villages: some, albeit a few, are in Gloucestershire and Worcestershire, but none of them more than a dozen miles from Warwick. Let us now see the number of villages destroyed in south Warwickshire. . . .

His list of depopulated villages runs to fifty-eight places, all of which I have been able to identify, with the exception of the ambiguous "Norton", and "Bosworth". In eleven cases Rous backed his statement by a comparison between the number of villagers listed in the Hundred Rolls of 1279 and the shrunken numbers which he knew. At Compton Scorpion there had been fifty-three tenants and a chapel to serve them: now none. At Compton Verney there were two tenants where there had been twenty-nine.

This list is, I think, unique. No other county, even others as badly hit by the conversion to sheep pasture, can boast such first-hand, incontrovertible evidence. It is at least twenty-five years earlier than the first Government Inquiry.[5]

Neither Rous' manuscript nor Hearne's text has been unknown to modern writers. Perhaps the best illustration of the depth of scepticism which the subject of lost villages had aroused is provided by Lipson. In his well-known three-volume *Economic History*, in its ninth edition in 1947, he quotes from Rous (in Hearne's printed text). But he discounts the list of village names by reporting an unidentified suggestion that they were inserted by Hearne! This cavalier treatment of evidence could have been avoided had Lipson gone from printed texts to the easily accessible manuscript copies, which have the full list of villages and no interpolations in eighteenth-century handwriting.[8]

There is nothing to show that Rous' work was known to administrators or others in the century after his death. He was not quoted by any of those pamphleteers who described the Midland depopulations in general terms. He was not brought forward as a witness by John Hales of Coventry, a Warwickshire man very zealous for witnesses against the depopulators.

There is a great deal written about Midland enclosure in Hales' *Defence* of his conduct in the Inquiry of 1548, and in the *Discourse of the Commonweal* (usually ascribed to him). We shall be using the *Discourse*[9] when we discuss the chronology and motivation of depopulation in later chapters. Here, we shall quote only the more succinct parts of his descriptive writing. The setting of the *Discourse* is in the heart of the countryside which Rous knew: the characters meet at a Coventry inn on an evening during the 1548 Inquiry. The

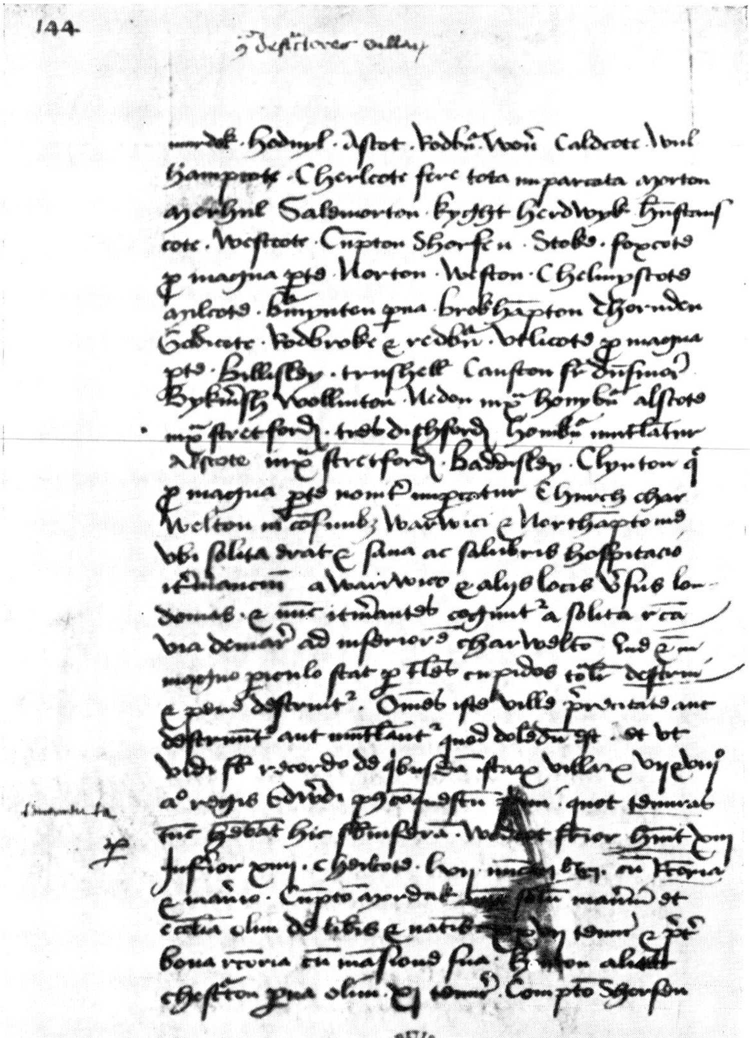

(9) JOHN ROUS' LIST OF DEPOPULATED VILLAGES

A page from the manuscript of The History of The Kings of England *written between 1485 and 1491. It is headed* destructores villarum. *For a translation see Appendix II B, p. 413.*

talk soon passes to the economic troubles of the time—inflation, enclosure, high wages, social unrest. The Doctor of Law chides the Justices for wasting their time on Inquiries when they might be looking to their lands. The Husbandman[10] defends those who object to enclosure:

> these enclosures do undo us all . . . I have known a dozen places within less compass than six miles about me laid down within these seven years; and where forty persons had their living, now one man and his shepherd hath all.

2

The shepherd living alone among the deserted houses is a figure whom we meet elsewhere, both in literature and in life. He is a figure which caught popular imagination, perhaps as the symbol of the changed economy of the village. We shall meet him in real life as Christopher Tiptoft the shepherd of Whatborough,[11] whose house was marked on the 1583 map.

We shall meet him in the person of the Argam shepherd who watched the institution of the incumbent to the grassy church. We shall meet him in real life in the Northamptonshire shepherd whom the jurors of 1517 found looking after the fields at Pilsgate.[12] He returns later in the *Discourse* when the Coventry master-capper says:[13]

> instead of some hundred or two hundred persons that had their livings thereon now be there but three or four shepherds and the master only.

He was cried abroad in the Proclamation[14] of Edward VI:

> of late by the enclosing of lands and arable grounds . . . in some places a hundred or two hundred Christian people hath been inhabiting . . . now there is nothing kept but sheep and bullock . . . and scarcely dwelled upon with one poor shepherd.

He appeared again in Latimer's Sermon preached before King Edward the Sixth in 1549, where the Bishop deliberately attacked covetous enclosers:[15]

> for where there have been a great many householders and inhabitants there is now but a shepherd and his dog.

He appeared a year later in John Coke's *Debate of the Heralds* where he says that[16]

> in England some one man keepeth in his hands two or three farms, and where hath been six or seven persons in every farm he keepeth only a shepherd or wretched herdman and his wife.

(Although there was no statement by a wife at Whatborough, there was a shepherd's wife at both Argam and Pilsgate.)

We find the shepherd in the preamble to the 1488 Act against depopulation, together with many of these commonly used phrases, such as the hundred or two hundred people who had lost their living by "the pulling down of towns", and he appears for the last time as late as 1597 in the headings of "Notes for the Present Parliament" in the Salisbury MSS:

> depopulating of whole towns and keeping of a shepherd only.

Other contemporary accounts were still more generalised. Thomas Becon's *Jewel of Joy* spoke of

> towns so wholly decayed that there is neither stick nor stone standing as they use to say.
>
> Those beasts which were created of God for the nourishment of men do now devour man. The cause . . . the greedy Gentlemen which are sheepmongers and graziers, the caterpillars of the commonweal.[17]

Becon's devouring animals are the man-eating sheep of More's *Utopia*:[18]

> the sheep that were wont to be so meek and tame and so small eaters now, as I hear say, be become so great devourers and so wild that they eat up and swallow down the very men themselves. They consume, destroy and devour whole fields, houses and cities.
>
> One shepherd or herdsman is enough to eat up that ground with cattle to the occupying whereof about husbandry many hands were requisite.
>
> Look in what parts of the realm doth grow the finest and therefore dearest wool, there noblemen and gentlemen: yea, and certain Abbots . . . leave no ground for tillage, they enclose all into pasture: they throw down houses: they pluck down towns and leave nothing standing but only the church to be made a sheep-cote.

In the *Dialogue of Pole and Lupset* the decayed villages are drawn into the perennial argument as to whether the country is underpopulated and whether men work as hard as they used.[19]

> There is lack of people and scarceness of men . . . if you look to the villages of the country . . . you shall find no small number utterly decayed

says Pole, and Lupset counters:

> this . . . argueth nothing the scarceness of people, but rather the negligent idleness of the same.

It will be noticed that in none of these comments since Rous was there the name of a single lost village. Where figures were given, there was a suspicious roundness, as Tawney observed when he quoted the Dean of Durham's neat 500 ploughs down in fifty years and 8000 acres converted to pasture by 1597. Even a pamphleteer with a very provincial theme could do no more than speak of "counties depopulated" and indulge in some very shaky arithmetic. This pamphleteer was the anonymous author of *The Decaye of England only by the Great Multitude of Shepe*,[20] published between 1550 and 1553.

This pamphlet bewails the high prices of goods and blames the sheep which occupy the land where other crops might grow in abundance. It concentrates on Oxfordshire, Buckinghamshire and Northamptonshire and declares that forty ploughs have been displaced in Oxfordshire since 1485, with the eviction of six people in each case, and a total loss of 240 persons. The author could not have known the returns to the Inquiry of 1517, where he would have found many more than forty ploughs laid down in Oxfordshire since 1485. The author's remedy was a law to declare that there should be as many ploughs everywhere as in 1485. If this proposal recalls the Act of 1489, the pamphlet's next point recalls the preamble of that Act, where national security had been seen as jeopardised by enclosure:

> it is a great decay to artillery: for that we do reckon that shepherds be but ill archers.

The theme of "the shepherd a poor archer" was a common one. Men recalled the traditions of the English husbandmen who had been the backbone of the victorious archers of the Hundred Years' War. At the end of the century, D'Ewes *Journal*[21] reports Cecil in the House of Commons as saying:

> I think that whosoever does not maintain the plough destroys this kingdom . . . I am sure that when warrants go from the Council for levying of men in the counties and the certificates be returned unto us again, we find the greatest part of them to be ploughmen.
> And excepting Sir Thomas More's *Utopia* or some such feigned commonwealth, you shall never find but the ploughman is chiefly provided for.

Cecil was perhaps forgetting how he might have found an ally for his own argument in the passage of *Utopia* we have already quoted.

3

But the statesmen, and those who sought to be the mentors of statesmen had not been silent. We shall postpone until a later chapter the examination of what was said by those who drafted the preambles to anti-enclosure legislation, for these garrulous Tudor preambles are always informative about the overt motives of the Crown and its advisers.

We have already quoted Bishop Latimer seeking to instruct Edward VI in statecraft. Latimer was the son of a Leicestershire yeoman, and no one growing up in that grassy shire just before 1500 could fail to be familiar with enclosure and depopulation. More than one sermon was built around the symbol of the Plough and "Enclosure, which is to let or hinder . . . the ploughing".

Poets were not averse to offering political advice, and we have the *Epigram*[22] in sonnet form, addressed to Queen Elizabeth by Thomas Bastard in 1598:

> I know where is a thief and long hath been
> Which spoileth every place where he resorts
> He steals away both subjects from the Queen
> And men from his own country of all sorts.

Houses by three and seven and ten he raseth
To make the common glebe his private land:
Our country cities cruel he defaceth
The grass grows green where little Troy did stand;
The forlorn father hanging down his head
His outcast company drawn up and down
The pining labourer doth beg his bread
The plowswain seeks his dinner from the town.
  O, Prince, the wrong is thine, for understand
  Many such robberies will undo thy land.

The theme was a favourite with Bastard. He developed it in two other shorter *Epigrams*:

Sheep have eaten up our meadows and our downs
Our corn, our wood, whole villages and towns.
Yea, they have eat up many wealthy men
Besides widows and orphan children:
  Besides our statutes and our iron laws
  Which they have swallowed down into their maws.
Till now I thought the proverb did but jest
Which said a black sheep was a biting beast.

When the great Forests' dwelling was so wide
  And careless wood grew fast by the fires' side,
Then dogs did want the shepherd's fields to keep;
  Now we want foxes to consume our sheep.

Bastard's advice to his Queen may stand alongside another lesson in statecraft. In the second Act of *Pericles, Prince of Tyre* the Prince is shipwrecked. Lying exhausted on the strand he overhears a conversation between fishermen. Their conversation is not unworthy of a prince for (although they seem to talk of fishing) they are talking in allegory of politics. Indeed, the Prince observes

How from the finny subject of the sea
These fishers tell the infirmities of men.

Among these infirmities are the destroyed villages: the first Fisherman puts it this way—

I can compare our rich misers to nothing so fitly as a whale. A' plays and tumbles, driving the poor fry before him, and

> at last devours them all at a mouthful: such whales have I heard on i' the land, who never leave gaping till they've swallowed the whole parish, church, steeple, bells and all.

Pericles adds, aside: "A pretty moral".

There were others who wished to influence the Crown to act more vigorously. A number of correspondents in Tudor and Stuart *State Papers, Domestic* argue this way. Typical, although late in the day, is the letter[23] from Richard Sandes to the Council of Charles I.

> I will give you the names of many decayed towns in the counties of Leicester and Northampton etc., and who decayed them. And now the Lord hath swept away the enclosers and their posterity out of all, and strangers have their houses and pastures.

Sandes is obviously writing after the event. His offer has something of the eagerness of an observant antiquary to air his discoveries. Had the village-sites been well known, he can hardly have thought that the Council would have been so ignorant of provincial life.

4

The principal character of contemporary comment which we have cited is, then, a general familiarity with the existence of lost village sites but little sign of detailed knowledge. There is one possible explanation which, I think, can be dismissed: that the names of deserted villages were so well known to their readers and listeners that authors did not bother to cite any. There is no evidence of Tudor reticence to repeat the familiar when they addressed an audience on any other subject.

In a later chapter it will be suggested that public awareness had this limited character principally because of the time which had elapsed since the worst depopulation. If Hales could write in 1548 that the principal part of depopulation had occurred before 1485; and if John Rous, by 1491, could already assemble fifty-eight sites depopulated in 530 square miles, then it is not surprising that Elizabethans were vague when pressed for exact information about a site.

We can demonstrate this vagueness when we have interrogatories put to local witnesses in lawsuits involving the lost village; or on occasions when local juries were called in to assist surveyors. We have already seen this uncertainty in the minds of the jurors at East Lilling in 1625:

> it hath been a hamlet of some capacity though now utterly demolished . . . *how long since doth not appear.*

Many miles from East Lilling, down in the Isle of Wight, another jury[24] in 1559 was as vague:

> we heare of many old streats and villages bothe of artificers and others cleyn dekeyed and no signe of eny howsinge whiche have had a Begynninge longe agoo out of eny mans knowledge . . . we cannot saye what sholde be the verie cause.

The county maps of the sixteenth and seventeenth centuries were on too small a scale to mark many villages, let alone the sites of decayed settlements, so that we shall not derive much help from these cartographers. But by a piece of good fortune, comparable to the survival of the Survey Book of East Lilling, a lawsuit of the fifteen-eighties did cause a "compotent" surveyor, Thomas Clerk (or Clark) of Stamford, to take his instruments out into the fields of Whatborough (Leics.), where a village had once stood, and to survey it on a large scale, with an attention to detail which bears comparison with the modern 6-inch Ordnance map. It was surveyed in 1586.

The map is preserved among the muniments[25] at All Souls College, Oxford, and is reproduced in Plate 5, together with the same fields photographed from the air in 1947. It does not show the sites of houses other than conventionally, contenting itself with the outside boundary of the village. Only the house of the shepherd is shown at the north end. Outside the village perimeter the former open arable fields are drawn, furlong by furlong. Other fields which had gone down from arable to grass at an earlier date beyond the memory of witnesses were assumed to be arable from the ridge-and-furrow of strip ploughing which could be seen in the grass in 1583: "theis groundes doe lie ridge and forrowe"; "Theis groundes have likewise bene arrable". The ridge-and-furrow of these former open-field strips still shows clearly on the photograph and the blocks of ridge-and-furrow can be compared and identified with the *furlongs* of the open-field arable as delineated by the surveyor of 1586.

I do not know of any other visit of a surveyor to a deserted site until a party of us, as amateur surveyors, carried our haversacks, measuring chains and marking rods up the side of Whatborough Hill in 1946. The principal features of our survey—the hollow depressions and the ponds—can be seen on the air photograph; and the ponds appear as sources of streams on the 1586 map.

The village of Whatborough stood on a small plateau at the summit of the second-highest hill in Leicestershire.[26]

> The extraordinary position of the village of Whatborough can only be adequately explained as an early foundation in the Old English settlement, possibly early in the sixth century.
> In 1222 it had a chapel. When the tax quota of 1334 was fixed . . . Whatborough was put down at only 5*s*. 6*d*.—a mere hamlet. In 1446 we see a further serious decline: the quota is cut from 5*s*. 6*d*. to 3*s*., a drop of 45%.

Dr. Hoskins and Dr. Parker have shown that the hamlet was depopulated in 1494–95 by Launde Priory who held the land on long lease from All Souls College. A lawsuit between the College and the post-Dissolution owner of Launde Priory was the occasion for the visit of Thomas Clerk the surveyor.

There is little about the sites of lost villages in those Tudor topographers whose work has been christened by A. L. Rowse, "the Elizabethan Discovery of England". The antiquities which interested them were of an earlier age. Leland and Camden must have ridden near many lost sites without recording them, and no doubt dined on their journeys in the Halls of the depopulators. Only in an allusive sentence in Camden have I found any echo of the depopulated village. He arrived at Halifax and was impressed to find it the very reverse of depopulated. Of its swarming hillsides he wrote (c. 1585):

> Halifax maintains more men than other kind of animals, whereas elsewhere in England in the most fruitful places you will see many thousand sheep and but few people, as if men had given place to sheep and cattle or had been devoured by them.[27]

5

In the next century Dugdale rode the fields of Warwickshire searching for material for the *History*. Like Richard Sandes he disapproved of the profit-seeking landowners, particularly those who had stepped into the shoes of the monasteries. He carefully noted when such landowners' families had died childless, and he helped to perpetuate the myth that the purchasers of monastic lands were awarded this fate by divine justice. He was, perhaps, not aware that the Warwickshire Abbeys, like the Leicestershire priory of Launde, had been themselves great depopulators in their day; nor that there was on the Statute Book that curious measure of 1402 declaring that monks should no longer be insulted by being called *depopulatores agrum*.

But Dugdale's interest did produce a county *History* with a careful attention to depopulated villages, and in the eighteenth-century edition the publisher provided maps by Beighton on which a special symbol was reserved for "depopulated places".

In his side-notes appears "the MS of John Rous' Historia Regum Angliac" and many of the comments in Dugdale's book show that he had used Rous carefully, even to the comparisons with the population in the Hundred Rolls. The British Museum copy of the Rous MS. has "Wm. Dugdale" on an outer leaf, and it is likely that this was the copy from which he worked. We know also that Dugdale's interest in enclosure had brought him to make his own transcripts from the Commission of 1517 and 1518, and we owe our knowledge of the Warwickshire returns of 1548 solely to his notes.

Later in the century the Nottinghamshire doctor,

Thoroton, rode his county making notes for his *History*. He shared many of Dugdale's interests, and the lost villages of Nottinghamshire are not forgotten in his pages.

> The plow upheld all till that stupendous Act which swept away the Monasteries . . . gave more frequent Encouragement and Opportunities to such Private Men further to improve and augment their own Revenues by greater loss to the Commonwealth viz. by enclosing and converting arable to pasture which as certainly diminishes the Yearly Fruits as it doth the People

wrote Thoroton in 1677. As he rode by Thorpe le Glebe, down by the Leicestershire border, he saw the ruined church of Thorpe with the shepherd selling ale in the former churchyard. The Ordnance survey mark the site of this church on the 6-inch map. The ruin, and some other churches on deserted sites, were sketched by Throsby for his engravings in the 1797 edition of Thoroton.

Thoroton preserved the name and date of the depopulator. He blamed Gabriel Armstrong, whose family had become sole proprietors of the parish early in the fifteenth century. In 1491 he had depopulated the lordship:

> so ruined and depopulated that in my time there was not a House left inhabited of this whole lordship (except some part of the Hall) but a Shepherd only kept ale to sell in the Church.

The transcript of the evidence presented to the Nottinghamshire Commission of 1517–18 only mentions 90 acres enclosed in 1491 and no persons evicted. But a membrane of the Commission's papers which Leadam did not print is headed "Names of suyche parsons summoned to appear" and the last name is "Gabryell Armestrang for Thorp in the clottes". This less elegant name for the parish links the *Clotts* of a 1287 document (=clods) with the Latin form *in glebis* (*gleba*=clod, lump of earth) and the French form of the modern name. Although no poll tax return is legible for this parish (and it is still a parish) we have the tax quota of 1334 which was 13*s*. 3*d*. Eight of the thirty neighbouring villages in this part of the county were of a comparable size. As late as 1434 the village was receiving no bigger tax relief than its fellows, so that the evictions of Armstrong may have fallen upon a fairly full community. It is an excellent site to visit. It lies near Church-side Farm.[28]

Of the other Midland county historians, Lipscomb, Nichols and Bridges have references to desertions although, in general, the more recent the *History* the less likely the mention of the village. There seems to have been almost a conspiracy of silence among the county historians of Yorkshire. At one time it almost seemed as if the Victoria County Histories would become life members of the same conspiracy. Dr. Hoskins has hard words to say about the *VCH*'s treatment of this subject, but I would not go quite so far. Oblique references to vanished villages can be detected in the nooks and crannies of the *History*, although it sounds incredible that the Hampshire volume could devote its pages to the Isle of Wight without ever mentioning the Act of 1488 against the decay of towns in the Island, the first anti-enclosure statute, with its graphic preamble; or without commenting on the fact that ten of the vills assessed to the medieval Lay Subsidies are now nothing but farm names. As we have seen, the islanders of 1559 knew better. This indifference can be paralleled in other county volumes and it is a monument to a school of local history writing which felt itself self-sufficient without a dose of the classic remedy traditionally first prescribed by Professor Tawney: a short dose of boots. An honourable exception can be found in the fifteen volumes of the *Northumberland County History* which has lively contemporary surveys of the late Tudor depopulations.

Two other travellers merit inclusion in our list: Stukeley and De La Pryme. Stukeley visited the site of Cestersover in Warwickshire in 1776 to see the chapel converted to a barn and, straddling the valley, the fishponds of the medieval village. The barn has now become part of a farm and the railway has helped to destroy the symmetry of the pond-dams. The moat of the Manor House was deep enough to drown an unlucky tractor-driver in 1950. Dugdale had seen

> the manor house reduced to a mean condition and the grounds for the most part converted to sheep pasture.

The encloser was Henry Waver, a London draper, later Sheriff of that city, who obtained permission to enclose in 1460 and 1467. But the tradition of Dugdale's day had not survived, and Stukeley thought the site Roman. This was perhaps permissible, since the Watling Street formed the northern boundary of the parish.[29] The site is shown in plate 15.

6

By a coincidence a similar mistake was responsible for the first air photograph of a lost village site. The Vicar of Welton, Lincolnshire, reported to Dr. O. G. S. Crawford in 1924 that there were ancient earthworks to the side of the Roman road which runs from Lincoln to the Humber. He suggested that these might be a Roman camp and worth photographing. On April 3, 1925, Dr. Crawford took a photograph from 4000 feet altitude. It was reproduced in the *Antiquaries Journal, 1925*, with a short note.[30] Dr. Crawford at once saw that this could not be a Roman site, but he had the skill and good fortune to know of an account of the site in 1697, when Abraham de la Pryme had described a visit in his Diary, published by the Surtees Society in 1870:

> This day I took my horse and went to a place called Gainstrop which lies in a hollow on the right hand, and about the middle way as you come from Kirton to Scawby. Tradition says that the aforesaid Gainstrop was once a pretty large town, though now there is nothing but some of the foundations. Being upon the place I easily counted the foundations of about two hundred buildings [reduced in a later account to a hundred!] and beheld three streets very fair. About a quarter of a mile [away] is a place called the Church Garth.

The diarist's diagnosis of the disease which had killed the village is interesting:

> Tradition says that that town was, in times of yore, exceeding infamous for robberies, and that nobody inhabited there but thieves; and that the country having for a long while endured all their villanies they at last, when they could suffer them no longer, rose with one consent, and pulled the same down about their ears.

(10) GAINSTHORPE, LINCS.

Photographed from the air by O. G. S. Crawford, the first abandoned village to be so recorded. It lies in Hibaldstow parish, 400 yards west of the Ermine Street.

This was an up-to-date version of the common myth of destruction by Cromwell or Henry VII, but it was not acceptable to de la Pryme who managed to sum up the whole history of the site in a pleasant phrase:

> But I fancy that the town has been eaten up with time, poverty, and pasturage.

Dr. Crawford's photograph (Plate 10) was an excellent one, and excavation of houses from it would have been simple. But it passed unnoticed (as far as I can judge) among economic historians and geographers—to name only two interests most concerned.

At the very same time, also in Lincolnshire, work on the listing of abandoned sites was being carried out by Canon C. W. Foster. His definitive list was published as an Appendix to the Lincoln Record Society's edition of the *Lincolnshire Domesday* in 1924, although he had published an interim list with his earlier volume of *Final Concords*. The list shows that Canon Foster was tracing his lost villages both in documents and in the field, and these parallel investigations were reinforced by a close study of the 6-inch Ordnance map. This must rank as the pioneer work on the subject and it makes the study of the deserted villages of this extensive county a more manageable task. The list does not prove to be complete, and some of the more important additions to it are listed in the Lincolnshire section of my Appendix. The list was concerned with any site, whatever its size and however early its disappearance, and some of the sites named in it were never more than single manors.

After this burst of activity in 1924 and 1925 a silence descended.[31] Here and there, the research workers for the English Place-Name Society were finding and recording lost vills. Here and there, the research workers for the Victoria County Histories were finding empty parishes and noting the isolation of churches. But, by and large, it was only with the publication of Dr. Hoskins' *The Deserted Villages of Leicestershire* (now reprinted with additions in his *Essays in Leicestershire History*) that the villages were incorporated in a narrative which took into account the general economic conditions causing these depopulations. As Professor H. C. Darby has said:[32]

> I think Foster's work was a remarkable pioneering effort; in a sense we were not ready for it.

Judging from work published between 1925 and 1945 this is true. No new general sketch of English economic history of any stature appeared between these years, and we have seen that Lipson did not disturb the general judgment of Tawney and Gay that the depopulations, although important, were not as extensive as the Tudor writers had claimed. Indeed we have seen that he printed (an anonymous) suggestion that Rous' list of village names was an eighteenth-century forgery.

No one knew better than Sir John Clapham what was being written in the twenties and thirties on the economic history of the provinces. Sir John was also an acute observer of the physical landscape as he walked and travelled. But his verdict which we have quoted is a memorial to the unforeseen results of the zeal with which the Elizabethans cried "Wolf"; and a chapter heading in W. H. R. Curtler's book reads:

> What Modern Research has to say about Tudor Enclosures. The Contemporary Outcry Exaggerated.

7

No account of the history of our consciousness of the deserted villages would be complete without some discussion of the poem in which the adjective and noun were immortally joined.

Oliver Goldsmith's *Deserted Village* was published in 1770. In the Dedicatory Note to Sir Joshua Reynolds, the poet wrote:

> I have taken all possible pains in my country excursions for these four or five years past to be certain of what I allege. Some of my friends think that the depopulation of villages does not exist, but I am myself satisfied.

Commentators have examined the poem in an attempt to identify his deserted village where wealth accumulated and men decayed. Goldsmith had named an *Auburn*, and although there is a depopulated village of that name in the East Riding there is nothing to suggest that Goldsmith's village was in Yorkshire. Commentators have suggested that he was describing Irish evictions, and if his allegations were about places so distant from literary London it is not surprising that his friends were sceptical. It would seem likely that an English depopulation could have been proved to them by an invitation to a journey by coach along a good turnpike road.

On the other hand, as we shall show when we discuss the chronology of depopulation, there were a number of depopulations of a particular type which might easily have come to Goldsmith's notice. These were those which removed a village to make way for a Great House or for a rebuilding of an older House; or to give an uninterrupted vista from the windows across the planned acres of the landscape gardeners. Such a removal might be followed—as it was at Harewood—by the building of a new (and often model) village outside the walls of the park. But there were villages which were not rebuilt in this way. Two of these were Hinderskelfe and Wotton Underwood (see p. 140). The same fate overtook Stowe and its hamlets; it overtook Wimpole; and Goldsmith may have known of any of these without difficulty. But exactly where his country excursions lay, and exactly where "the prey of hastening ills" was to be found we must leave in doubt.

In any of his country excursions it would not have been difficult for Goldsmith to hear some of the folk-myths which had been constructed around the deserted sites. We have seen that in the seventeenth century the fact but not the cause of desertion was still in lively remembrance, and as time passed men explained the deserted site which they could not help seeing in terms of their own experience. They had forgotten the enclosing sheep-master, so the agent was re-christened. Sculthorp in Rutland is said to have been destroyed by the Parliamentary Army in 1642; Bridges reported that Steane in Northamptonshire was firmly believed to have been destroyed by the Danes; Gainsthorpe in Lincolnshire by outraged neighbours; Stretton Baskerville had been burned by Henry VII in revenge for non-assistance at Bosworth Field; and most common of all looms the figure of Cromwell. As Dr. Hoskins has written

> any "trenches" said to have been dug by him are to be suspected as a lost village site, or the site of any building said to have been destroyed by him.

In October, 1951, we stood, on a misty morning, on the site of Bescaby, to the north-east of Melton Mowbray. Surely enough, the farmer who approached us out of the mist told us the story of Cromwell. Even the boundary furrows of the plough-lands became his entrenchments during a battle. If the strength of this myth is any guide, the Lord Protector must have made an indelible impression on the country mind.

Second only to Cromwell is the Devil. Where a church stands isolated (because a village has been destroyed or removed) then the popular explanation is often that the Devil malignantly moved the building overnight from some other centre. This is similar to the myth at Oldbury in Thornbury, Glos., where the church at the top of the hill is explained by the fact that each night the Devil destroyed what had been built in a day. The village was then told to yoke two heifers never milked, and where they fell exhausted was to be the proper site for a church: it was at the top of the hill.

Another way in which the village's memory has been handed down from generation to generation is in a field-name. "Town" or "Township" Field is always a clue worth following up, and there are corrupt forms of these names (such as *Downslip*) equally significant. At Hamilton, east of Leicester, the Ordnance map has always marked "the Town of Hamilton" in grassy fields, and this Tudor phrase may represent a continuous tradition. Mr. H. S. L. Dewar, who has been investigating a Somerset site, tells me that Bineham has been known locally as Bineham City. In all these deserted sites, of course, there are likely to be the common folk-myths of underground passages and buried treasure which preserve the memory of buildings and community life in an acceptably romantic dress.[33]

8

We shall conclude this chapter with a description of what must have been almost the most picturesque of all visits to a deserted village site. The village of Argam lay on the crown of the Yorkshire Wolds. To the east the land drops quickly to the coast. To the south and west the flat table-land is now broken by the wind-break belts of trees. Villages are far apart, and it is a hot, dry countryside in summer. In winter it knows the isolation of snow drifts. The site has not been ploughed, although almost every other field for miles is under a corn crop. The site was clear enough to be marked on the First Edition of the 6-inch Ordnance map.

A number of lost village sites were recorded on the First Edition of this survey, probably due to an archaeologically minded surveyor in that part of the county. Outside the Wolds and the Masham district this Edition failed to note any of the lost Yorkshire sites. The sites which were noted had their earthworks plotted but the type of village was merely described as "Ancient". It was probably identifications such as these which aided R. H. Skaife in his careful annotations to the Surtees Society's edition of the Yorkshire *Nomina Villarum*, published in 1866.

The exact date of the depopulation of Argam is not known, and as we shall see, it had been forgotten as early as 1632. Bardney Abbey had owned land here, and their cartulary speaks of

> *capellam nostram de Ergum et decimas unius carrucae terrae.*

Meaux Abbey also held land in the village and the *Chronicles* of Meaux have many references between 1190 and 1340 to houses and open-field lands in Argam. Argam with Bartindale (also lost) had a tax quota well above its neighbours in 1334, and a low relief in 1354. It is unlikely, therefore, to have been a Black Death destruction, but we cannot precisely date the event.

The church at Argam continued to have its parson inducted long after the parish had been enclosed and the parishioners diminished, and it is in a lawsuit about the holding of the living that depositions were taken from "divers ancient men of Kilham and Rudston", adjacent Wolds villages. It is from these depositions that the strange proceedings can be reconstructed. The induction of the priest to the non-existent church in the non-existent village gave rise to a symbolic transaction. The institution, said the witnesses,

> was by cuttinge upp a sodd or peece of earth in the place where the Church of Argam is supposed to have stood, and delivering the same to the said Master Pulleyne.

The field was at that time almost bare grass;

> there is a cottage house where some people dwelt near adjoining the place

testified one witness, and another witness was more explicit about the occupation of the cottager:

> there was only remaining a cottage where a shepherd and his wife lived

said William Harrison of Rudston. Asked where the Church was thought to have stood, one replied:

> Upon that very place

and another said:

> The place where the parish church stood being now quite demolished . . . and upon view of the same place . . . (there) did appear to have been anciently a wall.

Harrison had seen

> part of the walls of the Church of Argan standing in his time,

and Pulleyne's predecessor as incumbent had occasionally fulfilled his canonical obligations by reading prayers there. The formal obligations of the institution ceremony were met in the way we have described, but in view of the uncertainty in the traditional location of the site a curious double insurance was made:

> Lest that the induction should be mistaken, Mr. Gibson did cut up a sod or piece of earth upon either side of the place where the wall stood and another in the midst thereof.

The patron of the living, Robert Ellis, acknowledged to the court that he held glebe lands worth forty pounds a year, but that his allowance to the incumbent was only a thirtieth part of that sum. He may have considered it sufficient payment for occasional prayers in the open air. It is possible that his predecessor had conducted the occasional baptism of the shepherd's children on the site, for one witness recalled a font stone which he had once known.

The final question put to the witnesses of Master Pulleyne's journey is one at which any historian could be pardoned for drawing in breath in anticipation as he unfolded the paper. But the record of the witness' reply[34] is none the less disappointing for being as familiar as it is curt:

> how longe is it since the sayd churche was demolished and the inhabitants of the sayd paryshe depopulated?
>
> *Nescit*, he knoweth not.

Chapter Four

THE KING'S PROCEEDINGS

. . . our statutes and our iron laws
Which [sheep] have swallowed down into their maws.
    Till now I thought the proverb did but jest
    Which said a black sheep was a biting beast.

Thomas Bastard (1598).

I

IN this chapter we shall be concerned with State action against the destruction of villages. We shall examine the legislation, the Commissions of Inquiry, the prosecutions in the Royal Courts and the administrative measures of the Council against the depopulator. We shall examine the character of the records of this State action only in so far as they illuminate the character and effectiveness of the action. In other chapters we shall use these records for other purposes: to illustrate the fate of individual villages; to examine the period and the locale of the movement; and to discover the motives and identities of the depopulators.

Before 1489 it would have been difficult to argue in an English court of law that enclosure was an offence proscribed by statute. There was the Statute of Merton of 1235, a time when villages and fields were still growing. The statute was directed against men who encroached upon the common pastures and wastes as they drove their expanding arable fields outwards from the village. Appropriate as a restrictive influence in a period of colonisation, it was not fitted to justify action against those who were attacking those very arable fields in the advancing movement of grass against corn in later centuries.

John Rous, whose disapproval of enclosure we have already seen, claimed that he had presented a petition to Parliament asking for legislation in 1459. Even earlier there is the petition from the village of Chesterton to the Parliament of 1414 anticipating many later stories of the shepherd and his dog inheriting the empty village fields:

> there was made great waste in the same Manor . . . of housing —that is to say of halls and chambers and other houses of office that were necessary in the same manor—and none housing left standing there but if it were a sheepcote or a barn or swine-sty and a few houses beside to put in beasts.[1]

But no general prohibition resulted until 1489.

Individual citizens who were aggrieved by depopulating enclosure might have found their way to the common law courts or to Chancery to obtain redress. Such cases seem to be few, but since the fifteenth-century records are poorly calendared and indexed this verdict may some day be upset. There are a few cases in Chancery between 1485 and 1517 in which individuals present petitions alleging damage from depopulating enclosure, but before 1489 they had no statute to plead in their support. The Chancery Petitions of this kind, such as that of the inhabitants of Shuckburgh, were concerned only with the fact that legal rights of common had been usurped. They strove to assert rights, rather than base their case on a view that depopulation is illegal by statute or contrary to the welfare of the commonwealth. We find the same inhabitants proceeding against their depopulating landlord in the Court of Requests; and there are cases in Star Chamber, and also indirect evidence that the Council of the North was also used by aggrieved villagers. These individuals had been fortunate enough to obtain access to a court in defence of their property rights. Many of the dispossessed could not have hoped for such redress: the sole owner of a lordship peopled by tenants-at-will might find little more than a shadowy custom to restrain him, and during the Wars of the Roses many customs as well as laws had been effectively silenced.[2]

The motive for the first intervention by the Crown was not the defence of individual property rights, but the fear of danger to the State if depopulation were allowed to continue. It is significant that the Act of 1489 was preceded by a similar measure for the Isle of Wight alone. The chalklands of the Island were attractive to graziers, but shepherds and sheep pastures seemed to endanger military security. These fears are expressed in the preamble to the Act of 1488.

> It is to the surety of the Realm of England that the Isle of Wight . . . be well inhabited with English people . . . the which Isle is late decayed of people by reason that many Towns and Villages be let down and the field dyked and made pastures for beasts and cattles. The same Isle . . . is desolate and not inhabited but occupied with beasts and cattle, so that if hasty remedy be not provided that Isle cannot be long kept and defended but open and ready to the hands of the King's enemies, which God forbid.

The Act did not mention sheep specifically, and it is curious that although pasture is mentioned as the root of the evil, the Act did not make conversion an offence. Penalties were to be imposed only if holdings were taken into one man's hands so that total value exceeded ten marks a year:

> many dwelling places farms and farmholds have of late times been used to be taken into one mens' hold and hands, that of old time were wont to be in many several persons' holds and hands.

No new machinery for discovering offenders or levying fines was set up, and I have not been able to trace any enforcement of the Act. We have only a Proclamation of February 1492/93 in admonitory terms. Nor does there seem to have been any serious attempt to enforce the general Statute of 1489 until after the supplementary Act of 1515. Polydore Vergil, looking back from 1534, gave no hint of vigorous enforcement. For him these were years when[3]

> the abuses were not checked early in their development, and afterwards they hardened and became more durable.

The general Statute of 1489 was principally directed against the offence, not of engrossing (as in the Isle of Wight Act), but of depopulation. It was the decay of "houses of husbandry" which created an offence. Such a house was one which had with it 20 acres of land "normally" (that is, for three years past) under the plough. Until these houses were rebuilt, the overlord of the offender was permitted to take half the profits of the holding as a penalty, the other half falling to the Crown. The assumption was that overlords would take action. In fact the identity of interest between overlord and an enclosing tenant seems to have been close enough to prevent any action. The main interest of this Act lies in its preamble, with its long description of the ills attending depopulation.[4]

> Great inconveniences daily doth increase by desolation and pulling down and wilfull waste of houses and Towns within this his realm, and laying to pasture lands which customarily have been used in tillage, whereby idleness—ground and beginning of all mischiefs—daily doth increase, for where in some Towns two hundred persons were occupied and lived by their lawful labours, now be there occupied two or three herdmen and the residue fallen in idleness; the husbandry, which is one of the greatest commodities of the realm, is greatly decayed; churches destroyed; the service of God withdrawn; the bodies there buried not prayed for; the patron and curate wronged; the defence of this land against our enemies outwards feebled and impaired: to the great displeasure of God, to the subversion of the policy and good rule of this land.

Every one of these phrases could be illustrated many times over from the villages described in this book, and we shall often have to return to the themes here stated.

Government interest in the restraint of enclosure did not become active again until 1514, when two drafts were prepared for the Council. In the preamble of the first, a Bill, the blame was thrown on town investors and speculators who were buying up land to enclose it for pasture.

> Many merchant adventurers, clothmakers, goldsmiths, butchers, tanners and other artificers and unreasonable covetous persons do encroach many more farms than they are able to occupy. Farms and ploughs are decayed . . . and no more parishioners in many parishes but a neat-herd and a shepherd.[5]

The same theme is stated in the draft Proclamation.

> [There is] scarcity of grain by converting and engrossing [by those who] for their own lucre neglecteth tillage.

The Act of 1515, made perpetual in 1516, concentrated upon the offence of conversion from tillage to pasture: land which was tillage in February 1515 was to remain so, or to be turned back to the plough if it had been converted.[6] As in 1489, failure involved forfeit of half profits, but if the over-lord was not zealous in the cause of the commonwealth then the next superior lord could seize.

2

It was the failure of this zeal which helps to explain the Commissions of Inquiry set up by Wolsey in 1517 to investigate offences up and down the country, and the supplementary Inquiry of 1518. From the facts found, the Crown could set an example by suing for half profits from its own tenants. Since the findings of these Commissions were still giving rise to prosecutions in the reign of Elizabeth I, and since the evidence which it collected was virtually country-wide, we must devote adequate space to the subject. The greater part of the findings of the Commissions was printed in 1897 by I. S. Leadam from the Chancery files. He christened the documents "*The Domesday of Inclosures*". In 1892–94 he had published three articles in which he had transcribed notes of other proceedings at the Commissions from a manuscript in the British Museum, probably the summary of other 1517 and 1518 proceedings prepared to guide the later Commission of Inquiry in 1548.[7]

Even taking these articles and the book together, the findings of the Commission are not completely printed. The fault did not lie with Leadam, for membranes in the Chancery files had not all survived their long immersion in a sack in the company of an old boot from the Tower. These missing proceedings can, however, be restored for villages where proceedings against the encloser subsequently took place in the Court of Exchequer. The record of the hearing always began with the verbatim recital of the findings of the Commission. These records had not been explored when Leadam first wrote, and E. F. Gay, who initiated their study, carried on a vigorous controversy with Leadam over the interpretation of the findings.[8] Even when proceedings did not take place in Exchequer, we now have other files of Chancery documents arising from the Commission which were not available to Leadam or Gay. These are described in Chapter Nine.

The Commission itself derived its authority from Letters Patent, which were printed by Leadam.[9] They open with a preamble very similar to the Acts of 1489 and 1515, and then instruct the Commissioners:

> We order you, or any two of you, to enquire from a jury of men in these counties upon their oath as follows: which and how many villages, which houses and buildings have been cast down since the Feast of St. Michael, 1488? how much and what sort of land was in cultivation and now lying in pasture? how many and what type of parklands have been enclosed for feeding wild animals? by whom? when? and of what value?

The many hundreds of reports from the juries are the answers to these questions, usually preserved in the record in a common form, but with some interesting elaborations where a particular point had caught their attention. Such detail offered at Stretton Baskerville was quoted on p. 64. Many findings are easily available in Leadam and we need do no more here than give a translation of the routine form of report.[10]

This case concerns Wretchwick, a hamlet of Bicester (Oxon.) whose remains are well preserved in the grass surrounding Middle Wretchwick Farm, and for which a fifteenth-century rental is printed on p. 295.

> Indented inquisition taken at Culham in the said county of Oxford on 3 August 1517 before John Vesey, Dean of the Chapel of the Lord King at Windsor, and Roger Wyggeston formerly of Leicester, Commissioners of the King by virtue of letters patent (which are recited) before Thomas Lenthall, gentleman (and eleven other jurymen) and at an adjourned meeting on the nineteenth of October at Henley on Thames agreed to by the jurors.
>
> Who say upon their oath that the late prior of the Monastery of Bicester held five messuages and 200 acres of arable land with their appurtenances in Wretchwick [Wrecchewyke] in

> the parish of Bicester in the said county of Oxford; which lands used to be ploughed and sown with grain, and along with each messuage there were at least thirty acres of land ploughed as far back as man's memory goes. He held this land on the second of March 1489 when those messuages were laid waste and thrown down, and lands formerly used for arable he turned over to pasture for animals, so that three ploughs are now out of use there, and eighteen people who used to work on that land and earn their living there and who dwelled in the houses have gone away to take to the roads in their misery, and to seek their bread elsewhere and so are led into idleness etc. [*sic*]. And those tenements are worth ten marks a year. They are held from the King as of the Honour of Wallingford; and John, now Prior, possesses them.

Such an allegation provided all the material necessary for a successful prosecution under the Act.

The next step was an order from the Court of Chancery to the Sheriff to cause the offender to appear. This was done by means of the writ of *scire facias* which we shall illustrate from a Warwickshire case, that of William Willington of Barcheston, whom the jury had accused of enclosing 530 acres and destroying four houses and a cottage so that[11]

> almost all the hamlet of Barcheston is laid waste and made as nothing. Twenty four people have been expelled from their houses and tearfully seek food and work elsewhere.

The writ was issued on February 24, 1518, the spring following the visit of the Commission to Warwickshire. It recited the findings of the jury (as printed in Leadam) and continued:[12]

> we order you to make it known to the said William Willington that he should appear before us in our Chancery on the quindene of Easter next to show cause why he should not pay to us half the annual profits of these houses and lands from the first of March 1508 (which was the date of the depopulation) and what houses and cottages he has rebuilt according to the force, form and effect of a certain Act of Parliament of the fourth year of the reign of our father, late King of England etc.

These writs and the note of the appearance of those summoned to Chancery have survived for the counties of Bedfordshire, Berkshire, Middlesex, Buckinghamshire, Gloucestershire, Leicestershire, Northamptonshire, Oxfordshire and Warwickshire.[13] For some offenders the plea which they entered is bound with the *scire facias* writ (the plea is sometimes called "the traverse of the inquisition"). Also in these bundles are petitions to the Chancellor from offenders, which we shall describe later.

3

The proceedings against enclosers are most conveniently studied in the rolls of the Court of Exchequer. Even cases which were heard in Chancery or before the King's Bench were transcribed in Exchequer since the collection of fines might be a revenue matter. If a case like Tyringham's case in 1519 was sent down to be decided at the Assizes, the verdict of the other court would be recorded in Exchequer to show whether proceedings for recovery of the fine should proceed or be restrained. The number and scope of these Exchequer hearings will be indicated in Tables 13–15 in the Appendix.

It will be convenient to survey the prosecutions between 1517 and 1565 as a whole, and for that purpose the Memoranda Rolls of the Court of Exchequer have been searched for enclosure proceedings. This tedious reading of more than a hundred rolls, each of between 300 and 500 membranes, was lightened in its later stages by the discovery of the *Repertories*, which transcribe only the subject matter of the case as it appears at the top left-hand corner of the membrane in the Memoranda Rolls. The rolls were searched by E. F. Gay at the beginning of this century, and, for Leicestershire cases only, by Dr. Parker.[14] Unfortunately Gay did not publish more than a total of cases for the whole period and for the country as a whole. A new analysis by years and counties has been made in the course of the present work, partly to assist in an assessment of the vigour of Crown action, and partly to assist those who will wish to use these unindexed rolls for the study of a particular county's enclosure history.

The Crown's proceedings in the Court between 1517 and 1565 fall into two parts: before and after the Act of 1536 came into operation, so that we shall examine the form of proceeding in the years 1517–36, and then the differences after 1536.

The form of action which the rolls record is one for levying the statutory penalty of half the net profits of the holding since depopulation. An Exchequer record of a case of this kind has not previously been printed in translation, and the proceedings can be illustrated by taking the case of Sir Richard Knightley as the roll describes it. The record[15] has a number of repetitions (particularly of the 1517 and 1518 Returns) and for ease of reading they have been omitted from the translation in Appendix 2a.

The other cases in the rolls follow the same general form (although, as we shall see in Fig. 6, decreasing in number) until the Act of 1536 gave a fresh stimulus to action and new grounds on which to proceed.

The 1536 Act remedied a substantial defect in the Act of 1489. This defect is summarised in the marginal note to the printed *Statutes of the Realm*:[16]

> the said Act enforced only on lands holden of the King but neglected by other lords.

No case has yet been found of lords suing their tenants for half profits as the Acts of 1489 and 1515 had entitled them to do; the Act of 1536 now gave the King the opportunity of stepping in where angels had feared to tread. He was authorised to proceed against *any* encloser of any land converted from tillage since 1488 and against any fresh enclosures after the end of April 1536. The Act selected fifteen counties only for its operation, and they are the Midland counties with the addition of Cambridgeshire and the Isle of Wight. This group of counties is a significant choice, and in the analysis of cases in the diagram (page 115) it will be seen that it was in the Inner Midlands that most cases lay.

The Crown could now proceed. It initiated no new Inquiry, but turned to the reports of the 1517 and 1518 Commissions which lay on record in Chancery and in its own

Exchequer files. Before examining the vigour of the prosecution under this Act, we must mention another measure[17] aimed at the sheep-master which had come on to the statute book in 1533, since prosecutions under this earlier and distinctive statute are intermixed in the Exchequer record. We shall then be in a position to survey the Crown's proceedings as a whole.

The 1533 Act was titled "An Act concerning Farms and Sheep". The measure against sheep was simple: after Michaelmas 1535 no one man might keep more than two thousand sheep by the long hundred—2,400 head. The penalty was 3*s.* 4*d.* a head for any excess. The measure against the accumulation of holdings—so often the prelude to depopulation or even to less harmful enclosure—fixed a similar sum to be forfeited weekly by any man who took more than one farm into his hands. The problem of the large flocks was tackled again in the poll tax on sheep imposed in 1549 but repealed within the year. Another attempt in 1555 (2 and 3 Philip and Mary, c. 3) ordered one milch cow to be kept for every 60 sheep feeding on enclosed pastures. Many informations were laid against this type of offender in the Elizabethan Exchequer.

But whereas the 1536 Act was to rely on the Crown's zeal for prosecution, the Acts of 1533 and 1555 brought in the private enterprise of informers. A successful informer could share the penalty with the Crown. This delegation of public prosecution was not uncommon. It was to yield a good income in later years for informers against a wide range of prohibited offences from cutting down oaks to not planting the statutory acre of hemp.

The Act of 1536 was formally enrolled in the Memoranda Roll at the end of the business for Trinity term[18] 1537. Such an enrolment of a statute was not usual and the Crown must have wished to draw the Court's attention to the provisions under which offenders might now be summoned.

In Easter term 1539 the first case which specifically mentioned the 1536 Act was heard. The record of the Inquiry of 1518 was read in which the depopulation of Papley, Northants., had been presented.[19] This recital was followed by a recital of the Act of 1536 and a statement that the decay of houses at Papley had not been remedied. The Court ordered the sheriff to distrain for half the profits as a penalty. In the next case which they heard, that of Grimsbury in the same county, their inquiries showed that repairs had been carried out before 1538: the date of the return of the plough

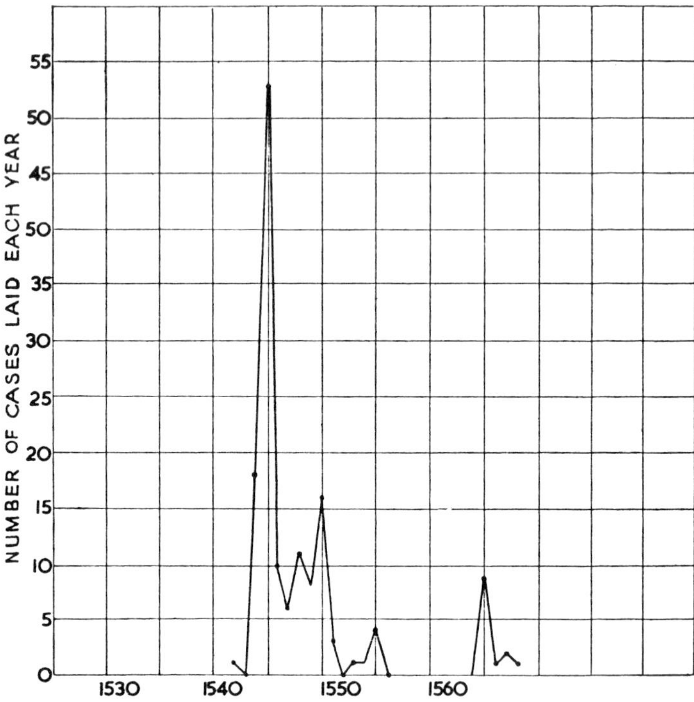

(Fig. 4). *Number of cases of offences against the Act of 1533 heard in the court of Exchequer each year.*

was given as August 22, 1534, and these facts were confirmed by a local Commission of Inquiry in April 1541; one of the Commission was Roger Wyggeston, presumably the Commissioner of 1517–18. In other cases revived that term (Compton, Berks., Norton, Northants., Weston-by-Cherington, Warws., and Ascott, Oxon.) distraint for the penalty was ordered. At Kempton, Beds., the local jury declared that the land concerned had not been under tillage within the memory of man and that the 1517 jury had been mistaken in their statements. Similar local inquiries are frequently recorded in the next three reigns, and were a principal determinant of the Court's verdict. A certificate of rebuilding and reconversion was the surest way to a verdict of acquittal —*visis premissis . . . eat sine die.*[20]

At the same time that the Act of 1536 was being enforced there appeared in the Court of Exchequer a number of informations under the Act of 1533 which had forbidden flocks of more than 2,400 sheep and laid penalties for the engrossing of farms into one man's hand. In the majority of these the

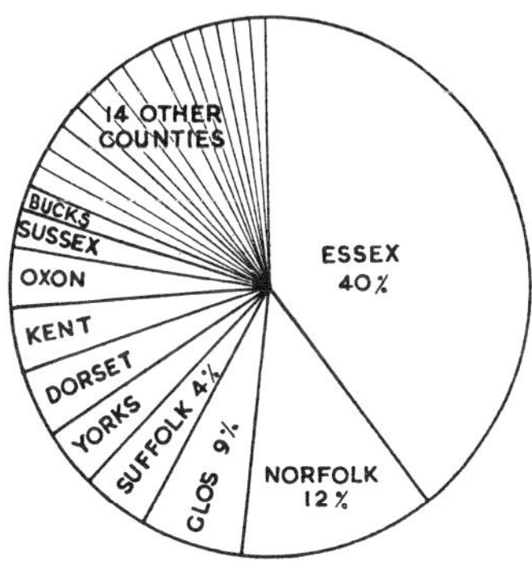

(Fig. 5). *The locale of the cases heard involving offences against the Statute of 1533 banning large flocks and engrossing of farms.*

action was initiated by the informer in pursuit of his half-share of the penalty. A small number were initiated by the Attorney General. Cases of this kind are distinguished in Table 13*a* and Fig. 40.

The first to be recorded was in Easter term 1542: the case of John Leek of Northamptonshire.[21] It was 1544 before another case was enrolled,[22] but this (as Table 13 shows) was the beginning of a steady flow. Only a few were for the offence of large flocks. It was the engrossing of holdings which informers seem to have been more successful in detecting. The character of this enclosure offence was very different from the depopulating enclosure of whole villages.

It differed in scale: the offences presented were all by men who had acquired one or two holdings, and small holdings at that. This in itself would not differ from the early stages in the ambitions of any grazier aiming to depopulate: but it was *not* followed by further acquisition, and—more important—the locale is different. Table 13*b* and Fig. 5 show that

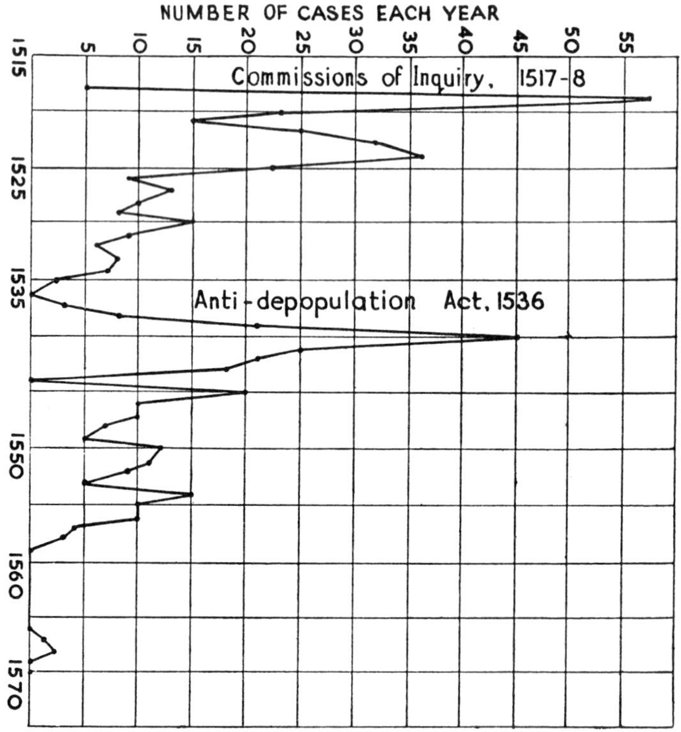

(Fig. 6). *Number of depopulation cases heard in Exchequer, 1518–68.*

these cases under the 1533 Act were principally in the very counties which the 1517–18 Inquiry had either not thought worth while visiting, or which had yielded only a small crop of small offences too trivial to be followed by prosecution. They represent not the engrossing of holdings in open-field counties, but the activity of the prosperous yeoman who is in the land-market of the old-enclosed counties, and is unlucky enough to find himself the victim of the enterprising informers. This small group of men could not muster more than a trivial collection of offenders. The principal contribution to the story of enclosure of informers like Michael Rust the London shoemaker is to cloud it, and this digression has been necessary to explain why Table 14 has deliberately omitted some "enclosure" cases of an alien kind. The "large flocks" offence offers more hope of being relevant to the subject of this book, but here again the number of cases turns out to be trivial and the Act does not seem to have been taken seriously. Single informations continued to be laid until

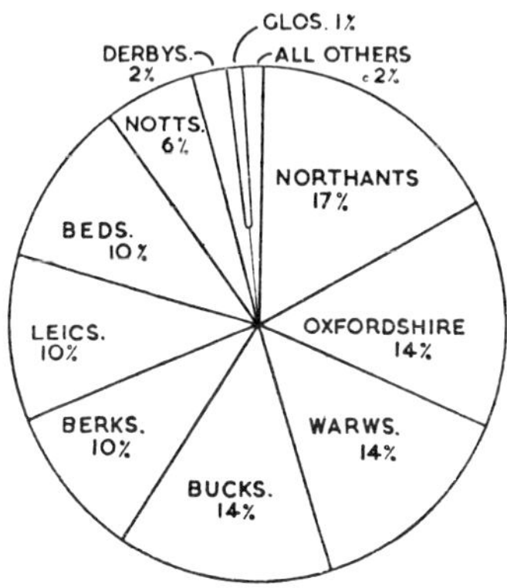

(Fig. 7). *The locale of depopulation cases heard in Exchequer, 1518–68.*

1624. We may now return to the enforcement of the Acts of 1489, 1515 and 1536.

In Table 14 (Appendix 1) 583 cases of depopulation heard in the Court of Exchequer between 1518 and 1565 have been analysed, year by year and county by county. Fig. 6 will show that there was an early burst of activity from 1518 to 1530, then a lull, with renewed interest in 1539 maintained until 1556, after which even Enclosure Commissions failed to bring a great deal of business into this Court.

When we examine Fig. 7 to see what parts of the country were sending depopulators to Westminster we find that seven Midland counties were responsible for 89% of the cases, and that if we add Nottinghamshire and Derbyshire's smaller contributions, the nine counties embraced 98 % of the cases. This significant emphasis on the Midlands will be explained in Chapter Seven.

In Table 15 we have taken four of the counties from which cases were numerous, and examined the cases in question to see what sort of depopulation was being alleged. Was it the eviction of dozens of families? Only rarely does such a case appear. As the Table shows, out of 482 cases, 340 involved the destruction of only one house. Cases in which six or

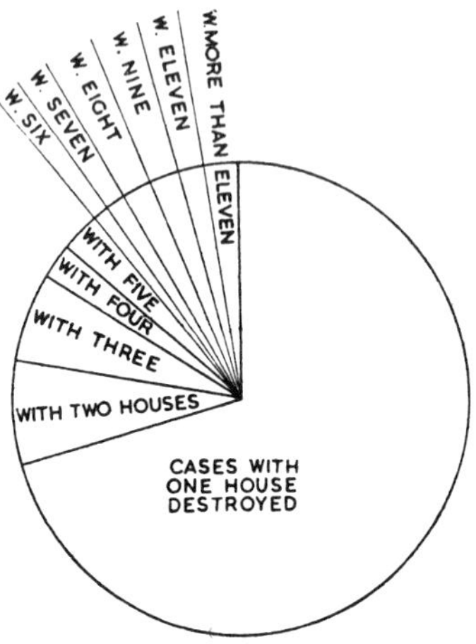

Fig. 8. *Size of depopulations alleged in Exchequer cases, 1518–68.*

more houses were destroyed number only forty-seven, about 10% of all enclosure cases heard in these forty years. Not many big fish are in the net. We even know of some that got away. Among the juries' returns for Northamptonshire in 1517 and 1518 were the depopulations of Catesby where sixty people were evicted; Thorpe in Norton with seventy-two and Glendon with sixty-two. In the first two cases the offender was a monastery and no action was taken against the laymen who received the pastures after the Dissolution. At Glendon no action was taken until twenty-seven years after the evictions had occurred.

We have another opportunity of confirming the impression that big fish had escaped the net. John Rous' list of deserted Warwickshire villages was drawn up between 1486 and 1491. Only a handful of these villages appear in the 1517 returns, and where they do, it is for the decay of the single house and the enclosure of the few odd acres, the last stage in the evictions.

Gay's analysis[23] of the juries' returns of 1517–18 showed that 68% of the 1090 cases in the Midland counties involved fewer than 100 acres. In Table 15*c* we have taken four Midland counties (Warws., Bucks., Berks. and Northants.) and analysed the 1517–18 Returns, looking not at acres but at the number of houses alleged to have been pulled down. In Warwickshire, the worst-hit county, 60% of the cases involved one house or no house; in the four counties taken together, 70% of all cases were of this insignificant order. Only 8% of all cases involved five or more houses destroyed. If we had only this evidence to go upon we might be pardoned for thinking that the depopulation movement was a pygmy affair and that all Tudor commentators had wildly exaggerated.

4

There are two separate problems. If we keep the metaphor of the fish and the net, they are these: we now know that big fish escaped, but was the net drawn in such a way that big fish escaped? and, were those fish which were caught, later able to escape easily from the net?

The 1517 Inquiry proceeded according to certain instructions. It reported, as a legal inquiry should, on those on whom it was told to report. These were the men who had enclosed and depopulated since September 1488, and this limitation would seem to be the main reason why the catch was so poor. The Commission was in time to trap some offenders, but many escaped for the simple reason that they, or their ancestors, had enclosed *before 1488*. Their enclosures had left their record in the empty fields and the tumbled houses, but no record in the returns sent to Chancery.

This limiting date was probably beyond Wolsey's control.

1485 was the date named in the first anti-enclosure Act, before which there was no statutory offence. As it was, there was murmuring and muttering at the Court, and the Commission was remembered as a grievance against the Cardinal at his fall, just as in the next century Archbishop Laud was to have it remembered in the hour of his impeachment that[24]

> he did a little too much countenance the Commission for Depopulations.

The grazing interests were strongly entrenched at court and in Parliament, although the day had not yet come when a Member would note the ears of the sheep-masters at the door of the Commons.[25] The effect of these land-owning interests as a brake on agrarian reforms has been demonstrated by Professor Tawney[26] and the point need not be laboured. It is illustrated by the dumb defiance of the lords who did not take the opportunity which the Act of 1489 allowed them, and failed to proceed against their depopulating tenantry. It was 1536 before the Crown could get—or wanted to get—the opportunity to proceed in their default. The same point is illustrated by Hales' spirited attack in his *Defence* on those who had sought to obstruct the Commission of Inquiry of 1548 and to blame him as the radical instigator of the riots of that year.

With strong interests in danger from the Commissions of 1517 and 1548 we must ask whether part of the small catch is not due to suppression of truth. In 1517, were juries all that far from the Bad Old Days? We know that in 1548 Hales had charged the jury not to show favours and promised protection:

> God, King and Commonwealth will defend you against the Devil, the World and Private Profit.[27]

Some lords had put their retainers on the juries. Hales quotes one as saying of him

> Nay by God's blood—he put one of my servants from the jury.

Other jurymen had been threatened with eviction, and we happen to know that the 1517 Inquiry had been followed by the victimisation of at least one witness. The constable of

Ascott in Milton, Oxfordshire, was Nicholas Eustace, and together with a husbandman from that village, John Rede, he went to Abingdon to present evidence of depopulation in their village. They would have heard the proclamation

> to encourage obtaining information against lords nobles and others of counties adjoining London who have since the King's reign or before dismissed their husbandmen tenants whereby parish churches are decayed and some turned into sheep houses:

and they were duly encouraged. But when the Commission was over they were expelled from the lands "by the cruel and malicious mind of Robert Dormer of West Wycombe" and by John Wilmot who had taken all the lands of Ascott to farm. The two villagers took the matter to the Court of Requests and their allegation and depositions in support have survived. They allege that Dormer and Wilmot, now that the village is all in one man's hand, plan to enclose—

> by them the holl township is and shalbe shortly leyd unto pastur and so ye said suppliants and other of their nygbours be desolate.

If we turn to the Oxfordshire Returns of 1517 we find:

> the jurors say that John Wilmot held one messuage and forty acres from Robert Dormer, gent., on 21 March 1516 . . . and has converted that land to pasture with the decay of the house.[28]

Those who turn to the 6-inch O.S. map of Oxfordshire, (sheet 46 N.E.) and see the fishponds marked by the side of the "site of church", and the Manor House alone in the parish will see how successful Dormer and Wilmot were. In 1279 there had been at least thirty-one men in the village, and the community's corporate legal existence is recalled by the description of Nicholas Eustace as "constable of Ascott" at the head of his depositions.

But the possibility of wholesale suppression seems unlikely, although we must allow for some constables who were less courageous than the constable of Ascott. The very number of allegations which did find their way to the Commission means that the landlords had not succeeded in erecting a very large barrier of intimidation. I have not been able to find other Eustaces with grievances to bring to the Court of Requests.

The accessibility of the prerogative courts, particularly in the Midlands, is testified by the sheer volume of cases, and if men could reach the court to complain of riots in Westmorland, it seems that someone with an enclosure grievance in Buckinghamshire would not have found it difficult. Indeed the files of Star Chamber and Requests have many enclosure cases: they form the greater part of the sources which have been used for describing the agrarian grievances of the sixteenth century. But all in all, the number of new depopulations which are alleged in those courts provide a very small supplement to the information collected in 1517.

Much the same conclusion was reached by John Hales in his *Defence* of 1548. His Commission had sat and received evidence. If we can judge from the Warwickshire evidence —we have very little else—he cannot have been encouraged. There were fifteen pieces of evidence.[29] In only four places was there depopulation to report since the 1518 Inquiry had visited Warwickshire, and these four places only reported ten houses destroyed between them. The other evidence was repetition of cases reported in 1517 or 1518 with small variations. No scandalous suppression was brought to daylight.

Commenting on the result of his work, Hales said clearly that the fault did not lie in the weak enforcement of the law nor in the obstructions which the covetous and proud had placed in the way. It lay in the law itself. It lay in the limiting date of 1488 beyond which inquiry could not pass. His words deserve careful study, and we shall return to them again when we attempt a chronology of depopulation in Chapter Five.

> It is not the execution of the laws already made . . . that shall restore the Realm to his perfection and replenish it with such abundance of towns and parishes and houses as have been in the time of King Edward the first which the survey of the Realm then made will plainly declare.
>
> For the chief destruction of Towns and decay of houses was before the beginning of the reign of king Henry the seventh.

I am sure that the "beginning of the reign of king Henry the seventh" was in Hales' mind because of its fundamental relevance to the barrier against inquiry and prosecution of the worst cases. These were cases which (as I have attempted to show in Chapter Three) still remained in popular memory and which coloured grievances as late as 1607. As Professor Tawney showed, the "agrarian problem" had begun as a problem of enclosure and eviction to the roads; but after the great inflation of the 1540's and the great redistribution of monastic lands it had become a problem of resisting rack-renting. It is not surprising that the battle slogans of one campaign were still on the mouths of those who fought the second.

It is interesting in this connection that an anonymous Parliamentary speaker of 1607 made the same point[30] as Hales, even though he was speaking in favour of allowing enclosure in the Midlands.

> A new law to reach all (depopulators) is most just, since by no reason Antiquity ought to turn mischief into conveniency, when it were more fit that he that by longest offending hath done the most prejudice and received the best Benefit, should in the punishment undergo the greatest Censure.

Like the Doctor in the *Discourse* this speaker also urged a new survey of houses on the pattern of the Hundred Rolls of 1279 so any future depopulator could be immediately noted. These suggestions, it must be repeated, come from a protagonist of the enclosing cause who argued that

> by redressing the fault of depopulation and leaving enclosure arbitrable . . . the poor Man shall be satisfied in his end, Habitation, and the Gentleman not hindered in his desire, Improvement.

5

After that discussion of the reason for the absence of some spectacular depopulations from the 1517 Returns we must now see what success the Crown achieved in its prosecution of those against whom its Commissioners had collected evidence. In our metaphor of the fish, this is an examination of how many fish, once caught, got away.

We cannot measure the deterrent effect of these prosecutions. Deterrent legislation which is successful results in law-abiding citizens, and law-abiding citizens do not become involved in the type of lawsuit whose records satisfy historians' curiosity. There is no silence like that of the well-behaved citizenry. Nor can we separate the fear of prosecution from the renewed profitability of corn in the second half of the sixteenth century, for each force pulled the landowner the same way: further depopulation was not imperative to his prosperity. What of remedying earlier depopulation?

We have already seen the easy terms upon which a writ of *supersedeas* could be obtained upon the promise to rebuild. What this promise was worth we cannot be certain. There was rebuilding at Wormleighton (where we have the Spencer petitions). There was rebuilding at Weddington near Nuneaton.[31] But if we examine the biggest depopulations reported in 1517 (such as those we have shown in Table 15) we find no village rebuilt there today.

The chief reason for easy acceptance of a rebuilding plea between 1519 and 1530 may have lain in the lack of machinery to carry out inspection, to see whether the promises had been kept. There is some hint of this in a number of cases resurrected after the Act of 1536 as if the Crown doubted whether the terms of the recognizances of 1520 and 1526 had been fulfilled.

In the Exchequer proceedings after 1536 it was common for the issue of rebuilding to be put to a fresh local inquiry. In every case I have found that the jury reported some rebuilding and conversion to arable. It is noticeable that they do not report the full rebuilding of all the houses reported lost in 1517; but the Court was satisfied. On the evidence the Attorney General moved for an adjournment *sine die*. Such a certificate[32] is:

> the sertyfycate of Roger Wygston George Radeley William Danvers and James Bury Esquyers commissioners appoynted by vertue of the kynges commission hereunto annexed is as hereaftyr foloweth. In primis that Anthony Cope Esquyer after the Inquysycon in this Commissyon specyfyed that is to say the xxth day of Septembre in the xxii nd yere (1530) of the

> Raygn of our Soveraign lorde the kynge that nowe ys (when) three messuages in Hardwyk (had been) by William Cope decayed, well and suffycyently he did newly cause to be reedyfyed and buylded mete and apte for husbandry and tyllage and that the said Anthony Cope . . together with iiii score acres of erable land xii acres of medowe xxiiii acres of pasture with thappurtenaunces in Hardwyke aforesaid and contynually from the sayd daye hath sett to and caused to be occupyed in husbandry tyllage and sowing of corne to and by tenaunts in the same tenements dwellyng and inhabytyng . . true not only by the vyewe and syght of the seyd messuages lands meadowes and pastures reedyfyed . . but also by the oathes and examynacons of the tennant and inhabitants inhabytyng and dwellyng in and on the same. .
> (3rd April 1541).

These alleged rebuildings are puzzling. It is unlikely that jury after jury was suborned or terrorised into perjury and we must accept their evidence. Two suggestions may be hazarded. One we have made already: that a small amount of rebuilding—perhaps a cottage or two for the servants of the manor house or for the shepherds—was accepted as "new building". A good deal of rebuilding of domestic cottage property was beginning all over the countryside, and there is no reason why a lord who was rebuilding the cottage of his husbandmen in his corn-growing villages should be any the less considerate for his shepherds in his pastures.[33] Other lords were building for the servants of the great house (as at Wormleighton). It may be suggested that the Court was equally easy about the interpretation of "reconversion" of pasture. The Act, indeed, had left a loophole. It ordered reconversion to arable to be "according to the course of husbandry in that part of the country accustomed". It was not too much of perjury—perhaps men felt—to swear that pasture which had seen the plough once in ten years was arable according to the custom of the country.[34] It may be here that Latimer got his story of the "ploughed" land which had but to see a single furrow sliced in order to qualify it as "arable" and protect its owner from prosecution. It was also possible that men rebuilt and later reconverted again to grass.

In 1565 a Buckinghamshire jury remembered that

William Sheppard's depopulation of tenements at Littlecote had resulted in his appearance in Chancery and the promise to rebuild two houses. This he had done; but after his death his two sons had reconverted.[35] They were well able to do this for it was a one-owner estate, "sole lordshipp there".

It is also possible that some reconversion to arable (and building of houses) did take place for the simple reason that the balance of economic advantage was beginning to move again towards corn-growing as urban populations grew and offered a good return for corn. In the not-infrequent years of dearth, when corn prices soared, many a pasture—as in 1918 and 1941—must have seen the plough again for a season. Such a stimulus rather than the stimulus of fear of prosecution might explain the rebuilding which seems to have come to some village sites.

But until we know more about costs, selling prices and profits to be made in sheep and wool at that period this must only be the luxury of speculation. The only stimulus we can be certain about is the fear of the Act of 1536, which we can be certain set many graziers anxiously questioning their surviving relations about exactly what had happened in 1491 in the Stretton Baskervilles and the Lillingstone Dayrells of the sheep-walks. But the evidence is in favour of the view that the fears would soon abate, and that only the unfortunate, like the Countess of Shrewsbury, paid their annual attorney's account for representing them at adjourned hearings in Exchequer through the reigns of Henry VIII, Edward VI, Mary, and Philip and Mary, to land finally at an Elizabethan haven. Only the unfortunate few heard awkward questions put at Quarter Sessions like those in York in 1573 or in the North Riding in 1609.

We have a contemporary witness to the zeal of enforcement in the historian Polydore Vergil. Writing in 1534, he described Wolsey's measures as "exemplary", but added

> The decree soon afterwards lost its worth. Since the nobles were afflicted by the reversion to the old husbandry they began to buy immunity by giving money to Wolsey, and rapidly many were allowed to retain what they pleased. So the great hopes entertained by many were frustrated.[36]

6

Not all who were summoned before the courts pleaded guilty. Some pleaded rebuilding; some might plead, as Tyringham had, that the land was not held of the King, and before the Act of 1536 this was sufficient bar to Crown action; some might plead that the depopulation was older than 1485 or 1488. This was a common plea, and one which is likely to have been true.

Some of the pleadings in Chancery have been preserved. Among the Buckinghamshire file are the pleadings of Thomas Tyringham who said that he had rebuilt one house and reconverted 30 acres to arable; of Sir John Longueville who asked leave to bring witnesses from Wolverton in his defence; of John Godwyn who pleaded that he was not tenant of the Crown and that the land was in tillage "according to the customs of Chiltern country" (presumably in a grass–corn rotation); of Robert Lee from Fleet Marston whose defence is the most interesting. He claimed that the fields of Fleet Marston had been enclosed "sixty years or more ago" and that the fields had mainly been under grass.

> It hath bene contynnually used in medowes and pasture this lx yeres and more, and no more in tyllage but onlye the sayd cxl acres.

This 140 acres, he claimed, had been the sole arable in 1485;

> there was no moo plowes in the said towne of Marston but only iiij at no tyme syth the ffirst yer of the raigne of kyng henry the vij

so that he had been unfairly saddled with the accusation of evicting forty-five persons, many of whom had left earlier in the fifteenth century.

Appendix IIA (page 410) shows how Sir Richard Knightley used this defence. In another county Sir Edmund Bray was pleading that

> iii of the seid ix meses hath ben dekeyed long tyme by fore the statute of anno quarto of owre seid late kyng and iii yers before the seid statute. He confesseth the dekey of the vi meses and the cxx acres of arrable lond put to pasture.

Others pleaded that the jurors had exaggerated and requested a fresh jury to be empanelled. Others, like the Prior of Daventry, were able to prove that they had no legal interest in part or all of land described in the Inquiry. He was discharged of two of the three houses in Staverton which he had been accused of destroying. Others pleaded that their tenants had done the casting down, but this was no defence in law, as the judges decided in Claypole's case. Others—particularly in the revived cases—would plead that the land was no longer theirs: in one case they were able to show that it was part of the royal park. The most common plea is that the damage had been done before 1485, and that the property was already

debilitatem putridam et corruptam[37]

It was common for a pleading to end with a request for the benefit of the statutory pardon, and we may quote in full the petition of William Willington, and then examine, without a verbatim quotation, the interesting petition of John Spencer of Wormleighton.[38]

> In the most humble wyse sheweth unto your Grace William Willington that wher as it was ffownde by Inquysicon in your Countie of Warr' and nowe in your Chancery of recorde remaynynge, That the said William was seased as of hys fee of the manner of Barcheston in the said Countie and iiii messuages one cotage DCCC (i.e. 800) acres of heyrable londe in Barcheston within the countie afore said, parcell of the said mannor; and that to iii of the said meses was used to be layen to tyllage with anye of them ii yerde lond, and with the fforth mese iiii yerde lond; and he so being seased the ffirst day of marche in the xxiiii yere of the reigne of kyng henry the viith the said mes. and cotage wylfully wasted and (fallen) in ruen to decay, and the herable londs afore said used to be letten with the said meses converted into pasture; and also that all the premysses were holden of your grace as by the said inquysicon remaynyng of recorde in your courte of Chancery more pleynly doyth appere; the said William will be redy to prove accordyng to the tryall of the court that he is seased of the said maner in hys demesne as of fee, wherof the cotage in the said inquysicon specyfyed is parcell, and also the said DCCC acres is parcell of the said manor, and the said William seyeth that the princypall place of the seid

manor and the seid cotage and all other howses parcell of the seid manor be sufficiently rapayred and at all tymes syth, and he seyeth that ther hath been used syth the seyd tyms to be occupied in tyllage within the seid manor and howses CLX (i.e. 160) acres, parcell of the seid DCCC acres, and ther as nowe but only wer used in pasture and medowe at the tyme of the said Statute and iii yers next before, and never syth put in tyllage; and he seyeth that the servyce of God is as well mayntayned in the Churche of the seid towne as it was at any tyme within this xl yers and the Churche well and sufficyently repayred and the ornyaments of the Churche nessary and convenyent for the same; and also noo persons ther nowe dwellyng and hath so ben contynued this xxti syth that the Inherytance and the ffrehold therof is in the persons named in the inquysicon which hold the same of the seid William by rent and suyte, and that he hath nothyng in the same but only of parcell therof at wyll and the resydue for terme of yeres, and this is the ole trewyth as the seid William will prove, and the seid William in his most humble manner submytteth hym selfe to be ordered and tried in the premisses as it shall please the kyngs highness and his most honorable cownsell. And by this his peticon relynqyseth his travers triable by the courte of the common lawe in exchaynge his greate costs and charges for the advoydyng of the seid untrue inquysicon in parts, and for the residue wher in he hath offended and the same confessyth he prayeth the benyfit of the great pardon by oure sovereigne lord nowe last granted by auctorite of parliament as it shall please his grace for the dyscharge of his offens above confessed.

This lengthy and verbose self-justification is the longest defence which we have from an encloser accused before the Court. In the record of the Exchequer cases the plea is usually summarised. It will be noted that Willington felt it necessary to reassure the Court about conditions which were not touched upon in the Commission's finding. There had been no accusation that the church was in disrepair. It will also be noted that Willington signs away his rights to be tried by common law procedure because of its expense, and is satisfied to be tried as the Council should direct.

His case rested mainly on two foundations. He alleged that only 160 of the 800 acres were under the plough in 1489 and that the jury had exaggerated. He also pleaded that he had done his duty and rebuilt the damaged houses. His final gambit was to plead the General Pardon of 1515.

The other Warwickshire petition came from John Spencer of Wormleighton, where the Commission had found twelve houses, three cottages and 240 acres affected by the enclosure, with consequent decay of twelve ploughs and the eviction of sixty villagers. The enclosure had raised the value of the land from forty to sixty pounds a year.

Spencer admitted that he held the land at the time of the Inquiry although the depopulator (in September 1506) had been William Cope, a previous occupier. He claimed that four of the fifteen dwellings had been rebuilt. Two others had been replaced by his new Manor House, and by four other cottages connected with the House in which forty people were employed. This is as many, he said, as the twelve houses had held. "The earthworks of the former village and the old Manor house lie by the canal on the hill-slopes below the present Manor." As far as the other twenty missing villagers were concerned, he submitted himself to the King in Council and (like Willington) relinquished his common-law right of too expensive self-defence and pleads the statutory pardon.[39]

The Crown appears to have been satisfied with the appearance of an encloser in court and his promise to rebuild. Upon such a promise or a statement that rebuilding had taken place, the levying of the penalty of half profits was halted. A writ of *supersedeas* was directed to the Barons of Exchequer whose Court would be responsible for the distraint and collection of the fines. (At half the profits of a thirty-year old enclosure, such fines were formidable.) On occasion the encloser bound himself by recognizances to undertake immediate rebuilding. These will be found on the Close Roll for 1520 and 1526, as well as in Exchequer.[40]

But by 1526 there was another burst of interest, prompted no doubt by rising corn prices. A proclamation of July 1526 ordered all who had converted to pasture and destroyed houses, and whose case had not been concluded, to reconvert and rebuild before Michaelmas; and in November the Court of Chancery summoned recalcitrant offenders before it.

There were more recognizances taken; and more protestations from enclosers that more good would come to the Commonweal if the hedges were suffered to remain. An unpublished membrane among the Northamptonshire file of the 1517 Returns is a note (dated 6 October 1526) of those who were to be summoned to explain their conduct to the Court:

> warne all personnes whose names be expressyd in a scedule indentyd to this precept annexyd . . and yf they be ded or have sold or departyd with their estate and interest . . than to somon and warne the owners and possessors of the same . . to appear before us in Chancery at All Souls' Day next.[41]

The schedule reveals that the Bishop of Lincoln and three others had been sent as a Commission into the county to report those who had converted land "to pasture of bestes".

No other county seems to have been visited at this time, if the extant records are any guide, but there were other occasions when *ad hoc* Commissions were sent to particular counties. Roger Wyggeston wrote to Thomas Cromwell in July 1539 that he was intending to view the enclosures complained of in Warwickshire, Leicestershire and Northamptonshire before Michaelmas,[42] and we have seen that from this time onwards local Commissions often had to ascertain whether rebuilding had actually taken place.

The loophole offered by the Proclamation of 1526 was to those owners who could

> justify and sufficiently prove by good true and unfeigned allegations and approved reasons (before the Lord Chancellor) that the continuance of their hedges be not prejudicial hurtful not to the annoyance of the King's subjects.

This qualification, which implies that reasonable enclosure will not be censured, is an echo of the Proclamation of July 1518. This had excepted those who could prove in Chancery that enclosure and "the standing of the same" shall be[43]

> more beneficial for the commonwealth of this realm than the pulling down thereof.

It is of the same spirit as the passage in the *Discourse* where John Hales, the Commissioner of the 1548 Inquiry, makes his Doctor deny that his face is set indiscriminately against all enclosing:

> I mean not all enclosures but only of such enclosures as turneth commonly arable fields into pastures;

or as the speech where the Doctor says that to go over one-hundred-per-cent to corn would be as foolish as a rural economy where you had "breeding of sheep only occupied". In Hales' *Charge to the Jury* (1548) he had said that he was not concerned to inquire into enclosure of land which had not interfered with the rights of commoners:

> enclosure is not where a man encloses where no others have common.[44]

As well as the loophole offered by these Proclamations to those who could prove that their enclosures had not harmed the welfare of others, there was the opportunity of obtaining a pardon, and we must turn aside to see how this could affect the relationship of the Crown and the depopulator.

The General Pardon embodied in the Statute of 14 and 15 Henry VIII c. 17 (1523) extended to

> fines amerciaments profits and all other things due or that ought to grow to the King our Sovereign Lord by reason of any decays or letting down of Houses, enclosures and converting of lands from tillage to pasture or any of them

and the pardon could be obtained

> so the same enclosures were put down and the lands put to tillage and the houses decayed re-edified, before the said eighth day of August next (1524) . . . or else the offender . . . come before the King in his Chancery and show reasonable causes why he cannot re-edify . . . abiding the order of the said Court . . . and in refusal or default . . . the party to take non-advantage of this pardon.

Clause five of the Act empowered the Court of Exchequer to respite any cases pending for the period of grace (until August 1524) but after that date the fines

> to be levied to the King's use in case that the said enclosures be not pulled down and the houses decayed re-edified or appearance made . . .

Earlier general statutory pardons had not specifically prescribed for fines resulting from enclosure prosecutions, but in many of the pleadings in 1521 in Exchequer (and in the Chancery petitions which we have already quoted) these wide general pardons are cited in mitigation. The Bishop of Winchester, faced with an accusation of decaying three houses in Oxfordshire, confessed the decay of one, denied two others, and pleaded the Statutory Pardon of 1514, which can only be the General Pardon of that year. In 1523 one-third, and in 1524 one-fifth of the cases heard in Exchequer pleaded pardons.[45]

Statutes of Pardons after 1523 did not include any specific wording relating to enclosures, and in Exchequer proceedings it is general pardons which we find being pleaded.

Individual pardons were also granted by Letters Patent after payment of suitable fee. Well before the first anti-enclosure legislation of 1488, the enclosure of Cestersover was authorised by a patent which was first cousin to the many medieval patents for enclosing and emparking.[46] After the legislation of 1489 the patent took the form of a pardon. In 1508 Sir Edward Belknap of Burton Dasset, Warws., was granted an immunity from prosecution under the Act of 1489 and the pardon was produced to the Commissioners in 1517. No doubt for safety, Belknap obtained a second pardon in 1519, and when the Commission of 1548 were in the county the pardon was again read to them with its apologia for a former Crown Surveyor:

> this decay of Tillage was no prejudice but benefit to the public for whereas before that Time they were able to entertain but 20 strangers upon occasion, they could afterwards entertain sixty as well . . . and that the benefice was better and more of value to the Incumbent than when the lands did lie in tillage by three pounds yearly.

The 1548 Commission found another 240 acres enclosed since the initial 360 acres of 1498.

Among the Chancery Proceedings is a petition from Sir Nicholas Vaux to have the benefit of the King's pardon for his decay of houses and conversion to pasture at Stantonbury, Bucks., and in the Patent Roll we find the pardon duly issued. Pardons appear in the same roll as late as 1553 (John Godwyn for Over Winchendon, Bucks.), while in 1550 the depopulation of Hogshaw in the same county was pardoned in the same roll in which the Belknaps obtained their third and final pardon for the conversion at Burton Dasset.[47]

7

Our examination of the King's proceedings has shown that they did bring to light and record many of the depopulations carried out between 1488 and 1517. Of these, the majority were petty, but the minority spectacular. Some other offences escaped record by a process of threats and bribes, but we have assessed these as few in number. The King's proceedings were less successful than they might have been. Their flaw was that they could not look back beyond 1488, by which date there is reason to suspect that a good deal of large-scale depopulation had been already achieved. The proceedings were not as vigorously pursued as they might have been, and promises to rebuild seem to have been lightly accepted. Only in a minority of cases were the full penalties exacted. A revival of activity in 1538 has been noticed, but with more profit to court fees and defending attorneys than to the cause of re-conversion of pasture. We have also put forward the view that State action might have acted as a deterrent to others who had recently manœuvred themselves into a position ready to enclose; and that the study of economic advantage might not lead a late sixteenth-century landowner so certainly towards grass as it had led his father and grandfather.

The explanation of this weakness in consistent action against depopulation is in part no different from the explanation of the intermittent execution of many other Tudor policies. It lies in the Crown's need to conciliate interested parties and the many distractions of other administrative duties and political bargains which had to be made during these years. It must not be forgotten that the Exchequer Rolls which bear our enclosure cases are those which hold the record of other proceedings arising from a Church reformed; from monasteries appropriated; from wars waged against the King's enemies inward and outward; and from another campaign waged against inflation. These matters were powerful competitors for the limited attention of the King and his advisers. Only when corn prices rose and the rioters sang their ballads of *Nowadays* did the question of enclosure come back on the Council agenda as of urgent importance. The pattern of action and inaction may seem more rational in some such context as this. It resembles the response of administrators to a crowded sea of trouble in other times and other places.

PART TWO

IN these chapters we must pass from the description of the lost villages and their impact on contemporaries.

When de la Pryme was called upon in 1697 to explain the grassy site of Gainsthorpe he had to hand a local tradition cast in terms of personalities: outraged neighbours had destroyed the village. This explanation he rejected in favour of a more complex explanation which aptly summarises the argument of the succeeding pages. The cause, he said, was "time, poverty and pasturage". We shall have to make an arbitrary separation of the threads of time, place and personalities, answering separately the questions, when? where? and who?

Chapter Five

THE OCCASIONS OF DESTRUCTION

. . . the time, When?
. . . when beasts most graze . . . so much for the time,
When.

Love's Labour's Lost, Act I, Scene 1.

I

IN this chapter we must pay more attention to the points in time at which villages were depopulated. Village mortality has not been evenly spread over the years, and particular social and economic conditions have been more favourable than others for the destruction of villages. We shall examine the nature of these conditions further in Chapters Six and Seven, but it will be useful first to form an idea of the occasions when villages were most likely to fall.

It is much easier to prove that a depopulation had taken place than to assign a definite date to the event. Even where detailed local investigations have been made it is often impossible to do more than assign a limit of dates between which depopulation took place. Although, for example, Dr. Hoskins was able to prove the depopulation of sixty-one Leicestershire settlements he was only able to suggest dates for twenty-one of these, the majority within the better-documented period from 1450 to 1603.

Precise dating is made difficult by the poverty of material evidence for those villages which were depopulated before 1485. Only after 1485, when the State Inquiries collected information which included the exact date of the final evictions, have we any systematic attempt to give a year and a month to the event. In other sources men speak more vaguely of "sixty years since" and "in ancient times". Nor, as we shall see, can we rely on the survival of manorial records where we can search for the early disappearance of villagers from the manor court or of their rents from the annual accounts. Excavation can do no more than suggest an "horizon" by showing that pottery beyond a certain date has not been recovered. Such an horizon is likely to be expressed in centuries rather than decades and it would depend, even if we had many more excavations in our sample, on knowledge of the chronology of local styles in medieval domestic pottery, a study which may be fairly described as in an interesting but pioneer stage.

For more narrow limits we must look mainly to the tax records; or in single cases to the survival of isolated documents which enable us to single out a definite point in time when a village was still flourishing, or a definite point by which it was destroyed. A rental of houses; deeds which convey strips of arable land; a bishop complaining of an empty church; the prosecution of a felon for house-breaking: these are isolated and single pieces of evidence which reveal a village still flourishing and thus enable us to narrow down the limits between which the depopulations occurred.

This process leaves us with a range of years, in any one of which the village might have finally decayed. Although we must emphasise the date at which the village was finally abandoned, we must not overlook the fact that only the very fortunate and strong-willed depopulator could destroy a village overnight. Only a would-be encloser with great political strength, a strong and loyal body of retainers, a deaf ear to local protests and a firm grip on local juries could hope to evict scores of people in one sweep. We do hear of such cases in the Returns of 1517: but more commonly the story is of the eviction of the last survivors.

The departure of the other villagers might well have been a slow process, and we shall show later that it often began with a voluntary movement away by peasants who saw better opportunities elsewhere; others would not be averse to selling out; offers of holdings in other villages could be used to persuade the more reluctant. There is no doubt that depopulation, like repopulation, took time. The depopulation of a village would be the last act in a chain of circumstances: in some villages the rising hopes and ambitions of a would-be grazier; in others the falling hopes of villagers who had suffered misfortunes, bad weather and poor crops.

In 1485 we can see villages in all stages of depopulation standing side by side with villages with their full strength still in them. There is village A already depopulated; there is village B which was not to be depopulated for another twenty years; there is village C which was to have its enclosure delayed until the 1550's when the new hedged fields were wanted not for sheep but for more efficient arable or mixed farming, and village C would do no more than shrink. Alongside and between these three villages is village D whose open fields would survive until the late 1700's. It may seem difficult to explain why near neighbours should experience such different fates.

The answer probably lies not in any difference of moral scruple between one village and the next nor in any failure to perceive where economic advantages lay. It may have been due to differences in the obstacles rather than differences of will. In Chapter Six we shall examine more closely the motives of the depopulators and some of the incentives and barriers which they knew: but there is no doubt that Time was an opponent to wrestle with, and our dating can do no more than suggest how long the fate of the village hung in the balance, and within what periods the depopulator was most successful in his ambitions; or the village least attractive to its inhabitants.

2

It may simplify the argument and narrative if we look first at that small number of villages which were destroyed for the mixed motives of beauty and utility, mainly in the eighteenth century. The removal of villages from before the windows of the great house is similar in effect to earlier depopulations, but the motive was rather different. The necessary steps would have been similar, but in a century when Property had been erected as King it was rather more difficult to override the veto of any freeholder than it had been in the more careless days of the Wars of the Roses.

These emparking depopulations flourished where the great landlord was sole owner, where he stood as monarch of all he surveyed.

It is likely that such depopulations were in Goldsmith's mind when he came to write *The Deserted Village*, but if so, it is curious that the prefatory letter suggests so much scepticism on the part of his London friends. In the letter to Sir Joshua Reynolds he wrote:

> I have taken all possible pains in my country excursions for these four or five years past to be certain of what I allege. Some of my friends think that the depopulation of villages does not exist, but I am myself satisfied.

It is difficult to imagine that the news of the removal of villagers had been so well concealed. Many aristocratic patrons of London writers must have visited the country houses and looked out over the lawns and lakes where the art of the landscape gardener had concealed the village scars. There was Castle Howard, where we have the Archbishop of York's acre of glebe lying underneath the lake. There was Wotton Underwood which we can reconstruct from the pre-enclosure plan. There were others which had been replaced by a newly built model village outside the park pale, as at Harewood or Wimpole. There are others, like Stowe, where the villagers are said to have been moved to other neighbouring villages. There was Milton Abbas; there was Nuneham Courtenay; there was Wimpole; there was Ickworth.

But these emparking depopulations are simple to detect, since local and county administrative records have left plenty of easily accessible material which will show whether a village was still flourishing in the early eighteenth century. The great house standing alone in its park, bearing the name of a former parish and perhaps including a lonely parish church within the park-walls, is not an uncommon feature of the English landscape. At Birdsall the ruins of the former parish church abut on the terrace of the Hall and the remains of village streets can be detected in the grass. A new church has been built some distance away, and a scattered village of

(11) HOLME ARCHIEPISCOPI, YORKS., E.R. (*above*)
HINDERSKELFE, YORKS., N.R. (*below*)

At Holme (south of Fridaythorpe), the crofts of the village appear only as a crop-mark in fields where the plough brings pottery to the surface every year. There were eleven households in 1381 and the village once maintained a prebend of York. The position of the former street and crofts of Hinderskelfe has been taken from a late seventeenth century estate-plan and sketched for comparison with the modern Ordnance Survey map. There are now only the house, gardens and lakes of Castle Howard.

estate houses will be found on the modern road. Only if there is no village outside the park-walls is there any case for further investigation. Should it appear not to have been flourishing at the beginning of the eighteenth century, then it is likely (as at Burton Constable) that the depopulation does go back much further, and that the ornamental parkland is the heir of the graziers' pastures and the site of the former village. Indeed the motives of beauty and utility may well have combined even in the sixteenth century. The parkland which pleased the eye would also have grazed the sheep and cattle. The Fairfaxes who lived on the site of Steeton, as we have seen, bred sheep on the Old and the New Park which stretched from their door, but they did not scruple to lose a little grassland for the making of their Great Pond.[1]

3

These depopulations apart, can we put any finishing date to the main current of depopulating enclosure? We shall try and show that in general the destruction of villages was coming to a standstill in the Midlands by the 1520s and in the North by the 1600s. But there is one confusing practice of sixteenth and seventeenth-century writing which has often clouded the acceptance of this thesis. It lies in the ambiguous use of the word "depopulation". There is no doubt that all through the sixteenth century men are describing (and usually denouncing) enclosure and depopulating enclosure. In the seventeenth century the issue became more controversial and pamphleteers were found to argue that depopulation was not the result of enclosure. But when we find titles like *Depopulation Arraigned* it is easy to imagine that villages were still being destroyed.

Yet if this literature is examined more closely it is clear that men were using the word "depopulation"—and quite properly—to mean not only a total loss of villagers, but *some* loss of villagers. A *depopulated village* to them was not a grassy earthwork, but a village with perhaps a score of husbandmen fewer than it had had a generation earlier.

It is also quite certain that depopulation in this relative

sense was going on in both the sixteenth and seventeenth centuries and that it was the result of agrarian change. It is also unfortunate from the point of view of clear exposition that this change—again quite properly—was described by contemporaries as "enclosure". But such "enclosure" was often no more than the re-arrangement of the scattered strip holdings of the village into compact hedged fields. No doubt some of these fell down to grass (just as former pastures were coming under the plough). Fewer labourers were needed, and there may have been economies in working compact holdings which also reduced the labour force of the village and caused unemployment and some migration from the village: all this was considerably less than total destruction.

We may illustrate this "decay of hospitality" (to use a popular Tudor phrase) from the air photograph (Plate 12) of Cosford, a Warwickshire village in Newbold on Avon parish. The fields of Newbold remained unenclosed until the eighteenth century, but Cosford had gone over to hedged fields much earlier. In the process it had been possible to economise in husbandmen, although not to do without them entirely. Alongside the existing farms and gardens can be seen the earthworks of other farms and gardens long out of occupation. When added to existing farms these earthworks complete the pattern of the corn-growing community of the Middle Ages, surrounded by its open fields. Cosford is in fact the Shrunken Village *par excellence*, and it is not the only one: but the Shrunken Village is a separate study.

We may show in a number of ways that what Midlanders were discussing after about 1540 was the Shrunken Village and not the Deserted Village. The Inquiries which the Government conducted in 1548,[2] 1565[3] and 1607[4] did not fail to produce evidence of houses destroyed and fields enclosed, but they are single houses and not whole villages; they are tens of acres and not hundreds of acres. It was proper to apply the term "depopulation" to this movement, but it proved confusing and it even confused contemporaries.

It would be tedious to rehearse all the findings of the Inquiries of 1548, 1565 and 1607 here. The point can be made by examining two Returns, that for Warwickshire[5] in

1548 and Lincolnshire in 1607. We may imagine that in 1548 John Hales, a prime instigator of the Warwickshire Commission, would have lost no opportunity to trace and record any new enclosures in his county since 1518. What do we find? Some of the presentments are simple repetitions of the findings of 1517 and 1518; others complete the reporting of old depopulations passed over or only partially recorded in 1517. At Stretton Baskerville seven houses destroyed between 1485 and 1488 were added to the sixteen which the 1517 Inquiry had reported destroyed between 1488 and 1517. In only five of the eighteen other cases of which we have the record was any fresh enclosure reported from the years 1518–48. Three of these are for enclosures of 18, 10 and 9 acres respectively, and there can be no destruction of villages there. The other two cases concern lost villages. Four houses were reported to have been destroyed at Whitchurch in 1534, probably the final abandonment of a village for whose depopulation Sir Edward Belknap had obtained pardon in 1508. At Chelmscote both Rous and the Commission of 1517 had reported extensive enclosure; two houses are now recorded as destroyed in 1547, with three others reduced to cottages. Some other enclosure is recorded here as late as 1598. Chelmscote was an unconscionable long time in dying.

If this is all that the principal Edwardian opponent of enclosure could find in his own county, we shall not be surprised if the Buckinghamshire Commission of 1565 produced a report of the same kind: a large number of small enclosures. Nor was the anti-enclosure Act of 1597 strictly accurate[6] when it claimed that

> of late years *more than in times past* there have been sundry towns parishes and houses destroyed and become desolate.

Its recollection of time past was limited.

The agrarian rioters of 1607 made much of the depopulating activity of local landowners,[7] but neither the Returns to the Commission of that year nor the informations against enclosers laid in the Court of Exchequer have much to say about deserted villages. It was open to anyone to lay an information in the Court of Exchequer, and London had no shortage of semi-professional informers living on the half-fines which the statutes offered them for their pains. Any provincial magnate able to terrorise a local jury would have no protection against these men, and we may discount any suggestion that depopulation at this period could have taken place silently and unnoticed. Three such informations were laid in 1606 and the number for Northamptonshire and Leicestershire was suddenly increased in 1607 to fall away in 1608.[8]

There is a single lost village name among these informations: that of Onley in Northamptonshire, where Thomas Gregory of Holdenby had enclosed 500 acres for cattle. In the other forty-eight informations laid in the eighteen months from Easter 1606, there is no mention of a village destroyed nor are the villages named those in which we have reason to look for a depopulation round about this time. It is clear from the cases of Wymondham and Leighton Bromswold that an agreed enclosure had taken place in the villages, and that the informer in London had seized his chance to take his rewarding proceedings.

The evidence brought in by the Commission of Inquiry of 1607 was very little different in character from that of 1548 and 1565. The Returns are extant for six Midland counties, although only one set, that for Leicestershire, has been printed. Mr. J. D. Gould has recently discovered a summary of the Lincolnshire Returns with more than a thousand entries.[9] At first sight this looks promising, especially when we read a heading in the manuscript "Great depopulations and decay of husbandry". Of the twenty-nine places so described, only two Kesteven villages could now be described as lost, and in each case there is some doubt. Sapperton in the list may bc the lost Sapperton in Welbourn, but the manuscript continues "seven cottages only left" . . . "most of these depopulations done forty years since".

The second Kesteven case, Panton Parva, may be no more than the making of Panton Park, although Canon Foster tells us that there is a lost Hardwick to be discovered somewhere in Panton.

In the Lindsey section of the Returns only Calcethorpe and Little Limber are truly lost places, and since the Population Return of 1563 records only seven families in Calcethorpe and its two hamlets we cannot really say that it was depopulated in the years just before 1607. Limber Parva is now incorporated in Brocklesby Park and it may indeed have been depopulated at this time. Nor is this meagre harvest of "great depopulation" compensated for in the section of the manuscript headed "churches and chancels decayed". Only one of the seven places named is a lost village for certain, and "Geresby" from which the lead had been stolen is a doubtful reading, since Girsby, a lost hamlet of Burgh-on-Bain, does not seem to have had a church.

The Returns deal with simple cases of enclosure on a small scale. The average area in the thousand entries is round about 13 acres and the average number of houses decayed about two per entry. Lincolnshire was sharing in that widespread enclosure of small areas of common fields which Warwickshire, Buckinghamshire and Leicestershire were also experiencing. It was also experiencing the wholesale enclosure of a village's fields by the assent of the proprietors and without the destruction of the village. This is the "enclosure and depopulation" of 1607. It cannot rank with the huge enclosures and total depopulations of a century earlier, and the double use of the word "depopulation" must be carefully watched. The last large-scale State Inquiry into depopulation ends not with a bang but a whimper.

We know that right up to the Civil War the Privy Council in London and the county Quarter Sessions continued to be exercised over enclosure. An examination of the cases brought before these bodies does not add to our list of deserted villages. Even the most extensive of the enclosures was bringing hedged fields but not the empty village. Dr. L. A. Parker made this point neatly by contrasting two maps: the one of Whatborough, enclosed in 1495 and destitute of any village; and the other of Pickwell, enclosed just before 1615, but with Pickwell village standing at the centre of its neatly drawn and coloured hedged fields.[10]

When we find country correspondents[11] writing to the

Privy Council in the early seventeenth century and offering to provide the names of villages which have been destroyed, is not this proof that depopulation of the old-fashioned sort was still in progress? I think not. These gentlemen were not insulting the Council's intelligence by reporting contemporary enclosures, but were practical antiquaries, calling the old world into the argument to redress the grievances of the new. The villages were so long lost that a country gentleman might think the Council would not know of them. As moral examples of what over-zealous enclosers had achieved in the past they would be useful ammunition. The argument as to whether enclosure was a good thing was still a lively one, and was to remain so until the end of the seventeenth century. A moral example does not cease to be useful simply because time has passed. If you are in the company of sinners then it is quite proper to point out the results of past sin, and in the pamphlet war Depopulation was more than once Arraigned, to borrow the title of one celebrated tract for the times.

We are now perhaps in a position to explain why the Tudor, and especially the Elizabethan pamphleteers were necessarily vague in their statements about depopulation, and why none of them stooped to mention a village name or to give an actual date. They lived among men who inherited a lively memory of what had happened a generation or so earlier. Anyone who denied depopulation would have been shouted down. They lived among fields which still carried ruined churches and ruined cottages. There was no need to give names, men need only look around them. Yet since so few villages were actually still tumbling there were no names and places to quote in the argument. The argument was worth maintaining, thought such men as Latimer and More, for the flood might come again, and perhaps only the increased profitability of corn in the second half of the sixteenth century prevented its second coming. Depopulation of villages was unpopular in both peasant and educated England—we can see that from the fact that the depopulating landlord or tenant found no apologist even in an age when any of the Deadly Sins seems to have been able to hire a pamphleteer. Such an emotive word, carrying such overtones of bitterness, was too useful to abandon, even if, when pressed to give names, pamphleteers took refuge in vagueness.

This vagueness was not confined to London pamphleteers. The local jury at East Lilling; the jury at Kiplingcotes; the villagers who lived near the site of Argam; the witnesses at Eastburn: these men remembered that there had been a village, but were not sure exactly when. From Lillingstone Dayrell in Buckinghamshire we quoted the glebe terrier which was correct in its guess of the fifteenth century, but wrong in the decade it chose. All this seems to point to depopulation at least three or four generations earlier than the depositions, probably more. Depositions on other matters show a very keen communal memory for dates and names.

We may illustrate this point by an interesting example from the Isle of Wight where a Crown survey[12] was made in 1559, only seventy-one years after the Island's depopulation Act:

> We heare of many old streets and villages bothe of artificers and others cleyn dekeyed and no signe of any howsinge whiche have had a begynninge longe agoo out of eny mans knowledge and so dayly growynge in the same dekey we cannot saye what sholde be the very cause.
> But among others we conjecture this that when all the howses stoode and people repleinished, the Staple was kept at Winchester and thonly porte at (South) Hampton which Filled all the Countrey with see men and vessells. And they the countrey abrode by occupyinge. And nowe all goythe to London and Flaunders which killeth all this countrey alonge.

The explanation was in terms of economic change within their memory and experience. They do not mention any of the causes of decay rehearsed in the Statute of 1488.

A far better recollection of things past—although again pointing to a pre-1485 date—had been preserved at Pendley[13] (Herts.) where in 1506 it was remembered that

> about eighty years before, Pendley was a great town whereof part lay in the parish of Tring and part in the parish of Aldbury. There were in the town above 13 ploughs beside divers handicraftmen, as tailors shoemakers and cardmakers with divers other. The town was afterwards cast down and

> laid to pasture by Sir Robert Whittingham who built the said place (Pendley Manor) at the west end there as the town sometime stood, for the town was in the east and south part of the said place.

We know that in 1440 a licence had been obtained to empark 200 acres here, and this may have been the beginning of the end for the village.[14]

4

If there was very little total depopulation in the second half of the sixteenth century, and if the depopulation reported in 1517 seems to have been the end rather than the beginning of a flood, then we are very near to a sentiment expressed by John Hales in 1549. In the course of the *Defence* he criticised the provisions of the anti-enclosure legislation which had taken retrospective powers to 1485 or 1488. For Hales,[15] this was to set the limit too late:

> the chief destruction of villages was before the beginning of the reign of King Henry the seventh.

We must allow that Hales was in a good position to know. He had lived at the heart of the grassy shires of the Midlands. He had assisted in the attempt to track down the new enclosures in 1517 and 1548. He had the evidence of 1517 extracted from the public records to assist his inquiry. He had a lively experience of the ways of landlords in avoiding the penalties of the statutes. His mind had been exercised in drafting statutes which would reform the weakened arm of the law, the law which Latimer had said was good in itself but which brought nothing forth in administrative action.

Like Hales, John Rous had lived at the heart of the Midlands.[16] From 1445 to 1491 he had been near Warwick at the heart of the grasslands. In 1459 he had appeared at the Coventry Parliament, and there petitioned against the destruction wrought by the appetites of landlords. The fifty-eight villages which he names as lately destroyed had disappeared, he says, in his own lifetime. If we compare them with the much smaller number presented to the Commission of 1517 in that county we see at once that for Warwickshire

Hales was perfectly correct: the greater part of the destruction of villages had been in the days of John Rous who was dead by the seventh year of King Henry the Seventh.

The particular date chosen by Hales can be explained purely in terms of the particular point he was making in his argument, and it is not suggested that 1485 had any general significance in enclosure history. "The beginning of the reign of King Henry the seventh"—whether interpreted as 1485 or 1488—marked the limit of the retrospective powers of inquiry and punishment which successive parliaments had granted the Crown. In a number of pleas before the Court of Exchequer the defence put forward by enclosers was just this: that the destruction had been carried out earlier than 1485. The plea of Magdalen College, Oxford, before the Judges of King's Bench was, for example, that Sir Thomas Danvers had enclosed Golder three years or more before the Act of 1488 and before they took possession.[17]

It was no doubt the memory of cases such as these which made Hales despair of ever making an example of the worst depopulations, already fifty years old. He was angry enough that graziers should attempt to bribe and threaten the juries at the Inquiry. He was sarcastic at the expense of those who thought that they would be able to compound for their offences by a fine or the purchase of a pardon:[18]

> some was persuaded that the end of the Commission should be but a money matter as it had been in time past . . . some said the Commission was but a storm for a time and soon would pass over, as a great many hope.

His judgment was, however, not only that strict enforcement was called for, but that the law itself was potentially a weak weapon:

> it is not the execution of the laws already made that shall restore the Realm to his perfection and replenish it with such abundance of town parishes and houses as have been in the time of King Edward the first which the survey of the Realm made then will plainly declare. For the chief destruction of towns and decay of houses was before the beginning of the reign of King Henry VII.

Tawney's comment on this last sentence was:

> the remark can hardly have been true of the great and sudden evictions which caused rioting and depopulation and evoked the long series of statutes which begin in 1489.

It seems likely that Tawney was too cautious. In a footnote to this comment he admitted that we know too little of the nature of fifteenth-century depopulation, certainly less than of the sixteenth century when there was the printing press for pamphlet comment, and when the State was strong enough to encourage men to appeal to its courts.[19]

The evidence from these courts which we have examined does, however, suggest that few major depopulations were in fact accompanying the "long series of statutes" after 1517. This legislation was concerned with depopulation in the broader sense, although its ambiguous language has made it difficult—as we see in Tawney's case—for historians to accept Hales' judgment that the worst was over by 1485. It is true that the "great and sudden evictions" did continue (but at a sharply diminishing pace) until 1517; if we look for concrete evidence of depopulated villages after 1517 we find very little indeed outside the Border counties, and even the preamble of the last of the "long series of statutes" (that of 1597) was based on an unhappy memory of things past and a lively fear for the future, rather than on any present discontents arising from a new flood of depopulating enclosures in the English Midlands.

In Chapter Seven, when we come to look at the different local experiences of depopulation we shall return to the question of chronology. This is because Northumberland and Durham, for peculiarly local reasons, experienced depopulation at the end of the sixteenth century, a hundred years after the worst cases in the Midlands; and because the eastern counties of Lincoln and the East Riding (and possibly Norfolk) seem to have known extensive depopulation significantly earlier than in the Midlands. With these two reservations, one for earlier and one for later depopulations, we can now consider the limits of time within which the Midlands experienced their greatest loss of villages.

We have so far marched backwards in our attempt to limit the period within which villages were most likely to be destroyed. This has brought us to a period between 1485 and 1517 when depopulating enclosure was still taking place, with suggestions that worse depopulation had occurred a decade or so earlier. We must now approach the same point in time from the other direction. Moving forward to 1485 we must see whether there is any evidence by which we can narrow the period of depopulation or whether there are many much earlier occasions on which depopulation also took place. We can then conclude this chapter with some examples taken from those villages—the minority—where we are fortunately able to put an exact date to their final destruction.

5

There was probably never a decade in the Middle Ages which did not see the death of one or more English villages. A village was as mortal as a man. It had been created by men living together, making the best use of the natural resources surrounding them. If these resources became exhausted, then no sentimental ties would bind men to continue living there. If these resources became out of fashion or unprofitable to work upon, then other means of livelihood had to be sought; and that probably involved seeking other places of livelihood.

We know that the Norman Conquest and the subsequent suppression of the rebels created many wildernesses where there had been villages. We have seen that it was this destruction by the Conqueror which prompted John Rous to turn aside from his *History* to bewail the Conquerors of his own day. We also know that most of the devastated villages were re-settled, probably by migrant colonists from less fruitful places, and certainly upon attractive easy terms. Only a handful of places did not recover.

In the two centuries after the Conquest a good deal of secondary colonisation took place under the pressure of hungry mouths on land. New villages and hamlets grew out of forest clearings, but the number of new major settlements seems to have been small. Indeed, near the Cistercian estates some villages were being destroyed. The abbey of Combe in Warwickshire was given land within the parish where the villagers of Upper and Lower Smite tilled their fields. These two villages have disappeared, and the former church of St. Peter at Lower Smite is now built into a farm-house. The earthworks of Upper Smite are faintly discernible near a farm-house at Nobbs Wood. The parish name disappeared, and is now preserved only in Smite Brook, Smeeton Lane and Smite Hill.

There is no cartulary of Combe Abbey in print, but Dugdale knew of the depopulation here. He described how the foundation of the Abbey in 1130 had created

> pasture ground where anciently two villages stood, the depopulation whereof hath bene ancient, for the vestiges are scarce to be discerned.

At Stoneleigh Abbey the monks, according to their own Ledger Book,

> settled in the place where Crulefeld Grange now is, having moved away those who lived there to the village now called Hurst.

In the mid-twelfth century Revesby Abbey offered land in outlying villages to those of its tenants who would leave the villages of Stichesby and Thoresby which adjoined the monastery. They all accepted, and thirteen families left Stichesby and eleven, Thoresby. Neither was ever repopulated, although the sites are known. The two villages do not appear in Domesday Book nor in the Lindsey Survey, so they were probably post-Conquest settlements in an area of small settlements.[20]

In Yorkshire the creation of the Granges of Cistercian houses was often associated with the removal of the villagers. Mr. Bishop has shown how Baldersby was cleared, so that

> what were formerly vills are now made into a grange,

and from the Fountains cartulary the creation of a compact estate at Greenbery near Scorton can be watched progressing as gift was added to gift and purchase to purchase. Eventually the villagers were evicted. (By a curious irony the devastation by the Scots in the fourteenth century found Fountains too poor to spend money and men in the repair of these estates and papal permission was obtained in 1336 to pass them back to lay ownership. Baldersby was resettled at this time)[21].

The general reputation of the Cistercians was damaged by their fondness for creating solitude out of the ruins of villages, although (as at Revesby) there were places where they offered alternative sites. From the *Historia Fundationis* it would seem that Old Byland is one such village, erected up on the moor when the monks occupied the former village site down in the Rye valley opposite Rievaulx Abbey. If we read carefully what Walter Map, one of their most violent critics, wrote, it will be seen that the purpose of the monastic depopulation was not always sheep-farming.

> they level everything *before the ploughshare . . . not scrupling to sow crops* [my italics].

although in one of his celebrated passages—

> you could say "grass grows green now where Troy town stood"

the crop is grass.[22]

The Cistercians had begun by removing villages for the solitude of their Rule, but in the end their activities as sheep-farmers were bound to bring them to enclosure for grazing. In 1216 the monks of Fountains made a formal agreement with the chapter of Ripon that they would not convert arable to pasture in any land which they acquired within the widespread parish of Ripon where their House lay. In 1952 the Economic History Society made a pilgrimage to Dishley Grange where Robert Bakewell had carried out the experiments in sheep and cattle-breeding which revolutionised stock-breeding in England. Dishley Grange represents the village of Dishley with 33 households in Domesday Book. The village was given to the monks of Garendon Abbey who had converted it to a grange by 1180: in 1563 there were only four families in the parish.[23]

At Sempringham in Lincolnshire the whole village entered the monastery, men and women, and the village disappeared. The first air photographs taken to locate the Priory site revealed the village lying to the north-west of the church.[24]

For a number of medieval villages the sea was the agent of destruction. It robbed some ports of their livelihood by silting up their harbours; it washed away others. It swept one village from Carmarthen Bay. In the case of Ravenser and Ravenserod it first threw up a sandbank off Spurn Head on which a flourishing town grew up to steal trade from Grimsby and Hull, and then just as swiftly it washed it away. The east coast of Yorkshire below Bridlington has lost some dozen substantial villages, some of them quite early in the thirteenth century.[25]

Fire was another agent of destruction. Fire might come by accident as we know it did in 1285 to Bywell on Tyne,[26] or it might come by hands of the King's enemy. The French burned Excete in Sussex, and it does not seem to have recovered.[27] The Scots burned some Northumberland villages regularly each decade, and we know from the Subsidy Rolls that in the fourteenth century their visits to the northern counties (even as far south as Otley) brought complete destruction to a number of villages on their route.[28] The *Nova Taxatio* of 1318 was an attempt to re-assess the value of clerical property after the great incursus into the North of the preceding years. It is easy to exaggerate the permanent effects of fire and sword. When houses were wattle and daub they might burn well, but they could easily be restored. The villagers could drive their animals and take their families out of danger, and there is plenty of evidence that villagers on the route of the Scottish invaders were busy again within a season or two and contributing to the Subsidy within five years. Extents for northern manors often show reductions in value where the two armies had marched, but it is rarely a valuation that has sunk to zero. Of the scores of Northumberland and Yorkshire villages which we know were burned, only a handful failed to recover. Probably the lost Newby by Rainton in the North Riding is one of these.[29] It was burned in 1320. Gristhwaite, only a few miles away, has also shrunk to one farm, but the problem is complicated here by a categorical statement in the Quarter Sessions minutes for 1607 that it was depopulated in 1577 by an encloser.[30] It may be that the village had remained a small hamlet since the Scots had burned it and so formed an easy prey to an Elizabethan grazier.

Nor must we forget that Domesday Book which we have used so often as an initial point at which to count our village settlements was itself a record of the destruction of settlement. In the towns William I pulled down houses to enlarge or create his castles; in his punitive raids he laid waste villages and fields although, as Mr. Bishop has shown, these were not to remain waste long. In the New Forest the destruction of some villages was permanent. The evidence of Domesday Book is quite definite on this point. Of the size and site of the settlements nothing definite is known: later chroniclers speak of churches destroyed in the making of the Forest but this may be a pious and romantic gloss.[31]

6

We may hope to trace other early depopulations by watching for the disappearance of villages from tax collectors' lists. These lists become fuller and more frequent after 1279, and we may also use them to see whether villages which were later to be destroyed were already showing signs of smallness and poverty in the early fourteenth century. The calculating eye of the tax collector was directed on the very matters of man-power and taxable capacity which interest us in this inquiry. The *Nomina Villarum* (Names of Villages) drawn up for the Exchequer in 1316 provides another opportunity of noting which villages were thought to be in existence at that time.[32]

We can illustrate this type of investigation best by showing it in action for a small area. It would be tedious to print too much, but the wapentake of the Ainsty, the rural area to the west of York, has been taken in Table 16 in the Appendix. It is important to make such an investigation in order to avoid confusing any earlier depopulations with those of the fifteenth and sixteenth centuries, and to assess whether they form any substantial proportion of the lost village sites of England.

It will be seen from the Table that (as far as sheer number of settlements is concerned) the Ainsty added only two villages to its Domesday complement between 1086 and 1377. During the same period it lost five villages, a net loss of three out of thirty-nine. Both from their tax assessment and their surviving earthworks the villages lost by 1377 could never have been very large. The casualties after 1377 on the other hand were more substantial, with tax quotas approaching those of their neighbours (and in one case surpassing them).

A study of Canon Foster's list of Lincolnshire depopulations shows the same features: a number of Domesday vills, possibly never very large settlements, failed to survive on a scale large enough to be separate units of collection in 1297, 1332, 1334 or 1377. From the many examples we have of small communities which did receive separate assessment we can conclude that any place which was omitted was little more than one house or farm. When we have small communities of five, six or nine adults taxed in 1377 or villages with tax quotas of 5*s*., 6*s*. or 8*s*. in 1334, we can be satisfied that a place would have to be very small indeed not to be taken into separate account by the Exchequer. (In this connection "separate account" must include the places linked with another village in a tax list or silently indicated by *cum membris* after the name of the parent village.)

The degree to which there was a retreat of settlement between 1086 and the early fourteenth century cannot be accurately determined from tax lists alone. The tax lists earlier than the late thirteenth century which survive are few. The basis of assessment changed from year to year, and incomparability places heavy burdens on statistics already slight in stature. Far too many counties have no tax roll earlier than the reign of Edward II (1307–27), and these early Subsidy Rolls can only speak of a *minimum* number of taxpayers, since the exemption limit excluded all those with small amounts of property or no property at all. In the same way, the Hundred Rolls of 1279 give minimum populations for certain villages, and this is satisfying if we want to establish that a lost village was still living in that year, but these rolls confine themselves to a small area of the country. To feel our way backwards from the Subsidy Rolls of the early fourteenth century takes us towards a period when the records of single villages and single manors in single years replace comprehensive county-wide or country-wide documents like the poll tax receipts. Single places and single occasions make thin history.

Disappointing as it is not to be able to contribute further to the "public debate" on an early retreat of settlement for which Professor Postan's articles are a self-styled[33] "pretext", the dividing line of 1334 does enable us to take our stand at one firm point. In that year we have the assembled village quotas for every county. The plague years have not yet descended to speed any retreat already begun. In the calculations which we shall make in Chapter Seven, we shall often measure local intensity of depopulation by the proportion of villages which appear in 1334, but subsequently disappear. Fortunately a study of the 1334 tax list does show us, as still alive, the vast majority of lost village sites which claim our attention from their earthworks; it also shows us in existence the vast majority of settlements mentioned in Domesday in addition to other late-comers on the scene. Taken in all, it is not a bad time to call the roll. We know that we shall miss a few absentees, but to trace them is a separate study. Only in isolated cases like Casthorpe, Great Conesby (Lincs.), Aldeby, Andrechurch, Ambion and Weston (Leics.) do we have positive evidence for earlier depopulation[34] although this may be more common outside the Midlands.

In those counties where attempts have been made to trace every lost village, we can essay a measure of the early depopulations. In Leicestershire, 61% of the lost villages were still listed in the 1334 tax roll as separate assessment units; another 18% were listed as one of a pair of places treated as one unit; another 9% which did not appear in the 1334 roll did put in an appearance in the 1316 *Nomina*

Villarum. This leaves only 12% unaccounted for, with a *prima facie* case for an early depopulation. In the East Riding the parallel figures are 55%, 15% and 0%, leaving 30% of the lost villages and hamlets to be presumed already dead by 1334. (These percentages are of all the places we know to be lost: the lost villages as a percentage of the living must be sought for in Tables 17 and 18.)

In Mr. Allison's study[35] of Norfolk he found that 35 of the 726 places mentioned in Domesday Book had vanished from the tax list by 1316. This can be compared with the 58 other lost villages which were still listed in the tax list of 1334 but have vanished since.

Of the Warwickshire sites which I have listed elsewhere, six had been lost before 1400; ninety had disappeared by 1485; and twenty-four more after that date. Eight other sites had probably gone by 1400, and seven others probably date from the period 1485–1558. (These figures include all settlements, however small, so that the total is greater than that shown in Table 6, where only those villages are counted which were substantial enough to be separately taxed in 1334.)

It is because these villages do not appear in early fourteenth-century tax lists that they can be called "already lost". Their absence from the tax lists robs us of a yardstick to measure their relative size. Judged by their earthworks alone these early depopulations were very small communities, but every county can show one or two exceptions to this rule. Only a very detailed study of charter evidence could show whether these earlier depopulations were settlements which came late to the agricultural scene: that is, which stood on marginal corn-land.

7

It is crucially important to show that so many to-be-lost villages do answer *adsum* not only in 1334, but also in 1352–53–54, and again in 1377, 1428 and 1433. These are years after the Black Death's most severe visitations were over, and it shows that the Black Death had not emptied them. It is important to emphasise their survival, since whenever local historians have chanced to notice a lost village within their province there has been the temptation to look back into the Middle Ages for something catastrophic enough to explain such a catastrophe. The Black Death was well enough known even to those who had not studied the Middle Ages very thoroughly, and it was called into the narrative as a *diabolus ex machina.* If such an explanation did hold true for the majority of deserted sites which one finds, then the problem of chronology would be a simple one, and this chapter could end here with a note that Hales was right, and that the great destruction of towns *was* before the beginning of the reign of King Henry the Seventh: indeed that it was in the twenty-third and twenty-fourth years of the reign of King Edward the Third. We need have no more to do with sheep masters and their ambitions: they would simply have stepped into empty holdings and empty villages like an explorer among the creepers and undergrowth of a newly discovered City of the Incas.

But the Subsidy Rolls of 1352–53–54 tell a quite different story from this, and their story is largely corroborated by the rolls of 1433 and subsequent years when the capacity of a village to pay was re-assessed. At these re-assessments (when villages were granted relief from their tax burdens if they were considered to be impoverished)[36] a few of our "lost" villages do appear among those relieved. Indeed, a few have heavy reliefs and these few can be considered as suffering from the results of plague or the contraction of the economy in the fifteenth century. But a study of these re-assessments throws into relief how exceptional such instances are, and how many villages—later to be lost—were still being regarded as no worse off than any other.

It is important to give the Black Death its due, even if we depose it from the role of the chief enemy of villages. It will not do to erect a counter-myth that the Black Death emptied no villages at all when we have villages like Standelf or Tilgarsley. At Standelf the incumbent petitioned his archdeacon in 1447 asking to be relieved of the obligation to say regular services in the chapel there, since the hamlet had no more villagers after *pestilentia et ipidimia*; in the previous year the Exchequer had granted relief from the lay subsidy obligation for this depopulated place which is now no more than two farms (Standhill) at the northern end of Pyrton parish, Oxfordshire.

Tilgarsley had presented a similar problem to the collectors of the lay subsidy. In 1359 they reported to the Exchequer that no one had lived there since 1350 and they could not collect the 94*s*. 9*d*. tax. The status of the village was considered *De Banco* by the judges in 1370 and again in 1378 and 1383. The Exchequer was loth to give up the hope that villagers would be persuaded to resettle, but by 1422 the village was cut up into closes and leased out. It was never to be resettled.[37]

The owner of Tilgarsley was Eynsham Abbey, and the Abbots had the problem of recruiting settlers in other villages. At Woodeaton[38] they could only hold their tenants and attract others by scaling down rents and manorial burdens:

> there scarce remained at Woodeaton two tenants, who would themselves have gone away had not Brother Nicholas then Abbot, come to a new agreement with them.

On such manors where tenants could be attracted and held, there was no question of total depopulation, and Woodeaton is still on the map.

If tenants came to the Woodeatons of England they left villages behind them elsewhere, and in the general reshuffle after the plagues there was an opportunity for villagers who could to move from poorer land to better, from hard masters to easy masters. This general mobility was deliberately hampered by the Ordinance and Statute of Labourers, but it went on. With a shortage of labour there were always Brother Nicholases who would rather offer better terms than see the land go right out of cultivation. This internal movement from one place to another more attractive could result in the depopulation of a marginal village just as surely as if the plague had killed off every villager, and in many documents which speak of empty holdings the plague and the bad soil are linked in explanation. At the lost Wyville in Lincolnshire[39]

> the three carucates are worth little, for the land is poor and stony, and lies uncultivated for want of tenants after the pestilence.

When Lincolnshire parishes were amalgamated the petition to the bishop in several instances spoke of the poverty and sterility of the soil. Once the first shock of the plague is over and men—even if only some men—are moving from place to place, it is not sufficient to explain a lost village by the plague alone, for we must face the question, why was it never resettled? No document exists to answer that question, and we must risk guessing that the villages which were never resettled after 1349 were akin to those from which men moved away of their own accord: they were unattractive places in country where men were no longer so hungry for land.

In these cases, land tumbled back to grass not because anyone wished to convert arable to pasture as such, but because grass was the residual crop. The pastures at East and West Wykeham in Lincolnshire which Canon Foster thought the best site in the county must be explained in these terms: the church was not served after 1396 because the parishioners had gone.[40] By 1437 Dunsthorpe in Hameringham was in the same condition and when the glebe land of Hameringham was surveyed in 1601 all that remained[41] of the village was "one little close called chappell yarde". At nearby Fordington the livings were also amalgamated, but the land remained partly arable. The men of Ulceby took the strips of Fordington into their open fields just as the incumbent took the name of the two livings.[42] At Dexthorpe, again nearby, the depopulated village became a pasture and in 1577 there was[43]

> one pasture containing ii acres wherein did stand the churche and parsonage.

In other villages (like Wharram Percy) with many years of life between the Black Death and their final depopulation, there was a sufficient fall in population from the heyday of the thirteenth century for the side aisles of the church to be pulled down and the arcade walled up. North Scarle[44] was burned in 1341, but when it came to be rebuilt the church had no north aisle, no north transept and no south transept: a shrunken church ministered to a shrunken community. Whisby in Doddington[45] never rebuilt its church, burned in 1321; Cublington was abandoned early in the fourteenth century but resettled and rebuilt.[46]

These cannot be the only examples of total or partial depopulation which can be assigned to the period of the Black Death and its aftermath, but in general the plague has been given too much credit for destruction of villages, and many sheep-enclosures passed by unnoticed as long as the Black Death could be invoked as an explanation.

8

If the Black Death did not destroy, did it enfeeble? Did it reduce strong, well-populated villages to an inferior position and make them highly vulnerable in the next century? We have no direct means of comparing populations before and after the Plague. Our sole opportunity of counting heads, the poll tax, comes after the Plague. From the years before the Plague there is a different type of evidence not strictly comparable, the evidence from the village quotas of 1334. The examination of this evidence in Chapter Seven reaches a simple conclusion: if the tax assessments of 1334 had anything to do with size and prosperity then the villages which were later to be depopulated were not typical villages. Their average tax quota was well below the average of their neighbours fifteen years before the first visitation of the pestilence.

These villages, the to-be-lost villages, have among their number some whose payment reached and even exceeded the local average, but the group has far more small villages in it than would a group made up of the same number of villages taken at random from the local countryside. If we may summarise a Table from the later chapter, we find that in 1334 about one in eight (12%) of all Leicestershire villages paid 20*s.* tax or less, and Leicester villages were assessed very much in the same sums as other Midland counties. In contrast to this, we find that of 225 lost villages in eleven Midland counties nearly two out of five (38%) paid 20*s*. or less. The poll tax figures of 1377 show the same characteristic: the to-be-lost villages have a very high proportion of unusually small places among their number.

When this characteristic appears both in 1334 and 1377 it suggests that the Plague of 1349 was not responsible for the enfeeblement of the majority of lost villages. Again, the tax reliefs of 1352–54 were granted "according to necessity" but very few lost villages (large or small) rank high in the scale of reliefs. The same is true of the reliefs granted after 1436. Cases like Flotmanby are exceptional. At the lost Flotmanby,[47] lying at the foot of the Yorkshire Wolds, the whole tax quota was remitted for 1352 and 1354. Its tax quota was only about one-third of the local average to begin with, but after the Plague the village could not afford that much and the local assessors agreed:

> this relief is in aid of those villages which are the poorest . . . by counsel of the Justices assigned to this matter. This is the intention of our Lord the King and his Council.[48]

Flotmanby survives only in the name of a hall and park.

In such cases, where no poll tax population is recorded, we can take the information from 1352–54 at its face value: the village is dead. Where the recorded poll tax population in 1377 is substantial we can acquit the Black Death of complicity in the destruction of the village. Towthorpe in the Thistles does not sound a very fertile place: it was small in 1334, small in 1352 and still small in 1377 with thirteen adult taxpayers. It is now depopulated, but we must assign a date after 1377. Many surviving villages had poll tax populations no higher than this.[49]

9

What do the poll tax returns show? are there villages which flourished in 1354, yet vanished by 1377? The poll tax evidence is most useful in proving that a village was still in existence in 1377, but it is too patchy in its survival for us to be able to say: no poll tax receipt, no village. The mortality among the receipts has been very high in some counties and negligible in others. We have fairly complete sets for Northamptonshire, Nottinghamshire, Yorkshire and the Lindsey division of Lincolnshire, but some counties have lost every receipt. Among the surviving receipts only one *nil* return[50] has been found: the collector for Bolton by Bradford (Yorks.) wrote on his receipt *nemo manet ibidem.* Bolton is no longer a lost village: by the Census of 1801 the industrial revolution had peopled its fields again with 474 inhabitants.

The next opportunity to call the roll comes in 1428, when all parishes with fewer than ten householders were remitted the parish tax levied that year.[51] In the inner Midland counties very few of our lost village names appear. Stretton Baskerville, Quarrendon and other Midland parishes with churches now ruined did not apply for exemption in 1428.

In Lincolnshire (and to some extent Norfolk) the list of exemptions is longer, and lost village names occur in it. Lincolnshire—particularly the Wolds—had been granted high reliefs in 1352–54 and the amalgamation of parishes which had already begun in 1428 suggests that in the to-and-fro migration of men after the plague years this area was on balance witnessing a retreat of settlement. The ruined churches of west Norfolk and Suffolk point to the same conclusion.

From 1432 onwards Parliament acknowledged local pockets of depression by allowing reliefs from the village tax quotas fixed in 1334. In the collections of 1442, 1445, 1449, 1453, 1462, 1463, 1468, 1487, 1489, 1491, 1492 and 1497 each "impoverished place" was granted some relief. The order to the collectors[52] was quite explicit: they were to pay attention to local needs, and relief was not to be allocated at a flat rate . . .

> these are the names of those villages cities and boroughs desolate, wasted and destroyed or too impoverished or too heavily assessed to the fifteenth and tenth, and sums have been deducted as follows. . .

As far as we can tell, these instructions were conscientiously carried out. Where we have two or more surviving tax rolls within this period for the same county it is usual to find the amount of relief varying from collection to collection. Although this suggests that re-assessment did take place and that a conventional sum was not allowed year after year unquestioningly, another difficulty arises. What conclusion can we draw when a county has only one surviving tax roll from the years 1432–97? If we find a village in such a roll with 45% of its tax remitted, what conclusion can be safely drawn? Is the village permanently impoverished, or has it had a particular and transient misfortune?

In counties where more than one year's rolls have survived we might find a village with 35%, 45% and 25% relief in three successive collections. In these circumstances we can do no more than to compare these three figures with the general local relief and see whether it was an exceptionally high relief. The more rolls which survive, the less the chance of error in generalising from one year's surviving assessment.[53]

As we might expect, the fifteenth-century tax reliefs do not fail to show some lost village communities deserving large reliefs, just like Flotmanby in 1352–54. Martinsthorpe in Rutland was assessed at 25*s.* 6*d.* in 1327; 40*s.* 8*d.* in 1334 and had had 88 poll tax payers: but in the re-assessments of 1445 and 1489 it was relieved of half its tax obligation. Rokeby and Mortham on the Tees had not recovered from their wastage by the Scots in the fourteenth century, and their relief from the quotas fixed in 1334 was considerable.[54]

On the other hand, the general experience of the villages which we now call lost was quite different. The majority of them received no greater relief than their neighbours, and many of them received quite low relief. The Stretton Baskervilles, the East Lillings and the Wharram Percies received relief well below average and on occasions no relief at all. Unless there is strong evidence from elsewhere to the contrary this will be interpreted as indicating that the communities were still far from depopulation in the mid-fifteenth century. It is unfortunate that the survival of the tax records for the years 1432–49 has been better than for the later reassessments of 1487–97, of which only a handful of rolls have been preserved. The years between 1449 and 1487 are the darkest in the history of the lost village, with everything pointing to considerable depopulation just at this point.

9

We have now assembled the general evidence which points to a period between 1440 and 1520 as that in which the main flood of depopulation took place. The line of inquiry which began in the eighteenth century and moved backwards has converged upon that moving forward from Domesday Book.

In a sense, the crucial years lie half in a no-man's-land of English historical research. This is of less importance in the Midlands, for the evidence of John Rous and the Inquiry of 1517 is sufficient to be certain that we have caught the depopulations in full force. In the other counties where the Inquiry of 1517 came too late to record the major depopulations we could wish for more records from the generation before 1485. In that period the Government was not directly concerned with depopulation as an illegal act, and the records are poorly indexed and too formidable in bulk for random inquiry. The local government records are slim, and the owners of manorial records from lost villages had every reason to destroy them.

One or two later records do suggest, as they look back to the years before 1485, that depopulation was active at that time. The first of these is the first anti-enclosure statute, that of 1489, which speaks of depopulation as no novel ailment. We know from an autobiographical reference that John Rous had presented a petition to Parliament at Coventry in 1459 complaining of enclosures. The Lord Chancellor criticised depopulating enclosure in a speech in Parliament in 1483, and there is the curious statute as early as 1402 which forbade

> any clerk secular or religious or any other liegeman of the King

to be indicted as *depopulatores agrorum* or *insidiatores viarum*. It was the estate of the Clergy which had complained that they were being indicted in these terms.[55] In 1414 there were two petitions to Parliament which seem to involve enclosure. One,[56] at Ragnall and Darlton, Notts, does not at first sight seem to be depopulation, since both villages survive. Adjoining them are the lost Whimpton and Woodcotes, and it is possible that the petition refers to the enclosure of parkland here. Similarly, the second petition cannot be linked with a site which is now empty, since it is for Chesterton in Cambridge: but there have been many years in which this site could have been resettled since that complaint of[57]

> none house left standing there but if it were a sheepcote or a barn or swine-stye and a few houses besides to put in beasts.

Leadam analysed the dates of the enclosures presented to the Commission of 1517 which, it will be remembered, had retrospective powers to 1488. More than half the 7,200 acres reported in Warwickshire were enclosed in the years between 1488 and 1500, and in his analysis of the Nottinghamshire evidence[58] he pointed out that the greatest activity in the Midlands, measured by cases heard in 1517, came between 1491 and 1500.

Looked at in conjunction with the other evidence, the widespread Midland enclosures at the beginning of the sixteenth century are seen as waning well before 1517; and if we allow for the lost villages which had been depopulated before 1485, in the lifetime of John Rous, it is doubtful whether the period covered by the Commission's powers of inquiry saw the true peak of the movement.

10

We may sum up this short examination of the various occasions of destruction by listing one example of each type which we have considered, together with the form of supporting evidence which seems necessary to justify assigning a depopulation to a particular year or range of years.

TABLE I

SPECIMEN DEPOPULATIONS FROM VARIOUS PERIODS

Date or range of dates	*Place*	*Supporting evidence*
A. By early 13th century	Butyate in Bardney, Lincs.	Domesday Book f. 363c. 4 ploughteams, 10 villeins, 5 sokemen in 1086. The township was given by Robert Marmion to Bardney Abbey, after which there is no mention.
B. By early 14th century.	Pallathorpe by Tadcaster, Yorks.	D.B. Kirkby's Quest 1284 and 1302 Fees. Not mentioned in *Nomina Villarum*, 1316.
C. 14th century, before Black Death.	Little Stapleford by Brant Broughton, Lincs.	A *villata* with Broughton in *Nomina Villarum*, 1316, but in 1338–39 the bishop gives permission for the chapel to be taken down.
D. Immediately after Black Death.	Tilgarsley, near Eynsham, Oxon.	Collectors of Lay Subsidy report in 1359 that no one had lived there since 1350 and the 94*s*. 9*d*. tax could not be collected.
E. Consequent upon the Black Death, but not immediately after.	Fordington, Lincs.	Church united with Ulceby 1450 on account of the small number of parishioners *causa pestilenciae*.
F. Consequent upon parkmaking in 15th century.	Fulbrook, Warws.	John Rous reports the destruction by the Duke of Bedford, brother of Henry V, in 1421. In 1428 only four householders.
C. Consequent upon enclosure before 1488, and not reported in 1517.	Sunderlandwick, E.R. Yorks.	35 in poll tax of 1377. 70% relief in 1452. Good clear site.
H. Enclosure reported in 1517.	Stretton Baskerville, Warws.	Destroyed finally in Dec. 1494. Date given by jurors at Inquiry.
I. Destruction in late 16th century	Utchester, Northum.	Near-contemporary survey explicitly says 1579.
J. Destruction in the 17th or early 18th centuries for emparking.	Hinderskelfe, N.R. Yorks.	Evidence of a village map before the enlargement of the house and gardens.

TABLE 2

USE OF THE TAX LISTS AND ANALOGOUS DOCUMENTS FOR APPROXIMATE DATING OF DEPOPULATION

Name of Village	*Present in Lay Subsidy of 1334? M = taxed by itself m = taxed along with another vill*	*Low percentage relief in 1352–54?*	*Taxpayers present in 1377 poll tax?*	*Fewer than ten households in 1428?*	*Low relief in mid-15th century subsidies?*	*Reported in 1517 as depopulated since 1488?*	*Other evidence*	*Suggested dates*
1. Burton Constable, Yorks., E.R.	yes: M	yes	yes: 105	no	yes: 33%	yes		date given in 1517 evidence
2. Little Corringham, Lincs.	yes: M	yes	yes: 49	no	yes: 30%	no		c. 1450–85
3. Maidenwell, Lincs.	yes: M	yes	yes: 25	yes	no	no	United to Farforth parish in 1450.	c. 1400–28
4. Risby, Lincs.	yes: M	yes	yes: 33	yes		no		soon after 1377
5. West Wykeham, Lincs.	yes: M	yes	no			no	United to Ludford parish in 1396.	c. 1360
6. North Cadeby, Lincs.	yes: M	no: 100%				no		c. 1349

These approximate datings by broad periods could be considerably narrowed where manorial documents or inquisitions ***post mortem*** have survived for a particular vill.

II

So far, with the exception of a note on the Border counties, we have treated depopulation as if it were felt at the same time in all parts of the country. In fact, as we shall see in Chapter Seven, this is an over-simplification. It is true of the core of inner Midland counties where the worst English depopulation was experienced. But in the counties of the Eastern margin there is a significant difference.

When the Inquiry of 1517 visited the Midlands it found evidence that substantial enclosure had taken place since 1488, but in the eastern counties there were only trifling and scattered cases to report.[59] At first sight this looks as if these counties were immune from depopulation, but when we come to measure up the 1334 tax list or the 1377 poll tax receipts against the modern maps we find the same intensity of depopulation which marks the Midlands. The difference is one of time.

In Lincolnshire and the East Riding (and perhaps in Norfolk) a bigger percentage of places disappeared earlier. Of the ninety-nine sites lost in the East Riding[60] I am completely unable to date fourteen. Of the remaining eighty-five, only thirty-seven are definitely from the period *c.* 1450–1550; sixteen were lost by 1334; and thirty-two others probably before 1450.

When there is much depopulation before 1485 the attempt to assign dates is bound to be hazardous, but my reading of the Lincolnshire evidence[61] is as follows:

Lost before the Black Death	12
Lost soon after the Black Death	15
Lost early in the 15th century	18
Lost in the 15th century (probably latter half) . .	27
Small villages lost after 1334 (probably 15th century) .	41

This points to much more substantial early depopulation in the eastern counties, and this will be examined further in Chapter Seven.

Our tools for dating these eastern depopulations are crude, but the results point to a phenomenon rarely experienced in the Midlands, a retreat of settlement spread over the century after the Black Death. Even our most definite source for this statement comes from a point well after the first impact of the plague. At East and West Wykeham no priest was instituted after 1382. It was not until March 1396–97 that the Bishop of Lincoln decreed the union of the church with Ludford Magna on account of the depopulation. It was 1437 before Dunsthorpe was similarly united to Hameringham. The Rector's petition gave as his reason:

> the lack of parishioners, the fewness of peasants, their low wages, the bareness of the lands, the lack of cultivation, pestilences and epidemics with which the Lord afflicts his people for their sins, and it (the glebe income) is hardly sufficient for the eighth part of the salary of a stipendiary chaplain much less of a rector who has to bear necessary charges.

In May 1450 Fordington was joined to Ulceby and Beesby to Hawerby, again with the explanation:

> *propter raritatem parochianorum pestilenciae causa*

and:

> *sterilitate quarum terrarum et defectu culturae.*

About the same time South Cadeby and Calcethorpe were joined together. In the same way,[62] the disappropriation of the church at Thorpe by Newark in 1455 was attributed by the bishop to

> the fewness and poverty of the inhabitants as a result of which lands once fertile and arable are now sterile and fallen back to grass.

As the list in Table 11 shows, there were many Lincolnshire churches which were abandoned between 1350 and 1550, and if we find the village names also occurring among those receiving high relief in 1352, and among those named as having fewer than ten householders in 1428, we must count them as being the victims of the plague. Judging from the reliefs of 1352, this was very badly felt on the crown of the Lincolnshire Wolds. Eight villages had both high relief in 1352 and fewer than ten households in 1428, and five of the eight come from the wapentake of Howardshoe.[63]

These villages which the fifteenth-century tax collectors

found empty had been easy conquests. None of them had been very large, compared with its neighbours, in the early fourteenth century. The average for the whole district was itself smaller than in the west, some 50*s*., but none of these villages could muster more than 53% of that sum, and only two of the eight we mentioned above paid more than 25*s*.

We shall return to this important matter of relative smallness in Chapter Eight, and we need only note here that the many ruined churches in Norfolk suggest that its experience was similar to that of Lincolnshire. The East Riding is physically similar to the chalk wolds of Lincolnshire, but it has very few ruined churches and much less evidence of depopulation in the half century following the Plague. By elimination, this would imply that the East Riding depopulation is only a little earlier than the Midlands, and this is confirmed by a higher number of depopulations caught in the 1517 net compared with Norfolk or Lincolnshire.

12

We suggested earlier in this chapter that in the more northern counties there was a burst of true depopulating enclosure in the last years of the reign of Elizabeth, that is in the period when there was a burst of enclosure by agreement in the Midlands. We have two letters from the Dean of Durham to Cecil, written in 1593 from the diocese. He complains of cornland tumbling down to grass and whole villages suffering depopulation.[64]

When I first read these letters I put them in the same category as the complaints of the Diggers and Delvers. But a subsequent study of the admirable village histories in the *Northumberland County History* has shown me that I did the Dean a serious injustice. Ploughs were decaying in Northumberland at that time and at a rate which did involve wholesale destruction of a number of villages. We may take as an example the former village of Hartley in Earsdon, frankly described in the Delaval MSS.:

> Hartley being a great husbandry town wherein Robert Delaval esquire holdeth certain lands of the Queen . . . and

> where also other freeholders had lands and tenements. Which lands about the 16th year of her Majesty's reign were in the tenure of 15 several tenants at will . . . who were able men and kept their 15 ploughs going with 60 acres of arable land at least to every plough, 20 acres in every field as the tenants affirm.

That was the situation in 1573,

> since which time the said Robert Delaval at several times purchased all the said freeholders' lands and tenements displaced all the said tenants, defaced their tenements converted their tillage to pasture, being 720 acres of arable ground or thereabouts, and made one demesne whereon there is but three ploughs now kept by hinds and servants.

At Seaton Delaval the process of conversion was more drawn out. In 1311 only about one-third of the parish was under the plough, and there were twenty ruined cottages in an extent of 1353. In the early sixteenth century a survey shows about a dozen houses remaining. These, and their holdings were gradually drawn into the estate; one in 1588, one in 1591, one in 1593, one in 1594, four in 1595, one in 1599 and a tenth in 1601. By 1628 there were no houses, but a flock of 1,300 sheep. These dispossessions were obtained by all the pressure of excessive fines, increased rents and petty vexations.

Such proceedings must have been quite common in Northumberland in these years as the list in Chapter Ten shows. At Newham,

> Sir Thomas Graye of Chillingham in the latter end of Queen Elizabeth's reign expelled 17 score men women and children all upon one day as the report of the inhabitants thereabouts have it

says a note in the Dean and Chapter Library. It will be recalled that it was the Dean of Durham who had complained to London about mass evictions in the county.

At Utchester in 1579:

> the township in all times heretofore having 12 tenants dwelling . . . until of late one Thomas Jackson did wholly expell the said tenants and put the land thereof to pasture and so it remains.

West Chirton was depopulated some time before 1538 and the tillage converted to cattle pasture in two large closes. In a survey of 1559 the surveyor wrote:

> there are 2,000 sheep and as many beeves and muttons as a baron can conveniently spend in a year on his house, and it may very well keep also ten geldings and sixty milch kine.

When the members of the Berwickshire Naturalists Club visited Humbelton in 1878 their handbook, recalling Goldsmith, described the site as "this English Auburn". At Hetton we have an example of the arrival of a landlord who had learned his enclosing technique in a good Lincolnshire school:

> a report of 1627 says that in the peaceful times of King James did Mr. William Carre come from Lincolnshire. He decayed all the said farms (Dixons only excepted). He took all the lands that belonged to them into his own hands.

At Caistron and Weighill the tradition is that the inhabitants were all killed in a plague of 1675. This may be so, but Rous' *pestis avaritiae* had found its way to Northumberland. Nor does the county lack its emparking enclosures: Shawdon in 1779, Haughton in 1816, Clennell and Biddlestone at an unknown (and earlier?) date—these villages followed the path of the Hinderskelfes and the Wotton Underwoods further south.[65]

Although these eighteenth-century cases in Northumberland have parallels in the Midlands, the generally later arrival of the depopulating enclosure does stand out. It is very useful (as the extracts which we have just quoted have shown) to have this late enclosure at a time when our chance of reading contemporary descriptions of the process is so much greater. The purchases of Robert Delaval at Hartley must have had their parallel in hundreds of such ambitious purchases in the Midlands a century or more earlier.

Until Northumberland agrarian history has had the attention which it seems to deserve we cannot do more than suggest why the experience of this county should have been different from the Midlands.[66]

Northumberland had been an open-field county as much as had Durham and the North Riding of Yorkshire, with which it shared many important physical and historical characteristics. The distribution map of open fields in the Orwins' book is less than fair to the settlers who had turned the plains of the north-eastern counties into arable land.

There had been substantial shrinkage of population in the fourteenth and fifteenth centuries in the Border counties. In addition to the factors working in the Midlands there was the constant trouble of invasion and counter-invasion. There is hardly a village history in the fifteen volumes of the *N.C.H.* which does not number among its documents an inquisition or a rental with burned and vacant holdings. No doubt they were partly rebuilt, and this was no new experience for Bordermen, as Froissart reported the Scots to say after English invasions:

> if the English do burn our houses, what consequence is it to us? We can rebuild them cheaply enough for we have only to require three days to do so, provided we have five or six poles and boughs to cover them.

But the general impression—backed by a number of cases of complete tax remission—is that there was a retreat of population in the latter Middle Ages.

Although there had been retreat, the nucleated settlements seem to have held their ground, even if only at hamlet rank. Their final destruction came not at the hands of the Scots but of their countrymen. It might be asked why, in this case, the would-be graziers of the county and of other parts of England had not moved into the villages earlier than the 1580s and 1590s. The reason may lie in the late abolition of Border Tenure. Once this was abolished the position of the small peasant was much less secure, and rack-renting, calling in of leases, or downright eviction could proceed uninterruptedly. The dispersal of the ex-monastic lands by the Crown and the first generation of speculators no doubt assisted in the acquisition of properties well sited for grazing and only kept from grazing by a stubborn smallholder. The confiscation and sale of the lands of the rebel Earls provided another opportunity for acquisition at this time.

Something of the same experience seems to have befallen Durham and the North Riding of Yorkshire, although the number of deserted villages there at this late period is smaller than in Northumberland, and there are a number of earlier depopulations in the North Riding comparable in date and size to those of the Midlands. It may only be an accident that the records of the North Riding Quarter Sessions provide us with one of the rare examples of justices inquiring about depopulations in 1609. When the justices drew up their list they were able to do better than the Commission of Inquiry in the Midlands in 1607. They mustered names of villages, dates of destruction and names of depopulators.[67] The sample is a small one, but it has distinct affinities with the Northumberland experience, and Dr. Bowden has suggested to me that it may not be unconnected with the expanding demand by the West Riding clothiers at this time for the coarse wools of the North.

The history of enclosure by agreement in the Border counties is another study, but here again it would seem that things were very different from the Midlands, and indeed from the East and West Ridings. The Midlands had been able to begin enclosing for sheep at an earlier date, but the wholesale conversion had halted in the 1520s. Although there was some enclosure by agreement in the Midlands between 1520 and 1720—indeed more than the text books suggest—there was a good deal of firm resistance or reluctance to see any economic advantage; and a comparatively high percentage of parishes had to wait until Parliamentary authority could be obtained to over-rule the objections of the minority. In the Border counties, wholesale enclosure for sheep and rationalising enclosure for better convertible husbandry came later than 1520, but were taken almost together in two short, sharp draughts of medicine. When Parliamentary enclosure began in the 1720s there was hardly an open field left to be enclosed in Northumberland, Durham or the North Riding.

Chapter Six

THE MOTIVES FOR DESTRUCTION

Causa huius tanti mali est cupiditas. Nam pestis avaritiae modernos infecit, et avaritia eos caecavit. Non sunt Dei sed Mammonae filii.
[Greed is the cause of all this evil. The plague of avarice corrupts our generation, and avarice blinds them. They are the sons of Mammon, not of God.]
John Rous of Warwick, *Historia Regum Angliae* (*c.*1486).

I

IT may appear strange that it is necessary to devote a chapter to the motives which drove man to destroy villages when so much has been said already about sheep-masters and graziers. In fact we have proceeded very unjudicially. We have blackened the character of the depopulator without more than hinting at his motives.

That in itself would not be too important, for we are not concerned in passing moral judgments on those who pursued the maximisation of their economic advantage to the point of destroying villages. What is of more importance in an economic history is that there should be no ambiguity about the economic advantage which was sought. Doubts, both direct and indirect, have been cast upon this advantage. These doubts can be traced back to our uncertainties about the general economic situation in the fifteenth century. These are uncertainties about the size of population; about the quantity of wool which was going to make cloth for home sale; about the relative prices of corn and wool at different times; and our virtual ignorance of any general trend in the relative costs of producing corn or wool.

This is a formidable body of ignorance. Until it is dissipated by half a dozen badly needed books on fifteenth-century topics any account of the motives of depopulators and the exact circumstances in which they were able to achieve their ambition can be no more than hazarded suggestions and a handful of case-histories which might turn out eventually to be wildly un-typical. This is a period whose history is far from being well-known. One Ford's lecturer saw its central theme as one of promise prejudiced. Professor Postan sees the paradox of losses in general productivity alongside the social gains of a more equal distribution.[1] Over all hang the confusion of a long civil war and the complexities of sources poorly calendared and little worked over.

Fortunately there were men who discussed this widespread conversion to grass while it was still an active movement, and in their account of motives they were quite explicit. They thought that men were converting land from corn to grass because it paid better. They said nothing about men with lands left on their hands or men forced willy nilly into the role of grazier. Their discussion was in terms of human will creating the pastures and destroying the villages. It was in terms of a very strong will.

2

The evidence which we shall call cannot be that of the enclosers' own statements, for they were not very vocal. They did not argue publicly. They did not make out a case for the economies of specialisation, the optimum use of soils, the necessary place of wool in the national economy, or anything so sophisticated. When pressed in a law-court their most common defence was that no harm had been done; or that, if it had, it was the responsibility of a previous owner.

From their silence we must turn to the evidence of their opponents and to other signs that contemporaries took it for granted that enclosure for sheep was a paying proposition. If the silence of the depopulators were the only evidence, we might have to be cautious about accepting their opponents' *ex parte* statements, but the evidence which we have gathered in this book confirms all that the pamphleteers alleged: there *had* been great enclosures and there had been great depopulations.

We can see in a number of ways that everyone assumed

grazing to be a more profitable use for the enclosed land than corn. One of the tasks of the Commission of 1517 was to ascertain any increase in value which had followed enclosure. The old and new values were set down in many of their returns and substantial increases can be seen.[2] The very legislation which first set itself to discourage depopulating enclosure sought a remedy in taking away the profits of any conversion. Half the profits were to be forfeit. We have seen how the Crown began in 1538 to follow this same course in proceeding for half-profits against tenants other than its own. The same course was followed by Hales in 1548 when he suggested a tax of a penny on sheep in the common fields and 2*d.* on ewes and lambs in several pasture, with 1½*d.* on other sheep in enclosed pasture. Such a tax was enacted in 1549, only to be repealed soon after (although evidence of its collection has been found) as "unworkable."[3]

The greater profits of enclosed land were indeed used by some enclosers as a defence. One argued that it enabled him to pay the Crown more rent; another, Belknap, that it had considerably augmented the yield for the incumbent from acres of glebe no longer in tillage. The willingness to pay fines and buy pardons looks as if men thought they could nevertheless recoup themselves.

At Wormleighton the rents had been raised from eight to thirteen pounds when the fields went down to pasture. Spencer's petition against re-conversion stressed how the Crown as superior landlord had gained. He also described the hundred pounds which he had spent on a new manor house and on refurnishing the church. But the jury had found that the value of the lands had risen from forty to sixty pounds a year. To spend five years' increment on capital betterment was not so philanthropic as it looked.[4]

When the anti-stapler pamphleteer[5] wrote his *Treatise concerning the Staple* (*c.* 1533–36) he was not one to deny that the enclosers followed a profitable course. When he wrote that

> for the less profit they destroyed the more

he had ceased to think in terms of money profits. He was in the realm of social advantage and welfare economics. The "*more profit*" destroyed was the social asset of having villagers—

> in one village to destroy the labours and living of a 400 or a 500 of common people.

The conflict between private benefit and social benefit which this pamphleteer expressed can be put no more clearly than in the words with which Hales encouraged the jury of 1548. He set three opposites balanced against each other, and the last of these pairs was "commonwealth" and "private profit":

> for God, the King and the commonwealth, if ye serve them truly and faithfully, as they be able to defend you against the Devil, the world and private profit, so may you be sure they will suffer no person to do you injury.

In the diagnosis of enclosers' motives in the *Discourse* and in Hales' *Defence*, the leading theme is human greed. It was the theme of Rous, More, Crowley and Latimer.

> The Council saw what hurt had grown . . . if the greediness of Graziers and Sheepmasters were not in time resisted.

Covetousness must be attacked at the roots, he urged. The roots were the relative profitability of grass against corn:

> who will maintain husbandry which is the nurse of every County as long as sheep bring so great gain? who will be at the cost to keep a dozen in his house to milk kine, make cheese, carry it to the market when one poor soul may by keeping sheep get him a greater profit . . . who will not be contented for to pull down houses of husbandry so that he may stuff his bags full of money?

It will be noticed that the sheep is considered to be more profitable than kine because of its low labour costs. How much greater the advantage of sheep over corn when it came to labour costs!

When the characters in the *Discourse* came to argue the causation of "enclosure" they were concerned with more than one sense of that word, and the author took pains to show he did not object to enclosure which took away no one's rights:

> I mean not all Inclosures. . . but only of such Inclosures as turneth commonly arable fields into pastures.

says the Doctor, and he then turns to his programme for halting and reversing the conversion to grass:

> as long as they find more profit by pasture than by tillage they will still inclose.
>
> They see there is most advantage in grazing and breeding than in husbandry and tillage by a great deal. And so long as it is so, the pasture shall ever encroach upon the tillage for all the laws that ever can be made to the contrary.

and in reply to the Knight's request for a practical solution the Doctor says:

> to make the profit of the plough to be as good . . . rate for rate, as the profit of the graziers and sheepmasters . . . either make as little gains to grow by pastures as there groweth by tillage; or else make that there may grow as much profit by tillage as did before by pastures.
>
> We must understand that all things ought not to be forced or constrained by the penalties of the law, but some so, and others by allurements and rewards rather.

The husbandman supports the Doctor with a story of a neighbour who twelve years earlier had found that

> profit was but small by the ploughs . . . and turned either part or all of the arable ground into pasture and thereby waxed very rich . . .

In the third dialogue the Doctor returns to his policy of discouraging sheep and encouraging the plough:

> I showed before that there is more lucre by grazing of ten acres to the occupier alone than is in tillage of twenty and the causes thereof be many. One is that grazing requires small charge and small labour which in tillage consumes much of the master's gain

and the Doctor concludes by summarising the policy to follow for curing a society sick with the plague of avarice. Money had tempted men to convert to grass, and with money they should be tempted back to corn-growing:

> with lucre they should be enticed to occupy the plough, yea and with other privileges.

There is no doubt that Hales was in full agreement with John Rous that the cornfields had been abandoned because of the greater income from sheep farming.[6]

3

Why, in the face of this virtually unanimous contemporary opinion, have historians hesitated to conclude that the greater profitability of grazing brought about the depopulation of villages?

Part of the explanation can be seen when we recall that, in general, historians did not believe that there had been very much destruction. So long as this was believed, there was every reason for not putting too much weight on profit-incentives. The American historian Harriet Bradley, who wrote from New York in 1918 about English enclosure, shows this pre-supposition most clearly when she stated baldly:[7]

> it is to the credit of these landowners that there are so few authentic cases of the depopulation of entire villages and the conversion of all the arable land to sheep-runs.

One cannot say whether the depopulators would have been the more pleased at finding an advocate to plead for the insignificance of their misdeeds or piqued at finding their long-planned, and sometimes dangerous, schemes so lightly consigned to triviality.

When faced with the suggestion that—prices apart—lower wage-costs would have encouraged the encloser to move from corn to the crop tended only by a shepherd and his dog, Miss Bradley did not bring forward a set of wage-figures but an argument that "everyone knows" enclosure brought pauperism, and so wages could not have been high. This ignored the fact that Plantagenet England was not Tudor England, and that the pauperism arising from the agrarian problem of the sixteenth century did not keep down wages in the fifteenth.

Miss Bradley, like others, foundered also on the available figure for the price of wool relative to corn. Thorold Rogers' prices were taken from a very small sample, and not continuously from the same sample. The price of wool varied in England from district to district even at the same time; this was due to local differences in quality and price-lists showing these local differences have been well-known to economic historians for some time. These factors make it useless to construct a simple price-index for good quality wool one year and poor quality in another. This is what Rogers was forced to do. He was careful to note the limitations of his figures, but other writers armed with them found it easy to show that grass did not pay.[8]

It cannot be said that our price-indexes are yet near perfection. The wool data available at present[9] in the Beveridge Price-History files are small. In the course of work on the wool-supply Dr. P. J. Bowden produced an index constructed partly from prices quoted in contracts or sales disputed in the courts. In their nature, these are not continuous for every year and they embrace different quality wools. After allowances for known differences in quality, for credit and for middlemen-profits a standard price was arrived at. These calculations have now been published and, in short, they show that between 1490 and 1552 there were only two brief occasions when the price of wheat was high relative to that of wool; but after 1552 the relative prices begin to move in favour of wheat; only after 1581 is wheat unchallenged.[10]

Dr. Bowden's argument echoes that of an unknown speaker in the Parliament of 1607:

> for Corne being dearer than Cloath or meat comparatively—then only will the Husbandman plough, since his onlie end is Profitte.

In Armstrong's *Treatise*, written c. 1533–36, there is a very definite account of a man weighing carefully the relative advantage of corn and wool. He does so by calculating the cost and selling price of the two alternatives.[11]

> Upon such search accounted, ... they found so great yearly profits by the increasing of wool more than by occupying the earth with the works of husbandry.

On such sentiments and Dr. Bowden's index alone it would be dangerous to assert unequivocally that a differential movement in corn and wool prices was one of the causes of conversion to pasture and later reconversion, but our confidence is heightened when we find contemporary opinion never speaking with a contrary voice.

Discussions in terms of price alone, even if we had more satisfactory price-indexes, could never be more than superficial. Men do not only think of relative sale-prices when they turn over in their minds the advantage of two alternative crops on the same land. They must think of the relative costs of production; they must think of any extra outlay on the capital equipment involved in converting from the traditional crop to the novel; they must estimate how long the present advantages (as they see them) will hold; if they take an irrevocable step (and the eviction of a village was almost irrevocable, judging from experience) they must be convinced that the traditional crop will not come into favour again within their foreseeable future.

If we look into the year-to-year fluctuations of corn prices in the sixteenth century we see remarkable differences between the price obtained in a good harvest and the price in a bad year. It must have been more difficult to think of a standard price of corn than one for wool, whose year-by-year price fluctuated much less, for the very good reason that —murrain apart—the wool crop was not subject to all the natural chances which beset a growing and ripening stalk of corn, nor to the same short-term elasticity of supply. It is possible that this factor might make it doubly difficult for men to decide whether to convert.

Needless to say, we are not well equipped with available fifteenth-century material to watch men making such calculations or even to know how many rational calculations were (or could have been) made. All we can say is that when we find men expressing ideas about enclosers' motives in 1486, 1489, 1514 and 1548 they speak as if enclosure aimed at an income greater than from corn grown on the same acres.

Was there a demand for the increased quantity of wool which must have come from this increased number of sheep? Estimates have been used to throw doubt on the ability of all the new wool from new sheep on new pastures to find a market. (We may add that contemporaries say nothing of this. There are no stories of graziers with wool on their hands in this early period.)

Why is there doubt? The principal reason again is the inadequacy of the statistics, and then the interpretation of what statistics we may construct. Is it sufficient to deduce that men created new pastures if we can show more wool being consumed than thirty years earlier? or must we show that more wool was being consumed than a hundred years earlier? The question also hinges on the mechanism by which men calculate advantage. We know little enough about this in our own century, let alone the fifteenth. The crucial and many-headed question is: To what (if any) normal base or year do men refer when they judge whether demand is weak or strong, stationary or likely to rise? We certainly cannot answer that question in respect of the fifteenth-century landowner or his enclosing tenant.

The figures which we have of wool consumption are incomplete. They have to be based on figures themselves derived from taxes on the export, either of raw wool (a diminishing quantity) or on wool made up into cloth and then exported. We do not know what other quantities of wool were being made up into cloth for English markets for English men and women to wear.

Before we discuss whether this quantity of wool for home consumption was likely to be rising, we must look more closely at the export figures. These were summarised in a well-known passage in Eileen Power's book on the wool trade:[12]

> it is a remarkable fact that in 1481–82, when, according to Henry VII's legislation, the enclosure movement had already begun, the same calculations give us only 29,100 sacks, still well below the level of the beginning of the fourteenth century.

The comparison which Eileen Power made was between years 1481–82 and 1310–11, "taking two fairly normal years". In the earlier year as much as 35,509 sacks of wool (or their equivalent in cloth) had been exported. The drop of over 6,000 sacks (or nearly 20%) is indeed striking, but it seems insufficient to throw doubt on the fact that men were finding economic conditions in the 1480s such that they wished to convert to grass and destroy villages in the process. Eileen Power herself gives a silent clue to one such incentive when she showed on the same page that the 1447–48 figures for wool production came out at only 24,381 sacks.

If we compare this figure with 1481–82 we see at once that there was an increase in the thirty-three years from 24,381 to 29,100 sacks, or nearly 20%. By the mid-sixteenth century the figure was to be nearly 32,000 sacks. If we are to explain how men behaved in the 1450s and 1480s it seems more reasonable to look at things from their viewpoint. What mattered to them was that more wool was being demanded, bought and consumed than a *decade* earlier, not that the over-all figure might be less than a hundred and fifty years earlier.

In fact we cannot be all that certain that it was all that much less *in toto*. The unknown quantity of wool which was taken for home consumption in the English cloth industry stands silently in the background during all these discussions. Eileen Power thought that it might be assumed to be less in 1481–82 than in 1310–11 because population had fallen. The more recent estimates of Professor Russell[13] suggest that population had, indeed, fallen by 1430 to some 2·1 million compared with a figure of some 3·75 million in 1348.

But here again, population seems to have begun to move towards its old level at or about the 1430s (according to Russell) or the 1460s (according to Postan). Professor Postan does in fact allow that the rise may have begun earlier:[14]

> the evidence of wages and of land values makes it impossible to say whether the relatively high numbers of *c.* 1540 resulted from a steep rise in population after 1470 or whether they were the product of a cumulatively slow growth reaching back into the middle of the fifteenth century.

Judging from the evidence of the area under cultivation he suggests that the three decades of 1430–60

> were years of declining economic activity and population.

If this were true, it would put the beginning of the population rise at about 1460. From that time onwards we might expect the demand for cloth for English backs to have shown an increase, as Professor Postan has written in another connection:[15]

> it was not until the late 'sixties or 'seventies of the fifteenth century that the late fourteenth century levels of [cloth] production were decisively overtaken and the industry resumed its uninterrupted progress.

This is just when our other evidence has suggested that depopulating enclosure gathered force. More people and more incomes meant more cloth bought in the markets of England.

Any rise in the demand for wool by the cloth-makers could no longer be met as in the old days by drawing on wool which would otherwise have gone abroad for sale. The amount of raw wool exported in the late fifteenth century had become so small that it could not act as a buffer against home demand which could now only be satisfied by the graziers increasing their supply: by more sheep and more pastures.

The number of customers is not the only factor which is significant in estimating demand. The purses of the customers might also be growing longer, even if the numbers were only slowly rising. Studies which have been made of the fifteenth century have emphasised the degree to which greater equality of distribution of income arose out of a generally depressed economy. Now such a distribution downwards might very reasonably have added to the demand for cloth. The beneficiaries of what have been described as the "gains on the side of distribution rather than production" would not have come into incomes so high that they promptly hoarded all their increments. It is likely that their spending would follow the familar pattern of necessities first, and saving afterwards. It is also likely that they would have been more likely to spend the transferred shilling on cloth than would its former owner. It is from the side of income redistribution that we might also expect the demand for cloth to have shown some increase.

In the *Discourse* we saw that the Doctor had thought that

one of the attractions of sheep was the light labour bill. The shepherd and his dog whom we have seen figuring in the literature of the day represented (in economic terms) a minute cost compared with the cost of labour for ploughing, sowing, reaping and maintenance. As the Doctor put it:

> Grazing requires small charge and small labour, which in tillage consumes much of the master's gain.

The figures of the rising labour costs after 1360 which Professor Postan has brought together show that the upward movement continued until 1460, when his table ends. In money terms, his artisans' wages in the period 1440–59 were almost twice those of the period 1300–10. Beveridge's figures for skilled and unskilled rural artisans show that although the gap between skilled and unskilled wages was narrowing, both were rising all through the same period. The Statute of Labourers represents one attempt to halt this movement, and (judging from results) it failed.[16]

Although our figures have shown wool prices rising relative to corn, there have not been spectacular rises such as some writers have demanded before they believed that economic forces hastened the increase of pasturage. In order to demonstrate a steady (or, indeed, an increasing) demand, it is not altogether necessary to have spectacularly rising prices. Over a long period prices will only soar if supply lags badly behind. Economists have their technical term *elasticity* for the ease with which supply can be increased under the stimulus of greater profit. If the supply of wool-bearing sheep could be increased step by step with any increase in demand from the clothiers then there would be no need for our wool prices to show great leaps upwards.

Now we should not expect it to have been difficult to increase the supply of wool in mid-fifteenth century conditions. In its early stages it could be achieved without anything so violent as the destruction of a village by a simple increase in the peasant flocks or an increase in the demesne flocks. Extra pastures could be taken from marginal or already abandoned corn-lands. Only when this supply of grassland proved insufficient need men turn their eyes to the arable fields.

The time limit for expansion was set by the gestation periods of lambs and fleeces and by the number of lambs a ewe could bear and rear. In the short run, import of sheep from Wales or the hills would augment the flocks while the very luxuriance of the new pastures paid good dividends in longer and heavier fleeces.

We may now turn to the conditions of the later fifteenth century and see what we may gather and conjecture of the process of enclosure. In a later section of this chapter we shall return again to the subject of demand and relative price for a short discussion of the economic factors which contributed to the slowing down and eventual halt in depopulating enclosure after the mid-sixteenth century.

4

What type of man was in the best position to profit by these opportunities presented in the second half of the fifteenth century?

The statutes themselves were quite explicit: the depopulation arose from those men who followed their most profitable course. As the Act of 1515 put it:

> tillage and husbandry be willfully caused to decay . . . for the singular profit avail and lucre (of the owners).

Drafts among the State Papers for 1514 include one for a Bill whose preamble named the type of men attracted into this form of investment:

> many merchant adventurers clothmakers goldsmiths butchers tanners and other artificers and unreasonable covetous persons do encroach many more farms than they are able to occupy . . . farms and ploughs are decayed . . . and no more parishioners in many parishes, but a neat-herd and a shepherd.

A draft proclamation of the same date denounces those who for

> their own gain neglected tillage.

The preamble to the Act of 1533 had a very full theory of causation. It was the wealthy who were investing in land for their greater profit, which they find not in corn but in grass.

> divers . . . subjects . . . to whom God of his goodness hath disposed great plenty and abundance of movable substance now of late within few years have daily studied practised and invented ways and means how they might accumulate and gather together into few hands as well great multitudes of farms as great plenty of cattle and in especial, sheep, putting such lands as they can get to pasture and not to tillage whereby they have not only pulled down churches and towns (but also raised rents and fines and doubled prices).
>
> One of the greatest occasions that moveth and provoketh these greedy and covetous people . . . is only the great profit that cometh of sheep.

Men did not seem to doubt that their advantage lay in wool rather than corn. It is perhaps significant that in 1489 the Act did not yet speak of this urban and mercantile capital coming to buy up corn-lands as a speculation, although such enclosers figure large in the two later preambles we have just quoted. The Isle of Wight Act of 1488 and the Act against the pulling down of Towns of 1489 did speak of consolidation—

> many dwelling places . . . have of late times been used to be taken in to one man's hold and hands that of old time were wont to be in many several persons hands and hold

but they said nothing of "foreigners" coming to take up holdings. This silence may (by itself) mean nothing, but when we look at the personalities most often cited in the Returns of 1517 they are principally local men, indeed many of them come from families which had held land in and near the deserted villages for generations. Perhaps only later did the "pure investors" from the ranks of goldsmiths, artificers and "other unreasonable and covetous persons" move out into the countryside.[17]

Thinking of peasant enclosers, Eileen Power wrote:[18]

> whoever was enclosing in the last part of the fifteenth century it was certainly not the old landlord.

If she was including depopulating enclosure in her generalisation, it founders on the Knightleys, the Tyringhams, the

Darrells, the Greys, the Vaux, the Caves and the Pierrepoints. Robert Spencer, first Baron Wormleighton, could have stood on the slopes behind his Manor House and looked down to the level plain, where a hundred and fifty years earlier his ancestors had held property in the now deserted villages of Hodnell, Watergall and Chapel Ascote.[19] Dr. L. A. Parker has shown that in only eight of the forty-five Leicestershire villages enclosed before 1550 was the encloser not the Lord of the Manor. It was, he says,

> overwhelmingly the work of the squirearchy.

If the qualification for being an "old landlord" was an ancestry going back to the Conquest, then Eileen Power would be right: but if it implies that the principal depopulators of the period 1475–1500 were coming in from outside, then it would not be an appropriate text for this section, however appropriate for the 1530s. Those who came into the queue at that later date had fewer opportunities (judging by results achieved) to carry out that total depopulation which the Acts of 1515 and 1533 remembered and feared, and they are called "depopulators" only in the more general sense. There are few lost villages to mark the victory of their will.

If we look at some of the personalities involved before 1517 we in fact find a solid core of local men, usually—although not all—of some substance. Indeed the capital outlay of purchasing land and sheep was not an operation you could hope to manage without good reserves or good credit; and there is no reason to think that good credit was available for small men who were doubtful risks. To him that had, was given.

The occupations named in the draft of 1514 suggest that, even then, the capital being attracted into grazing came from men whose normal work brought them close to stock or the produce of livestock. The exporter of wool, the maker of cloth, the exporter of cloth, the purveyor of meat, the tanner of animal hides would have a long connection and interest in pasture lands. Tanners figure frequently as the sixteenth-century lessees of pastures created fifty years earlier. The same could be said of many of the landowners summoned in 1517. They had long experience of producing wool for sale, some of it on the pastures of their other villages which they had no intention or hope of completely destroying. Any many-manored landowner who had not abandoned his own demesnes for the role of rentier would be intimately in touch with the demand for wool when he met wool-dealers or broggers on their business journeys around the provinces.

If we turn for a moment to monastic houses we find them figuring in the Returns alongside laymen. Among the Midland houses who found themselves answering in Exchequer were Bicester, Bushmead, Bruern, Daventry, Eynsham, Goring, Kenilworth, Llanthony, Reading, Stoneleigh, Tewkesbury and Warden. These were old landlords, old in the ways of sheep and wool-sales.[20]

Dr. Hoskins has also shown[21] how ten of the fifty Leicestershire sites whose depopulators can be traced are attributable to monastic owners. The depopulators of Bicester and Evesham had their parallels in Breedon Priory and Leicester Abbey. It was the enclosure of Whatborough by Launde Priory which gave rise to the lawsuit between the heirs of the former Priory estate, the Cromwells, and All Souls College and occasioned the unique map reproduced in Plate 5.

Where we find merchants among the depopulators of 1517 we may sometimes find explanatory local roots.[22] Richard Fermor, merchant of the Staple, was also a grocer who traded in silk and wheat, but he was a Buckinghamshire man, twice sheriff of his county. The family of the depopulator of Cestersover, Henry Waver, had been lords there in the thirteenth century. He made his fortune in London; he was Master of the Drapers Company and a Sheriff of the City. He returned home to build his manor house and destroy his village. William Cope had bought Wormleighton from the Crown in 1498; he was Cofferer of the royal household; but his wife's cousin was a Spencer, and it was to a Spencer that he made the sale which was to cause the Spencers so much trouble in the 1520s. William Willington, another Stapler, numbered Barcheston and Whitchurch among his Warwickshire purchases; he depopulated them. Belknap of

Burton Dassett had acquired half the village in 1473 from his uncle and owned it all by 1498.

One of his sisters was the wife of a Chief Justice of Common Pleas. We have already seen Chief Justice Fairfax of the Common Bench depopulating at Steeton; and he was presented in 1517 for evictions at South Holme in the North Riding. It was Mr. Serjeant Piggott who bought Doddershall and destroyed 24 houses there. It was an alderman of London, Henry Keble or Kebill, who depopulated Weston by Cherington. The Shephard family who depopulated Litlecote (Lidcote) were related by marriage to the Piggotts. Sir Richard Fermor of Easton Neston was the father-in-law of Sir Richard Knightley, the eldest son of Sir Valentine of Fawsley. Knightley lived on the site of a depopulated village, and from it engineered the destruction of others. Sir Thomas Green of Green's Norton, another depopulator, was the father-in-law of Sir Nicholas Vaux, first Baron Vaux, whose name was often called in the London courts. Vaux had married a great territorial heiress in 1507 and as the text of the *Dictionary of National Biography* quaintly puts it

> actively devoted himself to agricultural improvement.

The *Epitome* of the *D.N.B.* is more explicit:

> he enclosed much common land in Buckinghamshire and Northamptonshire.

We have (*c.* 1530–40) a document headed "a statement concerning the wool trade", which gives the names of the bigger growers in various counties. Among these names are several who have figured in these pages. We find William Fermor with his "growyng and gatheryng" of 150 sacks—each of from 120 to 180 Cotswold fleeces: the produce of anything from 18,000 to 27,000 sheep. Anthony Cope "of his growyng" had 10 sacks—from the backs of perhaps 1,500 sheep on his new pastures. The Abbot of Oseney and the Abbot of Bruern had 10 sacks each, the same quantity as Robert Catesby. In Warwickshire, William Willington (whom we know as both encloser and Merchant of the Staple) grew and gathered 100 sacks; Sir William Spencer and "my lady hys moder", 60 sacks; in the western Cotswolds we find the Abbots of Cirencester, Hailes and Evesham; and the Mr. Hunkes of Gloucestershire whose name was often called in the corridors of the Court of Exchequer. In Northamptonshire there was Lord Vaux, Sir Richard Knightley (30 sacks, or 3,600–5,400 sheep), Sir Robert Lee, Mr. Robert Dormer and Mr. Anthony Cave. Many of the fleeces in these sacks came from animals who had grazed among tumbled houses and weedy crofts.

When such men died, their inquisitions *post mortem* did not need much space for their holdings in the deserted parishes: a phrase or two dismisses the closes and pastures which cover the thousand acres or so of former arable fields.[23] Sir Richard Knightley left his choice pastures and parks of Fawsley, Charwelton and Snorscombe to his wife. Snorscombe had cost him a deal of money in lawyers' fees when the enclosure had been in question in Exchequer. The Tyringham's inquisitions had no need to detail many messuages in their village, and the Thomas Tyringham who died in 1526 left the rule of his three daughters and his three young sons to his uncle Sir Robert Brudenell, himself from a good enclosing stock. When Baron Vaux died in 1524 his possessions included the peopleless manor of Stantonbury for which he had been prosecuted, and for which his heirs were to make several appearances. And just as Knightley was anxious for his wife to enjoy the depopulated Fawsley, and John Spencer left his wife the free use of Wormleighton and Althorp, so in 1648 Grevill Verney of Compton Verney made a will by which his wife was to have part of the land where the village of Compton Verney had once stood. He must have valued the land highly as grass, for there were two things which, if his wife did, would forfeit his gift. One was her remarriage, the other was that

> if she shall plowe up any of the lands or grounds called the *Townes* upon both sides of the pools . . . the devise shall be void.

Indeed, the social life of country houses, country hunting and country market towns makes it quite unnecessary to suggest how the knowledge of the profitability of depopulation would spread. It was such knowledge, spreading from mouth to mouth, that the Commission of 1517 spoke of, when it put among the evils of depopulation

> . . . an evil example to others who might be so minded.

Dr. Hoskins has pictured the gentry of Leicestershire hawking together:[24]

> Villers, Faunts and Turpins all knew each other and went hawking together . . . all of them were enclosers, and so too were the Brooksbys of Shoby across the valley, and the Purefoys of Fenny Drayton at the other end of the county who were also friends and confidants of the Villers.
>
> The country gentlemen of Leicestershire, a small county in which everybody of some social position knew everybody else, and in which there was a great deal of inter-marriage, were not slow to learn from each other the new way of doubling their incomes by turning their estates into sheep and cattle pastures, and driving away their tenants from the one-time arable fields.

Alongside this picture of depopulators riding, hawk at wrist, over the lands they had enclosed, discussing the prospect of enclosing more, we may set that of a celebrated social event bringing enclosers together. The second (Cavendish) marriage of Bess of Hardwick was celebrated at Bradgate, whose owner had been called to the Exchequer to answer for depopulation there in 1520. Bess, as Countess of Shrewsbury, was herself to appear later to answer for the decay of Bittesby, "an evil example to others who might be so minded", or, in the words of the Act [25] of 1536,

> to the most perilous example of all others being in like case.

Indeed, there had been perilous examples ever since the Cistercian depopulations had shown what profitable use could be made of grasslands. There were to be perilous examples as long as men heard covetously of the celebrated enclosed pastures like those farmed at Creslow. There would be those who had heard of the depopulated fields and sought to be their tenant. Such was Sir Thomas Gargrave who wrote to Sir William Cecil twice within nine days in March 1570 asking:

> let me have Dale Town, worth twenty nine pounds a year, to keep some sheep for my house . . . by purchase or otherwise.

As its name indicated, this sheep farm had once been a village. In 1570 its former owner, Leonard Dacre, had forfeited it, and it was at the Crown's disposal, just as thirty years earlier many other former village sites had been at the Crown's disposal when the monastic owners had been themselves evicted, much as they had once evicted others.[26]

An interesting comment on the spread of perilous example among the Midland gentry comes from a letter[27] from a Brudenell of Deane to the Privy Council in 1636. He had been arguing that the enclosed lands in his estate were inherited already in that condition and that he was not to be blamed. He then moved to the *tu quoque* argument that other lords had also inherited enclosed lands. The names he cites are familiar to us: Spencers; Fitzwilliams; Shirleys; Greshams; Hattons; Knightleys; Catesbys; Griffins; Caves and Elmes.

5

The growth of depopulating enclosure in the second half of the fifteenth century shows the opportunity which had previously come to a few men being avidly sought as a goal by many. This happened at a time when there was internal political disorder giving powerful men opportunities to do what they liked with their own within the law, outside the law or on its fringe. There were as yet no anti-enclosure statutes, although there were men like Rous who were urging them. Many of the evicted tenants would have no legal title to redress in any court, and there were many ways of barring the suit of any who possessed the title and the means to seek the judgment of a court.

If our story is to be cast in the form of a slowly-dawning opportunity it must take its roots much further back than the actual years of eviction. As Professor Tawney has said:[28]

> the great pasture farms which aroused the apprehension of More and Latimer had their precedent in the small flocks of 30 or 40 sheep which had long been run (by peasants) on the common waste or pasture. . . .
>
> The movement towards pasture farming as a specialist branch of agriculture is one that proceeds gradually for a hundred years before the demand for wool becomes sufficient to produce the body of capitalist graziers.

What general economic conditions made possible the early extension of grassland? When was the demand for corn slack enough for the first defeats of arable to be registered? How could grass defeat corn without encroaching on the vital bread supplies or without running undue risks in times of bad harvests? When did the regional markets for corn become so well organised that it was safe to contemplate turning over to specialisation in grass, to move from Tawney's "small flocks" to a "specialist branch of agriculture"? Did the early conversions involve pressure on husbandmen to leave their fields, or were there villagers willing to be bought out and customary tenants anxious to move elsewhere, like Robert Graves'

> warden of sick fields that once
> sprouted of their own accord?

For how long was there grassland simply for the taking at a peppercorn rent?

As we have already said more than once, the extant manorial material which would answer such questions for the deserted villages is very tenuous, and the monographs which would assist the inquiry may be unwritten, and are certainly unpublished. This section of the chapter must inevitably have an element of speculative debate in it. If subsequent work shows that its suggestions are false and its guesses off-centre, then it will be a sign that fifteenth-century studies have reached a certainty which is now lacking. The cautious reader will note that the argument of the rest of this book does not stand or fall by the next few pages.

In a later chapter we shall discuss what physical conditions seem to have provided the greatest opportunity and incentive to depopulating enclosers. These opportunities and incentives were not equally active or equally successful in all places, nor were they equally active or equally successful in all years or in all families. What can be pieced together to suggest why some men could proceed to total depopulations in the second half of the fifteenth century while others waited—or had to wait—till the eighteenth or nineteenth centuries before they enclosed their open fields?

Much of what we have to say is related to the general retreat of settlement which began in the early fourteenth century and gathered speed with the Plague years. This was a movement known elsewhere in Europe and it contributed to the deserted villages of Germany and France, even if the circumstances of the depopulations on the continent do not mirror ours in all respects. Even in England it was possible for some villages, some towns and some districts to feel very little of the depression, but as Professor Postan has said:[29]

> contemporaries obviously believed that they were living in an age of contracting settlement, and there is no reason why we should not accept their belief at its face value.

It was the fall in total population which created village economies in which the balance between corn and grass was so different from that of the thirteenth century. Even if this contraction in its early stages emptied only a few villages, its results were felt far beyond. Not only was a new balance between corn and grass worked out in the years after the plagues, but the new economic and social relationships in those years of shrunken man-power were to be highly influential in determining the vulnerability of tenants in the years when the advantages of the sheep-walk were coming to the front again.

Many years ago Professor Tawney showed how the evictions of the Tudor period were made possible by the precarious tenures which peasants had anxiously sought and cheerfully accepted in the land-market of the fifteenth century. The fathers ate the sour grapes and their children's teeth were set on edge. If we inquire how certain tenements fell easy victim to the would-be depopulator in the 1490s we are driven back time and time again to conditions of tenure accepted by the occupier of that tenement a century or so earlier, at a time when lords were disposing of lands rather than seeking to engross them.

When there is better land or better terms to be had elsewhere, tenants will evict themselves. Such "self-evictions" were undoubtedly common in the years after the plagues, and in the marginal lands no one came to occupy all the empty spaces. Was there self-eviction in the late fifteenth century? Have the landlords been unnecessarily abused for the roofless cottage when in fact it was roofless because its occupier had voluntarily gone elsewhere?

This is not what contemporaries thought. Were they wrong? It does not seem so. The contribution of the peasant to his own destruction is limited to the weakness of the tenurial position he (or his forbears) had accepted. It is limited to the degree in which his own efforts to consolidate holdings had made it easier for the final engrossment to take place. It is limited to the degree to which large peasant holdings had already grown up in the village.

Confusion may have arisen because in one sense of the word "enclosure" the tenantry of the late fifteenth century were its supporters. In the laying of holding to holding; in the extensions of hedged fields assigned by agreement; in the division of common pastures and meadow: in these reforming activities peasants, large and small, took part. This type of enclosure they accepted, as Hales was to accept it. It is for this reason that some small landholders are presented in the 1517 Returns: they have converted arable to pasture. If their holding is large enough to have on it a second farm house or a labourer's cottage they may have destroyed that in the course of their re-organisation and so brought themselves within the shadow of the statute.

This, the "decay of hospitality", is far from being the depopulation of a village. In so far as it accepts radical change in agricultural custom and weakens some of the traditional safeguards of custom it may prove dangerous to other men or other generations: but it is far from the virtual suicide which the defenders of the landlords would suggest. Men only depopulate a whole village when they are lured away by better conditions elsewhere or when they are forced away by their landlord.

In the late fifteenth and early sixteenth century it was only the second of these two alternatives which operated. Houses were not empty because there was no one to occupy them but because the occupiers had been evicted. Land was going down to grass not because there was no other use for it, but because new uses and profits were envisaged. The peasants with substantial holdings shared in the desire to adopt new uses and gain new profits: but these men were not in the position, even if they had the will, to carry their enclosures as far as depopulation. That possibility was the monopoly of the landowner who owned (or who had on long lease) the village and its fields. He was the man who pushed the frontier of grass well out into the ploughlands of England.

In the early fifteenth century the frontier between the two land-uses was drawn in a very different place and it is to the earlier balance between corn and grass in the years after the plagues that we must now revert.

6

In our discussion of prices and profits we saw that in essence the conversion to grass was a simple change in land-use. Now, in our description of the medieval village in Chapter Two we saw that there were (in general terms) three contenders for the use of every acre. One contender was in almost continuous retreat: this was forest, scrub or rough heathland. Since even this use of land had economic uses—and for the aristocracy recreational uses—it was a contender with at times powerful support. Its successes were greatest when plague, war or technological change made men forsake old ploughlands. This contender then achieved a silent reconquest.

The second contender was four-legged. It was the animal

population: the ox, the sheep, the goat, the cow, and eventually the horse. These could make a poor living off scrub and heath, and they demanded grassland for their maintenance. In lowland England such pasture or hay-ground was limited so long as another, the third, contender was in the lists, a two-legged contender. For man, cleared land was the place where corn was grown. At any time where land was felt to be scarce; at times when population pressed on land: at such times, corn was the most powerful of the three contenders with the backing of men who feared hunger for themselves and their families. Since the plough was weak without the ox and the back naked without wool, some concessions were made to the claims of pasture and hay. But the price of grass ground in medieval extents shows how highly it was prized. In the pastures on the fallow fields we can see a compromise between two contenders which was a practical and not a sentimental truce. The grazing animals manured the land for its next corn crop as they fed on the stubble and weeds. That this is a truce and the war not over, we can see from the annual autumn slaughter of stock which the pastures and the hay could not maintain through the winter.

The competition for available cleared land seems to have been at its height late in the thirteenth century when the plough scars show in remote places that have never since known a furrow. Under such pressure it is likely that grassland was hard pressed to maintain its limited area, except in those upland regions where the plough had never been a serious contender. Only the abbeys of the Pennines and the villages of the Cotswolds were able to have their cake and eat it. In the Pennines there was abundant grass above the high-water mark of ploughing. In the Cotswolds the settlements, as can be seen still on the 1-inch sheet, were stepped far apart. In between there was room for extensive grazing grounds as well as ploughlands. To a lesser extent the hills of Lincolnshire ceded a greater place to grass amid the cornfields than in the Midlands. Once away from these uplands, the balance struck between corn and grass was weighed heavily in one direction. No doubt the demand for wool even in the thirteenth century was making the balance quiver: but no more.

In the years before the Black Death there were signs that the pressure of population on land was easing. Some writers have suggested that climatic changes were making it difficult to hold on to marginal land which had been colonised in the land-hungry thirteenth century; others that the marginal land was being overworked. After the Black Death the situation was even more radically changed. Professor Russell estimated that a population of England and Wales that had been 3,750,000 in 1348 was down to 2,250,000 in 1374 and about 2,100,000 between 1410 and 1430.[30]

Studies which have been made of empty holdings after the Plague have shown that on the more attractive soils it was not unusual for the majority of holdings to be taken up within a generation of the first pestilence. But there was some consolidation of holdings in the hands of the more prosperous who felt they could manage a holding-and-a-half or two holdings: and Professor Postan has suggested that there was a good deal of moving up the queue. Landless villagers took the opportunity. Those whose parents had been cottars working for a wage were now tenants-at-will in their own right.

But the queue had an end, and it is not unreasonable to see our examples of genuine Black Death depopulation and villages never resettled as being at the end of the queue. Here were villages to which no one wanted to come. No doubt there were a few lords who preferred to have no tenants rather than tenants on the revolutionarily easy terms which men were growing bold to ask. But such a stiff-necked attitude could not have lasted, and some income would have been better than none.

The two areas where post-Black Death depopulation is best documented, the Lincolnshire Wolds and the Brecklands of Norfolk, offer an opportunity to test this hypothesis of the marginal land which no one wanted for corn. Even today the Brecklands have not tempted War Agricultural Committees. In Lincolnshire (and in parts of the East Riding) the attractiveness of the soil to medieval eyes is more difficult for us to assess. We see these fields today, many of them good corn land, only in terms of the improved conditions after the Agricultural Revolution. We see the Yorkshire Wolds after Sir Tatton Sykes had carried out his improvements and brought the fields back from grass to corn again.

If we judge the productive capacity of these areas by the simplest tests we shall ask, how many men could they maintain in the Middle Ages? What was the relative tax quota paid by these villages fifteen years before the Plague? What do their poll tax receipts tell us of relative size after the main force of the plagues was over?

There is no doubt that these particular lost villages, even those which stood among quite prosperous neighbours, were regarded in 1334 as being already less able than their neighbours to contribute to the tax of the "fifteenth", as we shall see in the next chapter. The wapentakes of Lincolnshire which stand at the southern end of the Wolds were those where, after the Plague, least recolonisation took place. This is the classical district of ruined churches and lost village sites, comparable with the Brecklands. The average village tax payments in 1334 for the three wapentakes of Bolingbroke, Horncastle and Hill were 39*s*., 38*s*. and 32*s*. respectively. Their average village poll tax receipt numbered only 66 people. The other wapentakes in Lindsey had tax quotas of between 50*s*. and 73*s*. per vill, and poll tax payers averaging 100 per vill.[31]

These averages are of *all* vills, lost and surviving, and it is clear that the wapentakes of the southern Wolds had long had a general condition of smaller settlements. It is in this environment of settlements smaller than elsewhere that the plague was able to empty villages which were never resettled, so that the decree of union of Fordington and Ulceby parishes can speak both of the plague and of the poverty and infertility of the ground.

As we shall show later, the natural residual crop on land which had been abandoned was grass, so long as you had enough animals to keep the scrub from encroaching. Lindsey was an old and famed wool district, with pastures intermingled with its corn-fields even at the height of land-hunger in the thirteenth century. Even with the reduced population of the fourteenth century there were probably enough villages and villagers to put the abandoned fields of the empty villages to good grazing use. Sheep which knew transhumance were not averse to being shepherded a score of miles over to a new pasture.

After the plagues had passed, the re-cultivated lands and the re-occupied houses of the Midland villages were not unchanged. The new occupiers occupied on easier terms. They were recruited from the landless who had been the paid-labour force of the thirteenth century village. They had moved up the queue. If they stayed in their village, as old cottar turned new husbandman, their move was merely one of status. If they had migrated from more marginal land then their move was also geographical.

The abandoned margin did not lie easily to the view like a shore where the sea has retreated. We cannot plot with any certainty a fringe of hamlets and holdings lying side by side in some upland or some marshland region. We may have come nearest to it in the Norfolk Breckland or some of the high, dry hamlets which had clung to the crown of the Yorkshire Wolds or the Lincolnshire chalk.

Instead of any single high-water mark with a line of wrack and sun-dried seaweed we seem to have the retreat showing itself in many scattered places; a few acres here, a block of strips there, an extension of woodland here, and pasture augmented there. This is a retreat revealing itself not in a long thin high-water mark, the whole length of a shore, but in many scattered rock-pools.[32]

Of the three contestants for land whom we named, the prize goes always to the forest when the other contestants relax their efforts. In this sense, the second contestant, grass, stands half-way between the others. Abandoned corn-fields tumble first to grass and weed. For the first few years they would not differ much from the fallows. Men had been accustomed to seeing animals grazing on old corn acres one year in three, even on the best corn acres. The flocks which had been stinted could now have their stint enlarged. No agrarian revolution was involved in a silent extension of pasture which dealt lightly with men and houses and occupied only abandoned or half-wanted land.

This new balance between corn and grass may have been reached somewhere between 1420 and 1440. It was a balance which suited the existing reduced labour supply; the existing number of mouths to be fed; and the existing number of looms to be supplied with wool. It was clearly a different balance from the balance of the late thirteenth century when labour and mouths were plentiful, land scarce and looms fewer.

It was this new balance which was to be thrown out of equilibrium in the next sixty years. Some writing on enclosure and depopulation has seemed to suggest that the depopulator attacked a village with the land-use and tenurial relationships of the high Middle Ages. Recent work on the fifteenth century has shown an active land market among the small peasants, both for their own holdings and for any ex-demesne land which *rentier* lords were prepared or anxious to lease. It is this restless scene of buying and selling, profit and loss, trial and error which forms the background to the first attempts to turn a parish over entirely to grass.

In many villages we know that the lords reacted to land left idle in their hands either by reducing rents or letting out their demesnes in large or small parcels to any comer. In other villages there was another way out. Lords might keep the demesne in their own hand as a park or as pasture, or refrain from further annual leasing once it was seen that demesnes could be put to a profitable use for grazing. We can see the type of the former in Wiverton or Pendley or Fulbrook where the village finds itself on the edge of a new park enclosed with full permission of charter or letter patent. Wiverton remained as a small community until its sixteenth-century destruction. Within a generation Pendley village was only a memory—the 1506 survey shows—Fulbrook was down to four householders seven years after the Duke of Bedford's emparking, and the church was down by 1543. Ironically enough the castle in the park was in its turn demolished and the stone taken to build Compton Wyniates, itself on the site of a deserted village. In a court roll of the parish of

Barford which faced Fulbrook across the Avon, a perambulation of the bounds at Rogationtide, 1635, shows that opposite the lost site of Fulbrook the Avon was still called "Fullbrook Town Water".[33]

In this land-market, fluid at all social levels, the task of the encloser might be simple or insuperably difficult. It was simple if villagers could be persuaded to move; or if there were few villagers with a solid legal title to a freehold; or if local political power made it easy to evict without intervention by a court or by an aggrieved rival. It would be difficult if the process of buying up, exchange and threats was impeded by the presence of a substantial number of freeholders or by peasants who had the ear of a powerful local rival. These almost chance factors may help to explain the almost random distribution of lost sites within areas which are physically homogeneous. We are not surprised to find more depopulation in good grass country, but how else can we explain the fact that of three adjacent parishes in good grass country, one falls to the depopulator, another is not enclosed until the late 1500s and the third waits until the 1780s? Such a trio of diversity is not imagined for the sake of argument. It is a fact visible all over the country, and illustrated by our distribution maps.

Dr. Chambers has shown the close connection between a small number of freeholders and the early achievement of enclosure by agreement in Nottinghamshire of the seventeenth and eighteenth centuries,[34] and it seems likely to be equally true in the fifteenth.

If numbers and legal title were the obstacle to rapid enclosure we might expect to find corroboration by examining the size of villages which were depopulated and their legal and social structure. The latter task is made almost impossible by the disappearance of manorial documents for the lost villages. Single extents and rentals can be quoted, but these are open to the gravest criticism as a base for generalisation. Nor are we well informed about the "normal" social structure to make very much of figures for the percentage of freemen even if we had them for all our lost places.[35]

We are in a better position to assess relative size, and here the evidence is overwhelmingly in favour of the generalisation that depopulation came more commonly to villages which were smaller than their neighbours. There were striking exceptions; and "smaller than their neighbours" does not mean that the depopulated villages were tottering on the edge of extinction when the landlord enclosed them.

7

The disappearance of so many manorial records makes it impossible for us to cite more than a handful of examples of what was happening in the years when lords were manœuvring for position. We have already quoted the contemporary description of the Delavals' strategy, but it came from the late sixteenth century when documents survived to throw a single flash of light on what occurred on the eve of depopulation. At Stormsworth in Leicestershire, Selby Abbey[36]

> systematically bought out the surviving freeholders or acquired their land by gift until they had obtained possession of the entire land of the manor, which they then proceeded to enclose and convert to pasture. . . . The procedure agrees . . . with what was done by Leicester Abbey at Ingarsby and by Merevale Abbey at Weston . . .

We know that this was the method of the northern Cistercians. We know that this was the method of Breedon Priory at Andrechurch. It was to be the method of would-be enclosers in the eighteenth century. It was the logical policy to adopt if a planned course of action to convert and depopulate was in mind.

Once the depopulation was over there was a good chance that there would be a "sole lord" for many centuries. Only the dissipation of an estate or the cutting up of parkland into tenant farms would bring back more households. There were many surveys which would report in terms like those at Riseholme, Lincs., where Sir George St Paul[37]

> is owner of all the town.

In some of the Chancery petitions of the early sixteenth century the plaintiffs claimed that a would-be depopulator had first offered to buy them out or to exchange lands, and when they refused, resorted to eviction or sharp practice. This was the complaint of the Abbot of Lavendon about Thomas Tyringham at Filgrave. This was the complaint of four husbandmen and divers freeholders of Over Shuckburgh against Thomas Shuckburgh:

> all thys he hath doon to wery yor seyd besechors to dryfe theym from the seyd towne to the entente he myght laye it all to severall pasture. . . .

The depopulation of Hanging Grimston in Yorkshire followed soon after the surveyor of Dacre's estates there had written:

> there is none that hath any fre lond in the said lordshippe butt only this ferme of my lord Dacres.

We do not know whether this sole lordship was a recent achievement or the result of tenants abandoning holdings which had become unattractive through infertility or high rents. At the neighbouring Little Givendale, extents at intervals of a generation spoke of land "stony, waste and uncultivatable".

There were many who were seeking to angle themselves into the position which Dacre had either achieved or had thrust upon him. Such a one was the Abbot of Hailes who was harrying his copyholders at Longborough in Gloucestershire. They reported his intentions in a Chancery petition. The intentions were never realised, but they are familiar to us:

> he dayly stodyth to followe hys cruell intentys to decaye mynyche and distroye the tyllage of the said lordship which is the livyng of the kings subjects and the destruction of youre power oratours.
>
> He hath (900 sheep) and dayly exacteth requyreth and oppresith with divers exaction to the intent too dryve them oute of the said lyvingys because he wolde have the said manor holy decayed and convertid into pasture contrary to the kyngs lawes and statutys.

There are extensive pastures at Longborough, but between them and the river Evenlode the village and church still stand: but not far away was Sezincote, already enclosed by 1486, and Brook End and Grove, once hamlets belonging to Eynsham Abbey.[38]

Information drawn, as ours must be, from records of evictions challenged in the courts or recounted after the event to the itinerant Commissioners of 1517 may tend to exaggerate the degree of force necessary to turn some villages into sheep-runs in the economic conditions of the mid-fifteenth century, and parallel evidence cited in earlier chapters has suggested that some final depopulations might be the last act in a long series stretching back as much as half a century.

Although we must speak of many deserted villages as the product of human will, there must have been a few cases where the landlord found himself in possession of empty fields through the action of others. If Mortham or Rokeby or Gristhwaite were destroyed by the Scots we cannot blame the landlord. If his terms were still set so high after the raids or after the plagues that settlers were not attracted to his fields, then in a sense he has some responsibility for the continued desertion, although we cannot imagine many landlords remaining so stiff-necked that they would prefer an empty rent-roll. In the immediate conditions after the raids and the plagues it is not likely that the demand for wool was such that any lord forced to leave his land under grass could immediately do well out of misfortune. Yet such a man—or his heir—was well placed when talk began of higher wool prices as the fifteenth century grew older.

Where we have villages completely abandoned after the Plague it is not sufficient to say that the lord was an obstacle to their resettlement. Had there been any land-hunger on the thirteenth-century scale, land would have been resettled. The villages deserted for ever in the mid-fourteenth century must have had particularly unattractive fields like those at Givendale in the East Riding which inquisitions *post mortem* had been describing as stony and uncultivatable for years before the Plague. Here was the margin for arable cultivation at the prices ruling at that time.[39]

8

If our argument is correct—that depopulation came to villages where there was already a good deal of grassland alongside a diminishing number of husbandlands of corn; and that enclosure and depopulation might be an aim only slowly achieved—then we should expect to see signs of that in the late-fifteenth-century evidence. They are not wanting.

No doubt pleas that land was already in decay of tillage well before 1485 should be taken with reserve when they appear in the pleas and petitions of enclosers in court, but they are too frequent to be ignored, and they do have an air of honesty when they are coupled with admission that some further depopulation had been caused by the accused. Edmund Bray sounds credible when he pleads

> iii of the seid ix meses hath ben dekeyed long tyme by fore the statute of anno quarto of owre seid late kyng and iii yeres before the seid statute . . . he confesseth the dekey of the vi meses and the cxx acres of arrable lond put to pasture.

William Willington pleaded similarly that the 800 acres at Barcheston were already pasture by 1485. The Countess of Shrewsbury pleaded that there were only 150 acres of arable left at Bittesby when she had enclosed in 1488.[40]

At Wiverton, licence had been obtained as early as 1445 to make the demesne lands, some 200 acres, into a park. Alongside this park and the manor house there still remained villagers, but probably considerably fewer than when the demesne had been cultivated by villein labour. When George Chaworth was accused of depopulating the village in 1510 by enlarging his park by a further 254 acres—110 of which were arable—he was specifically said to have enclosed the whole township. In terms of houses depopulated the "whole township" was by then only four houses and a cottage. In 1377 there had been 47 taxpayers, and the area of ground covered by the earthworks of the former village, in Fig. 3, p. 51, shows that Wiverton had once been more than a four-house hamlet.[41]

Fortunately we do not have to explain how the landlords learned that wool was profitable and grass a possible crop.

No campaign of persuasion like that launched by agricultural journalists in the eighteenth century was necessary. Grass was not an exotic crop, and there seems to have been no methodical sowing of grass seed in the Middle Ages. Grass was a residual use. When extents wanted to be really pessimistic about the value of a piece of arable they said: "It is worth nothing, not even as grass, for there is plenty of grass in the surrounding district".[42]

Nor did sheep need to be imported, and the mechanics of conversion would have been simple, and (as long as the village remained standing) the process was reversible. The village not so completely turned over to grass could have maintained a balance between corn and grass able to swing quite widely from decade to decade. It seems likely that it was this type of village, and not one still resolutely pledged to

> the servitude of being forever ploughed,

which faced the would-be depopulator when the cause of one-hundred-per-cent grass became lucrative and attractive. Instead of being the residual, the heir of abandoned cornfields, grass became the aggressive and in some places the dominant contender.

In all changes of agricultural technique, particularly in a society without the printed word, much importance must be placed on the factor of imitation. The farmer changes a technique because he has seen others do so. He encloses, he tries root-crops, he tries artificial fertilisers, he tries tractors, he tries prisoner-of-war labour, because he had heard in the market place that others have done so successfully.

There were not lacking examples in the fifteenth century of those who had already done well out of wool. The Cistercians' example must have been well-known. There was the example of those estates large enough and well-enough organised to make one or more of their constituent manors wholly a sheep-manor, just as the Cistercians had granges wholly given over to sheep, even to single age-groups of sheep. There were few lowland areas of England not neighboured by chalk or limestone uplands with a thin scatter of settlements, and with extensive commons or inter-commons attached to each village. In the Vale of York the landowner of a few manors in the plain could look east to the Wolds or west to the Pennines and in each case see the profits of sheep-based farming, "an evil example to those so minded".

9

If the balance of advantage lay in the direction of conversion to grass it is very reasonable to ask why the depopulation ceased, and why there is even some evidence that grasslands went back to corn in the late sixteenth century.

When we examined the king's proceedings we found that they were more effective in bringing publicity to bear on enclosers than as vigorous and relentless prosecutions. If the length of Exchequer proceedings is any guide, the war which the Crown conducted was a war of attrition.

There were others among the publicists and pamphleteers who were endeavouring to keep alive hostility to depopulation. Unhappily, no would-be depopulator has told whether he was more deterred by fears of Star Chamber than Exchequer, or more by rioters than by sermons; and we can do no more than say that these impediments had been absent in the heyday of depopulation.

It is also clear that wholesale depopulation had to stop somewhere. Tudor England was in no position to carry the international division of labour so far as to make England all one sheep-run, importing corn to feed the shepherd, the sheep-master and the cloth-worker. The fear (and indeed the occasional reality) of a dearth of corn was still present in the 1590s. There was another fear; in every Tudor monarch there was something of the Recruiting Sergeant.

The first anti-enclosure statute had been grounded on a fear of insufficient men to resist invasion. A century later we know that the usefulness of husbandmen was at the front of Cecil's mind;[43] he knew that the muster lists depended on husbandmen; shepherds meant a great "decay of artillery".

Just as the years after the Black Death had seen a reallocation of men and land and a new working balance between corn and other products, so the mid-sixteenth century seems to have reached another balance. The very transfer of land from corn to grass would have helped to bring about an equilibrium point. There would have to come a point, even with a stable population, where the remaining cornland became insufficient and corn prices rose. In such circumstances men who had built up compact properties just ripe for enclosure would hesitate on the brink and then perhaps enclose; but for more efficient corn-growing.

It must have seemed as unrealistic by 1550 to aim at an England which was all sheep-walks as it had seemed unrealistic and profitless a century earlier to aim at preserving an England of open-field arable. The easing of the pressure on land as population fell (*c.* 1320–1410) and then the conversion of more cornland to grass (between 1450 and 1520) had resulted in something of a general post. The tendency to think of England as ideally one huge corn-bearing area had been broken down, until a speaker could say in the Commons debate of 1597:

> it fareth with the earth as with other creatures that through continual labour grow faint and feeble-hearted . . . and this did the former law-makers overslip, tyeing the land once tilled to a perpetual bondage and servitude of being ever tilled.

Men who could say that tillage might be a "servitude" had moved far from the earlier anti-enclosure acts which had sought to stabilise the area of corn and grass by prohibiting the creation of any more grassland than at some earlier date, be it 1488, 1515 or 1536.

Francis Bacon, writing at the end of the century, expressed the same attitude in his *History of Henry VII.* Commenting on the Act of 1489, he wrote:

> Enclosures they would not forbid, for that had been to forbid the improvement of the patrimony of the kingdom; nor tillage they would not compel, for that were to strive with Nature and Utility, but they took a course to take away depopulating enclosures and depopulating pasturage.[44]

In this general post the land-use of much of the Midlands, the grassy shires, could be considered afresh. Men could decide what was the optimum use with a freedom which they had never previously had, so long as land-hunger, tradition, sentiment or fear of bad harvests had kept them in their perpetual bondage and servitude of for ever tilling.

If they decided that grass was the optimum crop for some areas then we need not reproach them. The continuity of much of that land under grass until 1940 goes to show that their calculations were fairly sound. Regret that their social consciences did not match their acumen of calculation or their energy in destruction is another matter.

But by the middle of the sixteenth century the calculations which men were making began to give different answers. The mid-sixteenth century saw a peak reached in cloth exports after decades of expansion: then the quantity fell rapidly to a level about three-quarters of that in the peak years. This must have been reflected in the fortunes and optimism of graziers. There was no longer that clear advantage in growing wool rather than corn. Indeed in some districts the movement began to be towards more ploughland. We know that the late sixteenth and early seventeenth centuries saw much reclamation of heaths and fens in the north and east, and that the new land went under the plough. This was another contribution to the general post of land-use and the redeployment of resources.

This must mean more than that the diminishing area of cornland had begun to raise corn prices. It is certain that population was rising after 1550 and that new mouths needed feeding. If there was a shift—however small—towards towns we would expect to find a further stimulus to the demand for corn. Town-dwellers always include many who are too busy getting and spending to lay waste their powers in tilling.

It is true that all towns had their circle of fields, and in the text books every townsman has been given the character of something between a smallholder and an allotment-holder. But an allotment tends to grow cabbages rather than corn; and when we look at the people harvesting town fields in the engraved views the representatives of industry seem to be wives, daughters and apprentices rather than busy *entre-*

preneurs. The smoke from shops, offices and workrooms is still rising, and all Tudor towns had an alert eye on the engrosser of corn and strict control of badged corn-dealers. They needed the surplus of the countryside as well as the grain from their town fields. In York there were anxious prohibitions of butchers further extending their grazing ground in the villages of the plain. To the York Guildsman the countryside was *par excellence* designed for a granary.[45]

Just as there was a limit being set to the advance of pasture, so limits were set to the return march of corn. Some demand for wool was maintained, come boom, come slump: nor was it easy to reverse the initial conversion to pasture. This conversion had not involved any great effort of capital or construction if you owned the land or had a long lease of it. The gestation period for a fleece is not all that long.[46] Your biggest effort was the destruction itself, if you were so minded; but you could economise by letting time and straying animals do your work for you.

To turn pasture back to corn would involve considerable capital expenditure if the reconversion was to be on the scale of the initial conversion. It is true that for small areas

> land that had been converted from tillage to pasture could easily enough be reconverted into tillage.[47]

but the reconversion of a parish involved an effort of rebuilding houses for your husbandmen, outbuildings for their implements and barns for their grain. It is not surprising that while we hear of parkland being reploughed and some old pastures receiving the plough, we hear very little of the reconstruction of villages. Those who wanted more arable could achieve it elsewhere by going to other parts of their estate where there were still villages and villagers and increasing the proportion of arable there.

The difficulty of reconversion, quite apart from its expense, is stressed in the petition from Wormleighton against an order to reconvert and rebuild:[47]

> His hedges . . . be now twenty years old which be grown full of all manner of wood to great profit, and one of the greatest commodity in the country . . . and if the hedges were thrown

> down it should cause much variance betwixt the tenants of the lordship and towns adjoining thereunto which have no right of common.

We need not be surprised that when the area of land under the plough grew again in the late sixteenth and early seventeenth centuries it was not wholly at the expense of the Midland pastures but in the northern hills and heaths. Where the extra husbandmen were bedded and housed was in the old centres of population. Few lived in rebuilt cottages on a site formerly deserted. The more intensive use of the land in the seventeenth and eighteenth centuries did not bring the plough back to the sheep-walks. Men turned to the remaining open fields of their villages, seeking to use them more economically; seeking to enclose them by agreement where they could; others turned to the still plentiful areas of forest, heath and fen. In general this new war against the natural landscape was conducted from old and existing bases, and (the Fens apart) there are not many records of new settlements being founded or deserted ones refounded. Although the total population *c.* 1750 was greater than that of the early fourteenth century it was centred in fewer settlements. To add the villages of the fourteenth century on to the maps of the mid-eighteenth-century county cartographers is to see how far—in terms of the number of village units—the retreat of settlement has been carried, and how much of the ground won for grass by the mid-sixteenth century was never recaptured. In the same way a comparison of the Census of 1801 in rural counties with the poll tax receipts of 1377 is not always flattering to 1801, and 1377 was a year when (by all population estimates) more than a million fewer were alive than in (say) 1300. There must be many districts in Lincolnshire, Leicestershire and Northamptonshire which saw a greater density of population in the thirteenth century than at any time since.

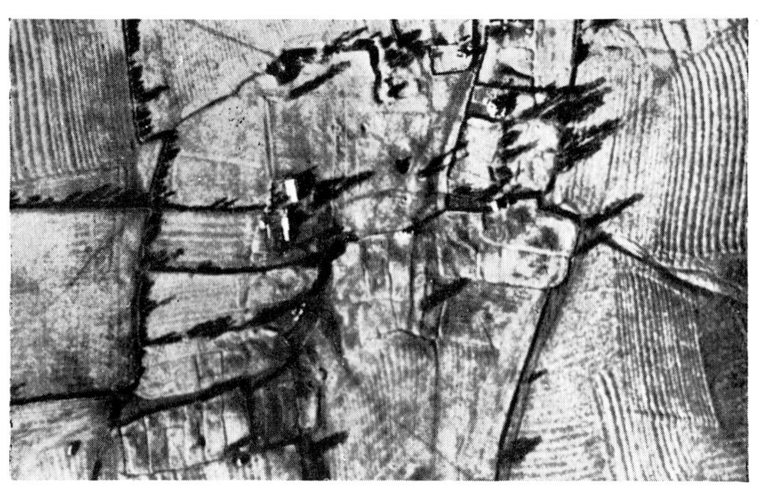

(12) THE SHRUNKEN VILLAGES

(Above). Faxton, Northants. (Below). Cosford, Warws.

In each, some houses remain, but surrounding them are earthworks similar to those of the depopulated villages, showing that the settlements were once much more extensive.

Chapter Seven

THE LOCALE OF DESTRUCTION

Now for the ground which . . . it is ycleped thy park.
Love's Labour's Lost, Act I, Scene 1.

I

IN this chapter we shall show that depopulation was strongly felt in certain English counties while it passed others by. For our facts we shall draw partly on the formal list of the more important depopulations in Part Four and partly on contemporary evidence and comment. When we come to attempt an explanation of such a distribution pattern we shall be brought very near to certain arguments which have occurred in earlier chapters.

This whole question of location brings us back to the royal inquiries and the royal prosecutions, since these were in their turn more concerned with certain counties than others. It brings us back to the motives and occasion of depopulation, since the agrarian development and the settlement pattern of some counties gave them immunity from the full force of the movement. It brings us back to contemporary comment, for Tudor legislators and publicists were well aware that depopulation was local in its emphasis.

It will be remembered that the first anti-depopulation Act was a local one, concerned only with the Isle of Wight. In a sense this Act can deceive us. It was passed not because the Island was feeling the force of depopulation more severely than other parts of the country but for the simple motive of military security, as its preamble makes plain. The Crown did not want this important prize for any cross-Channel invader to be left undermanned and unguarded. The Act tells us more about contemporary military fears than the pace and progress of enclosure.

There is no evidence of any proceedings against enclosures

in the Island, and when the 1517 Commission came to collect evidence their report on local depopulations speaks only of trivialities. Thirteen of the fifty-five vills in the Island are no longer any more than farms, the size of their tax quota and the recorded 1379 populations suggesting that they were never more than hamlets. The surviving earthworks, as seen from the air, are very unimpressive compared, for example, with the earthworks of the lost villages on the chalk of Lincolnshire. It will also be recalled from the documents quoted on page 147 that in 1559 a local jury had no coherent explanation to offer for the local decay of houses except the decline of Southampton as a port. They remembered nothing of depopulation for sheep.[1]

We have seen that other anti-enclosure legislation confined itself to certain counties, acknowledging that the threat of depopulation did not hang over all districts, and if we list the counties on which the 1517 and 1518 Commissions reported, we find notable absentees. If the Commission went to Surrey, Sussex, Kent, Wiltshire, Dorset, Devon, Cornwall, or Suffolk not a single vestige of its travels remains. In Hampshire it reported very little indeed.[2] From this evidence the downlands of the south do not seem to have been very familiar with the depopulations affecting the Midlands at that time.

A more precise measurement of the local intensity can be given by recalling the analysis[3] of the prosecutions which followed the Inquiry of 1517–18. The majority of the prosecutions were concerned with depopulation in a limited number of Midland counties, as Table 3 shows.

TABLE 3

ANALYSIS OF 583 PROSECUTIONS FOR DEPOPULATING ENCLOSURE 1517–65 BY COUNTIES

	%		%		%
Northampton	17	Warwick	14	Buckingham	14
Oxford	14	Berkshire	10	Leicester	10
Bedford	10	Nottingham	6	Derby	2
Gloucester	1	Middlesex	0·4		

All other English counties 1·6%

Contrasted with this group of counties is another where prosecutions are few, although other evidence points to quite severe experience of depopulation only a little earlier than 1485. We can relate this group to the Midland group by calculating the number of vills in each county which were taken as units of tax assessment in 1334 but which have since been depopulated. Table 4 summarises the results of a more detailed analysis[4] of these statistics.

TABLE 4

PROPORTION OF VILLS ASSESSED TO TAXES IN 1334 BUT SINCE LOST BY COUNTIES

	%		%
Warwickshire	13	Rutland	9
Leicestershire	11	Huntingdonshire	2
Northamptonshire	13	Cambridgeshire	5
Oxfordshire	11	Isle of Wight	22
Buckinghamshire	10	Lincolnshire	9
Nottinghamshire	5	Yorkshire E.R.	13
		Yorkshire W.R.	6
		Yorkshire N.R.	8
		Norfolk	9

The two columns show that although only those on the left figured large in inquiries and prosecutions in 1517–65, those on the right hand had had a comparable experience of depopulation. A third and truly contrasted column might be constructed of those counties with little evidence of depopulation since 1334 either from tax lists or from sixteenth-century inquiries.

Explanations of this diverse experience which we shall offer will be cast in terms both of time and space, both of geography and history. It will be seen that the counties dealt with in 1517–18 were grouped together at the heart of the Midlands, and we shall refer to them, for brevity's sake, as the Inner Midlands. The Table which follows divides the English counties according to their *general* experience of depopulation. Since geographical conditions within certain counties (such as Warwickshire) are far from homogeneous we shall later have to carry the examination a stage further and see whether the experiences of different districts within these counties show any divergence. But the Table will be useful in bringing together in a generalised form the evidence for various groups of counties, which is also shown in map form in Fig 9.

TABLE 5

LOCAL EXPERIENCE OF DEPOPULATION

Counties	*1517 Visit*	*1517 Returns*	*1517–58 Prosecutions*	*Tax list of 1334*	*Suggested diagnosis*
Group 1. Southern Margin Northern Margin Devon, Cornwall, Dorset, Wiltshire, Sussex, Surrey, Kent and S. Suffolk, Westmorland, Cumberland, Lancashire, Cheshire.	NO	NONE	NONE	A FEW ABSENTEES TODAY	VIRTUAL IMMUNITY
Group 2. Western Margin Shropshire, Herefordshire, Somerset.	YES	TRIVIAL	NONE	A FEW ABSENTEES TODAY	VIRTUAL IMMUNITY
Worcestershire.	NO	NO	NONE		
Group 3. Eastern Margin Norfolk, Lincolnshire, Yorkshire, N.R., E.R. and W.R., N. Suffolk.	YES	TRIVIAL	NONE	MANY ABSENTEES TODAY	EARLY DEPOPULATION i.e. PRE 1485. MEDIUM INTENSITY
Group 4. Outer Midlands Middlesex, Hertfordshire, Bedfordshire, Berkshire, Cambridgeshire, Rutland, Huntingdonshire, Staffordshire, Gloucestershire, Hampshire, Derbyshire.	YES	YES, BUT FEW	YES, BUT FEW	SOME ABSENTEES TODAY	DEPOPULATION *c.* 1450–1520 LESS INTENSE
Group 5. Inner Midlands Northamptonshire, Oxfordshire, Warwickshire, Buckinghamshire, Leicestershire, Nottinghamshire.	YES	VERY MANY	VERY MANY	VERY MANY ABSENTEES TODAY	INTENSE DEPOPULATION *c.* 1450–1520
Group 6. North-East Margin Northumberland Durham	NO	NONE	NONE	SOME ABSENTEES	LATE DEPOPULATION

It may be useful to summarise Table 5 in another form.

SUMMARY OF TABLE 5

AREAS OF HEAVY DEPOPULATION, visited in 1517, followed by prosecutions.

Group 5. Inner Midlands.

AREAS OF LIGHTER DEPOPULATION, visited in 1517, followed by prosecutions.

Group 4. Outer Midlands.

AREAS OF LIGHTER DEPOPULATION, not visited in 1517. (Probably depopulated earlier and later.)

Group 6. North-East Margin.

AREAS OF MEDIUM DEPOPULATION, visited in 1517 without subsequent prosecutions and with trivial findings.

Group 3. Eastern Margin.

AREAS OF VERY LIGHT DEPOPULATION, visited in 1517 with trivial findings.

Group 2. Western Margin.

AREAS OF VERY LIGHT DEPOPULATION, not visited in 1517.

Group 1. Southern Margin. Northern Margin.

In later sections of this chapter we shall try to explain why these six broadly different experiences can be found. Since physical conditions and the systems of tenure and farming

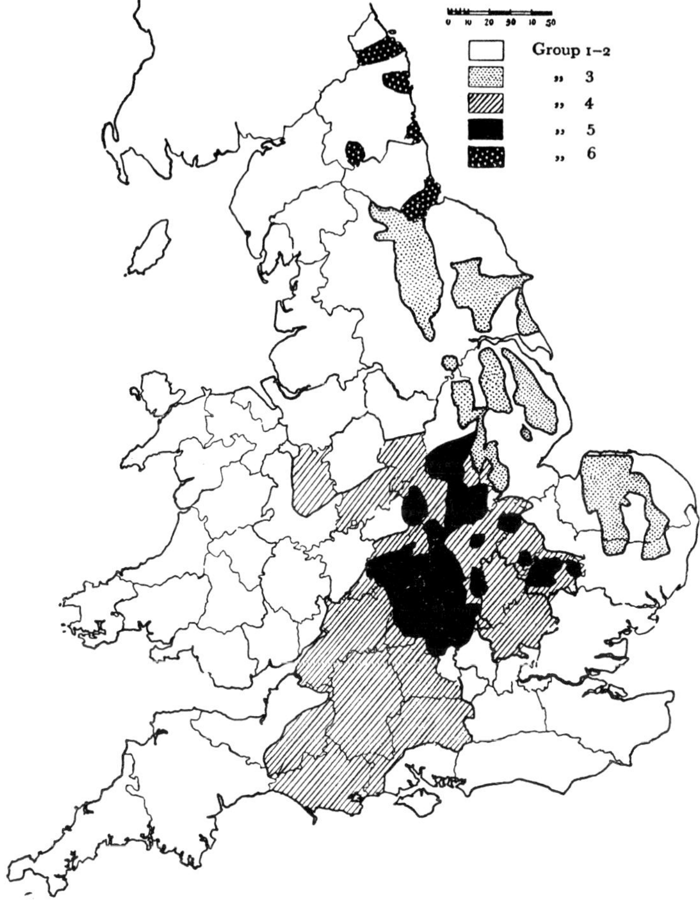

Fig. 9. *English lost villages, diagram summarising regional experiences as detailed in Table 5.*

arising out of those conditions are important determinants of this distribution pattern mapped in Fig. 9 we shall then have to see whether our explanation holds good when characteristics of one group intrude into parts of another group (e.g. the forest area intruding within Group 5, the classical counties of depopulating enclosure, as shown in Figs. 11–13).

2

Were contemporaries aware that depopulation was thus localised? The answer is certain. The Commission of 1517 does not seem to have been sent to certain counties of the north and west at all. When its reports were received and the Attorney General was instructed to take action against the King's own tenants who had been enclosing, the trifling Returns from the counties of the Eastern Margin[5] were ignored, as Table 3, p. 218, showed us. Even after the Act of 1536 when suits were instituted against other depopulators and the Returns of 1517–18 were scrutinised afresh, no cases from outside the Midland counties were revived. The Act of 1536 had itself been limited to the thirteen Inner and Outer Midland counties, with the addition of Cambridgeshire and the Isle of Wight.

The Doctor in the *Discourse* specifically exempted the old-enclosed counties of Essex, Kent and Devon from his strictures:

> I mean not all Inclosures, but only of such Inclosures as turneth commonly arable fields into pastures.

and in the second dialogue he denied that his policy was to set the plough in every corner of the kingdom, a policy as bad as bringing to every locality "the breeding of sheep only".[6]

In the pamphlet literature it is the Midland counties which are cited by name. The author of the *Treatise concerning the Staple* (*c.* 1533–36) put his deserted villages[7]

> in the middle parts of the body of the realm:

Rous had used the same metaphor when he described enclosure as principally

> *in umbelico regni*,

and if we wanted to enliven the vocabulary of historical geography we might, on his priestly authority, write "the Midland Navel" for "the Inner Midlands".

When Richard Sandes wrote to the Council complaining about seventeenth-century enclosure he adduced the examples of earlier depopulations as showing what would happen if men were free to convert the grass.[8] Like the Doctor in the *Discourse* he was aware that the Midlands were different from the south-east, where

> [land was] inclosed when yer was but few people, and these maintain tyllage husbondry and hospitality . . . but ye depopulation in ye champian countrys destroy all means of doeinge help or service for the Kinge.
> Depopulated townes [are] in the best naturall corne countryes which affore supplyed ye wants of others every way, beinge in ye middle of ye land. . . .

It was from examples in two Midland counties, Leicestershire and Northamptonshire, that he proposed to make the Council's flesh creep.

The pamphlet on the *Decay of England* which we cited on page 85 also used only Midland examples.[9] Beginning in Oxfordshire it estimated that 240 people had been evicted there.

> Now these twelve score persons had need to have living: whither shall they go? into Northamptonshire? and there also is the living of persons lost.

and in the next argument Buckinghamshire was adduced as a county where there was a dearth of corn through lost plough-teams.

It was in the Midlands also that the riots principally came, and although these were often later than the peak of the depopulating enclosure movement it was here that we saw the deserted village figuring in the rebels' programme of action as a remembered evil. In the northern counties on the other hand, the agrarian demands of the Pilgrimage of Grace were against the enclosing of commons and unlawful "intakes". The Articles have nothing about depopulation.[10]

The Commission of 1548 does not seem to have moved further than the Midlands. Hales himself was on the Oxford circuit, and the *Discourse* is set on an evening after a day's sitting in Coventry. The characters in the *Discourse* are Midland men speaking of Midland depopulations, just as Rous had spoken of those local depopulations centring on the Avon valley.

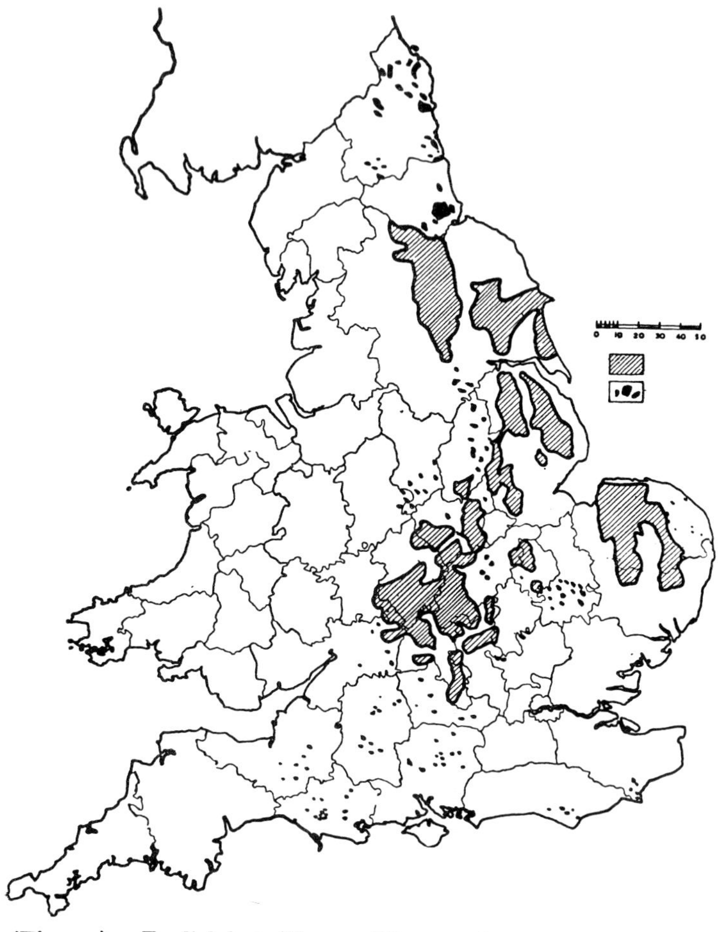

(Fig. 10). *English lost villages. Diagram showing local variations in the intensity with which depopulation was experienced.*

LINE SHADING: *areas with more than 11 % of villages lost since 1334.*

SCATTERED DOTS: *between 5 and 10 % of villages lost since 1334.*

Half a century later the Elizabethan legislation prohibiting enclosure was not specifically aimed at depopulating enclosure, but an interesting clause in the Act of 1597 "for the maintenance of husbandry and tillage" limited its operation to 23 English counties, the Isle of Wight and Pembrokeshire. It did not apply to Norfolk, Suffolk, Essex, Kent, Surrey, Sussex, Cheshire, Lancashire, Wiltshire, Devon, Cornwall, Westmorland or Cumberland. Northumberland was withdrawn from the act by an amending statute later that year.[11] This area in which nothing was said against enclosure is precisely the area of "old enclosure": the area inoculated against enclosure of open fields because it had already virtually lost them; and the area inoculated against further enclosure for pasture by the nature of its terrain and ample concessions already made to non-arable production within it.

3

We must now face some of the questions posed by Professor W. G. East:[12]

> a geographer would examine very carefully to see whether any regional or physical considerations were relevant to the matter; he would be concerned to study the changing soil pattern and drainage pattern of the different areas concerned, and he would study very carefully whether the distribution of land which was good or bad for grass farming entered into the story of depopulation. A physical explanation of that kind is not necessarily to be found, but I think it has to be looked for. Would one find for example that areas best fitted for arable cultivation did not suffer depopulation? whereas areas that were marginal for arable cultivation suffered to a much greater extent?

Clearly, geographers are the professional men best fitted to answer a geographer's questions, and the suggestions which follow are based only on that minimum of geographical knowledge which comes to economic historians.

As far as broad distribution is concerned, I think enough has been said already to show that geographical factors were crucially important, and this section will examine some of these in more detail. When it comes to explaining the distribution pattern of a narrower locality, then clearly the influence of personalities, of tenure, of village size and other adventitious factors will compete with the simpler physical factors of soil and drainage. It is interesting to note that Professor K. C. Edwards' study of land utilisation in Nottinghamshire found that the early enclosures of South Nottinghamshire had

> a diversity of soils involved . . . and no specific type of land appears to have been particularly liable to enclosure.

Nothing short of an intensive examination of a large number of lost village sites with an eye on conjectured Tudor soil and drainage conditions could solve this problem, and this is pre-eminently a geographer's task. (It is possible that local examination of physical factors may even give a clue to the origin of what (we shall see later) turned out to be an important determinant of whether a village survived: the factor of relative smallness.) The economic historian may name and date the sites, but since we have no large-scale maps of past soil conditions he must give way to other craftsmen here.

For that reason, none of the physical factors discussed below is intended to apply to a distribution pattern other than the broad pattern displayed in Table 5, page 220, showing that whole areas of England were virtually immune from depopulating enclosure; and even within the Inner Midlands—our classical area for depopulation—there were depopulated sites alongside villages which retained their open fields until the eighteenth century. This immunity we must now attempt to explain.

Nowhere can this contrast be seen more clearly than at Whitchurch, Warwickshire, where the mother village was depopulated in the early sixteenth century, the church now standing alone in the fields: but at the daughter village of Crimscote the fields were still unenclosed at the time of the Tithe Award map in the middle of the nineteenth century, so that Victorian surveyors who had elsewhere to plot only hedged fields were there faced with more than a thousand scattered strips to measure, draw and tabulate.[13]

Even where sharp contrasts of this kind were absent there were depopulated villages whose neighbours had open fields retained until the late eighteenth century. It is sometimes disconcerting for students who have been told about the relative intensity of Tudor depopulation in the Midlands to return to the subject of enclosure in the mid-eighteenth century and find that the Midlands is also the classical area of Parliamentary enclosure. We may set two maps side by side, and see how similar they are. The one is the map in the *Oxford History of England*, volume viii (which takes and expresses more simply the detail accumulated by Gay on a rather too-intricate map, with its fifty-eight different symbols). Each dot there represents an enclosure case—not necessarily a depopulating enclosure case—between 1485 and 1607. A distribution map of deserted villages would have perhaps fewer dots, but the pattern would be similar: a concentration in the Inner Midlands and the Eastern Margin.[14]

By the side of this map we may set one showing the areas most affected by Parliamentary enclosure, such as the well-known map in Gonner's book.[15] The two maps are very similar. The two movements had their greatest impetus in the same area of England. Outside this area, neither was felt intensely, although Parliamentary enclosure did reach smaller but significant proportions in the counties of the Outer Midlands.

We thus have the apparent paradox that the area which felt the depopulating enclosure most acutely was the very area which had more of its open fields remaining until the mid-eighteenth century than any other part of the country. Why did only a limited number of victims fall to depopulators in the Midland core? and why did those villages whose open fields survived this first storm of the period 1450–1550 stand a good chance of weathering another 200 years, despite the fact that enclosure by agreement after the early 1600s would no longer bring one before a judge and jury?

Earlier, we used the metaphor of inoculation in another connection. It might the more properly be used here. If depopulation was, as Rous said, a plague, then the weakest victims fell to it. Later we shall show that smallness of size was one such weakness. We have already suggested in the last chapter that a low proportion of freeholders was another weakness which left a village vulnerable. A landlord with connections in the wool trade or an eager acquisitive appetite was—for the purpose of this metaphor—another fatal weakness.

In the years between 1450 and 1520 the weakest went to the wall. As we showed in earlier chapters, the death rate for villages then slackened. Royal action or the movement of corn prices made depopulating enclosure less possible or less attractive.

After a serious epidemic it is often noticed that men are apparently healthier. The plague has killed off the weakest, and the longevity of the survivors pushes up the average expectation of life. How does this analogy apply to the plague of depopulation? In the period of depopulating enclosure those men with opportunities to enclose were those without formidable obstacles. Those with formidable obstacles in their path were forced to wait. As time passed, the obstacles, the stubborn freeholders, were in an even stronger position to resist suggestions of enclosure on the landlord's terms. When a Parliament of squires believed that Property was King, every small freehold had something of the divinity which hedged kingship, and it would have been a bold man who attempted to ride rough-shod over his freeholders to achieve a forced enclosure in the seventeenth and eighteenth centuries. In the end, wherever freeholders could not be educated to their own self-interest in an agreed enclosure nor be persuaded to part with their property for cash, only the creation of private Act enclosure made it possible to override their opposition and force them to accept hedged fields in exchange for their scattered strips.

If a village and its freeholders could survive the first plague of unwanted enclosure they were well inoculated against any recurrence, and we have the resulting pattern of such a map as that in Fig. 11 (1). The depopulating enclosures of the Caves and Faunts in Leicestershire stand intermingled with the quieter enclosures by agreement of the seventeenth

COUNTY DISTRIBUTION MAPS 1–4.

ıded to illustrate the general distribution of lost 'n a county. They could not be published on a ıgh to serve as a guide to the exact location of de will be found in the six-figure National Grid County Lists of Chapter Ten. The areas shaded ıaps are the exact areas of the townships whose tlements have been depopulated.

ʌn of the enclosure history of the county to n, by line-shading, of those townships en- ent between 1550 and the beginning of losure in 1730. The townships left white ts. There is an obvious concentration of "agreement" enclosure in the east and rliamentary enclosure in the central areas: dominated by Charnwood forest. The ıt and non-lost villages will be noted.

concentrated in the Avon valley and the uth. The north and north-west (the late- ea) is virtually immune.

T RIDING

lages are concentrated on the Wolds and erness. Virtual immunity in the former outh-east and south-west.

TH RIDING

nity of (*a*) the Pennines, (*b*) the north ıd (*c*) the late-surviving Forest of Galtres Riding immediately north of York.

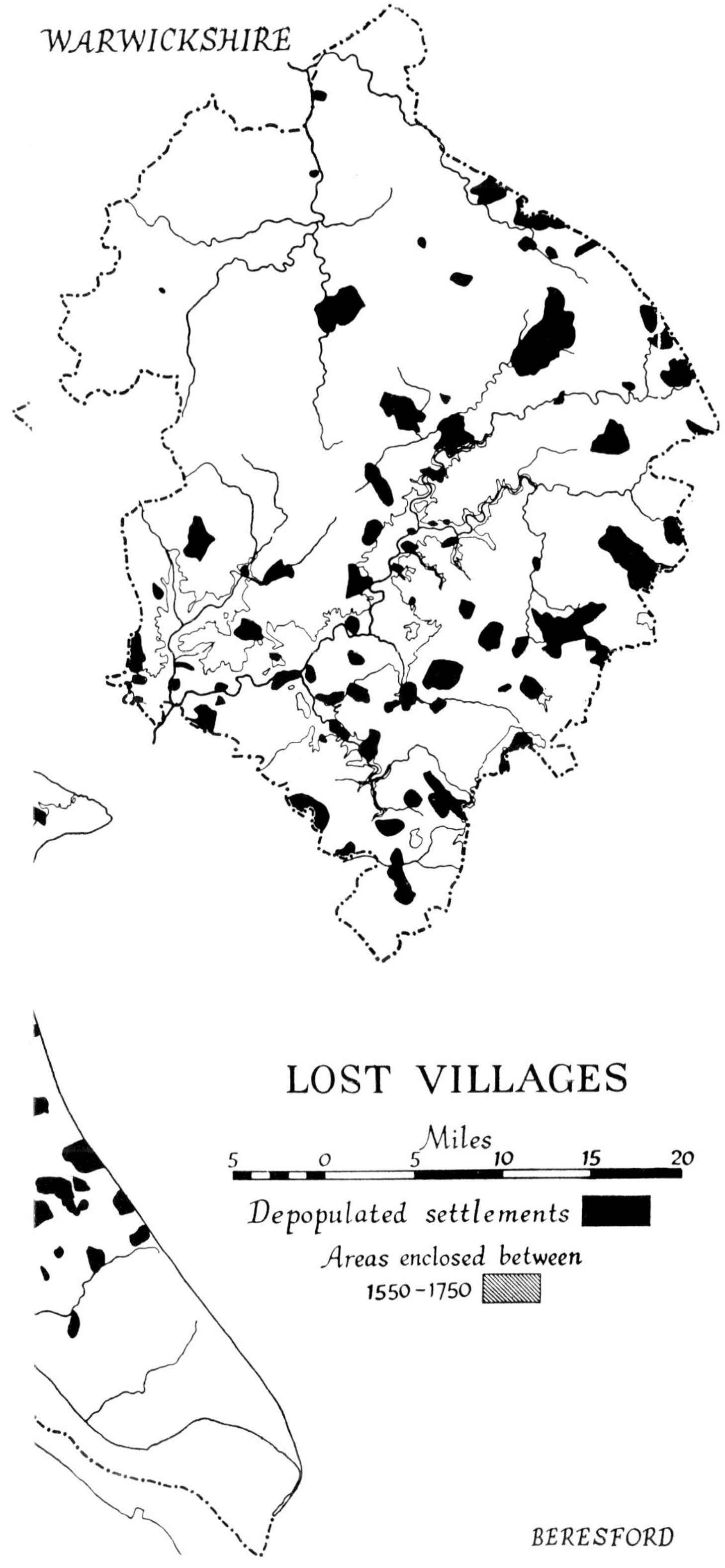

century and the statutory enclosures of the eighteenth. Those who had survived the whirlwind were well able to look after themselves in a mere high wind.

4

So much for the fortunate survivors amid a landscape of desertions: what of those areas with almost wholesale immunity? How was this immunity won?

We shall not be surprised, of course, to hear very little of depopulating enclosure among the higher uplands where pastoral pursuits had always dominated the economy. None of the 113 villages in three upland hundreds of the West Riding of Yorkshire has been lost. In such places there was little corn to be displaced and plenty of room to expand the grazing grounds without destroying villages.

Elsewhere there were forest villages whose form of agriculture was biased away from arable husbandry. Extensive areas of uncleared forest remained to provide a profitable source of income without any temptation to think in terms of sheep walks. In this category would fall areas like the Weald, the Forest of Dean, Sherwood and much of Essex and the Chilterns. As Dr. Hull has said of Essex in the sixteenth century:

> it was an agricultural economy which was sound enough to be encouraged rather than destroyed with sheep-walks.

In such districts it was very unusual to find much open-field arable, so that

> the early development of consolidated holdings contributed to the relative strength of the peasantry.[16]

If the physical and settlement conditions in woodland were so unfavourable to the activity of the depopulator, what of the wooded areas which stood at the very heart of the Inner Midlands? Counties which we have so far taken as unities were far from homogeneous in terrain. Although each of them possessed extensive areas of champine country, there were smaller areas with soil and drainage conditions favouring late-surviving forest.

The county distribution maps in Figs. 11–15 demonstrate that this factor was as important within the Inner Midlands

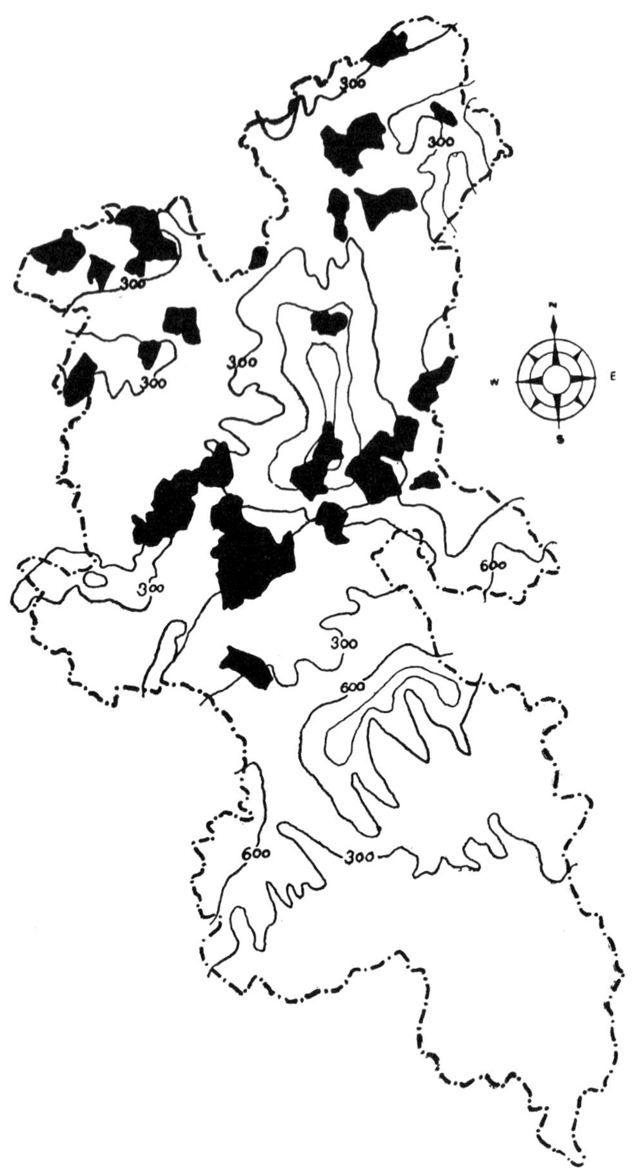

(Fig. 12). COUNTY DISTRIBUTION MAPS—5, BUCKINGHAMSHIRE.

Note the immunity from depopulation in the Chilterns at the southern end of the county. The wooded country between Bicester and Bletchley in the northern half of the county separates the main area of depopulation into two broad belts. (*Scale, approx.* 1 *inch* = 9 *miles.*)

as we have suggested for the country as a whole. Warwickshire shows the contrast most sharply. North of the Avon was the Forest of Arden, south of the river was the classical champine country. By the fifteenth century, Arden was no longer a continuous forest mile after mile, but (as now) it had blocks of woodland interspersed with clearings and villages. The influence of the forest on the life of Arden men has been shown in a number of studies. Professor Kinvig's Domesday map[17] shows it as the principal area of woodland, while champine, or *Felden* Warwickshire abounded in the plough-teams which were so few in the Arden vills. Dr. Hilton has shown[18] how the forest vills knew much less of the routine and arduous villein obligations of the open-field villages of the *Felden.* Lady Stenton showed how the "custom of Arden" was tolerant of enclosure in the thirteenth century, and I myself have examined the irregular field-systems which the terrain produced in the north of the county on the borders of Cannock Chase.[19]

When we come to examine the villages and hamlets of the county for depopulation the same division is immediately apparent.[20] The Arden villages were relatively immune. The forest Hundred of Hemlingford had only nine lost sites while Knightlow and Kington had forty-two and thirty-three respectively. Barlichway Hundred had twenty-nine lost villages, but if the river-side sites are omitted, it is as bare of them as Hemlingford.

It was the field-land, the champine part of Warwickshire, which was the battleground between corn and grass. The late-surviving forest parishes of other Midland counties conferred the same immunity as Arden: in the Chiltern counties the lost villages cease when the scarp slope is passed and the woodlands of the dip slope are reached.

Marshland settlements were equally immune. Not a single vill in the Holland part of Lincolnshire has been lost, and the immunity stretches from West Norfolk through Lincolnshire and Nottinghamshire to the marshes of the East and West Ridings of Yorkshire.[21] Only Romney Marsh seems unable to hold its own, and soon after the Black Death there were the ruined churches whose sites are still visible.

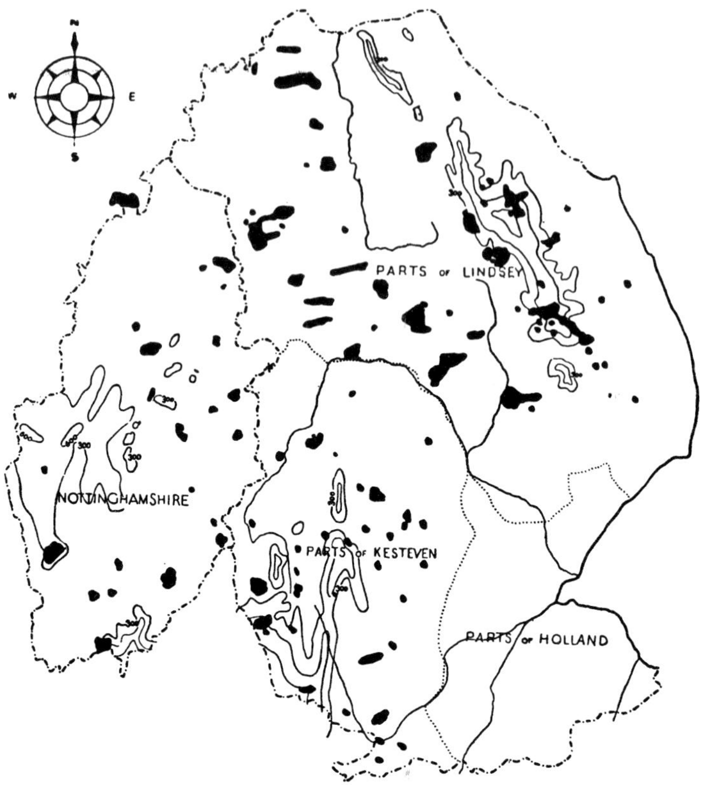

(Fig. 13). COUNTY DISTRIBUTION MAPS—6 AND 7, NOTTINGHAMSHIRE AND LINCOLNSHIRE.

Note the immunity of the reclaimed fenland in south-east Lincs. and the concentration of depopulation on the uplands of west and north Lincs. (Scale, 1 inch = 17 miles.)

In general we may say that land which was enclosed early or brought straight from the natural state into hedged fields was the type of terrain where immunity from lost villages is found. As R. A. L. Smith wrote:[22]

> newly-cleared land and newly-reclaimed and embanked lands are the two types of land that should be most constantly before the mind of the student of medieval enclosures.

One such district is the plain of Lancashire. Here, at first blush, we might seem to have nothing but a countryside of compact, nucleated villages. How did these escape the depopulation which descended on similar communities south of the Trent? Their immunity seems to have come from their early enclosure. If we read twelfth and thirteenth century charters there is no doubt that Lancashire had its open fields lying in strips. By the time we come to the enclosure troubles of the sixteenth century Lancashire had hardly an open field to be seen.

The open fields which had existed in Lancashire were only superficially similar to those of the Midlands. The Lancashire villages had always reached a balance between corn and grass (or between corn and wood) which enabled both to live together side by side. (The Tudor husbandry of the chalklands of Wiltshire successfully maintained such a marriage, as Dr. Kerridge has shown.) In the plain of Lancashire and Cheshire there was no scarcity of grass-ground; rough pasture lay easily to hand and in abundance. The open-field strips of thirteenth century documents seem to lie in a small number of "in-fields" while more extensive arable crops were taken from outlying fields, cropped for a while and then reverted to grass. When more is known about the pre-enclosure economy of these districts we shall be able to relate it more precisely to the positive fact that when the Midlands began to feel the force of depopulating enclosure these lands were already enclosed.

Their enclosure could not in itself have saved villages from destruction had their enclosed cornfields been in great demand as pastures; but demand for pasture of the quality which their fields could supply was already amply met by the abundant pastureland in its unimproved state.

In the Inner and Outer Midlands, on the other hand, strong forces were mustered against the champine village. Its extensive, cleared areas suggested rolling pastures comparable in sweep to the rougher pastures of the downland, but incomparably richer and lusher in their grass. The principal barrier was the scattered land-ownership and occupation rights of the open-field peasantry, but when they themselves acquiesced in changing the traditional courses of husbandry and in loosening the traditional bonds of land and man, they were making themselves highly vulnerable.

5

The degree of immunity and vulnerability can be measured by examining various districts and calculating the percentage of all villages within that area which have been depopulated.[23] In Table 6 we have only included those lost villages which were separately assessed to the taxes of 1334 or 1377. Had we not done so, we would have figures showing even more impressive percentages, but it would have been at the cost of comparability with the later Tables 17 and 18, where the same tax material is used to estimate the relative size of lost and surviving villages. Wherever low percentages are recorded in the following table we shall find ourselves in districts where the champine village was never firmly and characteristically established.

TABLE 6

LOCAL EXPERIENCE OF DEPOPULATION BY COUNTIES AND DISTRICTS

Proportion of vills separately assessed in 1334, but since disappeared.

	Vills in 1334	*Now lost*	*Percentage lost*
INNER MIDLAND COUNTIES			
WARWICKSHIRE:			
Champine hundreds:			
Kineton	71	17	24
Knightlow	107	13	12
Barlichway	63	5	8
Forest hundred:			
Hemlingford	45	2	5
TOTAL	286	37	13
LEICESTERSHIRE:			
Sparkenhoe hundred	59	10	16
Guthlaxton	42	7	16
Goscote	74	7	9
Gartree	97	8	8
Framland	47	5	11
TOTAL	319	37	11

	Vills in 1334	*Now lost*	*Percentage lost*
NORTHAMPTONSHIRE:			
Fenland and forest hundreds:			
Nassaburgh	7	0	0
Willybrook	18	0	0
Huxloe	19	0	0
Spelhoe	7	0	0
Wymersley	22	0	0
Hamfordshoe	10	0	0
Higham Ferrers	7	0	0
Other hundreds:			
King's Sutton	29	7	24
Navisford	19	4	21
Chipping Warden	12	4	33
Rothwell	26	6	24
Green's Norton	11	2	18
Orlingbury	16	3	19
Fawsley	21	3	14
Guilsborough	19	3	16
Newbottle Grove	20	3	15
Cleyley	17	2	12
Corby	26	1	4
Towcester	6	1	16
TOTAL	312	39	13
OXFORDSHIRE:			
Chiltern hundreds:			
Benefield	12	0	0
Langtree	11	1	9
Lewknor	14	1	7
Other hundreds:			
Bampton	30	0	0
Bloxham	16	0	0
Wotton	55	6	11
Chadlington	52	7	14
Ploughley	35	6	17
Bollingdon	41	6	15
Ewelme	25	6	24
Banbury	20	4	20
Thame	10	1	10
Ancient demesne (scatter)	14	0	0
TOTAL	335	38	11

(Fig. 14). COUNTY DISTRIBUTION MAPS—8 AND 9
NORTHAMPTONSHIRE AND OXFORDSHIRE.

Note the concentration on the high ground near the junction of the two counties and the low degree of depopulation in the fens of north-east Northants and the woodlands of central and south-east Oxfordshire. (Scale, approx, 1 inch = 17 miles.)

	Vills in 1334	Now lost	Percentage lost
BUCKINGHAMSHIRE:			
Chiltern hundreds:			
Stoke	10	0	0
Desborough	16	0	0
Burnham	12	0	0
Stone	9	0	0
Risborough	4	0	0
Aylesbury	11	0	0
Yardley	6	0	0
Champine hundreds:			
Stotfold	14	5	35
Cottesloe	15	4	27
Ashendon	16	6	37
Waddesdon	10	2	20
Ixhill	14	2	14
Rowley	10	1	10
Buckingham (Lamua)	10	0	0
Moulsoe	16	0	0
Bunsty	14	1	7
Seckloe	19	1	5
Mursley	16	1	6
Ancient demesne (scatter)	8	0	0
TOTAL	230	23	10
NOTTINGHAMSHIRE:			
Champine hundreds:			
Rushcliff	27	1	4
Thurgarton	45	1	2
Bingham	36	1	3
Newark	35	2	5
Forest or mixed hundreds:			
Bassetlaw	83	5	6
Broxtow	27	3	11
TOTAL	253	13	5
SOME OUTER MIDLAND COUNTIES			
RUTLAND:			
Martinslee hundred	22	4	18
East	9	1	11
Elvestow	12	0	0
Wrangdike	13	0	0
TOTAL	56	5	9
HUNTINGDONSHIRE:			
Leightonstone hundred	23	1	4
Normancross	24	1	4
Fenland hundreds	42	0	0
TOTAL	89	2	2

	Vills in 1334	*Now lost*	*Percentage lost*
CAMBRIDGESHIRE:			
Chesterton hundred	6	1	16
Arningford	17	1	6
Wetherley	12	2	16
Other hundreds	100	4	4
Fenland hundreds	28	0	0
TOTAL	163	8	5
ISLE OF WIGHT			
East Medina hundred	26	4	15
West Medina	29	8	27
TOTAL	55	12	22
PENNINES AND YORKSHIRE PLAIN			
YORKSHIRE, WEST RIDING			
Vale of York and plain:			
Ainstey wapentake	28	4	14
Barkstone Ash	54	6	11
Claro	88	8	9
Osgodcross	51	4	8
Strafforth	90	7	8
All other areas in Riding	272	7	3
TOTAL	583	36	6
EASTERN COUNTIES			
LINCOLNSHIRE, PARTS OF LINDSEY:			
Plain and upland wapentakes	440	34	8
Fen and fenland borders	29	0	0
PARTS OF HOLLAND:			
Fenland wapentakes	33	0	0
PARTS OF KESTEVEN			
Plain and upland wapentakes	260	29	11
TOTAL, excluding fenland	700	63	9
TOTAL, including fenland	762	63	8
EAST RIDING OF YORKSHIRE:			
Holderness (Plain)	81	5	6
Wolds and slopes	198	33	16
Other areas	87	11	12
TOTAL	366	49	13

	Vills in 1344	*Now lost*	*Percentage lost*
NORFOLK:[1]			
Breckland hundreds	74	16	21
Goodsands hundreds	80	14	17
Part greensand, part marsh:			
Freebridge hundred	36	3	8
Clacklose hundred	29	3	10
Other areas (centre, east and south):			
Hundreds of East and West Flegg, Diss, Humbleyard, Launditch, Mitford, Forhoe, Wayland, Holt, Blofield, North and South Erpingham and Eynsford	302	27	9
Hundreds of Happing, Taverham, Walsham, Loddon, Knavering, Depwade, Henstead, Ersham and Tunstead	163	2	1
TOTAL	684[1]	65[1]	9

[1] *N.B.*—This table taken from Mr. K. J. Allison's study is calculated on a different basis from the other counties. It takes *all* lost vills named in the tax list of 1334, whether or not they were linked with another village for assessment purposes. This gives a slightly higher percentage than figures calculated on the same basis as the other counties.

6

The separation of Durham and Northumberland into a separate Group in Figs. 9 and 10 and Table 5 was necessary since, it will be recalled, we found signs in Chapter Five that a final wave of depopulation hit this area towards the end of the sixteenth century for very local reasons connected with social custom, tenure and the security of copyholders: factors which were not directly determined by the type of physical condition which we have been discussing in this chapter.

Nor have we yet explained the curious experience of our Eastern Margin: of parts of Norfolk, Lincolnshire and Yorkshire. Here the trivial enclosures reported in 1517 and the absence of prosecutions might make us imagine that we are in a country of very slender depopulations comparable to the outer fringes of the Outer Midlands Group of Table 5: yet

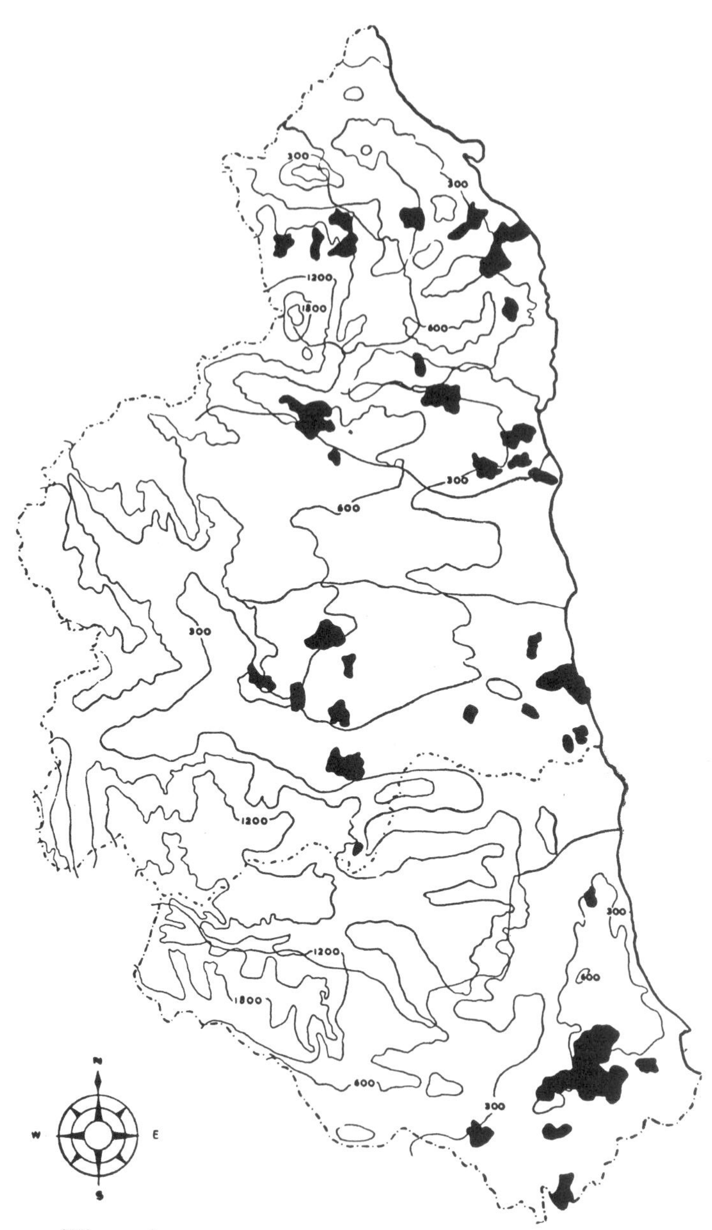

(Fig. 15). COUNTY DISTRIBUTION MAPS—10 AND 11
NORTHUMBERLAND AND COUNTY DURHAM.
(Scale, approx. 1 inch = 17 miles.)

when we come to examine the tax lists, poll tax receipts, ecclesiastical records or extant manorial documents we find that this area was as marked by depopulation as parts of the Inner Midlands.

In every respect except the timing of depopulation these counties might claim to be one with Warwickshire and Northamptonshire. Certainly they have sites as clear on the ground as any in the Inner Midlands, and the very frequency with which documents from these areas have already been used as illustrations in previous chapters will have prepared readers for the inclusion of these counties among those badly hit by depopulation.

The time-table of depopulation in these eastern counties, like the time-table in the Midlands, contains sites which fell at all periods. There were some villages here which did not revive after the Plague, but everything points to many sites still being inhabited in 1377 and in the early fifteenth century. This must mean that such sites were deserted within the same broad period as the Midlands (*c.* 1450–1550) but early enough to have their main peak passed when Henry VII came to the throne. For them it was even more true than Hales' Warwickshire that "the greater part of depopulation had taken place before the reign of King Henry the seventh". In them the Commissioners of 1517, armed with powers of inquiry which went back only to 1488, caught only the last stragglers. The majority had fallen in the Dark Ages of the movement, unilluminated by Government Inquiries and prerogative courts.

If these changes occurred a little earlier in this Eastern Margin we shall not be surprised to find that it also has a rather higher proportion of genuine Black Death depopulations never resettled; as well as truly marginal sites which seem to have fallen in the even Darker Ages of the retreat of settlement just before the beginning of the fourteenth century.

We shall now try and use this fact of earlier enclosure in the Eastern Margin, combined with what we know of the Midland experience, to answer a question posed in Professor East's final sentence. We have discussed immunity, and we must now discuss the very opposite. What made the Inner

Midlands and the Eastern Margin "suffer to a much greater extent"? Was it because they were poor cornlands which men were anxious to turn to grass as soon as the opportunity which we outlined in the last chapter had arrived?

The very reverse seems to be true. The unhappy experience of the Midland ploughlands seems to have arisen from the very fact that the soil of those parts was so good for more than one thing, with the balance of advantage so delicately poised. Quite small movements in the incentives to grow one or the other of the two contending crops would then produce a transformation of land-use more striking than in any other part of the kingdom.

It does not seem likely that the areas of depopulation can be correlated with soils pre-eminently suited to grass. The deserted villages had been planted on soil well suited for either. That was their fatal charm. Like Macheath their owner might say,

> How happy could I be with either,
> Were t'other dear charmer away.

Soil which was suited only for good grassland, on the other hand, could easily have escaped in the years after the Black Death from "the perpetual bondage and servitude of being for ever tilled", but we should not find its pastures flanked with what we have seen in the Midland distribution maps: corn villages alongside sheep villages; villages still with open fields in the early nineteenth century alongside sheepwalks enclosed in the late fifteenth century.

This narrow balance between the two uses for land can be seen expressly stated in sixteenth and seventeenth-century topographers. When John Leland described the champine country between Edge Hill and the Warwickshire Avon, where we have seen such extensive depopulating enclosure, he called it[24]

> the very granary of the whole county.

That was true. Alongside the granary parishes, however, he could have seen the pasture parishes and the empty parishes.

When Burton described his Leicestershire in 1622 he found in the south-east[25]

> exceeding rich ground, yielding great increase of corn in abundance of all kinds. . . .

but the sentence continued,

> . . . and it affordeth many good and large sheep pastures breeding a sheep to (incomparable) height and goodness.

He expressed the Macheath dilemma again in the same paragraph when he wrote:

> it yieldeth great delight and profit every way

and in his account of the soils of the north-east and south-west quarters of the county he wrote:

> both good soil and apt to bear corn and grass.

Only in the north-west quarter was the balance of advantage less in doubt: but he was then in the Charnwood Forest area where a quite different set of physical factors intrude into the county. It will be seen from Fig. 11 that depopulation was relatively sparse in this area.

The delicate balance of advantage made it possible for a long war of argument and counter-argument to follow. The Act of 1536 had called enclosures in the fifteen Midland counties[26]

> the greatest abuse and disorder of the natural soil of the ground that by any manner of invention could be practised,

and this is a classical statement from the school of thought which held that the proper use of each Midland acre was arable. This view steadily lost ground in the later sixteenth century, and not long after 1536 juries were certifying that land had been[27] reconverted to corn "in tillage according to the nature of the soil and the course of husbandry used in that county". No doubt this phrase covered rotations which included arable at some one course, satisfying both the progressive and the conservative opinions.

The occasions in the debates of 1597 when men spoke of perpetual tillage as "servitude" are well known. Men who appreciated the advantages of some local specialisation in crops other than cereals were recognising that the counties where extensive pastures had been created were in fact putting their land to its optimum use. The greatest benefit, suggested a Commons' speech in 1607, would be

> by grazing, to which their Soil is more fit than other counties.

To such men the former legislators had "o'erslipped" in ordaining perpetual tillage.

The other school of thought would have been less outraged had the balance been unequivocally in favour of grass. We may suggest that they were outraged simply because the Midlands were so good at both tasks; had there been poorer corn soils no tears would have been shed for the vanished ploughs. As well as having soils bearing the sweetest pastures, however, it was what Sandes had called[28]

> the best natural corn country.

The Midland villages which retained their ploughs and their open fields demonstrate that this was not altogether a false view: yet the pastures of the deserted villages show that it was not altogether the correct view.

The delicacy of the balance is also illustrated by the subsequent land-use of those parts of Norfolk, Lincolnshire and the East Riding which went down to grass at this time. They are the very areas which in the nineteen-thirties the Land Utilisation Survey could map as corn-growing land *par excellence*. If the Land Utilisation Survey's map of permanent grassland in 1931–38 is studied, the absence of shading from north Suffolk, Norfolk, Lincolnshire and the East Riding is striking.[29] These very years marked a low-water mark in the demand for English corn, but even in such unfavourable conditions these areas maintained tillage—and yet they were the very areas which we have described as being subject to conversion to pasture even earlier than the Inner Midlands! How was this? Had pasture been reconverted at some point after 1600?

Although these counties had not passed over entirely to grass in the early enclosures, the course of the eighteenth and nineteenth centuries saw much old-enclosed pasture reconverted to corn. This was partly made possible by improved techniques, but these could not have made cornland out of what Arthur Young had called "rich grazing lands . . . the glory of Lincolnshire", were not the balance between the two alternative land-uses as narrow as we have suggested. These lands, says the Land Utilisation report, "are now the finest arable in Britain", and the comparison with Arthur Young's phrase underlines our argument.

The same cycle had been seen in the Wolds of Yorkshire: arable in the fourteenth century; converted to grass in the fifteenth and sixteenth; brought back into the first rank of arable by the reorganisation of tenure and the technical improvements of the Sykes family, whose Sir Tatton stands on his column near Sledmere, surveying a landscape which has seen in turn the victories of plough, sheep and plough.[30]

The Land Utilisation Survey's map of permanent grassland in 1931–38 shows that there has not been the same reconversion to arable in the Midlands which we found in the Eastern Margin. Neither in the nineteenth nor twentieth century were the Inner Midlands the "finest arable in Britain". They were the grassy Shires, the counties of the Leicester Sheep and the Pytchley Hunt.

Although the balance here was tilted to grass, there was still enough of the old fickle ambiguity to make it possible for the type of sharp contrast to exist which we described at Whitchurch, where open fields survived alongside Tudor-made pastures. Earlier, we ascribed these survivals partly to the tenacity of small-property owners whose ancestors had weathered the dangerous days of sheep-depopulations, and who could not be bought out or evicted. Due weight must be given to this non-physical, adventitious factor in explaining the patchwork pattern of Fig. 11 or Fig. 12. Yet the survival of the two uses for land, side by side, must imply that the balance was still fickle. There is no evidence that those who held on to arable, even to open-field arable, were suffering a martyrdom of low incomes in the eighteenth century for their devotion to the Old Cause of the plough. The "maintenance of tillage" was no longer the result of

Acts of Parliament to that end and with that title. The satisfactory incomes from tillage compared with pasture were a more effective preservative of the traditional forms. Grazier and husbandman could face each other in south Leicestershire or south Warwickshire and say, as Burton had said a century earlier,

> great delight and profit either way.

7

We have spoken of districts where the balance was narrowly poised, and of districts where the balance was firmly set towards grazing. What, finally, of districts where the balance was firmly set towards corn, so firmly that the depopulating enclosures passed them by? There is in fact one area of immunity which we have not discussed fully. This immunity was conferred not by stubborn freeholders or by woodlands and orchards. It seems to have been an immunity by sheer excellence of corn-ground. It was found in the reclaimed marshland of the Eastern Margin and the fringes of higher ground at the edge.

In Lincolnshire, Cambridgeshire and the East Riding there are whole wapentakes or hundreds which consist of fenland or reclaimed fenland. When the casualty rate for villages, wapentake by wapentake, is examined the fenlands fail to yield a single deserted village. This is as true of the Ouse and Derwent wapentakes of the East Riding as the parts of Holland in Lincolnshire, as true of north Cambridgeshire as it is true of West Norfolk.

This immunity was almost entirely physical in origin. On the one hand the reclaimed alluvial soils were fertile in corn, and this shows in their high poll-tax density and their high tax quotas in 1334. Late to be settled, they were populous village communities, and we shall see in the next section that sheer numbers conveyed something of an immunity. Topographers did not praise these lands for being as good for wheat as sheep. The balance of advantage was firmly towards wheat, and for those who wanted to graze sheep there were always the wetter marshland fringes on which the fenland villages intercommoned, so that these communities were able to have the best of both worlds, the arable and the pastoral. Yet each knew its place, and there was no suppressed movement to turn the alluvial cornlands over to grass.

Almost paradoxically there was also a high rate of survival of cornfields in the Margin counties of the west and south, the old-enclosed districts. In these counties the area under corn was initially small, but it does not seem to have contracted in the period 1450–1550. In these counties corn and fruit, sheep and kine, grass and timber grew side by side. It does not seem to have been the efficiency and cheapness of corn-growing which preserved it, so much as the nature of the company it kept, the mixed farming and the immunity which came from already-old enclosure. The countryside of orchards, timber and grass had already had an opportunity to cast off its open fields and decide how it would allocate its scarce resources of man-power and cleared land. The decision it had made was not one which gave a very substantial place to corn, but it did give a minor place to arable and nothing that happened while the Midlands were being depopulated seems to have made the counties of the Margin regret their decision or change their mind.

8

Our final sections must examine the lost villages in relation to their neighbours, but from a different standpoint. How did the villages which were later to be depopulated compare with their neighbours in size during the fourteenth century? Were they significantly smaller even a century before destruction? The answer must be an emphatic, yes. Were they pygmies? The answer must be equally emphatically, no. Were they brought down to this relative smallness by the visitation of the fourteenth-century pestilences? This is what Mr. Trevor-Roper seems to have misread[31] into Dr. Hoskins' Leicestershire evidence . . .

> decline through plague in the fourteenth century followed by extinction through enclosure.

In fact the figures quoted by Dr. Hoskins do not bear this interpretation, and Dr. Hoskins does not so interpret them. The statistics set out in the Tables below show that these villages were already smaller than their neighbours before the first visitation by the plague.

We must first show how these conclusions are reached and then examine their implication. Our first need is for some measure by which we can set village against village at some point earlier than the beginning of the fifteenth century, preferably earlier than the Black Death of 1349.

If we require comparability over a wide area there are only two measures of relative size which we can employ for medieval villages, and neither of these is without its imperfections.

When the central government in the Middle Ages organised a counting of heads it was for taxation; there was no census for its own sake, and the poll tax of 1377 is a very weak substitute for a census. It excluded all those who were less than fourteen years old, and any others above that age who managed to escape the collectors' notice.

We must assume that the proportion of villagers under fourteen years of age did not differ greatly from village to village. We must also assume that the degree of evasion was roughly the same in different villages. Only after these two assumptions can we legitimately compare one poll tax receipt with another and say that we are comparing relative sizes. Even then, we must use only the information from 1377. The information from the poll taxes of 1379 and 1381 is useful enough in establishing that a village had a minimum number of people, but the degree of evasion was so great and so different in different places that it would be hopeless to use these poll taxes for comparisons between villages.[32]

One other measure also derives from taxation and from lists which we have already met in another connection, the lists of village quotas to the subsidy of 1334. These quotas are sums of money. They do not directly number heads. The assumptions we have to make if we wish to use them for inter-village comparisons are more serious than the assumptions when we use the poll tax. The principal assumption is that the lay tax had some relation to the real capacity of the village to pay taxation. It will be remembered that this was the avowed purpose of the 1334 revision, but since the sum paid in 1332 formed a minimum for any village's quota there could have been places whose real relative capacity was already below the sum of 1332 and so of that actually fixed in 1334. That danger does not seem to be great when we find that nearly every vill was scaled upwards from the 1332 level, and not merely by a nominal halfpenny or penny. The seven individuals who were taxed under the old system on their moveable property in the lost Wilstrop[33] in 1332 paid 12*s*. But in 1334 the new assessment for the village was 17*s*.

A second assumption which we must make is that the 1334 quota was based on the expectation that everyone would be contributing towards it, that is, that it does represent the real taxable capacity not of a small group of wealthy people, but of the others who contributed some share, if a small one, and that when the quota was low it represented a poor village.

We cannot be certain that a whole village did contribute towards its tax quota. All we can say is that certain petitions for tax relief after hardships do speak as if everyone paid. In 1347 the village of Hardwick, Oxfordshire, pleaded that there were only nine people left in the vill to bear the standard quota of 49*s*. 11*d*. If this was not reduced, they said, no one would be able to stay in the settlement.[34] When the houses of 23 villeins were destroyed by fire in the Lincolnshire village of Bloxham only five remained, and their petition[35] argued that, although they had not lost their houses, they were in no position *between them* to pay the full village quota, which was 50*s*.

When we come to the more general reliefs of 1352–54 and of 1433 onwards, they always speak of the general inability of a village to pay, and not of the inability of a small part of the villagers.

A third assumption is that the capacity of a village to pay had some connection with its prosperity, other than a prosperity rising only out of sheep pastures. The 1334 figures would be useless to us if high tax payments represented only the wealth of a few occupied in grazing, or if a high tax quota came from a very tiny community actively pursuing some very profitable craft which made them wealthy and taxable. But where poll tax figures survive from 1377 we can examine those and make certain that the prosperous place in 1334 was not relatively small. Such a comparison favours our case, since in the intervening years there had been a considerable general fall in population, and a village with forty poll tax payers in 1377 can reasonably be expected to have been able to furnish at least another ten contributors to the subsidy of 1334. To some measure the lists of names of those who were wealthy enough to pay tax in 1327 and 1332 afford another check. Short as these are, they do give some guarantee that a prosperous village was not prosperous by one or two men.

If we think these assumptions for 1334 too venturesome, then we can abandon the concept of size and speak only of "prosperity". In that case we compare place with place in 1334, and place with place in 1377, but make no attempt to relate the village's tax quota of 1334 with its poll tax figures in 1377. In fact, the correlation between the 1334 sums and the 1377 numbers is very high for certain counties, Lincolnshire and the East Riding in particular.

The simplest comparison is between the average tax quota of *all* the village assessments in a county and the average tax quota at which the to-be-lost villages were assessed. This is a crude comparison, but it is useful for establishing a starting point, and it has been done for 14 counties in Table 7. For each county the entry under "*A*" gives an average for *all* villages; that under "*B*" for whatever lost villages there were in that county; and under "*C*" we have *B* expressed as a percentage of *A*. This figure enables us to see at a glance the relative position of the lost villages in 1334 and in 1377.

The information for 1334 is fuller than for 1377. This is solely due to the high proportion of poll tax receipts which have perished. Where we have both 1334 and 1377 figures it will be seen that they both point in the same direction.[36]

TABLE 7

COMPARISONS OF TO-BE-LOST VILLAGES AND NEIGHBOURS BY AVERAGE SIZE OF 1334 AND 1377 TAX PAYMENTS

County	*1334 Tax Quotas*			*1377 Taxpayers*		
	All vills. A	*Lost vills.* B	*B as % of A* C	*All vills.* A	*Lost vills.* B	*B as % of A* C
WARWICKSHIRE	54*s.*	34*s.*	63	not extant		
BUCKINGHAMSHIRE	74*s.*	44*s.*	59	not complete		
NORTHAMPTONSHIRE	98*s.*	49*s.*	50	140	64	46
OXFORDSHIRE	76*s.*	45*s.*	60	76	37	49
NOTTINGHAMSHIRE	23*s.*	27*s.*	117	not complete		
LEICESTERSHIRE	47*s.*	26*s.*	55	99	59	59
YORKSHIRE:						
East Riding	47*s.*	28*s.*	58	100	48	48
West Riding	27*s.*	15*s.*	55	67	33	50
North Riding	25*s.*	17*s.*	68	62	34	55
LINCOLNSHIRE:						
Kesteven	79*s.*	38*s.*	49			
Lindsey, W.R.	57*s.*	36*s.*	63	81	31	38
Lindsey, N.R.	73*s.*	18*s.*	24			
Lindsey, S.R.	60*s.*	30*s.*	50	103	40	39
RUTLAND	47*s.*	24*s.*	50	99	68	68
HUNTINGDONSHIRE (Excluding fens)	96*s.*	57*s.*	58			
CAMBRIDGESHIRE (Excluding fens)	110*s.*	72*s.*	65	160	83	52
ISLE OF WIGHT	61*s.*	32*s.*	53	not extant		

Such are the measures by which the comparisons set out in Tables 7–10 have been made. No other such relevant measure, whether it be manorial incomes or feudal assessments, is available for country-wide comparisons once we pass away from Domesday Book. Sources like the Hundred Rolls or the valuations of extents which promise well at first sight soon prove to be useless through incomparability of the material which they present or the extreme unevenness of their survival.

When we compare village with neighbour it is important to compare like with like. It would be useless to compare the tax paid by a small vill in Sherwood or Arden with that paid by a fenland community. If there were lost villages in the Fens we should only want to see how they compared with other Fenland villages and not with villages on the Border. On the other hand comparisons of this kind gain statistical security the larger the sample, and in general the size of the sample taken for comparison in Table 7 is a whole county or Riding.

TABLE 8

COMPARISONS OF TO-BE-LOST VILLAGES AND NEIGHBOURS BY AVERAGE SIZE OF 1334 AND 1377 TAX ASSESSMENTS. DISTRICTS OF THE EAST RIDING

Districts	1334 *Tax Quotas*			1377 *Taxpayers*		
	All vills A	*Lost vills* B	*B as % of A* C	*All vills* A	*Lost vills* B	*B as % of A* C
HOLDERNESS	44*s.*	23*s.*	52	110	56	51
HARTHILL	54*s.*	40*s.*	74	109	46	42
HOWDENSHIRE	45*s.*	24*s.*	53	not extant		
BUCKROSE	33*s.*	21*s.*	64	74	42	56
DICKERING	46*s.*	21*s.*	46	not extant		
Whole county	47*s.*	28*s.*	58	100	48	48

(Holderness comprises the plain of the east coast: Howdenshire is in the low river-side plain between Howden and the Derwent; Harthill lies on the western slopes of the Wolds; Dickering and Buckrose lie largely on the slopes and crown of the northern and eastern Wolds.)

These calculations treat the county as a proper unit to use in comparisons. Would it give a greatly different result if we took a more local unit of comparison, such as the parishes immediately contiguous to a lost village or the parishes within a five-mile radius?

Had the lost villages been exclusively concentrated in areas of a particular soil, drainage or altitude it would have been improper to compare them with other villages from all over a county within which quite different conditions might operate. As we have already seen, even in Lincolnshire and

TABLE 9

COMPARISON OF TO-BE-LOST VILLAGES AND NEIGHBOURS, DISTRICTS OF NORFOLK, BY AVERAGE SIZE OF 1334 TAX QUOTAS

Hundred (i.e. district)	*Average tax quota of lost villages (A)*	*Average tax quota of other villages (B)*	*A as percentage of B (C)*
BLOFIELD	—	70s.	—
EYNSFORD	—	92s.	—
N. ERPINGHAM	—	65s.	—
HAPPING	—	112s.	—
TAVERHAM	—	51s.	—
WILSHAM	—	78s.	—
LODDON	—	73s.	—
KNAVERING	—	81s.	—
DIPWADE	—	91s.	—
MINSTEAD	—	78s.	—
ERSHAM	—	119s.	—
TUNSTEAD	—	100s.	—
BRECKLAND:[1]			
Grimshoe	48s.	143s.	33
Guiltcross	55s.	85s.	68
Shropham	56s.	105s.	52
South Greenhoe	77s.	141s.	54
GOODSANDS:[2]			
Brothercross	62s.	104s.	59
Smithden	51s.	191s.	26
North Greenhoe	67s.	126s.	52
Gallow	38s.	105s.	36
PART GREENSAND, PART MARSHLANDS:			
Freebridge	157s.	267s.	58
Clacklose	30s.	149s.	20
CENTRAL, SOUTH AND EAST			
West Flegg	30s.	110s.	27
Diss	24s.	57s.	43
Humbleyard	32s.	52s.	61
East Flegg	40s.	128s.	31
Launditch	36s.	97s.	37
Forhoe	29s.	74s.	39
Wayland	60s.	118s.	51
Holt	36s.	86s.	42
Mitford	70s.	100s.	70
South Erpingham	39s.	70s.	56

[1] Unfertile and marginal sandy areas.
[2] A name given by Young to the better quality "improvable" sands.

the East Riding (where the local concentration of lost villages is most marked) the lost villages are dispersed, and in other counties the dispersal is very wide. Even where there is local concentration there are surviving villages of normal size still standing at the side of the lost villages.

We may test this argument by taking the figures just given for the East Riding and making the same calculations in Table 7 not for the county but for the wapentakes. It will be seen that the more local comparisons, where the wapentake units have more homogeneous conditions of soil, slope and drainage, do not differ fundamentally from the county figures (Table 8).

It will be seen that there was a greater range of relative size for the lost villages in Lincolnshire (24% to 63%) than in the East Riding (42% to 74%), and Table 9 from Norfolk shows that the total range there was even greater. We have lost villages paying 20% of their neighbours' tax, and lost villages paying 70%, but it will also be noticed that no simple connection between the soil regions and this range is apparent.

Table 9 is taken from Mr. K. J. Allison's study,[37] and it will be noted that his basis of calculations is slightly different from that in the previous Tables: he is comparing the lost (*A*) with the non-lost (*B*) and not (as above) with *all* villages in a given area. Had he adopted the other standard of comparison his average tax (*B*) would be rather lower, and his percentages in (*C*) all rather higher. In twelve Norfolk hundreds there are no lost villages with separate tax quotas.

9

Another method of comparison avoids some of the dangers in comparing averages. The average tax payment or poll tax number in Table 7 may conceal a wide range of actual sizes, and Table 10 (with 17 and 18 in the Appendix) may serve two purposes. They will show what range of size existed in both surviving and lost villages, and they will show how the majority of lost villages fall into the smaller-sized groups.

To construct Tables 10 and 18 all the surviving poll tax receipts for a county or Riding have been examined and the numbers of taxpayers extracted. These villages have then been divided up into groups according to the number of taxpayers. The lowest group had from 0 to 10 taxpayers, the next had from 11 to 20, and so on. The figures shown in the Table give the *proportion of villages* in each of these size-groups. Thus a county of predominantly small villages might be expected to have a high percentage of its villages falling in the first few groups; while a county with large villages will have high percentages spread over the later groups in the Table. The actual number of villages in each county which have left surviving evidence is given in the last line. It is unfortunate that the Midland counties have fewer extant poll tax receipts than the northern and eastern counties, but the counties concerned give information from 1,698 villages, 157 of which have been depopulated.

The poll tax receipts have not survived in sufficient numbers for us to be able to construct similar tables for Warwickshire or Buckinghamshire in 1377. These two counties and others are included in Table 17 which uses the tax quotas of 1334 in the same way, breaking them down into size-ranges of 10*s.* and then counting the number of villages in each of these ranges.

Since the Subsidy Rolls are available for almost every county, we are able to cover all those areas where depopulation was serious, and contrast the experience of the lost village with the general experience of the county. For this Table the tax quotas for 4,231 surviving villages and 350 lost villages have been extracted from the rolls.

These Tables show beyond doubt that the deserted villages were commonly drawn from among those which were already in 1334 and 1377 significantly smaller than the run of their neighbours. To take two examples by way of interpreting the Table: in the West Riding one-third of all the villages later to be depopulated had between eleven and twenty taxpayers in 1377; but only one-thirtieth of the general run of villages fell within a category so small as this; in Warwickshire only 17% of the lost villages paid more than 50*s.* tax in

1334, while the villages of the county taken as a whole had 36% of their number assessed at that sum or more.

Whichever county we look at, the story is the same: and it seems equally true on either side of the Black Death. Had we only the 1377 figures, we might attribute the relative smallness of the lost villages to the plagues; but their tax quotas exhibit the same relative smallness fifteen years before the Great Pestilence.

TABLE 10

RANGE OF SIZE OF 379 LOST VILLAGES IN 1334, AND OF 156 LOST VILLAGES IN 1377

Percentage in each range	*1334 tax quotas (in shillings)*	*1377 tax payers (by number)*	*Percentage in each range*
7	0–10	0–10	4
23	11–20	11–20	19
22	21–30	21–30	13
17	31–40	31–40	21
8	41–50	41–50	11
8	51–60	51–60	9
5	61–70	61–70	7
3	71–80	71–80	7
2	81–90	81–90	3
2	91–100	91–100	3
0	101–110	101–110	0
1	111–120	111–120	1
0	121–130	121–130	0
1	131–140	131–140	0
0	141–150	141–150	1
1	over 150	over 150	1

Important as is this relative smallness in explaining why some villages were more vulnerable than others, it is necessary to stress again that it is relative smallness which we have discovered, and not empty villages. The to-be-lost villages were not pygmies. The depopulators were operating in villages which in terms of numbers were smaller, but not in villages already deserted.

It will be remembered that in Table 7 we showed that the average lost village in various counties had 31, 33, 34, 40, 48, 68 and 83 taxpayers. If we use Professor Russell's multiplier we have 46, 49, 51, 60, 72, 102 and 124 souls in these villages. This point is brought out in Table 10 which brings together the information which we have for 379 lost villages in 1334 and 156 lost villages in 1377. It will be seen that about half the lost villages had forty or fewer taxpayers, and about a quarter had more than sixty. In terms of 1334 tax quotas, about half the villages paid less than 30*s*., and about one quarter paid more than 50*s*.

To be so small was dangerous, but it was not fatal. Although smallness made for danger it was not a guarantee of destruction. A glance at Table 18 will remind us that 20% of *all* Yorkshire vills in 1377 had fewer than forty taxpayers, while 29% of *all* Oxfordshire vills fell within this danger zone, if it were a danger zone. Yet not all these small villages were depopulated. To explain why a particular village was destroyed we must do as we did in Chapter Six and pass from factors of opportunity to factors of will.

10

What is the implication of this relative smallness which we have discovered in a large percentage of the to-be-lost villages? The most obvious one is that in so far as numbers were ever an obstacle to the engrossings of holdings or to the eviction of villagers, then these villages were weak in that protection. When the would-be encloser began to think of building up a compact property he was faced in these villages with a smaller scale of necessary effort.

As long as we have villages with poll tax figures of one hundred upwards suffering depopulation it is clear that numbers in themselves were never a complete protection, any more than smallness was a guarantee of depopulation. Many villages which were relatively small in 1334 and 1377 have survived and flourish, even in the heart of the grassy shires. In Somerset, Wiltshire or Westmorland the relatively small size of villages did not place their inhabitants in danger of eviction.[37] The fatal thing was to be small and in the right place. What exactly was "the right place" we have discussed earlier in this chapter.

If the numbers which were reported evicted in the Returns

of 1517 are recalled, it will be seen that few of those total depopulations involved large numbers. Evictions of eighty or a hundred people were reported, but such cases are exceptional. The small scale of the final eviction may, of course, result from it being the last in a long series of called-in leases, bribes and threats; but the evidence in the Tables above suggests strongly that it often resulted from the fact that the community had been relatively small at least as far back as 1334.[38]

We have no early sixteenth-century case to show a village offering successful resistance to an attempt at total eviction. Had we such, we might arrive at a minimum number for successful physical opposition to the would-be grazier. There is, however, sufficient early sixteenth-century evidence of general violence and anti-enclosure rioting to make it likely that a substantial community could have put up a good fight, and that numbers were a deterrent to all but the most determined of enclosers.

Happy, no doubt, was the landlord with only a few freeholders between himself and his objective; happier was the man with only tenants-at-will to deal with, for time and patience would bring its reward; happiest of all was the man who found himself with no freeholders and very few tenants, for he might almost name the day when Will and Opportunity would coincide.

There is another significance which we may attach to the relative smallness of the less fortunate villages. We have seen that the relative smallness is found both in 1334 and 1377. The Black Death had only accentuated the smallness of some villages. It did not thrust many "average" villages down into the "small" class. The conditions making for smallness in these particular villages were older than the Plague.

The tax data from the years before 1334 are based on a quite different system of assessments, and this makes it difficult to see exactly how much further back this relative smallness goes. Were these particular villages relatively small even in the early thirteenth century? . . . even in the early twelfth?

Difficult and hazardous as are inter-village comparisons based on the 1334 material, the earlier tax lists pose even more questions than they answer. Even if the individuals whose tax payments they list had been truly taxed in proportion to their total capital (or income), what measure is this of the number or wealth of that vast majority of villagers with property too insignificant to be valued for taxation, consisting entirely of a small stock of goods officially exempt from valuation? When even large villages produce only three or four names of taxpayers in 1297 and 1301, what is the significance of a village with only one name?

Even these tax assessments only take us a relatively small step backwards in time from 1334. In some counties the 1334 subsidy is the first to have left surviving documents. In many counties the tax of 1297 is the first with surviving records, and this makes a step of only thirty-seven years back. What we need is a step of a century back to see whether the relative smallness of 1334 was a recent phenomenon.

It is generally accepted that for most of the thirteenth century there was land hunger and active colonisation, but recent studies—while differing on the exact time-table of retreat—are agreed that this movement had halted early in the fourteenth century, and that population was checked even before the Black Death administered its savage reduction.

If we had some standard by which we could make inter-village comparisons in the thirteenth century we might then see whether our relative smallness was a product of this retreat, and whether these villages were as populous as their neighbours before that date.

The relative size of medieval villages is a study almost large enough for another book. The figures in Table 18 (page 409) show that there was a range of size—represented in 1377 by from forty to eighty taxpayers—which reflects the most common experience. In the champine plains this was the community size which had been chosen, or accepted or fostered. It is difficult to know which. The size of a community depended in the last resort on the number of mouths which its fields could feed. The capacity of its fields to fulfil this obligation would depend on the area of the township or parish, and on the fertility of the soil within these bounds. The fertility of the soil in this country can vary quite considerably within a few miles, and no doubt this factor contributed something to the settlement pattern of large and small settlements intermingled within a county. But there was an adventitious factor which goes back to the Dark Ages. The site of a village had been chosen by settlers who had not the man-power or the will to exploit the whole of the land surrounding it. Probably not until the thirteenth century did the whole of a modern parish come under cultivation. The territorial limits of the village on the other hand—the parish or township boundary—had been agreed upon (or fought out) well before the Conquest, and many Anglo-Saxon charters have descriptions of boundaries which can be equated with the modern parish bounds.

The extent of a village's fields might, therefore, depend on how near another community had settled at the initial occupation, or on how near other later settlements were permitted. The creation of daughter-settlements in the immediate locality would be another factor which would eventually restrict the area of fields open for exploitation once land became scarce and men land-hungry.

This sketch of an argument which needs much fuller treatment may be sufficient to indicate that we cannot explain the relative smallness of one village wholly in terms of some unfavourable geographical factor. If this is so, then the explanation of why a particular village was a target for the depopulator will not always be the simple one: that it was smaller because its fields were marginal to corn. It will be that older, and often non-physical, factors had made for some villages being smaller than others, and that the smaller numbers presented in themselves a more favourable opportunity for enclosers. If small numbers were associated in a given village with common fields of small area, then the obstacles to enclosure were less formidable still.

11

Our general conclusion in an already long chapter must be brief. We have not found it difficult to locate and explain those districts where depopulation was rarely experienced. We have also found that a group of Inner Midland counties shared a common experience of considerable fifteenth and sixteenth century depopulation in their champine parishes. In the east and north we have found depopulation both earlier and later than in the Midlands, and there is much more evidence in these areas for depopulation linked to a general retreat from the lands marginal to medieval corn-growing. We found high immunity from depopulation in the fertile reclaimed marshlands which were supporting large populations in their villages in the late fourteenth century.

We have also noticed a characteristic intermingling of lost and surviving villages which makes it difficult to fasten on any broad geographical factor as a determinant of local susceptibility to the attentions of a would-be depopulator. Relative size has been shown to be a significant determinant, although this immediately poses another question: what made one medieval village smaller than its neighbour? Was it an old-established inferiority, or was it the product of the early fourteenth century? Was it related to a village having more fertile and easily-worked soils? Or to an initial choice of the site where the earlier settlers placed their first huts and fields?

Even relative smallness was not fatal, and even large villages occasionally fell to the depopulator. This emphasises the importance of the personality of the local landowner and the tenurial security of the local villagers; it also emphasises local variations in the degree of violence and disorder, under cover of which the depopulator might work unchallenged until Wolsey's Inquiry of 1517. We are in fact back, as we would be in the history of any surviving village, at multiple causation and local variety of experience. If this is a complex rather than a simple end to an investigation it has the advantage of being not unlike what we should expect from life itself.

PART THREE

A single chapter returns to the theme of the first Part, the villages as they now lie among the English countryside,

Chapter Eight

THE FINAL JOURNEY

> The winter wind flows like a sea over the upland pastures, flows indifferently through the broken casements of the squire's house, and over the bleached grass that covers the lost villages.
>
> W. G. Hoskins,
> *The Deserted Villages of Leicestershire.*

IN this short and final chapter the narrative returns to the first person singular. In the first section I should like to make my own assessment of the significant things which this study has brought to light, and thus to gather together the conclusions of the more technical chapters. In the second section I should like to abandon the discipline of counting and listing for the pleasure of recalling a few isolated incidents in the seven years during which my country journeys have been rather like those described by Oliver Goldsmith in the dedicatory letter which prefaces *The Deserted Village*:

> I have taken all possible pains in my country excursions for these four or five years to be certain of what I allege. Some of my friends think that the depopulation of villages does not exist, but I am myself satisfied.

I

When I first began to look for lost villages in the fields of Warwickshire my task was not to satisfy sceptics. The fact that depopulated villages did exist had been shown by Canon Foster more than twenty years earlier, and it was seven years since the trenches had been dug across the main street of Seacourt. It was more than twenty years since O. G. S. Crawford had photographed Gainsthorpe from the air, and Dr. Hoskins' study of the Leicestershire villages was just about to appear.

My first sight of a lost village was caught in the pastures of Bittesby, which is a Leicestershire parish. The discovery was accidental and it arose from an attempt to survey the ridge-and-furrow of the parish. The particular parish had been chosen for the simplest of reasons: it was the smallest I could find within walking distance of Rugby, and I was anxious to do a measured survey of the ridge-and-furrow in the whole of some parish. The survey of the fields brought Mr. Peter Ransom and myself with our measuring tapes to the site itself. I cannot remember clearly whether the significance of the earthworks then struck me, but I can recall describing them to Mr. Levi Fox who referred me to Dr. Hoskins' paper which had just appeared. I am probably not the first person to catch enthusiasm from Dr. Hoskins' writing, which so happily marries time and space, history and place. In my spare time from other work I set out to track down the lost villages of Warwickshire much as he had explored Leicestershire, and before I left the Midlands in 1948 I had prepared the list of sites which the Birmingham and Midland Archaeological Society has published in its *Transactions*.

The Warwickshire membranes of the 1517 Inquiry are fuller than those for Leicestershire, and I was able to search the air photographs of the county at the R.A.F. Print Library. Apart from adding the names and location of the sites of another county, this Warwickshire study did not take the subject much further than Canon Foster or Dr. Hoskins had already taken it. There were too few poll tax receipts extant to tempt me into any study of relative size and I was only vaguely aware of the significance of the lay subsidy figures.

Occasional visits to Northamptonshire, Buckinghamshire and Oxfordshire had shown me that the sites there would be as clear as those near Warwick and Leicester, and the published *Inquisitions* of 1517 and 1518 made it clear that the Midland counties would bear investigation on lines parallel to the Leicestershire and Warwickshire studies.

I went north in April 1948 to become a University teacher, and this book would have been impossible without the opportunities for work among documents and fields which the

University of Leeds afforded and encouraged. Indeed, only when it became apparent that the deserted village was a phenomenon not confined to the Midlands did this study pass out of the stage of being a collection of sites and occasions. Outside the Midland counties the 1517 Inquisition gave no hope that deserted village sites would be more than occasionally found. When they began to appear thick on the ground in all three Ridings of Yorkshire the whole horizon of the study was lifted. Not only did this mean that more sites had been found, but that the simple causation and time-table of Midland depopulation had to be measured and tested against evidence which derived from sources other than the Inquiry of 1517.

My survey of the Yorkshire sites was almost complete before I turned back to the other Midland counties. By this time I had learned to use the Lay Subsidy Rolls as a directory or register of fourteenth century vills from which to begin examining the modern maps, census returns and gazetteers. I was able to work over the air photographs in parallel with the other inquiries, and the assistance of students and friends made it possible to make trial excavations at four Yorkshire sites and to gratify the curiosity which had been aroused by a short excavation at Stretton Baskerville in my last winter in the Midlands.

The compilation of county lists for Northamptonshire, Oxfordshire, Buckinghamshire, Lincolnshire, Cambridgeshire, Nottinghamshire, Rutland, Huntingdonshire and Northumberland did more than add some two hundred new lost villages to my list. From these investigations significant detail began to accumulate to make the problem of causation and chronology one for urgent attention.

From this need arose the search through the Exchequer Memoranda Rolls to see exactly what followed from the Inquiry of 1517, and exactly what that Inquiry brought to light. This search produced more than the Tables in Chapter Four : it showed that the depopulating movement was coming to an end in the mid-sixteenth century and that significantly large areas (where I knew depopulated sites existed) were not visited in 1517 and reported upon. The first positive conclusion of this study, which no single county studies have been able to show, is the total extent of the movement, and the very different intensity with which it was felt in different counties, and in different parts of the same county.

The figures given in the last chapter have, I hope, rehabilitated the deserted village as something more than the product of the dreams of Tudor pamphleteers or Fabian reformers. They add to the fourteenth-century landscape of eleven counties nearly four hundred villages and many more hamlets. They add in many counties another one to every ten villages and hamlets which we see today. To the medieval landscape they add settlements, fields, villagers, churches, houses and streets. They make the fair field a little fuller of folk. They set down another community on the already rather crowded map to fill in that space or this. They do justice to the colonising movement which created the English villages, and they do justice to the effort of those who deliberately depopulated them; or to the forces which made for empty villages and pastures on which the grazier entered by default rather than by desire.

Once it was possible to say where depopulation was trivial and where it was intense, I could begin to show what geographical setting seems to have made the village most vulnerable and where, on the other hand, the environment seems to have made for immunity. The county distribution maps also emphasise that the classical landscape of the deserted village is one where the deserted sites are neighboured by existing villages and late-surviving open fields. Even in areas where there was a high percentage of depopulation the losses are rarely side-by-side. The men and the forces which destroyed villages did not sweep their victims off the board: they struck here and there.

The search among the Subsidy Rolls and poll tax receipts which produced the distribution figures also yielded data which lend themselves to a simple statistical treatment. As well as being able to speak of losses as a firm percentage of all villages, I am now able to speak with some assurance of the relative size of the lost villages and their neighbours.

The tables in Chapter Seven speak unequivocally: the victim was usually smaller than the survivor, generally—we may say—in 1377 a little over half the size. In 1334 the tax quotas tell very much the same story, and in general I am able to buttress the argument that the Black Death has been credited with more complete destructions than in fact it achieved. This case is perhaps the stronger for being associated with a number of proven examples of sites definitely abandoned at this period. I can afford to admit this as "exceptional" when there are so many poll tax receipts for substantial communities after the passing of the plagues; and when I can adduce the light reliefs from taxation allowed to the lost villages when in 1352–54 and in 1433 the "impoverished villages" of England were allocated their tax relief.

If we have been able to put a firm terminal date for serious depopulation in the mid-sixteenth century, the starting date is less certain. At the one end the study impinges on the villages destroyed by the Cistercian houses in the twelfth century and those "vills" in Domesday which even by the late thirteenth century were not taken as tax units by the Exchequer collectors. In the absence of much manorial material from lost villages, dating of destruction is difficult when the event came after 1377 and before 1488, the limiting date of the 1517 Inquiry. We must depend on hints from the fifteenth-century tax reliefs and on argument from the analogy of Warwickshire, where we have the unique contemporary list from the pen of John Rous. For only a handful of sites, the record of the union of parishes or a chance survival of a rental or cartulary provide a narrower limit within which to set the final death of the settlement.

The sixteenth-century legal proceedings and the contemporary evidence which we brought together in Chapters Three and Four suggest that the final evictions might themselves be only the last step, either in the retreat from an unwelcome margin or (much more commonly in the Midlands) in the advance of the ambitious grazier-landlord. We have tried to assess the calculations of profit and loss which might so move a man, and we have found nothing to make us doubt the contemporary belief that it was the superior profit from sheep over corn which acted as the stimulant. If grazing was the defensive answer of a few early fifteenth-century landlords with land on their hands, it is clear that the vast majority of the sites in the Inner Midland counties date from the period soon after 1450 when the grazier is taking aggressive steps to remove the villagers.

In some ways this study is the end of the beginning of lost village studies. With the area charted, it is now possible to begin a systematic examination of sites from an archaeological standpoint. There is a wide range of settlement shapes and situations available for excavation. The list in Chapter Ten names more than a thousand lost villages or hamlets. Medieval villages of substantial size lie unencumbered by any later accretions or disturbances, ready for those who would peel away the layers of settlement or lay bare the plan of houses and streets. In return for this gift, we may hope that archaeology will in its turn help us to narrow the date-limits within which the individual village fell. A task which local historians might well find profitable is the important contribution from local manuscript collections yet only partly known and indexed. Chapter Nine may assist as a starting-point here. Since the completion of this book the Deserted Medieval Villages Research Group has been founded to bring together the various specialisms impinging on the subject and particularly to carry out excavation. The Secretary is Mr. J. G. Hurst, an Assistant Inspector of Ancient Monuments.

Local investigators may also find the county lists which appear at pages 338 to 393 useful as another type of starting-point. They and the inquiring traveller will find grid-references to the 1-inch Ordnance maps, those indispensable tools in this inquiry. The skill and observation of these map-makers have shortened many journeys and indicated the need for many more. The dog-eared maps on my shelves remind me of how I once put them red and shining into my pocket or haversack on their first journey to a lost village.

2

What villages remain vividly in the memory of a traveller who has tried in his country excursions to be certain of what he alleged and to satisfy the double demands of his friends' and his own curiosity? What sites particularly repay a visit even by those with only a general curiosity and with very limited time?

The memories of exploration inevitably include disappointments as well as unexpected finds. It was pleasant to find the site of Old Arras on the air photograph when I was looking for evidence for the depopulated site of New Arras. It is disappointing when the gardens of a great house extend over the area where a village stood and effectively bar any further inquiry. Perhaps the loneliest of all sites, although very near to human habitation, is the site of Milton Abbas, so effectively replaced by a landscape-gardener's creation. In the vestry of the church, one August morning, I found a map of Milton Abbas before its destruction; and Hinderskelfe and Wotton Underwood have particularly firm places in my memory since they could be compared with maps made before the removal of the village. The late seventeenth-century map of Hinderskelfe was recovered one afternoon from among the estate plans in the strong room at Castle Howard; the early seventeenth-century map of Wotton was first shown me in a basement of the Aylesbury Museum by Dr. Mead on a Good Friday morning and compared with the modern ground plan that very afternoon.

Sites which have been built over by aerodromes or Nissen huts inevitably arouse the feeling of "I wish I had been there when they did it". Anyone who has dug excavation trenches will know the feeling of pleasure when you hear that someone else is doing the digging. I should like to have been at East Lilling when the foundations for the pylons were dug; I should like to have been at Astwick by Brackley when the farmer turned a bulldozer into an earthwork which was harbouring rabbits. From the archaeologist's standpoint my presence would not have made it any less a vandalism, but I might have recovered more pottery than I did from the surface after the grass had begun to grow again.

Pleasant as it would have been to travel with Dugdale or Thoroton when the sites were two or three centuries fresher, the modern traveller has the advantage of the air photograph, which under favourable conditions offers information about the village plan only equalled by a visit to the ruins in the months immediately following their destruction. From that time onwards a shroud has been cast over the site by grass and the weakness of men's memory: for many sites the air photograph has been the means of returning for a moment to some of the conditions of the sixteenth century.

The sites which I remember with affection will not always be those which I would recommend to a traveller or even to a student. It would be unnatural if I did not think of Bittesby with the nostalgic affection reserved for a first love, but the railway embankment which bisects it has removed or covered over the very centre of the village, and what one sees can only be half the area once covered with houses.

Whatborough, on the other hand, can be recommended for the most impersonal reasons. Its isolation and its hilltop setting make the desertion even more credible. There are lost village sites which it would be a pleasure to resettle, but Whatborough could only be recommended to those who like living with a wind fresh and uninterrupted from the Urals. The availability of the Elizabethan map of this site makes it unique, and it was a very pleasant afternoon when I first unrolled the photostat copy of the map I had seen at All Souls' and looked over a landscape which still bore many of the features noted by the surveyor three and a half centuries earlier.

Two sites compete for mention as most strikingly delineated in earthworks. My appreciation of them may in each case be conditioned by the devious routes by which they were reached. The two sites are Thorpe le Glebe in Nottinghamshire and Calcethorpe in Lincolnshire. Keith Allison and I came to Thorpe late in an autumn afternoon when dusk was already falling. We had stayed too long by the isolated church ruins of Kinoulton and Colston Basset. We were faced with two farms in the empty parish of Thorpe, either of which might have indicated the village, and we chose the wrong one to visit first. A cross-country scramble across darkening fields brought us at last to consolation. The earthworks, accentuated by the long shadows of the disappearing sun, seemed tremendous. Ploughmarks, fishponds, boundary-mounds . . . all were on a gargantuan scale.

I came to Calcethorpe when I was alone. It was a very hot summer afternoon. I had begun the day badly with a walk through waist-high corn sodden with dew and a long dull walk into Louth to catch a mid-day bus. Down a deeply-cut side-lane from the Louth–Market Rasen main road the heat was quite oppressive. From the depth of this lane the surface of fields seen through the hedge was set out sharply against the sky. A tune ran through my head, Britten's setting of

> mountains seem molehills and the ant
> appears a monstrous elephant.

Accentuated in this way the first appearance of hollow-ways and earthworks was unmistakable, and when I climbed up out of the lane and over the hedge I was looking at my first site in Lincolnshire which could hope to rival the Midland sites in clarity. No doubt my elation was increased by the knowledge that Canon Foster had not noted or described this village. The traveller who wishes to stuff himself on a diet of lost village followed by lost village could do no better than go to Calcethorpe. At its southern boundary lie South Cadeby and Grimblethorpe, not to speak of the shrunken Gayton-le-Wold and Biscathorpe. To the west are East and West Wykeham, sites which Canon Foster chose as the most perfect examples of Lincolnshire depopulation. A little to the north, but still within an afternoon's walk, are Great and Little Tows and the interesting earthworks that extend south and west of the present village of Kirmond le Mire.

3

My early journeys to lost village sites were made singly in week-ends and half-days snatched from other work. In the later stages I was lucky enough to find friends with cars who were willing to brave the green and muddy lanes by which lost villages are approached. In this way I was able to take in a whole county like Nottinghamshire in week-ends of intensive exploration prefaced by the work on documents and maps; in another tour, Philip Sheard's car found itself parked near all the principal sites in Canon Foster's Lincolnshire list and even breasting one of Dr. Hoskins' sites in north Leicestershire. On another afternoon between the sessions of the Economic History Society conference at Oxford, Lawrence Stone swept me out to Wretchwick and Walton.

In the summer of 1952, together with Clive Semple and Keith Allison (himself blooded in Norfolk lost villages), a ten-day tour of the southern counties enabled me to visit all the major sites south of the Thames and to catch my first glimpse of the Dorset and Hampshire lost villages which I had previously known only from books and documents. We were never able to arrange our itinerary so that camp was pitched on a lost village site: the nearest we came was an evening as guests at a camp where Brighton and Hove archaeologists were excavating. Sitting in the shadow of a late Bronze Age village we were able to hear Mr. E. W. Holden tell us about his preliminary excavations at the lost medieval village of Hangleton, and to watch jealously the sorting of pottery from a lost village of another age which we had had no part in finding.

The sites of the southern counties, although more scattered than their Midland and northern brothers, include some of the most pleasantly situated in the country. At Hartley Maudit in Hampshire a large village pond provides the foreground for the photographer's ideal site: the church standing isolated across the water with the empty site at its side.

At Newton in Dorset the Rev. H. B. Cowl was able to show us not only a lost village but a lost borough, and the next day we had the pleasant surprise of finding in the vestry of Milton Abbas church the map of the market-town before its destruction. We lunched late that day, but we were fired with greed: and by nightfall we had seen the foundations of the Norman cathedral on the abandoned site of Old Sarum.

(13) LITTLE COWDEN, YORKS., E.R.

(*left*) HILDERTHORPE, YORKS., E.R.

Cowden has been attacked both by sheep and erosion. The sea is now eating into the crofts on the right of the former main street. Twenty-four persons were reported evicted by St. Mary's Abbey, York, in 1517. Hilderthorpe was depopulated by the Priory of Bridlington, the adjacent parish. The suburbs of Bridlington are now repopulating it. The southern end of the Promenade can be seen, top-left.

Later in the week, not a hundred yards from the cars streaming to Beachy Head, we admired the pioneer zeal of the Sussex Archaeological Society in erecting a stone on the site of the church at Excete; the next day we walked the lost streets of the shrunken Winchelsea and at dusk were lost in the lanes between Rye and the ruined churches of Romney Marsh. Next morning in Rye there was a full-dress traffic census. "Where from?" asked the enumerator. We dared not tell him. "Where to?" he asked after we had foisted off the first question with some plausible untruth. "Canterbury", we answered cheerfully: for the first time for ten days our principal destination was a living place.

In July, 1953, while the page-proofs of this book were piling up at Leeds I was introduced to the sites of Norfolk and Suffolk, and saw for the first time the strange beauty of a ruined Norman church—such as Bawsey near King's Lynn—where the cornfields have returned up to the very walls, a tribute to the return of the plough where it once retreated.

It is not necessary to take to ten days' car and camping to view lost village sites. For those who seek one comfortably near a town, there is the Midland Red Bus which will take them very near the Leicestershire "Town of Hamilton" as the 1-inch map styles it. Those who go to the south end of Bridlington promenade have only a few yards before they see the site of Hilderthorpe in the fields (Plate 13).

Those who demand a journey no more strenuous than to a railway station may hope that the level-crossing on the Watling Street holds up the Rugby to Leicester train (as it sometimes does). They will then be able to look down from the grandstand of the railway embankment to the earthworks at Cestersover. The Marylebone to Manchester train goes a little faster and has no trouble with level-crossing gates near Charwelton in Northamptonshire, but the traveller who has been forewarned can take up a corridor stance and see the isolated church and the deserted village which John Rous described 450 years ago.

For motorists there is the site of Steeton which lies only half a mile from the busy Leeds–York main road; or Stretton Baskerville lying just off the A5 with the scars of digging hardly healed. Yet the travellers who reach the sites so easily will be less fortunate than those who tread the more difficult roads of approach: they will miss much of the excitement of first seeing the tell-tale mounds in the distance; and they will miss the heightening of excitement which comes with the over-grown and thorny footpaths which were invoked in the first paragraph of this book. A few sites may be brash enough to stand near a public highway, but this is dangerous for a lost village wishing to preserve its distinctiveness. With ribbon-development, petrol-stations and road-houses it may find itself no longer the deserted village, regretfully expelled from that select company whose existence is the token of such human ambition and despair.

PART FOUR

IN the two chapters of this Part assistance is offered to those who wish to know about the sites in their own locality or to pursue further information about these sites for themselves. Chapter Nine is a commentary on the principal documentary sources with illustrative quotations. Chapter Ten is a list of sites arranged in alphabetical order of counties.

Chapter Nine

THE SEARCH FOR THE LOST VILLAGE

First ye shall enquire what towns, villages and hamlets have been decayed . . .

Instructions to the Commission of 1548.

I

THIS chapter is concerned with method. It tries to answer the questions: How may we hope to discover whether there are any deserted villages in a given district, and if there are, where may they be found?

It might seem possible to answer these questions by prescribing a visit on foot to every field in the district, watching for the characteristic earthworks of streets and houses. Even this would be unlikely to reveal every site, particularly in districts where considerable ploughing has taken place in the last century; but it would reveal the majority. The ploughed-out sites might become visible in air photographs, and the air photograph would considerably shorten the journey from field to field in search of the other sites. In fact, neither of these approaches is likely to prove completely satisfactory: there is not a complete set of air photographs of every field taken under the best conditions for archaeological inspection; and a journey on foot from field to field would greatly limit the area which could be inspected even by an inquirer with infinite leisure.

The area of inquiry can be considerably narrowed by the use of documentary sources, and it is with these sources that this chapter will be principally concerned. We can conveniently classify our material into two groups: documents which prove that a village community existed, with information about its size and appearance in the days before its destruction; and documents which provide evidence of the destruction either from contemporary accounts or from subsequent repercussions of depopulation.

In a sense, a complete village history of each deserted site is necessary, and for that history there is hardly a class of document in public or private archives which might not be relevant. It is no part of our purpose to provide a handbook to the materials for village history. But among these records there are some which have the advantage of being succinct and of covering a wide area, so that lists of villages flourishing at points in the past can be drawn up, and village compared with village: such are the tax records. Others—such as the manorial documents—will have the advantage of descriptive matter which enables us to add flesh and blood to a village which would otherwise be the rather abstract notion of a community of taxpayers. In the same way any medieval records of land being sold or transferred could be expected to include land sold and transferred in deserted villages before their depopulation, and since this type of record has been much used by genealogists in their inquiries we shall find much of it already printed and indexed for easy handling. In the records of the law-courts we shall find evidence of the names and occupations of the depopulators. In maps, plans and surveys we shall hope to find how the site of the deserted village looked to those who were two or three centuries nearer the event than we are.

In order to avoid a dull catalogue of documents which could be found useful we shall try and use actual examples. We shall take documents (both printed and manuscript) which have helped in identifying or establishing deserted sites. This will also enable us to amplify the detail of some of the major sites which can only be briefly listed in Chapter Ten.

2

It is possible that somewhere in the country there is a deserted village whose bounds were described in an Anglo-Saxon land-charter, but I have not myself met with one.

An early list of customs and obligations in the lost Over Winchendon, Bucks., was thought to be pre-Conquest by the editor of the St. Frideswide's Cartulary.[1] In it, 36 tenants and six cottagers were named. However, it is with Domesday Book that the general search can begin in earnest. Domesday Book is accessible enough in print and many of the *Victoria County History* volumes have maps giving the location of places mentioned in the Book. Some caution may be necessary with the identification of places with very common names—Aston, Preston, Newton—but the publication of the Place-Name Society's county volumes has made it possible to check the *VCH.* identifications, and the *Domesday Geography* of Professor H. C. Darby will no doubt carry us further towards accuracy.

Not every place named in Domesday need have been a substantial settlement. Only in the plains can we assume that a Domesday "vill" was a nucleated settlement. But when a Domesday vill can be linked with positive evidence for a village community at a later date the antiquity of that settlement does not seem to be questionable. In no case have we assumed that the naming of a vill in Domesday, unsupported by any later reference, is proof that there was a depopulation in the fifteenth century.

We may take a small area of the English plain and see what proportion of Domesday vills is no longer with us. The Ainsty stretched from the gates of York to the bridge at Tadcaster, an area bounded by the rivers Aire, Ouse and Nidd. In Domesday Book it contained 37 vills. But only 27 of these are now represented by village communities.

In the Midlands we could take villages mentioned in 1086 and see whether they are assessed in the Hundred Rolls of 1279, but the rolls for Yorkshire have not survived, and we have no comparable list of villages until the great feudal survey of 1284–85, Kirkby's Inquest. That year in the Ainsty, 37 vills had their tenures described. The editor of Kirkby's Inquest was an acute topographer who made good use of the first edition of the Ordnance Survey 6-inch sheets which were just becoming available when the Surtees Society[2] published his work in 1867. In his footnotes he showed that of the 37 vills seven could no longer be found on the map as settlements. He passed over two others, Steeton and Easedike, which have also been depopulated.

In the same volume Skaife printed the *Nomina Villarum* of 1316, and this list of vills was published for all English counties in the five volumes of *Feudal Aids*.[3] The occasion of the *Nomina* was the grant which the Parliament of Lincoln had made of a foot-soldier from every vill (except boroughs and royal demesne). We may take it for granted that the naming of a township in this list is evidence that a township did exist. Indeed in some counties the *Nomina* expressly separated groups of places which were being taken as one for normal Exchequer purposes, and wrote against them: *ii villae*.

The use of Domesday Book, Kirkby's Inquest and the *Nomina Villarum* is no more than a simple checking of a register to see whether a vill is absent or present. We must turn now to sources which certainly have this same "register" utility for our inquiry, but which also afford important opportunities for descriptive and quantitative assessments (Table 16, page 404).

The Hundred Rolls of 1279 were not a census: they were concerned with tenure and tenants. They cannot help us to establish the absolute size of a village in 1279, but they do enable us to establish that a village had a minimum number of inhabitants and a manorial organisation. Exactly the same comparison with 1279 was made by John Rous of Warwick to point his description of Warwickshire depopulation; Dugdale used the rolls for the same purpose; and they were known to the author of the *Discourse*, who looked back from 1548 to the year 1279 to see

> such abundance of towns parishes and houses as have been in the time of King Edward the First which the survey of the Realm then made will plainly declare.[4]

The Warwickshire part of the rolls has yet to be published, but Dr. R. H. Hilton tells me that (without allowing for the possibility of some double-counting) there were thirty-one manorial tenants in the lost Walton D'Eivil, forty-seven in the lost Fulready and twenty-two in the lost Thornton.

In Buckinghamshire, Tyringham was a village whose name was often heard in Tudor enclosure proceedings. In 1279 there were twenty-seven villein holdings and nine free tenants. In demesne were 350 acres and in villeinage, 250. The peasants cultivating such an area were no hamlet community. In Oxfordshire was the lost Clare in Pyrton, with seventeen tenants named in 1279, while at Gatehampton by Goring there were five *servi* and *custumarii*. At Golder hamlet there were nine demesne virgates and thirteen free tenants: Golder is now one house.[5]

3

In the years between the Hundred Rolls of 1279 and the *Nomina Villarum* of 1316 the number of extant local tax records begins to increase. We can use these as a form of register in which to mark villages as present or absent at a particular date; and we can also use them to obtain some idea of the relative size of the villages which were later to be lost and those which were to survive.

Since these tax records figure so much in the argument we must first say a little about their date and nature. The most useful tax for leaving information behind it was that known to contemporaries as the Lay Subsidy. The word "subsidy" did not carry its modern sense of a payment by a government to relieve the lot of its citizens. It was exactly the opposite. It was a payment in aid (subsidium) of the governmental expenses by those lay members of the community who were wealthy enough to make assessing and collecting worth while.

The Lay Subsidies, up to and including 1332, were granted to the King on the basis of an assessment of personal property. The tax collectors compiled lists of individuals and the value (sometimes also the description) of their movable property. The rolls were made up by vills and the names of the vills boldly written as headings. These lists are not complete lists of villagers, since only those with sufficient property of a particular kind were liable to be assessed.[6] In 1332 in the lost East Tanfield (N.R. Yorks) there were fourteen persons taxed, whose assessments totalled 33*s*. 4*d*. We can do no more than say that there were at least fourteen people substantial enough to pay the subsidy in 1332: it is perhaps permissible to compare the figures with neighbours' figures, and add that from eight to fourteen taxpayers was the local range, and that 33*s*. 4*d*. is more than the local average.[7]

In the West Riding the village of Givendale stands next to the village of Sharow in an earlier tax list, that of 1297. At Sharow the tax paid was 32*s*. 1½*d*.; at Givendale 32*s*. 0½*d*. The number of taxpayers at Sharow was eleven, at Givendale, eight. The possessions of Givendale men which were taxed included ten plough-oxen, eight and a half quarters of fine wheat, eighteen and a half of ordinary wheat, ten and a half of barley and twenty-nine and a half of oats. There was a small flock of fifty-seven sheep. This was clearly a village where the plough still sped. Only three of the twenty-nine villages within the Liberty of Ripon paid more tax; but in 1801, when the population of Sharow was 106, the census enumerator had only one house to visit in the township of Givendale.[8]

For the tax of 1301 we do not have a list of the possessions taxed, but merely a statement of the value of the goods *in toto*. In the North Riding of Yorkshire fourteen people paid tax at the Tees-side village of Barforth, whose ruined chapel and dovecote can still be seen. This sum was a quarter of that paid by the town of Richmond.[9] The deserted site was nick-named "Old Richmond" in the eighteenth century, and the legend ran that this had been the former site of Richmond with a tunnel connecting them. The story was untrue, but like a true myth it carried two seeds of truth. The place had once been a substantial village for which we are lucky to have a long series of family charters and deeds; while the building of Richmond after the Conquest seems to have been responsible for the disappearance of the vill of Hindrelac, certainly as a name, possibly as a settlement.

The tax of 1332 was the last of the medieval subsidies to yield a list of names. The low yield for that year induced the King to bargain with the townships for a single sum to be paid by each community, leaving the township to arrange how that sum was distributed among the inhabitants. The only proviso made was that the quota should be at least that of 1332. Comparison of the 1332 and 1334 payments shows that the 1334 village quota represents the personal assessments of the richer villagers in 1332 adjusted upwards to give a village quota which the village and its neighbours agreed was not unreasonable. These village assessments remained basically unaltered until the sixteenth century: when more money was needed, then each village simply paid two, three, four or five times their quota. It was the principle familiar to us as the rateable value of a house determining the relative share of tax which an individual unit bears towards the general rate fund.

It is unlikely that those men from township and borough who bargained with the royal assessors had any idea that the quota was to remain in force for more than three centuries. The royal instructions seem to have been based upon a wish to arrive at a sum which would satisfy both parties; the Exchequer by making sure that any quota would exceed the yield of 1332; and the taxpaying community by bringing them into the making of the bargain. This was a novel step, different from the older technique of assessing the value of individuals' moveable property by a local jury.

> The tax of 1332, and to a lesser extent that of 1334, may serve the economic historian as a very fair index of the prosperity of the nation and of sections of it at that time

wrote Charles Johnson,[10] but it will be our assumption that the 1334 figures are a slightly better guide to the relative prosperity of villages.

Not all counties have surviving tax lists for the years 1332 or 1334, but since the quota remained unchanged for more than a century the 1334 quota may be taken from later Lay Subsidy Rolls. These rolls, with their neat lists of villages arranged by hundreds and wapentakes, are indispensable in the search for lost villages. They are easily read, and the comparison of the list of villages with those on the 1-inch map is one of the most direct routes to a first list of suspects.

When we discussed the occasions of depopulation in

Chapter Five we utilised the Lay Subsidy Rolls in further ways: we examined the relief allowed to villages in the years 1352–53–54 for impoverishment due to the Black Death, and we examined the relief allowed in years following 1436 to villages

> desolate, wasted, destroyed or too poor or otherwise too heavily burdened with taxation,

as the collectors' lists are headed. It was more convenient to discuss the origin and utility of those particular Lay Subsidy Rolls there.

The sixteenth and seventeenth century rolls for the "subsidy" (as opposed to the conventionalised tenths-and-fifteenths) are also useful in establishing *minimum* numbers of taxpayers in a township at that date. But, like the pre-1334 rolls, the amount of exemption and evasion makes it difficult to use them for estimating populations.

4

Classed among the Lay Subsidy Rolls at the Public Record Office are the surviving accounts of the three poll tax collections of 1377, 1379 and 1381. These are of great help to us in dispelling any suspicion that more than a minority of the depopulated sites which we find in the fields owe their destruction to the Black Death.

Unlike the Lay Subsidies, these poll taxes were levied on individuals and not on their property. The tax of 1377 was intended to fall on every person over fourteen years of age in the country at the flat rate of fourpence. The poll taxes of 1379 and 1381 (which were progressively evaded) were graduated according to occupation and status. It is the lists of names from these two latter collections which have found their way into print in a number of counties through the interest of genealogists in the surnames of the taxpayers. Where these lists of names have survived there are actual names to be counted. But for 1377, where there are few nominal rolls, there are often the files of tiny pieces of parchment bound together with another thin parchment string.

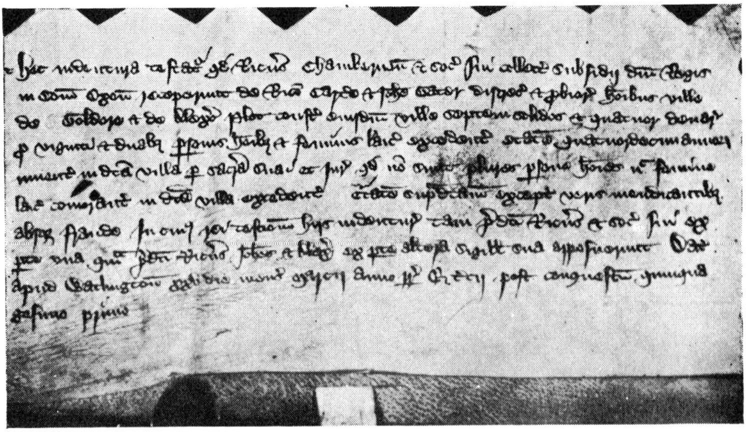

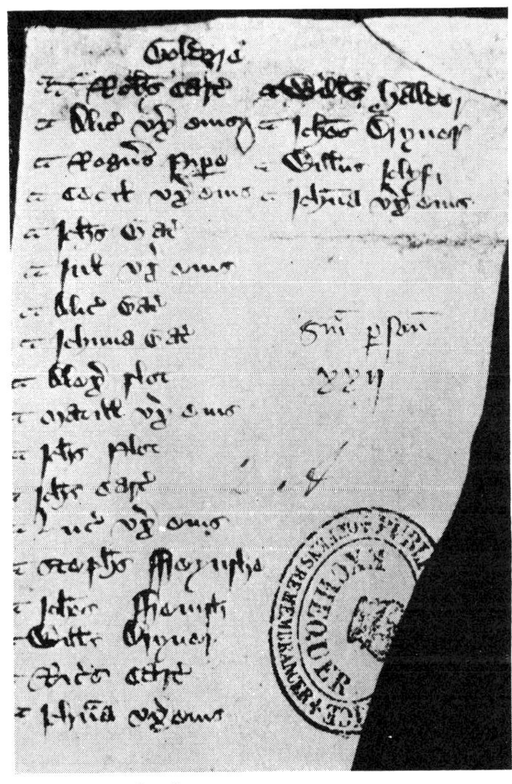

(14) GOLDER, OXON.

(Above). The receipt given to two discreet and honest men and the constable of the village by the collectors of the poll tax of 1377. Fourpence was paid by each of 22 villagers over the age of 14. (Below). A list of the names of the 22 villagers. There is now only one farm. A translation of these documents is given in Appendix II C, p. 413.

In at least one case they still remain in the leather pouch in which they travelled down from the North Riding of Yorkshire to the Exchequer audit. By a remarkable coincidence I found the receipt of Stretton Baskerville, a lost village of Warwickshire, strayed among a Lincolnshire bundle of receipts. The tax paid in the lost village came from fifty-five taxpayers. One such receipt is shown in Plate 14.

These dockets are the indented receipts from the collectors to the constables of the village, giving the sum collected and the number of heads concerned. For the village of Solbergh[11] near Kirby Wiske we read in 1377:

xi s. pro xxxiii capitibus

The 11*s*. was from the thirty-three adult villagers who paid their groat tax. But there is no village of Solbergh now. Its memory survives in a house name (44/355892). It is likely that these thirty-three villagers were renting the former demesne of the village; for in 1306 the Manor had been ruinous and the land held only by twenty-five bondmen. If we apply Mr. Bishop's test for a manor without demesne—the absence of any great inequality among the taxpayers assessed in 1301—it squares with this suggestion. If we compare Solbergh with its neighbours, we find that it was slightly smaller.

It is the evidence of the receipts of 1377, rather than the lists of 1379 and 1381, which can best be employed in comparisons and calculations. This has its disadvantages, since so few have been published, and the majority have had to be sought in manuscript, usually in faded pieces of parchment one inch by five. The lists of names which resulted from the taxes of 1379 and 1381 have been more popular with Record Societies since they were of genealogical interest, but the degree of tax evasion in these two collections was so great that the figures are useless for estimating even relative sizes of villages. In some districts where we have both 1377 and 1379 figures we find villages shrinking to less than half their size at the approach of the tax-collector, while others vary by only a few heads. The age limit had been raised to 16 years in 1379, and this creates another problem: How large was the body of youngsters compared with adults?

Professor Russell has suggested that we should add 50% to the 1377 figures to allow for youngsters.

The 1379 receipts are useful for indicating social classes in the lost village: at the lost Cestersover, where Stukeley turned off the Watling Street to see the ruined chapel, there were twenty-two names in the poll tax list for 1379, each paying the fourpence a head of the lowest social grade. No one in Cestersover came into the 6*s*. 8*d*. or the 20*s*. class, as did Thomas Cosford, *firmarius*, or William Poirfrey, *apprenticius de lege* of the next village, Churchover, where fifty-two names can be distinguished, fifty of them paying the standard groat tax.[12]

Imperfect as they are for some purposes, the documents from 1379 and 1381 have one advantage over the receipts of 1377. In the receipts of 1377 we have only the constables' names to add flesh and blood to the averages, modal ranges and medians of statistical calculations. But in Cestersover in 1379, although we may not know how many children he had, we do know that one of the husbandmen who went to plough the ploughlands of our air photograph was named William Pyryton. Although we do not know how many of his brothers took to the woods when the tax-collectors approached, we do know that they found Richard Thressher and took his fourpence to London, along with those of Walter Hert, Thomas Berton, Richard Scherd, John Day and seventeen others.

5

On no other occasion in the Middle Ages was anything like a count of heads organised. Historians of population step rapidly from 1377 to the Chantry Returns of 1545 or to the parish registers of the same period. Unfortunately 1545 is too late for our purpose except to confirm that empty parishes are empty. The registers of Wharram Percy show that the children brought to the font in the 1550s are not the children of Wharram Percy villagers; they come principally from Thixendale, formerly a hamlet of Wharram, now a substantial Wolds village.

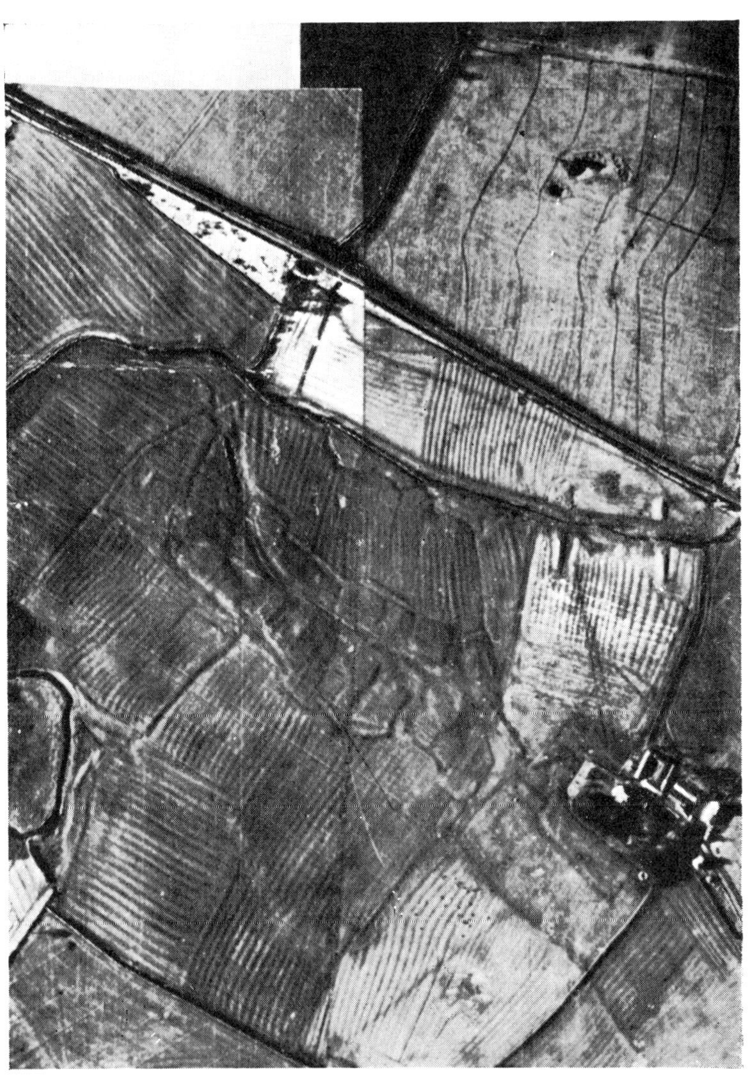

(15) CESTERSOVER, WARWS.

A site clearly marked in heavy clay. A fragment of the chapel is incorporated in a barn of the Manor Farm buildings, bottom right. The main street led from the Manor down to the stream. There are breached dams of a former pool near the intersection of the stream with the railway, centre right. Some crofts cut across the ridge-and-furrow, showing that they were taken in from arable fields.

The parish was the unit of assessment for a novel tax granted in 1428. This did not result in the counting of heads, but it did produce a return of parishes with fewer than ten households. The tax itself was a mixed one, partly on fiefs and partly on parishes. The parish tax[13] was levied on

> alle inhabitantz householders withynne every parysche o this saide royaume so yat yer be inhabited in ye saide parishe x persones there holdynge houshold

The actual rate of tax was connected with the current rate for the ecclesiastical tenth which does not concern us at the moment. But at the end of each list of assessments appear the names of parishes which had fewer than ten inhabiting householders. In Cambridgeshire, for example, we read:[14]

> Hundred of Barton . . . in Malton parish there are only three inhabitants holding houses and no more, and the said church is within the said hundred of Barton. It is worth only eight pounds a year and pays nothing therefore for the above reason.

Malton had been a Domesday vill and had been separately taxed to the Subsidy as late as 1250. In the Hundred Rolls of 1279 there had been twelve freeholders, four villeins and ten cottars. In the tax lists of 1316, 1327 and 1334 it had been linked with its neighbour, Orwell. The village was clearly reduced in size by the beginning of the fourteenth century. There is now only Malton Farm.[15]

In Lincolnshire there were eight parishes reported in 1428 as having fewer than ten householders which also received high relief from lay taxation in the years immediately after the Black Death. None of these eight villages is now anything more than a single farm, and the churches are completely destroyed. It seems likely that the Black Death and the succeeding returns of the pestilence had completely enfeebled these villages.[16]

Combined in this way with tax evidence, the 1428 lists are useful for establishing a reduction in population in the first quarter of the fifteenth century. Not all places so listed have since died; a number of them, like the small hamlets of the poll tax returns, have been able to expand since that date. Four of the Leicestershire villages with fewer than ten householders in 1428 are now flourishing.

We cannot use the 1428 evidence quite so freely when we lack support from tax documents or when we move away from the plains into the regions of orchard and forest, where settlements had always been scattered, churches often isolated, and parishioners few. It is unlikely that the long lists of small parishes in Somerset or Dorset in 1428 indicates particularly severe depopulation or economic *malaise* there. These were the non-nucleated parishes, the tiny hamlets which can still be seen shaken over the Ordnance map as if from a pepper pot.

A final limitation of the 1428 evidence is that, of its nature, it was concerned only with parishes. Very many to-be-lost villages did not have their separate parish church.

We have so far examined only those records which set out to survey a county or a district for fiscal or feudal purposes. There exist many classes of record which are concerned only with one particular village, manor or family: records of manor courts; reeves' accounts; transfers of land; sales of property; payments of rent; surveys of feudal obligations or the boundaries of a disputed area. When the villages with which they deal have not survived, they offer descriptive detail to supplement that of the eye and the spade in the deserted fields. But they are likely to be fewer in number and more elusive than records of the medieval Exchequer.

6

It has not been difficult to prove the existence of a village from documents which derive from the medieval Exchequer. We are less fortunate when we seek surviving documents from the lost manor. The Exchequer had a solemn permanence whether villages came or went. But the manorial organisation existed only to link together lord and tenants, the property-owner and those who cultivated his land. With the departure of the cultivators the manor court came to an end. The break in continuity made it less necessary to preserve the manorial court rolls or the reeves' accounts. In those surviving villages which have not lost their medieval court records it has been their practical utility as a legal record which has helped their preservation.

But in the conditions of the sixteenth century, with the prerogative courts actively curious about depopulation, it may well have seemed prudent for a landowner to destroy the manorial records of a depopulated village. They were proof that a village community had existed.[17] What makes the loss serious is that only from such records could we examine what happened in the village in the years before the final depopulation. Any conjectures which we make about these years will inevitably be based on a very small body of direct evidence.

The "extent" of a manor was a written survey of the potential sources of income within it. Extents are most commonly found in connection with the inquisition *post mortem* where the Exchequer made a formal assessment of the estate of a deceased tenant-in-chief of the Crown in order to value the feudal dues, or, if the manor was to come into the Crown's wardship, the income. The number of these documents extant is large, and landowners' property was so scattered that among the many thousands of manors for which we have extents, deserted villages are bound to occur. There are also extents which did not arise out of an inquisition *post mortem*. Among the *Ancient Extents* in the Exchequer is a roll for the Isle of Wight in 1298. In the manor of Bernardsley[18] (now one farm, east of Brading) there were thirteen houses; at Swainston[19] there were forty-two free tenants and eighty-one customary tenants. The demesne arable contained 288 acres in 22 furlongs (*culturae*). Swainston itself is now a country house in a park. Within its bounds was established the borough of Francheville (now Newton) with its seventy-seven and a half burgess tenements in the 1298 extent. Newton is little more than a few cottages, but its depopulation is bound up with its decay as a seaport. In another extent of the same reign for the Isle of Wight, the lost village of Penna,[20] north-east of Newport, had 124 acres of demesne, 12 of meadow, 28 of enclosed pasture and 37 of common pasture. There was a watermill, and six tenants' names were given in the extent.

In 1323 an extent of Lidcote (Bucks.) was taken. This hamlet maintained 140 acres of arable worth 3*d.* an acre; there was a manor house with a fruit garden; fifteen free tenants were on the rent roll: the former manor is now a farm, and the Chapel of St. Giles is traditionally said to have lain in a field near by. Depopulation was reported in 1517. The hamlet was *totaliter devastata* after William Sheppard had enclosed 100 acres of arable in 1507 and evicted eight persons.[21]

In 1327 a Northamptonshire extent included two neighbouring villages which were to be depopulated. At Barford there was a manor house and 65 acres of demesne arable. Five villagers held newly asserted land; there were thirteen customary tenants, each holding a virgate of land; there was one cottager; and the village possessed a water-mill in the river Ise. At Glendon, a mile away on the hill, there were seven cottagers and four customary tenants.[22]

An extent of any early date is useful in providing descriptive detail of the economy of a lost village in the days before its depopulation, and in assessing its minimum size. The later the date of the extent, the more useful it will be in establishing the date of final depopulation. For this reason extents of the mid-fifteenth century would be most valuable: but extents were feudal documents, and with the decay of feudal services the details of manorial assets and incomes were much less fully given. A single sentence giving the money income replaces the long descriptive paragraphs of the thirteenth and fourteenth-century extents. By the time of Henry VII, when the Inquisitions are again well calendared, the extents are virtually useless for our purpose.

For Wharram Percy, which we have already described from other points of view, we have a series of inquisitions conveniently spaced and running through to 1457, and in them some of the features which can be seen in Plate 1 are described.[23] The complex of rooms at the upper end of the photograph which we christened "the Manor", can be equated with

> *unum capitale messuagium in quo edificatur una grangia*

of the 1367 Inquisition, when the villagers were already leasing the demesne lands from their lord, and commuting their feudal service for a money rent:

> tenentes ad voluntatem et nativi qui tenent terras dominicas ibidem et omnia alia terra et tenementa manerii pertinenta cum uno molendino aquatico . . . et redditur per annum in omnibus, xxi li.

The water-mill is no longer visible since the construction of the railway along the valley.

The Inquisition of 1380 is much fuller. It described the partition of the manor for dower, and in the two-thirds assigned were

> a messuage held formerly by the vicar with a cottage, a close and land.
> a cottage which John de Cawood lately held with gardens and land.
> nine bovates (*i.e.* unit holdings of arable land with accompanying pasture rights) of demesne land lying throughout the whole field along the paths between the demesne lands and the lands of the tenants at will on the west side in a *cultura* (furlong) called "Medelgates" . . . and so on in the same way throughout the Field.
> a messuage formerly in the tenure of Reynold Martynson with three bovates.
> bovates in the tenure of John son of Robert.
> a messuage and three bovates of Walter del Hill.
> a messuage in the tenure of John Pryhet and Alice his mother.
> the like in the tenure of William del Hill.
> a third part of two bovates in the tenure of William son of Geoffrey.
> a cottage with land, in the tenure of Walter Cawood "Le cotegarth" at the end of the town.
> two cottages.
> three waste tofts.
> a water mill.
> a common oven.

a kiln.
a pond called Milndam.
another pond.
common pasture.

By 1436 there were sixteen messuages, and since the number of bovates was the same, these were probably the unit holdings. The value of the bovates was 4*s.* each, and the value was the same in another Inquisition of 1457, when there were also sixteen messuages. The rents of free tenants on each occasion totalled 3*s.*, but the corn-mill (a water-mill) had fallen in value from 13*s.* 4*d.* to 11*s.* In both years there were six acres of meadow at 1*s.* 8*d.* each, and 20 acres of woodland. Between them these Inquisitions make it possible to say confidently that the village still had the characteristic features of a corn-growing open-field village in 1457.

We may link photograph and extent[24] in a similar fashion for the East Riding village of Burton Constable, now swallowed in the grounds of the Great House. Two transformations of the landscape have conspired to hide the site of this village. In the early sixteenth-century enclosures the Constables destroyed the village which bore the family name, and in the eighteenth century Capability Brown surrounded the house with its formal landscape and park. But the air photograph reveals that the grass of the park land had once been something other than ornamental: the roads and a few houses are visible to remind us of the medieval village described in more than one Inquisition. In 1293 the windmill was already built: it can be seen in the bottom of the photograph as a central mound surrounded by a circular ditch. The windmill was worth 13*s.* 4*d.* a year to its owner in 1348, half the value in the Inquisition of 1336. The value of the bovate had also fallen between 1336 and 1348 from 9*s.* to 5*s.* In the 1293 Inquisition the bovates had been tilled by twenty-one villeins and fifteen cottagers; in 1336 twenty-three villeins and twenty-two cottagers with one free tenant; in 1348—the year before the Black Death—the number is not given, but the rent from them (£26 13*s.* 4*d.*) was a little greater than in 1336 when it was £22 8*s.* 10*d.* The dove-house of 1293 (still on 1st edn. O.S.) was not valued in 1336, but each extent had an enclosed and ditched wood of 49 acres. In 1336 and 1348 there were 11 acres of pasture in a clearing made within the wood, and 14 acres of meadow lying down by the river. In the Manor House was a chapel, and it may have served as a parish church for the villagers. In the early nineteenth century Poulson described it as dilapidated: it had been the place of worship for the 105 persons for whose groats the poll tax collectors gave their receipts[25] in 1377. The Black Death had not emptied the village, and the houses described in the extents could easily have sheltered this number of adults.

The inquisitions *post mortem*, although dealing with manors in the provinces, are Exchequer documents preserved in London. What of the manorial documents which have remained in or near their original homes? We have seen that they were subject to a double chance of destruction. There were good motives of concealment in the early sixteenth century; and in the last century these manorial documents have been as vulnerable to the bonfires and salvage drives as the manorial records of any other manor. The rentals, court rolls and reeve's accounts which we shall quote are a thin harvest.

Few proprietors can have thought it worth preserving the rentals of depopulated villages. It is fortunate that the fate of one proprietor was such that a fifteenth-century rental fell into the hands of the Crown and has been preserved among the Exchequer records. Bicester Priory owned the hamlet of Wretchwick near Bicester, and at the Dissolution a small paper rental[26] travelled to London with the other evidences. It covers the years 1432–37. Wretchwick is now no more than a number of mounds and a few depressions near Middle Wretchwick Farm, and we know from the Inquiry of 1517 that it was depopulated in March 1489 when eighteen persons were evicted from five houses and 200 acres enclosed.[27] The value of the land was given at £6 13*s.* 4*d.*

The rent roll for Epiphany 1432 was for a smaller sum:

from John Castell 6*s.* 8*d.*
John Gybbys 6*s.* 9*d.* and for a cottage 10*d.*

from a tenement of John Chesterton and a cottage: nothing, for they are vacant.
a tenement of John Bedale 2*s*. o*d*.
a tenement of William Skrene 2*s*. o*d*. and for "Frerehuwys" also 3*s*. 4*d*.
William Dyer 3*s*. 4*d*. and for half a croft "Dymonds", 1*s*. 8*d*.
William Sperman 3*s*. 4*d*.
John Sperman 3*s*. 4*d*.
Richard Benhull 3*s*. 4*d*.
Richard Seberne 7*s*. 11*d*.
a tenement formerly John Dey's: nothing, for it is vacant.

The Michaelmas rental for the same year begins similarly, with an extra 4*s*. now that Chesterton's land and croft were taken. But a second paragraph is headed:

Rents of tofts and vacant crofts there:—
Item,

John Gybbys for a toft next to Style Way	12*d*.
John Castell for 2 acres and a toft	10*d*.
John Bedale for 3 acres and meadow of his toft	18*d*.
Joan Sperman for half of Emyncroft	20*d*.
Thomas Gybbys for the other half of it	20*d*.
Thomas Gybbys for Redyscroft	6*s*. 8*d*.
John Sperman for Fowlyscroft	5*s*. o*d*.
William Skerne for Frerehuwys	3*s*. 4*d*.
William Dyer for Dymondscroft	1*s*. 8*d*.
William Sperman for Colynscroft	3*s*. 4*d*.
For Aynolfscroft	blank
William Sperman for land and meadow vacant	blank

These items do not appear in the rental for March 1433, but they occur in a slightly altered form in the Michaelmas rentals for 1436 and 1437. The rental shows a small community of perhaps a dozen families, of whom several were able to rent other holdings for which the Priory could not find tenants. This is probably a reflection of general economic conditions which we discussed in Chapter Five.

A rental of a village field from a date after the destruction is not likely to say very much about the former village. Indeed it is the silence which is likely to be evidence. When a rental purports to be the rental of a manor with a name going back to Domesday Book, yet has nothing to say of rents from villagers' houses or from village tenants, then there is a strong case for believing that the village has already been destroyed. Where the land is all pasture and where the parish is all in one man's hand the suspicions deepen. The rental of Creslow[28] in Buckinghamshire for 1607 is for

> One Manor House, seven closes of pasture being 699 acres, and . . . noe freeholder nor coppyeholder belongeinge to Creslowe nor leaseholders.

There had once been a parish church here for the villagers, but services ceased in the reign of Elizabeth, and the last presentation was in 1554. Some walls remained in 1713, but they were used for animals. The great closes of pasture which were the grazier's ambition and creation still show on the 6-inch Ordnance map, where the huge field of nearly 200 acres stands markedly different in size and shape from the more conventional fields of the district.[29]

A valuation of Thornton Bridge[30] (Yorks., N.R.) in 1586 tells the same story: the Manor House; the Park; a garden; nine closes of pasture, and two of meadow and the parish is surveyed. The fields of Easton Neston in Northamptonshire were reduced to the same simple formula when they were surveyed[31] in the reign of Henry VIII: the Manor Place, the Park, the Great Meadow, the Little Meadow, the Mills, Horseclose and the Coneygree.

We have a pair of rentals[32] for the village of Dale on the edge of the North Yorkshire moors. In 1387 free tenants to the number of twenty-three were named. The village had a water-mill and a common bakehouse. In the rental of 1433 the income is stable at just over £13, and twenty-two tenants were named. In the tax list of 1301 fifteen persons had possessed enough goods to be within the taxed group. In 1446 the rebate for Dale is the standard one of 16%: the county did not take Dale to be impoverished or overtaxed. But from the moorland road one can now look down into Dale with its two farms scattered in the narrow, deep valley. On the valley sides are lynchet-like terraces which look as if they mark where the ploughs moved. In Humberstone's Survey of 1569 the parish consisted of seven enclosed holdings, one of which was the "*messuagium vocatum* Dale Town", and the almost empty parish now has "Dale Town" printed across it on the Ordnance map. In 1901 the farmsteads mustered only thirty-seven souls.

We have seen that it is unlikely that a consecutive series of rolls or accounts will have been preserved for a lost village. We are grateful, therefore, to find two years' accounts for Kingston (or Little Chesterton) in Warwickshire: in these rolls of 1386–88 we are in a corn-growing village. The rents come from messuages where husbandmen are living, and from the arable holdings which they are cultivating.[33]

Ten years later, away in the East Riding, a monk of Meaux copied out the rentals[34] of certain of the granges. In each of them there was a substantial arable. At the lost Octon there were 410 acres of arable to a bare 25 of pasture: at Wharram Grange in Wharram Percy parish the proportion was 1128 to 110 acres.

The survival of a reeve's account is even more informative than a simple rental. We have such accounts[35] for East Tanfield from 1336 to 1500. This village lay on the banks of the Ure, just within the North Riding. Its neighbour, West Tanfield, stands by the bridge on the Ripon-Masham road and still flourishes. The meandering course of the river passes by a field marked on the map as "Town Gate": it was the main street of the village, represented now only by a single farm. In 1517 the enclosure of 400 acres and the destruction of eight houses was reported as having very recently taken place.[36]

The accounts for 1443–44 show that the shrinkage had begun. Of the 44 arable bovates, half showed some decrease in rent, presumably as a reflection of land surplus. Only two cottages are reported as empty through want of tenants, but others had only been occupied for part of the year, and the over-all reduction in rents is about one-sixth of the standard rents. We do not know, of course, from this single roll at what earlier point in time this accounting standard had been fixed. The tax quota of 28*s.* in 1334 compares very favourably with the average of 23*s.* from the twenty-five other villages of Hallikeld wapentake, but the reliefs[37] in 1439 and 1492 were 6*s.* 8*d.*: a proportion rather higher than the local average of 16%.

But on the back of the account roll we have the unusual pleasure of a record of expenditure on building in a lost village. Among its items are repairs to the tenements of Robert Christopherson, Robert Lethley, Robert Smith and William Harrison as well as to the kiln. The wages of labourers and the expenses of nails, wood, *lez watlyng*, *le lattyng* and *le dowbyng* are set out. It was seventy years before these would be thrown down.

7

Monastic records, although private, have something of the continuity of the Exchequer records. Those cartularies which survived the Dissolution have been the treasures of antiquaries and the delight of local record societies. Occasionally, as we have just seen, a single rental or a short run of rentals has been preserved by being copied into a cartulary or by passing to the Court of Augmentations with the other evidences of property.

Many cartularies date from a period before the Poll Tax, so that they are not likely to be called in to this investigation as prime evidence for the existence of a settlement at a particular date. They will rather serve to provide illustrative detail of a village and fields in the days before it was depopulated. The detail in charters granting land to monasteries was often minute, and it is clear that the gifts were in open-field villages when charters describe many scattered acres, each bounded and admeasured.

Monastic cartularies have been used extensively in this work, but the type of document is so familiar that it seemed better here to take examples from the rarer source, the lay cartulary. In essence the cartulary was no more than the copying and preservation of deeds and agreements which we might find surviving singly elsewhere. The single deed, like that[38] which details the eight small pieces of land given by

John Ward of Rippingale to Robert de Thorp of Ringstone (Lincs.), may be as good a pointer to a lost village as a whole cartulary. The Ringstone deed describes carefully how the 4½ acres were scattered among the furlongs when the village still had its open fields in 1377.

Compared with monastic cartularies, collections of charters for lay families are rare. Where the property included villages subsequently depopulated, the lay cartulary will be as informative as that of a monastic house. Such a cartulary is that of Boarstall,[39] drawn up between 1444 and 1449 for the Rede family. The second village in its pages is Standelf, represented now only by Standhill farm. In 1218 there were daily services in the chapel, but by 1424 only three times a week. The final decay of the village seems to date from the decade following. The earlier deeds describe a house between the lord's court-house and the house of another villager, with open-field and meadow land; this came to the Redes in 1433. In 1434 other tenements passed to Edmund Rede. In 1440 he acquired a small parcel of land and pasture. The lord of the manor, as Rede then was, appeared with the vicar of the mother church at Pyrton before the Archdeacon's court at Oxford. They pleaded that by reason of plague the village was empty. Agreement was reached that the vicar's obligation could be fulfilled by saying mass once a week. If at any time the hamlet should be resettled, then the thrice-weekly services should be resumed. Rede promised to continue to allow the vicar the tithes of the lands at Standelf. In 1446 Standelf was granted a reduction in its tax quota. The cartulary includes an unusual document from one of the commissioners assigned to allocate the tax-relief among the impoverished villages in the country.

> *deductimus de villa de Standelf ad dictum integram xv am. et x am. ac medietatem xv me. et x me. nimis graviter onerata de dicta integra xva. et xa. summam xxxvi solidorum et ix denariorum et de predicta medietate xv me. et x me. summam xviii solidorum et iv denariorum et oboli . . . datum vi to. die Novembris anno regni eiusdem regis xxv to.* [*1446*].

The former village consists now as it probably did in 1446, of one farm and 500 acres of grass land.

In 1402 Rede also acquired Gatehampton on the banks of the Thames near Goring. A charter dated before 1251 describes houses in the "vill" here, although the abbreviated summaries of later charters in the printed *Cartulary* make it impossible to see whether the frequent references to the "manor" include any tenements. Before 1251 there was a fulling-mill here and a ground for tentering cloths.

The Rede family seem to have been associated with other manors in which decay had taken place at the end of the fourteenth century perhaps making them attractively cheap and easily convertible to pasture-use. Shotover in Headington had twenty cottagers in 1358 and 1361. The manor may be represented by the 900 acres of Shotover Park today. Thirty-nine pages of the printed *Cartulary* are concerned with lands and tenements in Clopcote Manor, which also seems to have been destroyed and absorbed into Rush Court near Wallingford.

Boarstall itself is considerably shrunken, although we can hardly call it entirely depopulated. There is a very early example of an open-field map for this parish drawn in 1444 showing the three fields of the village, the manor, the church and areas of woodland. The cartulary contains many deeds conveying messuages and lands in Boarstall. *Evidences* for sixteen tenements are given, and an inquisition of 1432 gives twenty messuages as five-sixths of the Manor of Boarstall. In 1452 Boarstall is *villula sive hamletta* and twelve inhabitants put their seals to an agreement.

8

The West Riding site of Wilstrop is unusually well documented. We have the family papers of the lords of the manor in the thirteenth, fourteenth and fifteenth centuries, from which we can establish beyond doubt that Wilstrop was a village with houses and villagers, and not a disembodied "manor". We have also the list of those who paid the poll tax here in 1379; and among the Star Chamber records is a contemporary record of the occasion of the destruction of the village and the intention of the man who depopulated it.

Such a combination of evidence is rare for any one and the same site, and it is particularly useful in the West Riding where there were fewer sites depopulated than in either of the other Ridings.[40]

Our information about the destruction of the village comes from the mouth of Simon Robynson, parson of Moor Monkton, in 1514. Robynson petitioned the King in the court of Star Chamber for redress. The living was in the royal gift, and Robynson had gone there in 1511. Within the parish of Moor Monkton lay the site of the village of Wilstrop and the manor house of the depopulator, Guy Wilstrop. A dispute over Wilstrop's obligation to pay tithes for Wilstrop ensued. Such disputes were not unusual, but this dispute took a violent turn. Guy had destroyed the tithe corn while it was standing in the fields for collection, he had kept the parson's sheep from pasturing in the commons of Wilstrop and he had encouraged one Joseph Ughtred to assault Robynson during morning service in his own church. He had also stolen tithe corn from Moor Monkton as well as the parson's building timber and some of his animals. He had fined the parson without reason in his manor court and had vexed him with lawsuits.

A tithe dispute would be almost inevitable in a parish where the common fields had been turned to pasture, for the tithe obligation would be traditionally set in terms of corn and crops which would no longer be grown. Some of the detail of violence and threats we must take with caution, for this is the petition for the plaintiff: the defence has not survived. But from another suit in Star Chamber of 1499 we shall see that the Wilstrops were no strangers to violence.

It is in the course of his petition that Robynson suddenly brings in the destruction of the village as part of his attempt to blacken Wilstrop's character. His actual words may be quoted—

> in defraude hys father, Milles Willestrope, and he dydd caste doune the town of Willistrop, destroyed the corne feldes and made pasture of theym, and hath closed in the commen and made a parke of hytt.

Near the empty site stood the manor house, for the stolen sheep from Moor Monkton had been taken

> to Wylstrope to the afforesaid Guyes and my lady hys mothers hows.

No doubt Robynson hoped, with the anti-enclosure legislation on the statute books and the current of opinion so much against conversion to arable, that this complaint would weigh against Guy. As with so many Star Chamber cases, we do not know the outcome. In January 1522–23 Robynson exchanged his living for that of Doncaster, and shook the dust of Moor Monkton off his feet. No mention of the depopulation of Wilstrop is to be found among the surviving records of the 1517 Commission of Inquiry which visited the West Riding to seek out such cases: perhaps because the enclosure had occurred just before 1485.

Robynson's petition gives no precise date for the enclosure, but an earlier Star Chamber case would seem to arise from the event. In 1499 Miles Wilstrop was himself a petitioner to the Court. He complains of Sir William Gascoigne, of the Abbot of Fountains and of other local gentry who for three years have been waging a private war upon him. Apart from waylaying his relatives, the rioters had paid particular attention to the Wilstrop park. In 1497 eleven of them came and pulled down the fencing; on the next day a hundred or so persons came to Marston Moor

> to thentent to poule doon the pale of the parke of the said Milez at Willesthorp.

On another occasion 400 people had come by night and pulled down 380 perches' length of paling. In 1498 he had set up 180 perches again, only to have it pulled down, cut into pieces and carried away, together with 100 walnut trees and new apple trees two or three years newly grafted, and the young trees planted alongside the 180 perches of paling. In March they breached his mill-pond, and again in April; in October they dug up his rabbit warren, and in January 1499 pulled down another 40 perches of paling, came to Miles' house in the park and would have killed him had he been there. They went away to Tockwith vowing to slay him, and rousing opinion against him.

In this sequence of events there are clearly two causes operating: the family feud of the Gascoignes and the Wilstrops; but also popular local feeling against the new park with its fresh trees only a year or two old. It has in fact all the symptoms of an enclosure riot, with its objective the park for which the enclosure had taken place. It is doubtful whether 100, and on another occasion 400, people could have been brought together to help the Gascoignes with a personal feud, had not some other more immediate grievance moved them and "dyvers and many of thame . . . havyng unfittying language agayn the said Miles".

It would seem then that the crucial date lies before April 1497. What evidence is there that there was a substantial village for Miles to destroy?

Part of the answer must be sought in the fields themselves, where the length of the village site is some 400 yards. The earthworks do not splay themselves very far from the narrow central line of the main street, and the arable fields can be seen beginning immediately on their southern and western flank, and moving away in steady ridge-and-furrow to the parish boundary. The present area of the parish is quite large, and most of its surface shows sign of medieval arable cultivation: this in itself should show that the village was substantial.

In the poll tax of 1377, thirty-three people were taxed. In 1379 the names of twenty-five persons appeared, two of whom were fullers. It is therefore possible that the mill was then being used for fulling, since the village is perched on the south bank of the Nidd. For 1306 we have more information, since in that year Robert of Pontefract died possessing lands in Wilstrop which the Exchequer recorded. He had 130 acres in the arable fields, 10 acres of meadow, some pasture in closes, an oak wood (now Wilstrop wood?), a water-mill and fishery, and from the peasant tenants a total rent of 4*s.* 7*d.* and the obligation to do thirty "works", or units of villein labour, each autumn. This, in fact, is a quite typical medieval village.

We must now turn to the family papers of the Wilstrops. The family was careful to preserve the documents recording transactions in land, and later in the fifteenth century these were copied into a book. A note on the second page shows that the book was of practical use to later generations, for it was produced as evidence before the Council of the North at York in 1597.

> in the matter between Christopher Thwaite of Marstone and Sir Oswolde Wylstropp knyght concerning the enclosing by force and arms of a parcell of Marstone Moor called Broken Close. (The occupiers of four tenements in Marston claim that they have pasture rights on that part of the Moor.)

The book now rests in the John Rylands Library, Manchester, and it was used by Roger Dodsworth.

Its interest for our purpose lies in the references to houses, villagers and other details of the physical lay-out of the village in the centuries before its destruction. The documents comprise charters, indentures, concords, compositions, writs, inquisitions and pleas. The Wilstrop village documents begin at fo. 174 (old pagination). The first document (undated, but before 1263) concerns a water-mill. Document 6 is a copy of the Inquisition on the property of Robert de Pontefract described above. Documents 7 and 8 mention the mill-pond and an acre of land above it. Document 10 lists twenty-eight tofts and twenty-six adjacent crofts with 126 acres of land appertaining, and the services of free tenants totalling 100*d.* a year. This is our first and most important piece of physical information, that there were at least twenty-six separate dwelling units with their enclosed gardens behind them. The next document (unnumbered and dated 1318 by Dodsworth) repeats the figure of twenty-eight, but now assigns this number to tofts alone, no crofts being mentioned.

In document 14 we get two of the names of the open fields of Wilstrop, for the roods of land are described as lying in either *campo australis* or *campo de molendino* (*i.e.* South Field or Mill Field). An indenture numbered 15 (undated) is in Norman French and speaks of

> *la chapel, le manour de Wilsthorp et le stank de le molyn de Wyllestrop.*

We have already met the mill-pool, but this is the sole reference to a chapel, which was probably a private chapel in the manor house.

In document 23*a* we have more precise information about the size and position of the toft and croft village unit. A toft and croft is described as being of 2¼ acres lying between one man's toft on one side, and another named man's toft on the other. With it went 6 acres in the Field below the Town (? Mill Field), 4 of which lay in Westcroft. To them there was a right of entry and exit by a road passing between William Faber's toft and Wimarius' toft. Document 24*c* also describes the scattered portions of land in the open fields which went with six tofts; five lay side by side

inter toftum de Roberti de Marisco et Northlidchate.

The Northlidchate looks very like a form of *north lydiate.* The sixth toft is separate, being defined as that formerly belonging to Robert le Piscator (Fisher).

Document 24*e* is dated 9 Edward III (*i.e.* 1336). In it are a toft and a croft and

molendinum fullericum quod vocatur Walkmylne.

which lies on

via vocata Mylgate.

This confirms the suspicion that the mill was used for fulling cloth and joins the lawyer's Latin term to the colloquial English, "a walk mill". Document 26 (dated 1411) speaks of messuages and tofts and acres of land, and 27*f* (dated 1416) of a cottage with its croft.

The natural thing to ask is whether these physical details can be linked to any details of buildings or roads visible on the ground. We can better answer that with the aid of the air photograph. It does not reveal any significant features otherwise invisible as one walks over the fields near Wilstrop Hall. The village area is clearly defined: for it is the area which is not striped with ridge-and-furrow. Within this area, the clearest signs are those of the roads; the individual detail of house-plans is much smudged by time and by the washing of soil to smooth out right-angles, and the coming of grass to shroud other details.

9

From the records of the manor we may turn to those of the church. Documents which prove the existence of a church fabric may be crucial in any investigation. In those parts of England where the settlements were nucleated, evidence of a church is almost always evidence of a village. When we find the institutions of clergy to a medieval living recorded in the registers of the bishop, we may fairly deduce medieval villagers served by the church. Only in those districts where settlement was scattered among woodland or orchards were churches also scattered. The Herefordshire or Worcestershire churches which stand alone may have an explanation which hinges on convenience of access: their isolated site was convenient for all scattered farmsteads which they served, even if it was adjacent to none.

Before the Reformation (and even after it) we cannot always expect depopulation and the destruction of a church to be reflected in the immediate cessation of institutions. Incumbents might continue to draw the income in absence or while serving another parish. The absentee incumbent of Argam, whose picturesque induction in the open pastures has been described,[41] was also the minister of one of the Leeds chapelries. The institution of the incumbent at Dunsby (Lincs.) took place for the last time in 1506. In the taxation of 1526 the living is associated with Brauncewell, but the two names are not joined in the bishop's register until an institution of 1667. The Bishop of Lichfield in 1633, as we saw on page 63, had found the incumbent of a desecrated church drawing his stipend in London. But as church discipline tightened, visitations by bishop or archdeacon brought such instances into daylight.

Where the decay of a village through pestilence or enclosure emptied the church of its congregation it was possible for the bishop to be petitioned and an amalgamation of parishes decreed. On such occasions we are able to say with certainty: depopulation has already occurred by such-and-such a date.[42]

The record of the amalgamation may also record the

approximate date when the village suffered its blow. We have already described the case of Standelf on page 300.

South Cadeby in Lincolnshire was joined to the Rectory of Calcethorpe in the second half of the fifteenth century, and its site was forgotten until Canon Foster traced its homesteads along the sides of the disused medieval road running from Ludford Magna to join the still-used Blackstone Heath Road. Ironically, Calcethorpe itself was depopulated later, and among the earthworks which surround Manor Farm is a small group known locally as "Priest's Close".

As early as 1398 the Pope was informed that Middle Carlton, a few miles north of Lincoln, had had no parishioners for forty years and it is clear that this is one of the genuine Black Death destructions of a village. At Burreth, to the south-east of Lincoln, both the vicar of the parish church and the abbot of Tupholme Abbey died in the Plague, and we find no institutions recorded in the bishop's register after 1381.

The parish of West Wykeham in the chalk wolds near the source of the Lincolnshire Bain comprised the two villages of East and West Wykeham. In the Lincoln register in March 1396–97 the vicarage of Wykeham was joined to that of Ludford Magna, since West Wykeham had been attacked by divers pestilences; so destitute of parishioners that there were not ten households. "No priest would be joined to such a spouse" and the church and vicarage were said to be ruinous.

Even before the Black Death, there were hamlets with chapelries and dwindling congregations. Such was the case at Little Stapleford, which appeared in the *Nomina Villarum* of 1316 as a hamlet of Brant Broughton. But by January 1338–39 the rector of this Lincolnshire village was granted permission by his bishop to take wood and stones from the superfluous chapel at Stapleford for the fabric of his church or bell-tower a mile away. Much the same may have happened at Kiplingcotes at a date before the first surviving episcopal register.

In the county of Lincoln there were 622 churches and village chapelries to which institutions were being regularly made in the thirteenth century.[43] Of these, 77 no longer stand. Not all these lost churches come from deserted villages: seven of the Stamford and thirteen of the Lincoln churches are no longer standing: one at least has been swallowed by the sea, and one or two were pulled down when two churches in the same village were found to be superfluous. But the list below shows what the depopulation of this county has meant in terms of abandoned churches, and the proportion lost is only equalled by that of Norfolk. In the list the date of the last recorded institution or of the formal union of parishes is given.

TABLE II

LOST VILLAGES OF LINCOLNSHIRE WITH LOST CHURCHES, AND DATE OF LAST INSTITUTION OR OF UNION OF PARISHES.

AUTBY in North Thoresby	1416
BEESBY united to Hawerby	May 1450
BURRETH	1381
CADEBY ST. HELEN (North Cadeby)	by 1367
CADEBY ST. PETER (South Cadeby)	1457
CALCEBY by Alford	c. 1540–70 (united 1750)
CALCETHORPE	1660–62 (but depopulated earlier)
CAWKWELL	c. 1521–47
CARLTON, MIDDLE	union 1398
CONESBY by Scunthorpe	?
DEXTHORPE	1451
DUNSBY in Brauncewell	c. 1506–26
DUNSTHORPE	union 1437
FIRSBY, EAST	1640
FORDINGTON	union May 1450
HANTHORPE	?
HUNDON by Caistor	?
KETSBY	1597
MAIDENWELL with Farforth	union 1592
MALTBY by Louth	?
MERE	united by 1418
RAVENDALE, WEST	1367
RAVENTHORPE	1387
RISBY	c. 1521–47
SOUTHORPE	1521

STAIN	1660
STAPLEFORD PARVA	union 1338
WALMSGATE	*c.* 1435
WYHAM	1660
WYKEHAM, EAST AND WEST	1397 union
WYVILLE	1597

In addition, the following small villages which once had their parish church now have to worship elsewhere.

ABY	1640–2
APLEY	1427
ASTERBY	?
BILSBY ST. MARGARET	1560
BIRTHORPE	*c.* 1430
CLAXBY PLUCKACRE	1660–2
COCKERINGTON ST. MARY (North Cockerington)	united to South Cockerington December 1449
DALDERBY	?
HALLINGTON	1640
LAUGHTON in Folkingham	union 1562
SLEAFORD, OLD	1506
SWABY	1367
THORPE in Kirkby Laythorpe	1592

We have already seen that by 1428 there were parishes whose tax had to be adjusted because, although there was a church, there were fewer than ten householders. This is the same problem facing the tax-collector as that which prompted the abatements in the Lay Subsidy a decade later: a sum assessed in the conditions of one period was outdated by economic change.

The shrunken parish of Clopton (Cambs.) may stand as typical of those whose falling revenue from fees was making them unattractive to incumbents in the late sixteenth century.[44] The church must already have been neglected, for the Commissioners of Edward VI in 1553 found that the patron had removed the bells, and the only articles found were two old vestments and a silver chalice. The suppression of the chantry had further reduced the fees, and in 1561 the rectory was vacant. In November of that year the patron,

Mr. Oliver St. John, and the vicar of the adjoining parish of Croydon petitioned Bishop Cox for the amalgamation of the livings, very much as Wykeham had been joined to Ludford by another bishop in another diocese in another century. The petitioners stated that there were now only two houses in Clopton. Yet in 1352, only three years after the Black Death, there had been an outburst of new building of churches in this district, and another bishop had come to Clopton on October 7th to dedicate the new church of St. Mary. Its name and site are now preserved only on the 6-inch Ordnance map and cattle graze its mounds.

Ruined and falling churches came under official notice whenever reforming bishops and archdeacons took pains to hold thorough visitations of their parishes. At a visitation[45] of 1518 the church of Fleet Marston, Bucks., was reported *ruinous*: in Wolsey's Inquiry of 1517 the depopulation had been reported.[46] Similarly[47] we find the Dean and Canons of St. Mary in the Fields, Norwich, who were lords of the manor and Rectors of Bowthorp, petitioning that the church might be reduced to a chapelry,

> there being no inhabitants in the town but the college servants who tilled their lands.

But the dean and canons had themselves been presented for depopulation in 1517. At a Norfolk hamlet, Holt in Lesiate, the Commissioners heard in 1518 that the late Thomas Thursby had destroyed

> a whole hamlet with all its houses and turned all the land to animal pasture

while in 1474 the church was reported to be ruinous, and the living was annexed to Ash Wicken.

The seventeenth-century visitations reveal a number of churches in ruins ever since the villagers had left. At Wyville, south of Grantham, now no more than a cluster of farm and cottages, the Lincoln visitation[48] of 1603–4 learned:

> ther ys neyther churche nor Chancel neyther inhabitants nor have not beene theis xl or l years.

The Church at East Wykeham had

> both churche and chauncell in some decay and lykely to be in more want, for that there are few or no parishioners.

The poverty of the inhabitants in very small villages was often stressed as a reason why effective rebuilding was impossible. Such was the case at Ludford Magna. At Binbrook the absentee landlord was blamed—

> the groundes occupied by forreners.

At Riseholme, where the church now stands in the park, accompanied only by the Hall

> the churche ys utterly ruinated . . . there ys lytle hope to have the church reedified for that there ys not above one parishioner. Sr George St. Poll knight ys owner of all the towne.

At Somerby by Brigg (which has since grown a little)

> there ys no parishioners but only the lord, mr. Rosseter esquier justice of peace in whose hands are all the tenem (ents) and lord of the parish.

At Buslingthorpe, near Market Rasen, the same Visitation found

> no parishioners or very fewe there,

and on the Ordnance map today it has its church and its manor farm standing alone.

In west Norfolk and Suffolk the retreat of settlement left behind it an astonishing scatter of ruined churches, many of which are still marked on the Ordnance map and others can be traced. Many of these fell into disuse earlier than the sixteenth century, but one or two were reported upon in 1516, like that at Choseley where

> 300 acres belonged to the said houses and 60 were ploughed; but the rest are pasture now, and by this decay the church there has fallen down.

There are abandoned churches in Buckinghamshire, Oxfordshire, Warwickshire, Northamptonshire and Nottinghamshire, although to a much smaller extent than in Norfolk.

(16) TWO CHURCHES OF LOST VILLAGES

(Above). The church of Quarrendon, Bucks., engraved for Lipscomb's History of Buckinghamshire *(1847). Only a few courses of stone now remain.*

(Below). The church at Wharram Percy, Yorks. E.R., seen in 1952 from one of the abandoned roads. The church had its side-aisles removed in the fifteenth century when the arches of the arcades were blocked up. It is now disused and the tower is falling.

The institutions to these benefices will be found recorded in the bishops' registers. The point at which institutions cease is not always an accurate guide to the point at which a population had ceased to exist, for, as we saw at Argam, the institution could continue long after the reduction of the church to a single course of walling. The principal use of the episcopal registers is to see whether a church ever existed at a given lost village, and to note when a union of livings occurred.

The sums at which parish churches were taxed cannot be taken as proportional to the value of the village fields or village incomes. The taxation reflected only the size of the glebe lands, which would vary with the generosity of the original endowment and subsequent benefactions, or the size of the cash income of a vicarage. Only when the ecclesiastical tax-lists take care to show that a church is now unable to pay its taxes can we glean information relevant to the subject of the decay of its villagers. The occasions when the assessment of clerical taxation were revised were 1291–92, 1340 and 1535 (with a revaluation in 1318 in the northern dioceses, where the Scottish invasions had wasted crops and villages).[49] Mortham on Tees fell from £66 13*s.* 4*d.* to nothing, and Rokeby from £5 to £2.

We may also use the ecclesiastical tax lists of 1291 and 1318 as a check-list to see what churches were still reckoned to be standing. The lost Argam, Little Cowden and Thorpe-le-Glebe are to be found entered in the Diocese of York.[50]

In 1340 Parliament granted Edward III the ninth lamb, fleece and sheaf together with a ninth of moveable property in cities and boroughs. The basis of the calculation of the worth of this ninth was an assumption that it would come to about the same sum as the tenth of all clerical income in 1292, and local juries were called upon to explain whenever the 1340 sums did not come up to that amount.[51]

Had a parish been depopulated by 1340 it seems unlikely that such a cogent fact would not have been stated. Many other excuses were put forward, ranging from inundations by the sea, raids by the Scots and the dryness of the summer to the murrain in sheep and the mildew in the corn.

In a number of areas jurors did state that a proportion of the village lands were lying uncultivated and unsown. The reason here seems to have been not bad weather but sheer absence of general demand. But in only one case have I found a statement that the village fields were completely deserted, and in no case except on the northern border was the reduction in taxation anywhere near 100%. Many of the churches of our deserted villages appear in the 1340 list without any plea for consideration. Such were Stretton Baskerville, Steane, Hogshaw and Fulbrook, Dunsthorpe and Shelswell.

The one case of total desertion is at Cublington, Bucks. It was stated by the jurors[52] that

> there are two carucates of land in the said parish which lie fallow and uncultivated, and thirteen houses stand empty and their tenants have gone away because of their poverty. Sheep and lambs are few, and there is no one in the parish substantial enough to be taxed to the Fifteenth.

We do not know what had happened at Cublington, but the village seems to have been refounded soon after 1400. The institution of the incumbent in 1410 was "the first of the new church", and the earthworks of the old village adjoin the new. It was not among the villages with fewer than ten inhabitants in 1428.

10

The records which we must now briefly describe are those which show the individual or the Crown taking action against depopulation or the threat of depopulation. Here we are no longer using documents to show that a community of a given size was in existence at a given date; we are in the field of contemporary descriptions of enclosure and depopulation.

The destruction of a village might concern only those with tenancies-at-will, and their eviction would not be quashed by the courts before 1488 even if the victims could obtain access to a court. But a depopulation might include freeholders or others to whom the court would afford protection if its ear could be obtained. It will be in the records of Chancery and the prerogative courts that we shall find records of villagers seeking such protection and redress.

Of the prerogative courts, we have documents from Star Chamber and Requests in London, but the records of the Council of the North and of the Marches are few. We know from stray references in other sources that the Council of the North was looked to as a protection against enclosing, but no record of a total depopulation being presented to it has yet been found.

In both Star Chamber and the Court of Requests agrarian grievances figured largely. But the majority of these are grievances which arose out of other discontents than the complete eviction of a village, and the amount of assistance for our investigation is small.

One of the best documented of the depopulation cases is that of Wilstrop which stood on the banks of the Nidd in the West Riding of Yorkshire. We have quoted from the Star Chamber hearings in this case on page 302, but it will be recalled that even here the depopulation was only a side-issue, an attempt to blacken the defendant's character in a dispute over tithe corn. Even the earlier case of riot at Wilstrop, which would seem to have been a direct result of the final depopulation, brought no explicit mention of a depopulation when a Star Chamber matter was made of it. What have we more explicitly ?

The vicar of Tarringe in Sussex gave evidence[53] to Star Chamber that there had been sixty houses in Heene, a hamlet of that parish.

> James Graves of Tarringe, brewer, William Cooke of East Grinstead being lords of all or a great part of the said town, the inhabitants being customary tenants by copy of Court Roll, for their own private gain and lucre in the six years past have taken the said houses into their own hands, turned out the inhabitants by great fines and do forbear to keep court so that the heirs cannot claim their rights. The orchards are dug up, the town is depopulated and there remains no sign of the houses.

Heene (before its repopulation and obliteration by Worthing) was a small and empty parish of 400 acres. This account, which probably dates from the early seventeenth century, shows how the eviction of the tenants might be spread over a number of years, opportunities taken as leases fell in and the manorial court abandoned when there ceased to be tenants.

We have quoted from other Star Chamber cases in Chapter Four, and one of the comparatively small number of Tudor depopulations in Norfolk can be inferred from the case[54] of Henry Fermor who "let down the houses at Thorpland" and "allowed a number of houses to decay . . . to the destruction of the said town".

The value of a case in a prerogative court may only be that it provides a *terminus ante quem.* If its discussion of a rack-rent or a stolen deed or an abducted heiress speaks all of pastures and sheep and nothing of corn and villagers then it is likely that we are at a point where the village had already disappeared.

Many thousands of petitions to the Lord Chancellor have survived the late fifteenth and sixteenth centuries. These have been listed by the Public Record Office with a note of the place and county concerned. Among these places are some which figure in our lists of depopulated places. Only occasionally is there such a direct reference[55] to a depopulation as that at Over Shuckburgh (Warws.) where a number of freeholders complain that

> Thomas Shuckburgh of late of hys grete power and myght hath enclosed severed and taken from ye said orators the sayde certyn grounde . . . and all thys he hath doon to wey your seyd besechors to dryfe theym from the seyd towne to the entente he myght laye it all to severall pasture as he hath doon the forsayde grounde.

Such a complaint of encroachment on land might have passed for any of the other hundred agrarian complaints one could turn up in these files. But the motive alleged is that of *total* abolition of the village community of husbandmen, one of whom, William Makeries, heads the petition. The lord's defence was simply that he was entitled to the common land in dispute since it was part of the common waste of the manor. He said nothing about his intentions, which are only revealed when we turn to the Court of Requests and find that Thomas Shuckburgh was sued for enclosure at Shuckburgh in May 1516 and Trinity term 1517—that is, before the Commission of 1517. When the Commission visited Warwickshire it reported the eviction of six persons in the 1517 Return and twelve persons in the 1518 Return.[56]

The decay of Misterton and Poultney in Leicestershire has been investigated by Dr. Hoskins, and there is an echo of the event in a short petition to the Chancellor from the Abbot of Sulby, whose abbey lay across the county bounds of the Avon in Northamptonshire:[57]

> the fields were used with tillage and nowe the said towns be pulled down and laid to pasture . . . whereby the Abbot hath lost certain rents. . . .

Where there is no such direct evidence we can only note that an enclosure formed the subject of a petition, and where we know from other sources that the enclosure was a depopulating enclosure we may infer that the complaint comes from that occasion or from the preliminary moves by a would-be encloser. In a petition[58] against the lord of Filgrave, Bucks., the Abbot of Lavendon Abbey alleged that Thomas Tyringham had offered him land in exchange when he enclosed his lordship. The Abbot refused but was then sued for the title of the house and 30 acres concerned. Tyringham's defence included the fact that he and his father were sole proprietors of the parish. This helps us to understand the ease with which Thomas depopulated it and the frequent occurrence of the family name in the Exchequer rolls after 1518.

To supplement the common law and the prerogative courts Wolsey created the Commission of Inquiry of 1517. We have already described the work of this Commission in Chapter Four, and here we can only briefly describe the documents which resulted from it. One of the principal parts of the record was made accessible by I. S. Leadam's *Domesday of Inclosures*, published in 1897, and by other Inquisitions which he published in the *Transactions* of the Royal

Historical Society between 1892 and 1894, and by the Nottinghamshire Inquisition which he edited for the Thoroton Society in 1902–4. These summaries of the Inquisition which he printed in the *Transactions* were taken from the Lansdowne MS. i, 153, at the British Museum, but they seem to correspond with the returns (also in summary form) at the Public Record Office. One interesting membrane among the files which does not seem to have been copied is a list, dated 1526, of those who were being warned to appear and answer for enclosures in Northamptonshire. A similar list exists for Nottinghamshire.[59]

The main body of the evidence of depopulation came from the Midland Counties whose Inquisitions were printed in the *Domesday*. The two volumes cover the counties of Berks., Bucks., Essex, Leics., Lincs., Northants., Oxon., Cheshire and Warwickshire, together with the 1518 return from Bedfordshire. These will all be found in the Chancery files.[60]

Following the receipt of these various returns from twenty-three counties, writs were issued ordering the appearance of enclosers at Easter 1518. Eight files of these writs have been preserved.[61] The individual files represent counties as follows: 1. Beds.; 2. Berks. and Middlesex; 3. Bucks.; 4. Glos.; 5. Leics.; 6. Northants.; 7. Oxon.; 8. Warws. Among these writs are pleadings and petitions from which we have already quoted in Chapter Four. The form of the writ of summons may be illustrated from the case of Sir Richard Knightley whose petition [62] for benefit of the statutory pardon has been printed by Hubert Hall.

> Henry . . . etc to the sheriff of Northamptonshire, greeting. An Inquisition of the 13th August last was returned to Chancery by the Commission of Inquiry, and in it, they found that Sir Richard Knightley was possessed of seven messuages in the hamlet of Snottyscombe . . . where seven ploughs were maintained. It was worth 17 pounds a year and held of us as of the Prince of Wales. We order you to make known to the said Sir Richard that he should appear before us in Chancery three weeks after Easter to show reason why half the profits of the said messuages and cottages and land since the said 4th of February until the

day when they shall be repaired and rebuilt, should not be forfeit to us according to the provisions of the Statute of 4 Henry VII; and also to hear what our Court shall determine in this matter. You shall return the names of those who served him with the writ, and this writ. Witness my hand 24th February 9 Henry VIII.
[Endorsed: Sir William Parr.]

Answer of Sir Richard Knightley in Chancery (cp. pages 410–13).

> John Ernle, on the King's behalf, said that according to the Inquisition one messuage called Bodyngtons with 100 acres had been cast down by the said Sir Richard. He asked that there should be an inquiry by verdict of his neighbours. The said Sir Richard similarly. As to two messuages called 'Everdone' and 'Clerkes' John Ernle said that the plea was defective and asked for judgment. As to three others called 'Rusleys', 'Ryseley' and 'Aleyns', John said at the time of the Inquisition and for three years earlier only 19 acres had gone with each of the three houses, as the inquisition said. And he has another messuage with twenty acres in Snotescombe as found in the Inquisition. The King asks for a local jury to investigate. Richard Knightley similarly.

Pleadings in the Chancery cases are also to be found in two other files. The file C43/2/ has been calendared, and it consists of transcripts of pleadings from twenty cases in eight Midland counties. The file C43/3 is uncalendared, but those enclosure cases which have been examined (Littlecote, m. 51; Stoke Poges, m. 54; Waddesdon, m. 95) do not seem to differ from those in C43/28/3 (Bucks.).

On the Close Roll for 1520 and 1526 there are enrolled recognizances, and a few enclosure cases are recorded on the *Coram Rege* Rolls,[63] but here again the detail is usually repeated in the recital of the case when it came before the Barons of the Exchequer as a revenue matter.

The nature of the Exchequer proceedings arising from the Inquiry of 1517–18 has already been described in Chapter Four and no more need be said here of the information which these cases provide. They supplement the *Domesday of Inclosures* whenever they deal with a case from the lost membranes of the Chancery files; they give the date of the depopulation, the name of the depopulator, the area and number of houses concerned, the number of people evicted usually in the same form as the familiar *Domesday* entries, and where the case is contested they will illustrate the defences which were pleaded or the grounds on which pardon was sought. I have also found among the Miscellanea of the Exchequer a contemporary summary of the Warwickshire part of the 1517 Returns. Unlike the Chancery returns and the Exchequer recital it is in English and includes only the principal cases where land was held of the King. Its summary[64] of the Wormleighton enclosure of 1498 is

> Willm. Coope gent hath decayed in Wormleighton anno 14 Henry VII xii mess. et iii cotages ccxl acres of arrable lond and hath enclosed the holle towns and convertid it into pasture the value by yere lx li. Xii plowes. Lx persones. The state thereof nowe in John Spencer holden of the King. There remayneth yet a manor place newe bylded by John Spencer and vi cotages.

The nature of the proceedings can briefly be illustrated from the case of Lillingstone Dayrell in Buckinghamshire. For this village there is a *scire facias* writ of the form already quoted in Knightley's case, which recited the facts found by the Inquiry of 1517 held at Fawley in October and a second Inquiry to supplement it which had been held at Long Crendon in September 1518. The 1517 findings have been printed in the *Domesday of Inclosures* and will not be repeated here. In brief, it was shown that Thomas Darrell, holding the land from the Earl of Oxford, had depopulated eight houses and four cottages when he enclosed 164 acres in February 1493 and forty persons were evicted

> *dolorose abinde recedere coacti fuerunt et in occium perducti sunt.*

The enclosure proved the undoing of the village, and only the Manor House remained

> *tota villa de Lullyngton Darrell predicta prosternitur et totaliter devastata existit praeterque unum capitale messuagium in quo predictus Thomas manet.*

The enclosed lands were worth £40 a year to Darrell. The

supplementary Inquiry of 1518 valued them at £46, and showed the economic incentive to enclosure by a valuation before enclosure of £23.

The main record of the hearing against Darrell begins in Michaelmas term 1540. Darrell had obtained a writ of *supersedeas* at a previous hearing in Michaelmas 1519, after promising to rebuild. He was left in peace until the Act of 1536 brought a revived interest in the Inquiry of 1517 and 1518. In 1540 the Barons heard the findings of 1517 and 1518 re-read, and since the seven houses seemed to have been still unrepaired at Michaelmas 1538 there was a *prima facie* case for a penalty under the 1536 Act. The Court ordered the sheriff of Buckinghamshire to order the occupier of the land, whoever he might be, to appear. Paul, the son of Thomas Darrell, appeared to show cause why half the profits of the lands should not be forfeit, as from Michaelmas 1538. After the formal pleading by his attorney, Darrell showed that the 300 acres of the second Inquiry were the same as the eight holdings of the first, and the eight houses in the second were similarly merely repeated from the first. There was no mention of the four cottages of the *Domesday* and the 1519 hearing. He claimed that only five houses had been destroyed in 1493 and that in March 1535 three houses had been built at Lillingstone and 150 acres ploughed "according to the nature of the soil and the course of husbandry of those parts"—using the words of the Act in his plea.

The case was adjourned eighteen times, until in Easter 1545 the Attorney General spoke for the Crown. He recited all the facts once again and the Court ordered a local jury to be empanelled and the facts found. In Hillary term 1545 the depositions of three local witnesses were read: they said that three houses did exist and had maintained ploughmen on 160 acres since 1535. In face of this the Attorney General accepted Darrell's pleading and the Barons adjourned the case *sine die*.

In fact there is reason to think that the rebuilding and the reconversion may have been only superficial. It will be realised that the Court had retreated considerably in being satisfied with three houses rebuilt and 150 acres converted when eight houses and 300 acres had been in question. It is possible that part of the parish was temporarily under the plough in 1545. Indeed the plea had only been that it was ploughed "according to the local course of husbandry", which leaves a good deal of latitude in interpretation.[65]

In his study of Leicestershire enclosure cases, Dr. Parker found reason to doubt the affirmation of rebuilding, and at Lillingstone we are fortunate to have the evidence of the glebe terrier[66] of 1601.

> Touchinge the gleabe of the parsonage of Lillingston yt is the comon opinion . . . that theyre hath bene a gleabe but what shoulde be the quantity and where yt shoulde lye, not man can tell bie reason of the pullinge downe of the towne and inclosure of the whole Lordship aboute some hundred yeres bigon.

The terrier of 1625 shows the incumbent a little more discontented than those who had compiled the terrier of 1601.

> Bei the reporte of men of fower score yeres olde there have bene twelve ploughs goinge and some six score inhabityngs, until afterwards and that aboute som ix score years since as it hath bene comonly reported, Thomas Darrell Esquier the first of five generations bought out the freeholders, inclosed the Lordship, pulled downe the towne turninge the same into fish pondes, and also pulled downe the parsonage house as it doth credentilie appeare bie divers foundations of walles.

It adds that the vicar's house had become a dairy house and

> it was an easie matter for a gredie Lordship to swallow up a little glebe.

The incumbent concludes bitterly that Darrell

> in a blind zeale for his soules healthe hath given the pasture to Lovefield (Luffield) Abbey.

It will also be seen, comparing the findings of 1517 and the "common opinion" of 1601 and 1625, that there had already arisen something of that confused memory of the date of population which we have already discussed in Chapter Three.

The later official Inquiries have been described in Chapter Four. Both in bulk and in relevance to our theme they are slight. Warwickshire apart, we have nothing from the Inquiry of 1548 comparable with the information collected in 1517 and 1518. The returns for Buckinghamshire in 1566 are very full, but the enclosures which they brought in to the net are not total depopulations but small-scale enclosures. The returns of 1607 are very similar.

For the years after 1548 we have to rely on scattered references in family papers or on chance information among the State papers. Thus there is evidence taken from the rioters of 1596 in Oxfordshire who had cried:

> we wish the hedges and they who made them in the ditches; are there not a hundred good men who will rise and knock down the gentlemen and rich men who made corn so dear and who took the commons? . . . Mr. Fryer has destroyed the whole town of Water Eaton.

The lord of Hampton Gay was also threatened. These lordships had been Oseney Abbey land before the Dissolution, and from the cartulary we can confirm that there had once been husbandmen here to be ejected from their commons, and houses to be cast down.[67]

II

Our principal post-destruction evidence from the seventeenth century can be gleaned from some of the legal disputes which arose from ambiguities created by depopulation. We have seen that some local historians were visiting the deserted fields in the second half of the seventeenth century, but if History was riding to the deserted villages in pursuit of Truth, the Law came in pursuit of tithes or taxes. It can be imagined that in the century after their disappearance the deserted villages posed some pretty problems of rating. The important taxes were parish taxes. The levy was on a parish basis, and the parish officers were collectors and assessors. But what of a parish which (even if it had a church) had no parishioners? What of a parson presented to two livings who finds one all pasture, the chapel gone, but who maintains his claim for tithe? What if neighbouring parishes, saddled with some of the descendants of the evicted villagers, complain that the owner of the pastures is not being levied to any poor rate at all? All these cases arose in various parts of the country.

Of these disputes, those over tithe were the most frequent. We may meet these either locally in the ecclesiastical court or in London in the Exchequer of Pleas. The heir to the depopulating landlord possessed the whole parish. Indeed without this right *de facto* or *de jure* his ancestors could hardly have depopulated. The sole proprietor was sole tithe payer and sole heir to the responsibility of maintaining the fabric. If he were indifferent to religion or to the cause of the Established Church he might easily, as we have seen in Lincolnshire, allow the fabric to decay. If the living were in his gift, a pliant incumbent might ask no questions and raise no clamour. In Northumberland the Delavals continued to pay tithes on the depopulated villages rather than risk an awkward lawsuit. But elsewhere there were lawsuits, and some of the evidence which we have already used for other purposes was taken from the records of such disputes.

In May 1609 the Vicar of Bicester brought an action[68] in the ecclesiastical court at Lincoln against Sir Michael and Sir Richard Blount, the owners of Wretchwick. Now we have already seen how this hamlet was destroyed by Bicester Priory, and in the course of this tithe dispute both plaintiff and defendant referred to a depopulation still remembered in the district, although with no precise recollection of how and when it had occurred.

The defendant denied that he was the depopulator:

> there never was any such tenants or depopulating of the said hamlet in his time since the dissolution of the said Priory . . . if there was any conversion of the same from tillage it was done—as he the defendant had been informed —many years since.

The plaintiff was rather more precise about the size and status of the village but inclined to suggest that the Blounts were connected with the depopulation and the fall in the value of the tithes.

> the said manor or hamlet of Wretchwick had been heretofore well manured and inhabited with at least thirty several tenants or householders, freeholders, copyholders, and leaseholders whose small tithes yearly would at this day be worth unto the vicar of the said vicarage one hundred marks at the least. The said manor or hamlet was now depopulated and the same was come wholly to the lands and possession of them the said defendants.

When Kennett made his *Collections* for the history of the Bicester district he was able to see many court rolls from Wretchwick and manorial accounts which were then in private hands. The latest of these which he quotes is from 1424–25, when the tenants' rents brought the Priory 73*s.* 4*d.*, the rent of crofts 34*s.*, and the rent of lands in the fields, meadows and pastures of Wretchwick another 56*s.* 6½*d.* The Priory, like their successors the Blounts, were sole lords, and had been since 1272.

There was similar disagreement between incumbent and lord of the manor at Clopton, Cambridgeshire, depopulated by John Fisher between 1500 and 1518. The encloser had bought out and ejected the occupiers of the common arable strips, but there remained the glebe strips, scattered among them. This enabled him to put the parson in a double difficulty: the petition[69] to Wolsey explains this:

> the said glebe he can in no wise occupy in tillage . . . as the residue of the said lands in the fields be laid to pasture, and if he should sow the glebe lands it would have been destroyed by cattle, and if he had put in any cattle on his glebe lands they would not abide upon it because there are no hedges, and no defence made between the grounds of your said orator and the ground of the farmers, for the fields have always time out of mind laid open.

The "farmers" were Robert Morgan and Robert Brockwell to whom Fisher had leased the pastures. There had been a similar dispute about 1500 between Fisher and the previous incumbent, and it is not possible to say whether the whole depopulating enclosure had taken place so early. (An Inquisition of 1511 into the lands of Fisher's son names a number of messuages, but in the fashion of Inquisitions *post mortem* of that century does not make clear whether the messuages lay in Clopton or in neighbouring villages where he also had held property.) Fisher was a London lawyer who had bought the parish from the Clopton family in 1489 and then followed his advantage. Clopton has been the subject of a careful monograph by the late Dr. W. M. Palmer, published in 1933, with two photographs of the abandoned site. He was able to trace the manorial descent, date the enclosure, locate the site of the church and bring together the Lay Subsidy material for the parish—including a rare type of document, a list of villagers who contributed to the Lay Subsidy of 1341 when the village's tax quota to the fifteenth was collected in wool.

We have already seen the parson of Lillingstone Dayrell bemoaning that

> it was an easie matter for a gredie Lordship to swallow up a little glebe

and our accounts of Kiplingcotes and its transported bells were drawn from the seventeenth-century tithe dispute. On the eastern slopes of the Wolds was Eastburn, and among the papers at the Diocesan Registry at York is "an allegation[70] for Thomas Thomlinson gen."

> The Towne or village of Eastburne of the parish of Kirkburne did aunciently consist of a great many messuages cottages and dwelling houses, and that then the lands of grounds belonging to the same was very inconsiderable and consisted most of tofts crofts garthes and other backsides belonging to the said houses.

These messuages had come into one man's hands, for a second document continues:

> the said messuages and other dwelling houses were about twelve years ago totally demolished and the towne of Eastburne quite depopulated by John Heron late of Beverley Esq. the then owner of the same and the grounds therunto belonging made into meadow.

and the interest of the owner of the tithes appears from the final sentence:

> since the demolishment and depopulation of the houses and town of Eastburne . . . the tithes of hay there have been much more valuable worth about 50*s*. or 3 *li*. per annum (previously) not . . . above 10*s*.

The allegation is not dated, but from the hand appears to be from the first half of the seventeenth century.

Eastburn is one of those sites marked on the Ordnance maps as "Ancient Village". It had been a Domesday vill, and in 1304 there had been 40½ bovates in bondage, nineteen cottages and a free tenant in his own cottage with 2 bovates in the open field; the buildings included the Manor and two dovecotes in its courtyard. By 1401 the lady of the manor possessed all the manor except 2 oxgangs and two messuages. The gap between this date and the "allegation" is too great for us to draw any deductions from this fact; in 200 years of agrarian change in the Wolds it would have been possible for the lady Isabel's demesne to have passed into a number of peasant hands and then to have been recreated as a unified holding by some ambitious sheepmaster or Beverley merchant.[71]

The poor rate posed questions similar to tithes, and inter-parochial rating disputes involving a lost village have been found among Quarter Sessions proceedings. The justices in Sessions had the duty of seeing that there was a constable to each parish. In empty parishes this was difficult and shepherds resisted the office. The constable who should have collected the poor rate from the owner of Caldcote township in Grandborough parish (Warws.) was fined for absenteeism in 1680. In 1653 the same court heard

> a great complaint that . . . Hodnell being anciently an eminent parish having inhabitants and officers as other towns before the depopulation thereof by enclosure . . . but for many years past the estate being in great men's hands and in a manner without inhabitants save shepherds, those lands with Chapel Ascote (also depopulated) being worth 1,500 pounds per annum bear no charge . . . whereupon it is prayed that one of the shepherds be appointed constable.

The prayer was granted, but he refused to serve and was fined £10. Eventually another was appointed, but by 1679 Hodnell had been assigned for poor law purposes to Fenny Compton parish. Other depopulated parishes, such as Combe Fields in the same county, were held by the judges at Assizes to be extra-parochial and exempt from all poor-rate.[72]

Few counties have full Quarter Sessions records from the sixteenth century when the justices might have been making specific inquiries about depopulation. It is probably as a result of the national Inquiry of 1607 that the North Riding justices of Yorkshire recorded the depopulation of four villages, naming the depopulator in three cases. A fifth village (which is shrunken rather than deserted) was named and then erased. The loss of the Assize records of the sixteenth century has robbed us of what would have been most valuable information.[73]

The occasional tithe and poor-law dispute appeal apart, the deserted village passes from official notice early in the seventeenth century until in the nineteenth century two great surveys by the officers of the central government produced a body of printed evidence which greatly assists the search for a lost village. These surveys were the Census of 1801 and the first edition of the 6-inch Ordnance survey map beginning in 1846.

12

The columns of the Census table are quick to show which townships have exceptionally small populations. But because the unit of enumeration was the traditional one of the township, we have a list of townships in 1801 to check either against medieval lists or against the modern map. The preservation of the areas of townships as units of local government administration, and so of census enumeration, is a remarkable continuity in tradition. The nineteenth-century census material has been reprinted in the *Victoria County History* volumes.

In Nottinghamshire eleven townships had fifty-one or

fewer inhabitants in both 1801 and 1901. Of these the following are "lost" villages:

	Inhabitants	
	1801	*1901*
Haughton	41	51
West Burton	33	51
Thorpe Le Glebe	20	37
Wiverton	2	33
Kilvington	20	30
Meering	7	9

In the Buckinghamshire census of 1801, nineteen townships which had formerly been villages mustered fewer than fifty inhabitants, and one other village achieved the distinction of having its depopulation recorded:

> the now depopulated village of Ekeney cum Petsoe, not even a single house remaining . . .

It will be seen that the deserted villages have census populations as large as fifty-one. In case this seems a rather populous desertion, it must be explained that it includes the servants in the great house and the inhabitants of cottages and farms which have been subsequently built on the periphery of the parish. The fully inhabited village of this part of the country could muster a population (again including the great house and peripheral building) ranging between 60 and 400.

If we make a similar comparison for the East Yorkshire Wolds in 1901, and take families rather than total population, we find occurring among the smallest entries a number of names which we have already known as deserted villages.

Taken by itself, the census cannot be more than a pointer, but it is an easily accessible source and one quickly worked over. Every case where less than half a dozen families remain in a lowland parish is suspicious and requires further study.

The Ordnance Survey maps are a source whose importance I assess as highly as the air photographs. Without them this book would be unwritten. Their utility begins with the first edition of the 6-inch sheets. These maps carefully recorded civil parishes and extra-parochial places as

TABLE 12

LOST VILLAGES OF YORKSHIRE IN THE CENSUS OF 1901

Township name	*Area in statute acres*	*Families or separate occupiers, 1901*
ESKE	1088	6
ARGAM	559	6
EASTON	734	3
FORDON	464	4
BRACKEN	677	3
COWLAM	2052	8
EASTBURN	823	3
ROTSEA	806	5
TOWTHORPE	1712	9
BELBY	582	3
EDDLETHORPE	718	8
FIRBY	525	6
WHARRAM PERCY	1459	7
OUSETHORPE	333	3
THORPE LE STREET	676	4
WAPLINGTON	813	4
WAULDBY	1021	8

In the *North Riding*, apart from the thinly populated parishes of the high dales, there are such parishes as

LITTLE EDSTONE	171	2
HUTTON HANG	590	4
WATH	372	2
COTCLIFFE	133	2 (1911:1)
LEAKE	429	2

and in the non-Pennine areas of the *West Riding*

BILHAM	536	7
STOTFOLD	256	1
WIDDINGTON	701	4

they stood before the boundary amalgamations of the nineteenth century. They record the settlement pattern before the age of suburbia and ribbon development which have repopulated some deserted sites and obscured their topography. Their careful record of district names, farm names, and even field names helps the identification of places which did not have parochial status. In a few instances the archaeological interests of the Survey caused the earthworks of deserted sites to be surveyed and incorporated in the map. The continuing interest of the Survey in an archaeological record has been responsible for a number of other sites finding their way on to later editions and on to the smaller-scale maps. Reference has already been made to the occasions when the Survey has done good by stealth in marking village streets as "moats" and by recording the medieval "fish ponds". The Archaeological Officer has kindly allowed me to see the current Record maps on the 6-inch scale for a number of counties, and the Lists in Chapter Ten have profited from this kindness.

The parish boundaries shown on a modern sheet can sometimes offer a silent clue to the extent of a depopulated township. When all the local boundaries have a symmetry disturbed only by one parish with an extra "bulge", and a lost township is to be located, it is reasonable to infer that the bulge represents the old, lost township added to the parish. The Lincolnshire parish of West Halton has the irregular shape of a fallen "L"—thus: ┘. It contains the lost Haythby which forms the foot of the "┘", with West Halton itself contributing the vertical leg. There are many other instances where parish boundaries hint at former villages.

Nothing need be said here about the utility of the air photographs in the R.A.F. Library. Despite the fact that archaeological investigation was not their purpose, the Plates in this book will be a sufficient illustration of the value of their assistance both in confirmation and exploration of sites. In general, the air photographs have been used in this work as confirmation of suspicions already aroused. The time which I could spare to visit the Library made it impossible to examine methodically every photograph over a county area to see whether there were other sites which had been missed in searching documentary sources: only on one occasion did a photograph examined for one site yield another.

The Head of the Department of Geography at University College, Hull, Mr. King, has had the foresight to obtain a virtually complete cover of the East Riding (and some other adjacent areas) for research work. He kindly allowed me to examine this collection to supplement a shorter visit to the R.A.F. Library. I was examining the photograph of Arras, whose depopulation is well attested in Star Chamber records: Sir Robert Constable had evicted the husbandmen in 1532. Over the boundary, in Etton parish, I noticed a small group of significant earthworks. These consisted of not more than a hamlet, but clearly defined. In size and lay-out they resembled Holme Archiepiscopi or Raventhorpe, two other East Riding sites which disappeared probably as early as the fourteenth century.[74]

I turned to Kirkby's Quest to see whether there was an unidentified vill in Etton. There was: and what was more, from charter evidence, Skaife had placed it at a point where the parishes of Etton, Gardham, Arras and Hesseleskew met. This is exactly where the earthworks lay, a little to the east of the Arras belt plantation. The name of this site was Ald Erghes (Old Arras). It is possible that there had been a migration down to the other Arras. A similar move from Gardham to Newton in the neighbouring parish is well attested. The former site of Gardham has been marked on the Ordnance map ever since the first edition.[75]

Since this book was written, Dr. J. K. St. Joseph, Curator in Air Photography in the University of Cambridge, has added many deserted and shrunken villages to his collection. A list of these will be published in volume 2 of the *Cambridge Air Surveys*.

13

Even for surviving and vigorous villages, maps from a date earlier than 1700 are rare, and it is not surprising that we have so few for deserted villages. The Elizabethan map of Whatborough has already been described in Chapter Two. Most depopulations had occurred before the skill of the map-maker had grappled with large-scale plans. In the case of seventeenth and eighteenth-century depopulations there is a slightly greater chance that an estate map may have survived. It was usually the great landed families who carried out the village-destroying improvements in this period, and these families had strong-rooms, muniment-rooms and estate offices in which maps might be preserved and survive.

Elsewhere I have published the modern Ordnance map of Wotton Underwood, Bucks., with the outline of a 1649 map drawn over it. The detail of the earlier map runs to houses and open-field strips, but for clarity the individual strips were not shown. The original 1649 map is at the Museum, Aylesbury. Although the church has survived, almost every other house has been removed, and part of the former village is now under the lake.

It is likely that more than one village site lies under a lake before the windows of a great house. We have no map of the former site of the village at Compton Verney (Warws.) but all the signs point to it being where the ornamental water now stretches.

We have confirmation at Castle Howard that the lake there does cover part of the former village of Hinderskelfe. The magnificent façade of Castle Howard overlooks a fountain (the figures of which were brought from the Great Exhibition) and a formal landscape of lawns, lakes and trees. Under them lies the village.

Among the estate maps at Castle Howard is a plan of the village in 1694, before the building of the present Castle Howard. Houses line the street and their gardens run back to the arable fields. The church lies next to the Castle and the rectory is at the eastern end of the village street. In the next estate map, that of 1727, the village has disappeared and with it the church and rectory. An agreement between the lord of Hinderskelfe and the Archbishop of York had provided for the leasing of the glebe lands, which consisted only of a few acres; the church and church-yard, and the rectory house and garden. With this lease, several times renewed, there were no property rights standing between the ambitious builder and his landscape design.

In the reign of Victoria a curious private Bill was considered and passed by Parliament. It enabled the Archbishop to exchange this little island of land at Castle Howard for something more useful in the parish of Sheriff Hutton.

The Act had a plan affixed, and any members of Parliament who looked at the plan must have wondered. The plan shows the buildings and gardens of Castle Howard. The land to be exchanged is marked in red. It consists of a tiny square just outside the south-west corner of the Castle and a slightly larger square, five acres in area, 300 yards to the west. About half this square is under the lake! The two areas were, of course, the church-site and the rectory-site. Their ghosts were troubling the lawyers, and a Private Bill was to lay them.[76]

Before the art of the surveyor achieved large-scale plans there were verbal surveys such as that of East Lilling, which we have quoted. These surveys are methodical descriptions, usually accompanied by valuations or suggestions for improvements. They might arise whenever an improving landowner commissioned them; or they might arise in the Middle Ages when a change of ownership made it necessary to value the new property. We could hardly wish for a better topographical description of the houses of a lost village than in a survey[77] of Frickley (W.R.) where we read in 1426 of

> a messuage called *Fox Place* and a bovate of land; this messuage lies between the King's highway from Pontefract to Rotherham on the south side, and the road leading from Wakefield to Doncaster on the other (northern) side.

or later, of

> a messuage with a croft called *Panelcroft* and a bovate of land being sixteen acres; it lies between *Shepardcroft* on the east, and the road leading from Pontefract to Rotherham. It also abuts on the road from Wakefield to Doncaster at its southern end, and at its northern end upon *Halstokyng*.

The survey names the three open fields of Frickley among which the strips which made up the bovate were scattered; they were *Mylnefield*, *Cloghfeld* and *Kyrkefeld*.

A hundred and thirty years earlier a survey had been made of the estates of the prebends of York. One of these prebends was lord of the manor of Holme Archiepiscopi near Wetwang, on the Wolds. The survey of *c.* 1295 named eight tenants as holding 32 bovates at an annual rent, and a further 2½ bovates were let to tenants.[78] There was a prebendal manor house, but nothing is left of the village except a crop mark. (Plate 11.)

14

We have now described the principal documentary sources on which this investigation has been based, and the chapter might easily double its length if every single source which had yielded some item of information were rigorously listed. We might then describe the grant of a Tuesday market and an annual fair of three days for the lost Cestersover, which lay so conveniently near the Watling Street; or the complete desertion of Rowley when the parishioners betook themselves to America; or the affray at an ale-drinking in the lost Cleaving; or the murdered man found dead in the fields of the lost Gainsthorpe; or the sheriff commandeering wheat from the fields of Compton Verney in 1445; or the complaints when the lost Steeton was still extending its ploughlands over commons and woods in the thirteenth century; or the windmill at the lost Weedley which can claim to be the oldest recorded in the country.[79]

In the investigations which have produced this book, no exactly identical line of inquiry was followed in each county. In Warwickshire, for example, the quest moved on from the empty parishes suggested by the 1-inch map to the comments of the county historian, Dugdale, and to the list given by John Rous in the fifteenth century. Confirmation was usually obtained by a personal visit or by a friend's visit. In Buckinghamshire much more reliance was placed on air photographs, while in Northamptonshire the methodical study of the subsidy lists and poll tax receipts was the first avenue of approach. In Yorkshire it was possible to move through air photographs, maps, field-work and tax sources almost in parallel, and this type of combined attack is obviously the most satisfactory. The ideal investigation would probably begin with the 1-inch map and the 1801 census and move back to the subsidy and poll tax lists, with a glance at the findings of 1517–18. Enough *prima facie* evidence would then have been collected for a double attack: one on the visible evidence of the fields; and one on the documentary sources of the type described in this chapter, which would have to be sought wherever they could be found.

Chapter Ten

LOST VILLAGES: COUNTY LISTS

> Provincial History is the most liable to mistakes, having so much to do with dates, names and local statements that the man of candour who has a knowledge of the subject will not be offended when he discovers an ear of bearded barley raring [*sic*] its head amidst a fine crop of wheat.
>
> *Conclusion* to John Throsby's edition of Robert Thoroton's *History of Nottinghamshire*, 1797.

THE aim of the lists which follow is the location of the principal sites by a six-figure grid reference from the 1-inch Ordnance map, or by a sheet number of the 6-inch map for those counties where the courtesy of the Archaeological Officer made a set of these larger-scale maps available to me on loan. As much supporting detail has been added as space will permit. References for more than a thousand sites are presented.

Certain counties have been exempt from elaborate treatment when lists of lost villages have already been published or have hope of separate publication. In these cases only the most interesting sites have been selected for notice. Such counties are Norfolk, where Mr. Allison's list has a hope of publication locally; Leicestershire where Dr. Hoskins' list is in print; and Warwickshire and Yorkshire where my own lists are in print. In the case of Lincolnshire I found that numerous additions to Canon Foster's list were necessary, and since my approach was rather different from his I have not thought it extravagant to print a new list, taking as my standard those villages which still had separate notice by the fourteenth-century tax-collectors.

No investigation beyond a brief scanning of the 1-inch map has been carried out for the counties of Monmouth,

Cornwall, Middlesex or Hereford, although at Kilpeck, *445305*, in the last-named county there is an excellent example of a shrunken or migrated village site and the *Report* of the Royal Commission on Historical Monuments adds Upper Chilstone, *399395*. The Isle of Man has also been omitted. Further local study may well show that single depopulations here and there did occur in these counties, but I have not thought it worth while to devote the time to an examination of the subsidy rolls and poll-tax receipts in order to record the few exceptions to a general verdict. Both the agrarian history of these counties and the silence of 1517 support the inference from maps and contemporary opinion in the age of depopulation.

I have had assistance from Mr. John Hurst in checking these lists and map references. I should be glad to hear of any amendments to my list which I shall accept in the spirit of the quotation which heads this chapter, and which I shall try to incorporate if re-publication should ever be possible.

ABBREVIATIONS EMPLOYED IN THE COUNTY LISTS

CPE. These references are to air photographs from the R.A.F.

DB. Domesday Book.

LS. Lay Subsidy, usually of 1334 unless qualified by a date.

PN. The appropriate county volume of the English Place-Name Society's publications.

PT. Poll Tax of 1377.

VCH. The appropriate county volume of the Victoria County Histories.

123456 References of this kind in italics are the National Grid location of the approximate area of the site or of a name or feature suggesting a site.

BEDFORDSHIRE

The county was visited by the Commissions of Inquiry in both 1517 and 1518. Their printed findings occupy 18 pages, and twenty-five of the enclosers were summoned to appear in Chancery. There were also some Exchequer proceedings. None of these cases concerns a large area enclosed, and the number of houses decayed is small. The largest degree of eviction was at Wresslingworth, where ten persons left their homes, but the village was not totally depopulated. Almost every village in the printed tax-lists of 1309 and 1332 ranks today as a substantial village. Not every Domesday settlement still survives, but the number of casualties is small, and some (like Putnoe) became granges of Warden Abbey, which can also be held responsible for the shrinkage of such post-Conquest settlements as Limbersey. Eversholt had thirty-nine persons wealthy enough to be taxed in 1309, but later in the century was on the brink of depopulation. It is now flourishing.

The general immunity of the county must be ascribed partly to the favourable conditions which the Ouse valley offered to corn-growing; and partly to the form of settlement which gives us the characteristic "Ends". Here, farms are scattered and the countryside has the appearance of late-colonised lands and a farming community never gathered together for defence or reclamation. Such an environment would produce a high proportion of land individually held and a relatively small place for the open fields whose enclosure elsewhere precipitated depopulations.

The number of certain fatalities can be put at two:

HIGHAM GOBION *103327* A sixteenth-century visitation of the parish found only 1 parishioner. In the Census of 1901 the parish maintained 59.

HOLCOT *945388* In the fourteenth century taxed with Salford; is described in the *VCH.* as "barely a village".

Local research may solve the more dubious problems of:

STRATTON BY BIGGLESWADE *205441* 29 names in 1332 tax-list; 1334 quota was 54*s*.

CHELLINGTON *961564* Church stands alone. Local tradition has a village nearby, and the migration may date from the amalgamation of Carlton and Chellington manors in the Trailly family in 1359.

SEGENHOE *980360* May never have been much more than a manor house and cottages.

COLWORTH *98161*.

STONDON, UPPER *150355*.

BERKSHIRE

The force of depopulation was not strongly felt in this county. In 1517 the jurors reported that 670 people had been evicted and 120 houses decayed between 1488 and 1517, but when their reports are examined in detail it will be found that the majority of offenders had done no more than enclose a few acres with the consequent decay of one or two houses in a village. The village names which occur are the names of existing villages. Substantial evictions were few, and an examination of the 1-inch map and of the *Nomina Villarum* does not suggest that many villages had disappeared in the period between 1316 and 1488.

The inference is that Berkshire settlements were so firmly planted and (in the west) so linked to a degree of pastoral husbandry alongside the arable that opportunity failed to match any will to enclose that may have been present among the Berkshire gentry. The offences reported in 1517 reflect an early piecemeal enclosure movement of the kind that was to be felt in the Midlands half a century later, producing not the Lost Village but the Elizabethan "decay of hospitality". The prosecutions for enclosure in Berkshire which were heard in the years following 1517 confirm this conclusion, as Table 15 shows.

Depopulations reported in 1517 in villages not surviving:

FULSCOT *545888* 29 persons.

Other depopulations:

SEACOURT Deserted by 1439. There were corn mills here in the twelfth century and fulling mills in the thirteenth. Excavated by R. L. S. Bruce Mitford. *486075*.

Other possible sites:

There are a number of shrunken settlements such as CHAPELWICK, *255880*; EAST COMPTON, *525796*, where eviction was reported in 1517, but subsequently resettled; EATON HASTINGS, *260982*; GOOSEY, *357918*; SHOTTESBROOKE, *841771*.

BUCKINGHAMSHIRE

As one of the counties most affected by depopulation, Buckinghamshire demands some detailed attention, and this list represents a summary of a detailed investigation. References are given to the sheet of the Ordnance Survey 6-inch map.

The distribution map shows that both the wooded Chilterns and the long-persisting forests of the northern parishes were virtually immune from depopulation. EVERSHAW and OKENEY seem to represent early depopulation, possibly as a direct result of the plagues. Manorial histories will be found in the *VCH*.

ASTON MULINS (or Bernard) *769083* *33 S.W.* CPE.UK. 2436/4038.

BOURTON *710334* *13 S.E.* By 1517 Inquiry.

BURSTON IN ASTON ABBOTS *842188* *28 N.E.* By 1517.

COTTESLOE IN WING *860230* *24 N.W.*

CRESLOW *812218* *23 S.E.* Church site, last presentation 1554; one very large field hints at old pasture enclosure. CPE. UK. 2436/4090.

DENHAM *758205* *23 S.W.* There is a local legend of a church, which may have been a manorial chapel. The Old Park wall remains in parts. There are suspicious earthworks east of the farm.

DODDERSHALL *721202* *22 S.E.* The Tudor map in Lipscomb's *History* shows cottages near the House.

EVERSHAW *636384* *7 S.E.* Said to have been a separate parish till fifteenth century. Upper and Lower Chapel farm recall the former chapel of St. Nicholas.

FILGRAVE *871484* *5 S.W.* This village (and Tyringham) were the subject of much Tudor litigation. In 1585 the church (site north of Rectory Farm) was in occasional use. By 1636 it was roofless. In 1578 Thomas Tyringham was pardoned for enclosure here.

FLEET MARSTON *779159* *28 N.W.* Church virtually alone. Prosecutions in Exchequer after 1517 suggest decay all through fifteenth century. 15 taxpayers, 1332.

GROVE *918225* *24 S.E.* "No village proper" says *VCH.*, iii, p. 361. Open fields here in 1607. Query whether ever a nucleated settlement?

HOGSHAW AND FULBROOK *739228* *23 N.W.* In 1327 20 persons taxed. 314 acres under the plough in 1338 (*Camden Soc.*, lxv (1885) pp. 68–69). In 1517 depopulation dated as 1487. Church of St. John now gone; was in occasional use till 1650. See *VCH.*, iv, p. 54.

LENBOROUGH *705300* *18 N.E.* In 1517 dated as 1500 and 1506. Now one farm.

LIDCOTE (LITTLECOTE) IN STEWKLEY *834244* *23 N.E.* An extent of 1323 shows a normal arable village. Depopulated by 1517. Former chapel of St. Giles lies near the Mansion, now a farm.

LILLINGSTONE DAYRELL *706398* *8 S.E.* In 1517 whole village reported destroyed in 1490. Confirmed by glebe terriers.

LISCOMBE IN SOULBURY *885256* *20 S.W.* Hamlet went with making of park *c.* 1505?

OKENEY (OR EKENEY) *920490* *5 N.E.* The church site is in a pasture field to the S.E. of Petsoe Manor, called St. Martin's field. The benefices of Okeney and Petsoe, *q.v.*, were united *c.* 1459. By 1560 both churches had gone. Okeney is now "assessed and rated to the parish of Emberton".

OLNEY HYDE *874536* *2 S.W.* The parish has only 11 fields. Olney Park, which this may represent, was enclosed in 1374. In 1353 Olney Hyde was a hamlet "worth 90*s*. and not more on account of the Pestilence".

PETSOE *919494* *5 N.E.* Benefice united to Okeney in fifteenth century.

QUARRENDON *800155* *28 S.E.* Ruined church. In 1636 it was described as "a hamlet anciently enclosed and depopulated". The earthworks of streets and houses are very clear. There is said to be a Civil War encampment also on the hill-brow.

SHIPTON LEE IN QUAINTON *728213* *22 S.E.* Now shrunken to 2 or 3 farms. In a sixteenth-century map in Lipscomb there is a village cluster here. There was depopulation reported here in 1517, allegedly in 1504. In 1608 there were still 10 tenants.

STANTONBURY *835428* *9 N.E.* Well documented. Depopulated before 1517 and after 1487.

STOWE *678374* *13 N.W.* In 1710 there were 32 houses and a population of 180. The settlement seems to have been moved to Dodford, out of the Park. BOYCOTT, on the same sheet, is said by Willis to have been destroyed by 1735.

TATTENHOE *829339* *14 S.E.* The church stands practically alone with suspicious earthworks nearby.

TETCHWICK *679187* *27 N.W.* Now only 2 farms—shrunken village?

TYRINGHAM *859467* *5 S.W.* This depopulation is probably associated with the Tyringhams of Tyringham who depopulated Filgrave. The church stands alone in the Park. There are only the Hall and associated buildings besides. 7 messuages destroyed in 1562.

WALDRIDGE *783073* *33 S.W.* "A considerable hamlet", *Lipscomb*, ii, 166. CPE. UK. 2436/4038.

WINCHENDON, UPPER *746145* *Over 27 S.E. and 28 S.W.* Well documented. Destroyed by John Goodwyn before 1554.

WOTTON UNDERWOOD *868159* *27 N.W.* Much shrunken. Pre-emparking village plan in Aylesbury Museum.

Other suspect sites

ACKHAMPSTEAD (MOOR FARM) *805908* See *Records of Bucks.*, xv (1949), pp. 166–71.

ADDINGROVE, NEAR OAKLEY *665113* *32 N.W.* Once a chapelry of Brill, now a farm.

ASCOTT *900230* *24 N.E.*

BEACHENDON *759137* *28 S.W.* Domesday village.

BROUGHTON IN MENTMORE *900200* ? Leadam places a village here, which was depopulated in 1511.

CALDECOTE NEAR BROUGHTON, AYLESBURY *840130* *29 S.W.* *P.N.*, p. 147.

CALDECOTE NEAR NEWPORT PAGNELL *872421* *10 N.W.*

CHETWODE *640297* *17 N.E.* Scattered, with site away from modern church.

CUBLINGTON *843223* *23 S.E.* Migration. See p. 314 *supra.*

EYTHORPE *770140* *28 S.W.*

FOXCOTE *717358* *13 N.E.* Only shrunken?

STOKE MANDEVILLE *837095* Migration from near old church?

CAMBRIDGESHIRE

In the western half of the county there is a small number of sites whose history is similar to that of the Midland depopulations. The survival of the Hundred Rolls together with very full Lay Subsidy and poll tax material has enabled the assessments of size to be cross-checked.

Principal sites

CHILDERLEY, GREAT AND LITTLE *c. 357615* The village was destroyed by Sir John Cutts in the reign of Charles I for the enlargement of the Park. But in 1432 and 1489 heavy reliefs had been allowed from the tax quota of 66*s.* for the village and hamlet. In 1377 there were 76 who paid the poll tax. Five tracks meet at the site, a common pointer to a former community. There was still open field arable in 1417 and 1436 inquisitions *post mortem.* In 1279 there were 8 freemen and 16 villeins at least in Great Childerley and 4 free and 19 villeins in Little Childerley. Enclosure was also reported here in 1517.

CLOPTON *302488* This site has pride of place for the admirable monograph by Dr. W. M. Palmer. A new church was dedicated here in 1352, so that it is unlikely that the Black

Death had emptied the village. It was always taken with East Hatley for taxation purposes, although as the senior partner. The living was united with Croydon in 1561, since the enclosure *c.* 1500 had depopulated the village.

MALTON *373484* This village stood within Orwell parish. In 1279 there were 10 freemen, 4 villeins and 3 villeins at the least. The church stood in 1340, although in 1316 and subsequent taxation the village was always linked with Orwell. Some small evictions were reported here in 1517. The site is represented by Malton Farm. In 1428, 3 households.

WHITWELL *543545* This small village stood in Barton. It was a Domesday village, and in 1279 2 freemen and 11 villeins were named. In 1316 onwards it is linked with Barton for taxation purposes. (The village of WRATWORTH in Orwell is also said to be lost, but the Hundred Rolls show that this is not the same place.)

WIMPOLE *337510* The village has here been moved out of the Park, where some ruins are to be seen. There were 173 poll tax payers in 1377, and the village tax quota of 1334 was 145*s*. Only low reliefs were allowed in 1432, 1444 and 1489.

Depopulation in the Cambridgeshire fenland, like the fenland of Norfolk and Lincolnshire, is virtually non-existent. In the eastern half of the county identification is made difficult as nucleated villages give way to more scattered settlement on the higher ground and to fenland villages.

Among the possible sites in this part of the county are:

LANDWADE *622681* Enclosures of a small kind were reported in 1517 and there had been 44 people paying the poll tax of 1377. The tax quota of 1334 was 40*s*., well under the general average. The fifteenth-century reliefs, although rising from 8% in 1432 to 25% in 1489, are not spectacularly large. There was a chapel in 1279 (and 1340) and 29 names occur in the Hundred Rolls here.

BARHAM *575461* A hamlet of Linton which seems to have been of considerable size in 1279. In 1316 and later tax lists it is named only with Lynton.

BADLINGHAM *678709* Now a farm, had 37 poll tax payers and a tax quota in 1334 of 36*s*. Fifteenth-century reliefs were similar to LANDWADE.

HENNY IN SOHAM *557752* Was a Domesday village which never achieved separate mention in the tax lists. KENNET, *700683*, and SILVERLEY, *704602*, may be woodland and dispersed settlement or villages shrunken. CHILFORD in Linton, *567489*, suggests a village; similarly NOSTERFIELD in Shudy Camps, *c. 640443*.

CHESHIRE

This county of grazing and woodland was one of relatively late settlement with ample opportunity for combining pastoral pursuits with tillage. Like Shropshire and Lancashire, its small number of lost villages may be due to eighteenth-century emparking. The following sites have been noticed:

PLEMSTALL *456702* The church stands virtually alone on the edge of the Gowey marshes.

CHOLMONDELEY *545515* The former parochial chapel stands in the Castle Park.

As in the counties of the south-west, the scattered settlement makes it difficult to use isolated churches as evidence of former villages, otherwise SHOCKLACH, *432502*, and BRERETON, *781648*, would be candidates.

I have not been able to find any account of a depopulated settlement in Ormerod's *Cheshire*.

CUMBERLAND AND WESTMORLAND

These two counties shared with Northumberland some experience of destruction in border warfare and private raids. The survey of 1584, which is described under Northumberland, *infra*, singles out Millom and Uldale, but both of these have recovered. At LANGTON, a mile east of Appleby, *c. 710200*, the experience of the Northumberland villages at the hands of the sheepmaster was paralleled. The surveyors reported "the whole township decaied and converted into pasture, and nowe in the hands of the Earle of Cumberland". There had been earlier destruction here (Nicholson and Burn, *Cumberland and Westmorland*, i, p. 355. At ESTON in Arthuret, *433716*, there is said to be a "ruined parish" (Hutchinson, *Cumberland* (1794), ii, p. 545). SMARDALE, *734085* has a ruined chapel.

DERBYSHIRE

In the Census of 1801 only ten townships had fewer than fifty inhabitants, and some of these were moorland areas. Only in the Dove and Trent valleys are we likely to find conditions encouraging sheep depopulations. There are no returns for 1517, although two cases concerning Lee by Bradbourne, *194519*, were heard in the Exchequer. There seems to have been surprisingly little retreat of settlement from marginal lands in the Peak. The Parliamentary surveyors of 1649 knew that some villages or hamlets had gone (*VCH.*, ii, p. 175). Some small Domesday vills in the Chesterfield area seem to have disappeared (ex. inf. Mr. W. E. Godfrey). See also SP. 15/28/113 f. 13 (1584): 'the Earl of Leicester pulled down whole towns and villages for his pleasure'.

ALKMONKTON With a substantial tax quota of 22*s*. 6*d*. in 1334, this village must have been as large as any of its neighbours. A very large pasture field at *196386* is covered with remains of streets and houses. The Norman font now in the new church was dug up here at the point marked on the 6-inch O.S. map as "site of chapel". There has been some resettlement at a distance by the new church.

ARLESTON AND SINFIN. *335297* and *342312*. The two were linked for tax purposes. Neither is now more than a farm, although the growth of Derby may soon confuse the issue.

BARTON BLOUNT *209346*.

BENTLEY, HUNGRY *180388* A clearly defined set of streets.

BUPTON *c. 220370* Migrated?

CATTON *207155*.

EATON, COLD *148567* High tax quota in 1334. The wide green in front of the two surviving farms suggests a circle of houses.

EATON (OR EASTON) ON DOVE *118363* Old Hall appears on the O.S. map, *118363*. The nearby Sedsall, *111376*, was separately taxed in 1334.

FOREMARK *330265*.

Other possible sites:

ASHE *262326*.

AULT HUCKNALL *466652*.

DRAKELOWE *c. 240200*.

GRATTON *209619*.

HOON *c. 224300*.

MERCASTON *278424*.

SAPPERTON *186345*.

DEVON

Like Cornwall, Devon was not visited in 1517.

Dr. Hoskins tells me that there are examples of the retreat of settlement in this county, whose history he is now writing. Any estimate of the intensity of depopulation must await the publication of his book. Wholesale sheep depopulation does not seem very likely in this county of early enclosure and abundant upland pastures, but occasional depopulation by the Black Death or as the result of the fifteenth-century contraction cannot be ruled out. A site at Great Beere, *690034*, has been excavated by Mr. E. M. Jope.

DORSET

Like other chalk counties of the South, Dorset does not figure large in any contemporary discussions of depopulation. It was not visited in 1517. A small number of fifteenth-century depopulations have been recorded, with the characteristic amalgamations of parishes. A favourite county for gentlemen's seats, it can also offer a fair selection of churches standing alone in parkland such as HANFORD, *845110*.

In his *Civil Divisions of the County of Dorset*, published in 1833, E. Boswell carefully noted the depopulated parishes, and what little is known of their manorial descent or church fate can be seen in Hutchins' *History of the Antiquities of the County of Dorset* (3rd ed., 1863). References in the following list to that work are preceded by *H.* The *Report* of the Hist. Mon. Comm. (1952) has noted (p. 117) the shrunken village site at Frampton, *615955*.

FROME BELET near Dorchester *715891* The parish was united with West Stafford by 1470. There is a Frome Hill on the 1-inch O.S. map. (*H.*, ii, p. 514.) (Cp. 7 James I, c. 26.)

LACERTON *864105* The parish was amalgamated with Stour Paine in 1431. The site of the church has been noted by Dr. St. Joseph. It is locally known as Bones (Boons) Field. See also C. D. Drew in *Proc. Dorset Nat. Hist. and Arch. Soc.*, lxix (1947), pp. 45–51, for these vills and the lost RANSTON.

STEEPLETON IWERNE *862112* "Reduced to church and mansion". (*H.*, i, p. 298).

STINSFORD *715914* "Almost depopulated by the Earl of Ilchester". (*H.*, ii, p. 558.)

WIMBOURNE ALL SAINTS *c. 024126* The mother parish. Was united to Wimbourne St. Giles in 1733. All Hallows Farm suggests the location. Only the cemetery remains.

WINTERBOURNE CAME *705884* Has the classical symptoms of church in parkland.

WINTERBOURNE FARRINGDON *696885* The church was a half-mile west of Winterbourne Came. There are house-sites in the field (*H.*, ii, p. 519) which I have myself seen.

WITHERSTON NEAR POWERSTOCK *530970* Had its church in decay by the early 1500s. (*H.*, ii, p. 199.)

There are a number of other instances of chapels or churches decayed, and one promising folk-myth at East Chelborough where the church now at Lewcombe, *558075*, is said to have stood prior to its removal by fairies. Among fallen church buildings which I noted are West Woodyates (*H.*, iii, 614); West Bexington where the living was joined to Pucknowle in 1451; and Woolcomb Maltravers (*H.*, iv, p. 332). There are no doubt others.

It will be seen that sheep depopulation of the Tudor period is not likely to be the occasion on which many of these villages disappeared. The making of the great park is much more prominent. In the narrow sense of a "lost" village we cannot claim MILTON ABBAS, *800024*, among our number since the Earl built a magnificent compensatory village half a mile away. The market village of the Middle Ages is even more obliterated than the monastery alongside which it stood.

In the vestry of the abbey church hangs an engraved plan of the village before depopulation, from which its exact situation can be reconstructed. The work of Capability Brown has succeeded in replacing almost every inch of the market village by lawns and lakes, but a few house sites can be seen on the eastern slopes, a little below the line of the present road from the new village to the abbey and above the footpath.

Although not a lost village in the strict sense of the word, attention should be drawn to Dorset's lost borough of GOTOWRE. It was Edward I's intention that a new borough should be planted here on the shores of Poole Harbour, and although preliminary steps were taken to lay out a site and attract settlers, the venture never prospered. The name "Newton" is an indication of the general position of the borough, although the few houses which bear that name are the product of nineteenth-century clay workings in the hinterland, and the church marked on the map was a mission chapel. During the Second World War this area was taken over for battle practice, and little remains of Newton. The site of the thirteenth-century borough lay a little further to the north-west in what is now dense woodland and heathland. The name of the borough is preserved, slightly corrupted, in Goathorn plantation. The Rev. H. B. Cowl of Newton Cottage (which is much older than the Newton village and lies well to the west of it), kindly showed us the houses whose foundations he had observed in the woods and the clear signs of hollow ways and enclosure boundaries all over this area *c. 010852*. It would repay excavation.

Dorset also possesses in KNOWLTON, *024103* (*H.*, iii, p. 150) on Cranborne Chase one of the best examples of pagan and Christian occupation of a single site, with the church inside the prehistoric earthwork. The church is quite isolated, and there is no village; nothing could be seen in neighbouring fields to suggest village earthworks, but there has been much ploughing. Early Tudor surveys of the village and fields are to be found among the Wollaton MSS. (Univ. of Nottingham Library). See also P.R.O., E 178/699. Local investigations alone could authenticate MELCOMBE HORSEY, *748024*, where some earthworks suggest a *prima facie* case for a lost village, and at MELCOMBE BINGHAM where the church and Manor stand alone, *775021*. The houses in Hartfoot Lane may represent a migration from either or both Melcombes. Hutchins (iv, p. 367–8) had noted the double depopulation and the sites of former houses. At Melcombe Bingham he recorded the field name, *Town Hays*.

DURHAM

Although many village histories have been published in Surtees' *History* and (for the Stockton Ward) in the *VCH.*, they are too often reticent about the fate of the village or indeed whether a township ever had one. The medieval tax lists are few, but a detailed investigation of the records of the bishopric would probably repay effort.

The map shows examples of empty parishes and isolated churches, and re-population by colliery villages has come to cloud the issue in the last century. In general, the experience seems to have been half-way between that of Northumberland and the North Riding. Depopulation here is enumerated in the Border survey of 1584, which attributes decay since 1536 principally to the extortions of landlords, since the Scottish raiders did not come beyond Tyne. The principal sites which I have noted are:

CLAXTON *475280* *VCH.*, iii, p. 243.

EMBLETON *420298* *Ibid.*, p. 327.

GRINDON *395255* *Ibid.*, p. 247: "never a village", but Bishop Hatfield's Survey of 1382 (*Surtees Soc.*, p. 167) suggests a village.

LAYTON *377270* *VCH.*, iii, p. 323. Exchequer depositions at the P.R.O. (Trinity, 28 Eliz., no. 16) state that there had been a town here earlier in the century.

NEWSHAM *c. 383113* *VCH.*, iii, p. 228.

NEWTON, ARCHDEACON *255172* *Ibid.*, i, p. 360 for sketch-plan.

YODEN *433418* *Arch. Ael.* 2nd. Sr., x (1885), p. 186.

Among places whose situation suggests depopulation, but of which I have found no evidence are:

Old Burdon, *382505*; Butterwick with Oldacres, *385298*; Elstob, *340238*; Foxton, *363248*; Newbiggin E. and W., *376189 and 365185*; Shotton, *368254*; Slingley, *380480*; Whessoe, *276182*.

ESSEX

The evidence from the 1517 Returns is slight, and Dr. Hull thinks that Leadam was wrong in thinking that other returns were missing. Certainly there were no prosecutions in Exchequer until the day of the informer (1533–49), when, as shown on p. 113, *supra*, the "enclosure" cases were in fact the engrossing of a small number of adjacent holdings. Norden's *Description* (1594) said: "ther are noe great flockes of sheepe in this shire".

Some Domesday vills have disappeared, as Professor Darby has shown, but the map does not suggest that many medieval villages have disappeared. THUNDERLEY, *560360*, was amalgamated with Wimbish in 1425; Great and Little STANWAY, *952221* and *952206*, were amalgamated in 1366; OVINGTON and BEAUCHAMP ST. ETHELBERT in 1473, *c. 770420* (*VCH.*, i, pp. 403–4). Mr. F. G. Emmison tells me that SNOREHAM near Maldon, *c. 885996*, has disappeared. Wickham Bishops has an isolated church at *825113* in the fields, replaced by a modern church in the village. The church of LITTLE BIRCH, *951209*, is ruinous (Morant, *Essex*, ii, p. 50). In *Essex Review* lxii (1953), pp. 6–17, Mr. W. R. Powell has published a list of the county's churches and chapels in existence by 1300.

GLOUCESTERSHIRE

A few prosecutions followed the Returns of 1517, but no very startling evictions were disclosed. A group of depopulated villages lies at the northern corner of the county near to similar Warwickshire sites, but some of the villages in which evictions were reported in 1517 are still surviving. CLOPTON, *168455*, now in Warwickshire, is an exception, as is DIDCOT in Dumbleton, *002356*, where the Abbot of Tewkesbury evicted thirty villagers in 1491.

An excavation at HULLASEY, *974993*, has been mentioned in the text, *supra*, p. 68. The isolated church at OLDBURY ON SEVERN, *609919*, suggests a migration, and there is the usual folk-myth of the church that was destroyed in the night until it is built away from the village. The Rev. F. W. Potto-Hicks tells me that HARFORD by Bourton, *130225*, was formerly a village. WALL by Aldsworth was reckoned a village in the thirteenth century, *155106*. SEZINCOTE, *170310*, was listed by John Rous in his fifteenth-century attack on depopulation. Admirers of Mr. T. S. Eliot who have seen Little Gidding in the Hunts. list will be relieved to know that BURNT NORTON is also a suspect, although it may never have been much more than a manorial settlement, *145416*. LARK STOKE, *197438*, with twelve inhabitants in 1801, is now in Warwickshire, and there are suspicious earthworks. ICOMB in Church Icomb, *213226*, had thirteen people in 1801, and there may have been an amalgamation or migration here. The isolated "church-site" and manor house at LITTLE SODBURY, *760830*, suggests a similar event.

The Cotswolds have been remarkably free from depopulation, but UPTON, *c. 147348*, ROWELL, *074249* and NORTHWICK, *168365*, were formerly reckoned as villages. DITCHFORD TRES, *200370*, are now partly in Warwickshire; I have described the depopulation elsewhere. DAYLESFORD, *243259*, once in Worcestershire, is a marginal candidate for inclusion here.

HAMPSHIRE

The 1517 Commission of Inquiry visited Hampshire, but the seven membranes which the findings occupy have nothing but trivial enclosures to report. There are signs, as the list below indicates, that there was some sheep enclosure here in the late fifteenth century as well as some eighteenth-century emparking, but the total amount compared with the area of the county and the surviving villages is small.

ABBOTSTONE *565345* In 1340 there was a church here. In 1316 it had been reckoned a village, and in 1327 18 parishioners were wealthy enough to be taxed. The village tax quota of 1334 was 24*s.* 2*d.* The site is visible on the "green".

BLENDWORTH *712136* The village is described by the *VCH.* as "a small group" and the church appears to be disused. The basic tax was the high sum of 74*s.* 4*d.*, and 23 villagers were wealthy enough to pay tax in 1327.

BROWN AND CHILTON CANDOVER *576392* and *593401* Chilton Candover church was pulled down in 1876 but the village was destroyed soon after 1562 when it was bought by "one Fisher deceased who bought this place extirpating the inhabitants and pulling down the houses, there remaineth only the church and a farm". The fourteenth-century tax quotas have not survived except for 1327 when 15*s.* 1*d.* was paid by 8 people.

Brown Candover was destroyed in 1595 when "in like manner (to Fisher) beginneth one Corham to do with Brown Candover". The parish church, burned in 1845, stood on the left bank of the river, half a mile from the present church, opposite Candover House. Rebuilding has subsequently occurred here.

CHARFORD, NORTH AND SOUTH *c. 170190* Fewer than 10 households in 1428. Taxed as one village in 1316, but after that they are linked to a third village. The north church was in ruins by 1727, and the south church is known only by its site.

DOGMERSFIELD *c. 775515* The parish church stood in front of Dogmersfield House and was moved at an unknown date. The second church was rebuilt in its turn in 1843, and this third church is now dismantled and over-run. Basic tax: 44*s.* 6*d.* with 30 people able to pay tax in 1327. Relief t. Henry VI was 27%.

ELDON, UPPER *365278* In 1428 the parish had fewer than 10 households. The thirteenth-century church now stands in a farm-yard. It was reckoned a village in 1316.

FARLEY CHAMBERLAINE *395275* The village consists of the church, a farm and the school but the broken ground indicates settlement. In 1316 Farley was reckoned a hamlet, and the fifteenth-century tax relief was small.

HARTLEY MAUDIT *742361* The foundations of the manor house lie by the church in the fields. The village, says the *VCH.*, is "small and scattered". The quota of 1334 was 21*s.* It was reckoned a village in 1316, and in 1283 there are 27 tenants named, as well as an unspecified number not named. From the late fourteenth century, it was Duchy of Lancaster property. 1591: 4 Freeholders, 16 others. It is a picturesque site with its pool.

SWARRATON *570370* The church stood in the meadows and was finally removed in 1849. The rectory which stood near by was pulled down in 1820. The tax quota was 20*s.* 4*d.* and 15 villagers had paid tax in 1327. In the *Nomina Villarum* of 1316 it was reckoned a hamlet.

WESTON CORBETT *688470* The church was in ruins by the 1580s. In 1801 there were 10 inhabitants of the parish. The basic tax quota was the small sum of 11*s.* 8*d.* and fifteenth-century reliefs were small. It was a hamlet in 1316. Weston Patrick adjoins it, and has a church. The overgrown enclosure by the manor may represent Weston Corbett Church.

Other Suspects

GODSFIELD, *603371*, had a church or chapel in 1340, and in 1831 was reduced to one house; but it was a Knights Hospitallers' manor and may never have been more than a grange. The isolated church of LAVERSTOCK, *497490* (basic tax in 1334: 22*s.* 6*d.*), suggests a settlement once stood near by. WEST TISTED, says the *VCH.*, is "almost deserted" but the map, *650290*, does not reflect this. ELVETHAM church *783564*, stands in the park. BOSSINGTON, *335309*, has clear village earthworks to the south of the isolated church.

ISLE OF WIGHT

No depopulation was presented in 1517, despite the Act of 1488 which specifically applied to the Island. In 1559 a jury blamed the depopulation, not on enclosure, but on the loss of maritime traffic and employment, ". . . and nowe all goythe to London and Flaunders whiche killeth all this countrey along". However much this factor contributed, the language of the 1488 Act makes it clear that agrarian changes had also been important. There are folk myths of the loss of many Islanders in the battle of St. Aubin (July, 1488), the year of the anti-depopulation Act (*I.O.W. County Press*, Oct. 4, 1952). The low degree of mid-fifteenth-century relief suggests that the depopulation is after 1446, but the (imperfect) poll tax figures of 1379 suggest that the lost villages were already among the smaller. Their memory had all been preserved as tithing units as late as 1605.

East Medina

ASHEY *96 N.W.* Basic 70*s.* Reliefs 1438–46 small. Poll tax had 75 paying. This suggests a late-fifteenth-century depopulation.

BERNARDSLEY *96 N.W.* Basic tax: 40*s.* Reliefs 1438–46 small. Poll tax: in 1379 5 persons paid. An extent of 1297 gives the rents from 13 houses occupied by customary tenants, yielding £6 13*s.* 4*d.* in all. This suggests depopulation very near the Black Death.

HARDLEY Included with Yaverland in all tax figures. Said by *VCH.* (v, 162) to be in Bembridge Farm grounds. Excavations in progress near here at Centurion's Copse (1952), by Major Gordon Fowler, possibly of a lost WOLVERTON MANOR.

KNIGHTON Included for taxation with Arreton except for poll tax when Arreton had 97 and Knighton 92.

KURNE West of Brading. Included with Atherstone in all tax figures.

NUNWELL Tradition recorded in *VCH.*, v, 165, is that "a goodly house and great village of 50 houses" were consumed by fire in the time of Henry VI. (This village was not reckoned a tithing in 1605.)

PENNA AND FAIRLEE *90 S.W.* Basic: 50*s.* 8*d.* Poll tax: 36. Small reliefs 1438–46. There is a normal manorial extent t. Ed. I with 124 acres demesne arable.

STANDEN *95 N.W.* Basic tax: 22*s.* 8*d.* Poll tax: 16, but there had been 13 who were substantial enough to be taxed in 1327. In 1559 "the churche remaineth and is void". The tax reliefs in 1438, 1442 and 1446 were 4*s.*, 3*s.* and 2*s.* only.

STENBURY *98 S.E.* With Godshill for all tax purposes.

WYKE *98 S.E.* Included with Sandham except for poll tax when Sandham had 125 and Wike 107.

West Medina

ATHERFIELD West of Chale. Basic: 18*s.* 6*d.* No reliefs for poverty at all. Poll tax: 19, which suggests a late-fifteenth-century depopulation of a small village.

COMPTON *94 S.W.* Basic: 7*s.* 6*d.* which is very small. No reliefs. Poll tax: only 9 names.

SWAINSTON (HOUSE) Basic 233*s.* Reliefs all small. The high basic rate is due to establishment of the borough of Newton within the parish in 1255. The poll tax shows that Swainston was still substantial; there were 96 in Newton and 196 in Swainston. In the tax of 1327 seven times as many paid in Swainston as in Newton (Francheville). An extent of 1297 shows that Swainston had 288 acres of demesne arable in open field ("culturae"), 474 acres pasture, 300 acres wood and 22 acres meadow. The rents of 42 free tenants totalled £6 4*s.* 2*d.* and those of 81 customary tenants £2 16*s.* 5*d.* Newton had 77½ burgage tenements, yielding £5 2*s.* 8*d.* in rent. A rental of 1507 is ambiguously "Newton or Swainston", but suggests 50 tenants in Swainston. Swainston now lies within a park and the air photograph shows very little: it may be a later emparking case?

WATCHINGWELL now in CALBOURNE Basic: 18*s.* 2*d.* Small reliefs for poverty 1438–46. Poll tax: 15. A similar case to Atherfield? Extended at £7 3*s.* 5*d.* in 1300.

Other Sites

Complicated by rebuilding or scattered settlement pattern:

Billingham (*98 N.W.*; taxed with Chillerton but reckoned a township for taxation in wool of 1342); Kingston (*98 N.W.*; basic tax: 32*s*; no reliefs; forty-nine poll tax payers in 1379); Afton (*93 S.E.*; basic tax: 34*s.* 4*d.*; poll tax payers); Thorley (has isolated church. Village may have moved to Thorley Street or be resettled there. Taxed with Wellow.)

Other Notes

The air photograph evidence for the Island which I have seen (1951) is uniformly poor.

Quarr Abbey possessed many of the manors which appear in our list, and (like the Midland abbeys) may have contributed to the fifteenth-century depopulation.

HERTFORDSHIRE

In 1517 this county was immune from reports of depopulating enclosure, and there were no prosecutions later in the century. Comparison of the map with the fourteenth-century tax lists indicates that the lost settlements are few, and the wooded nature of the majority of the county would be sufficient explanation. A small number of sites lie on the more open chalk in the north-east.

The following sites have been noted:

BROADFIELD *c. 325310* A chapelry of Rushden once a parish, but then united to Cottered. There is a ruined church by chapel wood, which was decayed in the sixteenth century. The basic tax quota was 26*s.* 3*d.*, and a relief of 64% was given in 1446, suggesting desertion.

CALDECOTE *237385* 7 households in 1428. Tax quota 1334 was 42*s.* 4*d.* with *c.* 28% relief in 1446, which represents about the local average. 5 houses in 1801.

CHESFIELD *246279* Benefice united to Gravely, 1445 (*VCH.*, iii, p. 90).

CLOTHALL *272320* 6 households in 1428. Basic tax was 86*s.* 4*d.* with 45% reduction in 1446. In 1340 the greater part of the arable was said to be waste. The settlement is now very small.

ORWELL (or HORWELL BURY) *330364* Basic tax was 28*s.* 7*d.*, with 50% relief in 1446. This Domesday village lies in Kelshall parish, and now is part of the village.

PENDLEY *944117* Destroyed by Robert Whittingham, *c.* 1440.

THROCKING *338302* Basic tax 15*s.* 7*d.* with 75% relief in 1446. Only 8 householders in 1428. 10 persons in 1801.

THUNDRIDGE *368175* This small settlement was once a chapelry of Ware. The chapel ruin is shown on the 1-inch map. The church tower is fifteenth century, which seems to suggest a later enclosure as the cause of depopulation.

WAKELEY *341269* Last presentation to the living in 1454. Fewer than 10 households in 1428 and waste reported here in 1340. In 1801 Census the population was 7.

Other Sites

THORLEY *477189* The church stands alone, but a newer settlement, possibly a migration, has developed on the main road at Thorley Street, ¾-mile to the east. The basic tax was 70*s.*, with less than 30% relief in 1446. Average relief for the district was 16%.

The lost settlements, with the exception of Thundridge and Caldecote, suggest themselves as late fourteenth or early fifteenth-century desertions, probably as part of the post-Black Death retreat.

HUNTINGDONSHIRE

Depopulations here are small in number and probably early. The prosecutions following 1517 and the evidence of the Inquiry itself support this view. The eastern half of the county is allied to the "immune" fenland settlements of Cambridge, Norfolk and Lincolnshire. The western hundreds seem to have remained loyal to corn, and even to open fields: the percentage of open fields surviving until the age of Parliamentary enclosure in this county is as high as anywhere in England.

The sites which have been noticed are:

BOUGHTON FARM *198648 21 S.E.* A Domesday village with 6 villeins and 13 cottars in 1279. In 1316 it was linked with Diddington.

COPPINGFORD *165800 13 S.W.; 13 S.E.* Domesday village with 22 tenants in 1279. Church destroyed. In 1801 the parish, with outlying farms, mustered 53 people. The tax quota of 1334 was 54*s.* having been raised from the 36*s.* 8*d.* of 1332. In 1327 and 1332 28 people paid tax here; and less than 20% relief was obtained in 1448.

GIDDING, LITTLE *126817 13 N.W.* Tax quota of 46*s.* in 1334, representing 15*s.* 6*d.* increase on 1332. 18 paid tax here in 1332, but there were fewer than 10 households in 1428. In 1436 a relief of over 25%, and 38% in 1448. With outlying farms the Census of 1801 numbered 47 people.

SIBSON IN STIBBINGTON *096976* Domesday village. In 1279, hamlet of Water Newton and had 29 tenants. In 1316, as one of a trio. Not taxed separately in 1332 or 1334 onwards. Now re-building.

UPTHORPE *124720 17 S.W.* Former hamlet of Spaldwick. In 1279, 22 tenants. Not taxed separately in 1316 onwards. Plan in *VCH.*, i, 304, and in *Hist. Mon. Com. Hunts.*, p. 244*a*.

WASHINGLEY *135890 9 N.W.* In 1279 at least 42 tenants; in 1332 27 names paid tax, implying many more. The quota of 1334 was 60*s.* and the tax of 1322 and 1332 saw 27 and 25 taxpayers. By 1447 institutions had ceased, and the church had fallen by 1534. In 1512 the living was amalgamated with Lutton.

This seems to be an early fifteenth-century depopulation. Washingley was not named in 1428 as having fewer than 10 households, but in 1436 the relief from taxation was 50% and in 1448 it was 67%.

WEALD *230596* *26 S.W.* The shape of fields makes it seem that houses have been here fairly recently, perhaps before an eighteenth or nineteenth-century road diversion. If the track past the site were continued it would pass Croxton church, standing alone in the park with the village now outside.

Other Sites

There are a number of very shrunken sites; CALDECOTE, *141883*, *9 N.W.*, which was joined with Denton in medieval tax lists; LITTLE CATWORTH, *099728*, *16 S.E.*, which was a Domesday village, separately taxed in 1334 at the small sum of 14*s*. 8*d*., and with only seven paying the poll tax in 1377; STEEPLE GIDDING, *132814*, with its fishponds near the church; COLNE, *367762*, where St. Helen's church has been moved some 300–400 yards; and the Templar's manor of OGERSTON, *123897*, *5 S.W.*, probably no more than a grange farmstead. It was named as one of a trio in 1316. CONINGTON, *175857*, has also moved its centre, as the map in *VCH.* shows. MIDLOE, *162645*, may never have been more than a manor. WOOD WALTON has its isolated church near the Castle mound, *209821*.

Size of lost villages

The two lost villages which were important enough to be taxed separately in 1334 paid 54*s*. and 60*s*. as against an average for the district of 96*s*. This average, however, is inflated by the fact that 25% of all villages paid more than 140*s*. The median range is from 51*s*. to 60*s*. and thus the lost villages were not "untypical".

KENT

In this county of early enclosure, with ample opportunity for orchard and pastoral farming for the London market one would not expect to find many examples of villages depopulated in the course of a swing from arable to pasture. At the best there would be a few emparking enclosures and villages removed outside the park walls, leaving the church to companion the manor house. There may have been something of the kind near Aldington where two church sites can be seen within a couple of miles of each other (at *081351* and *093352*). Nearly a score of amalgamations of parishes are recorded in Hasted's *History of Kent* (1778).

The group of isolated and ruined churches on Romney Marsh are clear indications of a retreat of settlement since the day when the churches were built to serve the colonists of the reclaimed lands. In these conditions it is not possible to say that there were villages which the church served; judging from such surviving churches as Snave or Old Romney the number of houses immediately adjacent to the church was small, with scattered farms standing along the line of drains or on small islands raised a few feet above the old water-level. The ground adjacent to three of the ruined churches was carefully examined to see whether any house-sites suggested themselves. At MIDLEY, *031232*, the ground was completely ploughed out. Small fragments of pottery lay in the soil and there was a suggestion of a former hollow-way (the church lies well off any existing road). At HOPE ALL SAINTS, *049258*, and EASTBRIDGE, *074321*, there was again a possible road but little else. ORGARSWICK, *084306*, and the lost BLACKMANSTONE (P.T. 8) and ORLESTONE were not visited. The former was already too poor to pay its tenths in 1384, and the active life of these churches cannot have been more than two centuries. Orgarswick parish had six people in it at the Census of 1801, Eastbridge twenty-one, and Midley twenty-nine. The lost port of STONAR by Sandwich may also be noted (*Arch. Cant.*, lv (1942), pp. 37–52).

LANCASHIRE

Only two places had fewer than fifty persons in the census of 1801. Industrialisation has obscured the evidence from the ground; Accrington was depopulated when it became a Grange of Kirkstall, but it would be difficult to prove from the ground!

The general agrarian history seems to have been similar to that of Cheshire or Shropshire, with conditions producing immunity from depopulation through the ease with which they accommodated arable and pastoral pursuits within one framework.

LEICESTERSHIRE

The sites of this county have been very fully described by Dr. Hoskins, and some additional material on the size of the Leicestershire sites will be found in Tables 7, 17 and 18. The majority of sites in this county are well-authenticated depopulations of the period 1450–1550, and the sites have been well preserved in the undisturbed grasslands. The list below is intended as a guide for visitors, indicating some of the clearer sites.

WHATBOROUGH *767060* The classical site, with its Elizabethan map.

BESCABY *823264*	KNAPTOFT *625895*
INGARSBY *684055*	COTES DE VAL *553887*
HAMILTON *645075*	MISTERTON *556840*
BITTESBY *500860*	POULTNEY *582850*

LINCOLNSHIRE

This county has the distinction of being the subject of the pioneer list of lost villages by Canon C. W. Foster, which he published in its definitive form in 1924. In it, he listed 149 "extinct villages and places", but not all the places in the alphabetical list were ever villages, and some disappeared through other agencies than human will. More than one was drowned. The list also includes monastic granges and vills which have not been traced other than in Domesday Book.

Canon Foster's list is not strictly comparable with the other lists in this book, since he did not use any tax lists after 1332, nor the poll tax receipts nor the fifteenth-century tax reliefs for Lindsey; but it would be repetitive to reprint all the information given by Canon Foster, and the cause of comparability has been served by including Lincolnshire in the statistical Tables 17 and 18, pages 407–409, and in the tables giving local intensity. Mr. J. Golson is working on the history of settlement in this country.

It is hoped that the brief list below includes all the principal sites and the majority of the minor ones which disappeared after 1334. To save space and repetition the villages have been grouped according to certain important information which we have about them. It will be seen that Class (*a*) and Class (*b*) represent those villages badly affected by the plagues or already very small in 1334.

The sites marked * appeared in Canon Foster's list. Canon Foster described WYKEHAM and SOUTH CADEBY as "the best examples in the county" and they can be recommended to visitors. GAINSTHORPE, which Canon Foster did not list, was photographed from the air by O. G. S. Crawford, in 1924, and is well worth a visit. CALCETHORPE, which was the next parish to Wykeham, was also not listed, but there are excellent earthworks. The isolated churches of RAND, *106791*, and GOLTHO, *116774*, are partnered by very good village remains, and the "encampment" which is in reality SOMERBY village, *846897*, is well worth the trouble of obtaining permission to visit. It is not on a right of way, but the green lane from *850890* leads up to the fringe of the site. CALCEBY, *386758*, is also well worth seeing.

(Since the main portion of this book was written, an inspection of the unpublished files of the *Inquisitiones Nonarum* (E179/135/29) confirms the existence in 1341 of a number of churches at villages included in the following list: *e.g.* South Cadeby, East Wykeham.)

Class (*a*). Villages with more than 50% relief after the Black Death and also (if they had a parish church) mentioned in 1428 as having fewer than ten householders. The figure in brackets is the size of the village's original tax quota compared with its neighbours'.

CADEBY, NORTH *270960* (11%)
RAVENDALE, WEST *227997* (30%)
BEESBY *266966* (75%) 7 families in 1563.
HAWERBY *260975* (53%) 5 families in 1563.
AUDBY *280971* (27%)
CAWKWELL *282800* (36%)
*CARLTON, MIDDLE *950770*
*WYKEHAM, EAST AND WEST *225882* and *215890* (46%) 1 family in 1563.
ORFORD *204947* (27%) 24, PT. 1 family in 1563.
*HAVERCROFT *c. 830930*
SAWCLIFFE *912145* (58%)
MALTBY *314844* "Submerged village". *Kelly*, p. 299 (1937).

Class (*b*). Lost villages already having fewer than ten householders in 1428, but with relief small in 1354. Original tax quota expressed as a percentage of its neighbours'.

SKINNAND *940575* (33%) 3 families in 1563.
MERE *010652* (68%) Site described in *Kelly's Directory* (1932), p. 435.
DUNSBY *c. 035513* (30%) Former church. 5 families, 1563.
WYVILLE AND HUNGERTON *873302* (59%) Church now rebuilt.
KETSBY *370770* (57%) Had a fair and market.
GREETWELL *014715* (90%)
WALMSGATE *360775* (42%) 30 paid poll tax, 1377. 8 families, 1563.

RISEHOLME *980753* (42%)
SOUTHORPE in Edenham (66%) 1 family, 1563.
RISBY *c. 930150* (55%) 33 paid poll tax.
MAIDENWELL *322795* (40%) 25 paid poll tax. 4 families, 1563.
*CADEBY, SOUTH *244877* 2 families, 1563. Church down, *c.* 1450.
CALCETHORPE *248885* 4 families, 1563. Church down, *c.* 1450.
WYHAM *276951* (54%) 1 family, 1563.
COATES BY STOW *914835* (45%) 17 paid poll tax.
FIRSBY, EAST AND WEST *006854* and *978849* (72%) 25 paid poll tax.
DUNSTHORPE *302660* Church decayed by 1421.

From their inclusion in the 1428 list it may be inferred that all the above villages were rated as parishes. There are records of the amalgamation of some of these with their neighbours.

Class (*c*). This list contains only villages which were separately assessed in the Subsidy Rolls.

DUNSTALL *890936* (58%) 23 paid poll tax in 1377.
SOMERBY BY GAINSBOROUGH *846897* (67%) 54 paid.
CORRINGHAM, LITTLE *865903* (92%) 49 paid.
BRACKENBOROUGH *330906* (38%) 28 paid. Had a church.
GRIMBLETHORPE *238865* (22%)
FARFORTH *318785* (30%) 22 paid.
CALCEBY *386757* (32%) Had a church. PT. 60. 18 families, 1563.
DRIBY *390745* (31%)
FORDINGTON *420717* (18%) Had a Church. 3 families, 1563.
STOWE (NESS WAPENTAKE) Near Barholme. Not on 1-inch map.
HANDBECK In Wilsford (28%) Not on 1-inch map. 6 families, 1563.
*CASTHORP, EAST AND WEST *863356* (33%)
*BOWTHORPE (41%) There are two Bowthorpes, one in Manthorpe.
AUDLEBY AND HUNDON *110040* and *115025* (24%)
WATERTON *853180* 21 paid.
SANTON *940129* (62%) 58 paid.
GUNNERBY *215990* (28%) 5 families, 1563.
ROXHOLM *053505* (74%)
BULLINGTON *093780* (75%) 73 poll tax. 2 families, 1563.

Class (d). Lost villages which appear in the 1334 tax list only as junior partner in a pair of villages taxed together.

HOLME IN SUDBROOK *043762*
*CONESBY, GREAT *894138*
MANBY *936096*
*CONESBY, LITTLE *876144*
*HAYTHBY *890190*
GILBY *864933*
*BECKFIELD *190927*
*KETTLEBY IN BIGBY *034079* 1 family in 1563.
KETTLEBY THORPE *042079* 5 families in 1563.
*HARDWICK, WYKHAM and DRAYCOTE *c. 120990*
ROXTON *168126*
FONABY *109030*
*CAWTHORPE IN COVENHAM *c. 350960*
ALEBY IN RIGSBY *438770*
STAIN IN WITHERN *469848* Once had its church.
TOTHILL IN RESTON *419813*
DEXTHORPE IN DALBY *406717*
*HARDWICK IN PANTON *c. 175790* ?the "Panton Parva" of C 135/261/8 when 18 tofts.
BECKERING IN HOWTON *121806*
*BANTHORP *062110* (1-inch, O.S. sheet *123*.)
*RINGSTHORPE *925415*
CASEWICK *078090* (sheet *123*).
*TOWTHORPE *925385*
*DUNSTHORPE AND WESTHORPE *In and near Grantham.*
*OSGARTH IN ROPSLEY *Site not known*
*HOUGHTON AND WALTON *In and near Grantham*
*MILTHORPE *Site not known. F. p. lxi places it in Quarrington*
BACTON WITH ASGARBY *=Boughton 124455*?
*THORPE LATIMER *132397*
LOBTHORPE *954207* 9 families in 1563
*OUSEBY IN SEMPRINGHAM *104343*
WEST WILLOUGHBY *965435* 7 families in 1563
*THORPE PARVA *Site not known: in Westborough*
*STAPLEFORD PARVA *Exact site not known: near Broughton*
GUNBY *468667*
CROFTON *055401*

Class (e). Villages not separately assessed in 1334.

GAINSTHORPE *956011*
*CROSSHOLME *992917*

*COATHAM *155113* Cistercian depopulation? (*Monasticon*, v, p. 676.)

*STURTON, LITTLE *215755* Presented in 1517. 1 family in 1563.

GOLTHO *116774* Very clear site. 8 families, 1563.

*GANTHORPE *924291*

*THORESBY AND STICHESBY Monastic depopulation in Revesby.

SEMPRINGHAM *106329* The whole village is said to have entered the monastery with its founder.

SOMERTON *954586*

NORFOLK

With its very diverse geographical conditions, this county makes an interesting study in the distribution of lost villages. A preliminary study of the sites has been made by Mr. K. J. Allison (*Lost Villages of Norfolk*: unpublished thesis, Department of Geography, the University of Leeds), and in view of the possible publication of his work in *Norfolk Archaeology* no formal list is given here.

The Commissioners visited Norfolk in 1517, and reported a small amount of total depopulation since 1488, and Mr. Allison thinks that depopulation of this kind was felt principally in the centre and north of the county. In the south-west there is the Breckland where the situation may be parallel to that of south-east Lindsey or parts of the Yorkshire wolds: a retreat of settlement in the late fourteenth century in the face of marginal environmental conditions. In the Fens and in the dispersed settlements of the north-east there was very little depopulation at any period.

Norfolk is unequalled for the number of its ruined churches where villages formerly stood, and since most of these are marked in Gothic type on the 1-inch O.S. map they form a ready-made guide for the visitor. The return of the plough to East Anglia in the last two centuries has meant that sites have been much more disturbed than the Midlands, and a number seem to have been ploughed out. At others, as at PUDDING NORTON, *923278*, the field with the ruined church and street-earthworks is an island of grass in the parish cornlands.

The best sites to visit are:

BAWSEY, *662207*.
CALDECOTE, *745035*.
EGMERE, *897374*.
GODWICK, *905222*.
WELL, *750046*.
WEST WRETHAM, *899914*.

Good R.A.F. photographs exist of PUDDING NORTON, *924277*, CALDECOTE, *745033*, TESTERTON, *937267*, HOUGHTON ON THE HILL, *867053* and KEMPSTONE, *886160*. A pre-war photograph taken by the Norfolk and Norwich Aero Club suggests the site of a lost Domesday settlement, *896191*, although only excavation could confirm.

West Wretham's field system is the subject of a well-known article by H. C. Darby and John Saltmarsh in *Economic History*, iii (1935), pp. 30–44. My own attention was first drawn to the Norfolk sites by reading Mr. Saltmarsh's article in *Cambridge Historical Journal*, vii, p. 24.

Mr. Allison's provisional assignment of date to the depopulations shows that there were 726 separate places named in Domesday Book, 99 of which have since disappeared. Of these, 34 do not appear in the *Nomina Villarum* of 1316. By that time other settlements had been added to the map, and some of these have also disappeared. In the 1334 tax list 684 villages are named, and 65 of these (or 9%) are lost. From his maps I have calculated that:

45 villages were probably depopulated by 1400.
55 villages were probably depopulated after 1400.
15 others which were depopulated after 1400 can be provisionally assigned to the Yorkist and Tudor period.
10 have their dates quite uncertain.

There are a few cases (*e.g.* Houghton, *794285*) which are emparking enclosures with the removal of the village in the eighteenth century. The clearest cases of a Tudor depopulation are: the "whole hamlet" of HOLT, *676185*, reported on in 1517; CHOSELEY, *755408*, and THORPLAND, *938322*, in 1520.

NORTHAMPTONSHIRE

In view of the importance of this county's sheep-depopulations a full list of sites is printed here, with references to the sheet of the 6-inch Ordnance map. The distribution map and the tables printed above, page 235, show that, as in Warwickshire, there was immunity from depopulations in those parts of the county where forest persisted late, and in the fen-borders at the east.

While the majority of these sites were destroyed late enough for their fate to be presented in 1517, there are a few sites that had disappeared earlier. Steane's four households in 1428 contrasts with the fifty-one poll tax payers of 1377, and Sulby had similarly declined. Sibberston had only thirteen paying tax in 1377 and institutions to the church ceased in 1389. Others which had shrunk in the fourteenth and fifteenth centuries continued as small hamlets until their final destruction. Glendon, with fewer than ten householders in 1428, was finally depopulated in 1513. Faxton on the other hand has shrunken since 1746 (plate 12).

The first list includes the sites which are better documented and for which the location is less in doubt. A second list of less certain sites is appended.

APPLETREE IN ASTON *483497* *54 N.W.* Good, clear site.

ASTWELL (*see* FAWCOTE) *610440* *59 N.E.* In PT. joined with Fawcote.

ASTWICK IN EVENLEY *565333* *63 S.W.* District name on map. N.B. "Old Town Hovel" to north of road. Good site. Unenclosed t. H. VIII.

BARFORD *850820* *25 N.W.* *Bridges*, ii, 72. Church standing, 1625. 1517: *quasi tota villa destruitur.* 52 PT.

BROCKHALL *633626* *43 N.E.* Probably a post-Tudor depopulation. Enclosed, 1605. In Bridges' day there were 12 houses. In 1327 Harleston was *hamletta* of Brockhall.

CANONS ASHBY *578506* *55 N.W.* 24 persons evicted in 1492. In 1377 82 laymen paid the poll tax. 41 houses in 1343.

CASWELL IN GREEN'S NORTON *651510* *56 N.W.* Sir Nicholas Vaux enclosed the whole hamlet in 1509.

CATESBY *526594* *42 S.E.* In Upper and Lower Catesby in 1377 172 persons paid poll tax, and 126 in 1379. The Priory evicted 60 persons from 14 dwellings in 1491.

CHURCH CHARWELTON *545555* *49 N.E.* Earthworks near church. This part of Charwelton is recorded as depopulated by John Rous, writing *c.* 1490.

EASTON NESTON *703493* *56 N.E.* The church stands alone in the park with the hamlet of Hulcote outside the park. In 1327 60 paid tax in the two places, and in 1377 118 paid poll tax there.

EDGECOTE *505479* *54 N.E.* and *S.E.* 95 PT. (1377). 40 persons evicted by 1503. But see Baker, *Northamptonshire*, i, p. 495.

ELKINGTON *620760* *29 N.E.* Pre-Tudor? No prosecutions in 1517. 30 PT. Bridges says there was a church here. Institutions ceased before 1420.

ELMINGTON IN OUNDLE *063893* *19 N.W.* A number of enclosures in this hamlet were reported from 1494 onwards. PT. with Oundle.

FAWCLIFF *544679 35 N.E.* This may be Braunston Cleves. Mr. Franey suggests that it can be seen at the sharp bend in the lane to Barby.

FAWCOTE *595430 59 N.W.* This place is always linked with the equally lost Astwell in tax documents. In 1377 59 persons paid poll tax, and in the *scire facias* writs of 1517 9 depopulations are mentioned.

FAWSLEY *566567 50 N.W.* 90 people paid poll tax in this village in 1377; and 66 in the much-evaded tax of 1379. In 1327 52 paid the Lay Subsidy.

FAXTON *785752 31 N.W.* "No village" *VCH.*, iv, 167. With Mawsley 94 PT. Mr. King of the Northamptonshire Record Society kindly tells me that there is a map of 1746 showing about 32 cottages here.

FOSCOTE *662473 56 S.W.* Some depopulation in 1488.

FURTHO *774430 61 N.W.* *Bridges*, i, 296, says depopulated t. Jas. I with remains of the village still to be seen in his day. Sir Richard Empson had licence to enclose, 1498.

GLENDON *846814 25 N.W.* Fewer than ten households, 1428. Extensive depopulation reported in 1513. "Old enclosure" *Bridges*, ii, 13.

HALSE IN BRACKLEY *566404 59 S.W.* This Domesday village, said to be the mother settlement of Brackley, is now 3 scattered farms. 107 PT.

HOTHORPE *667852 15 S.W.* In 1377 57 people paid poll tax. Bridges speaks of about 20 houses, so this may be an emparking dcpopulation of eighteenth century? I have visited the site, which seems to lie to the west of the Hall.

KINGSTHORPE *080856 19 S.E.* *Bridges*, ii, 417, "marks of a village".

KIRBY (GROUNDS) in WOODEND *636495 55 N.E.* *Baker*, ii, 30, "traditionally a considerable village". 38 persons evicted, 1487. Faintly visible on ground today.

MAWSLEY *c. 800760 31 N.E.* This parish is now one house. It was a hundred meeting place. With Faxton PT.

NEWBOTTLE *524368 62 N.E.* 36 expelled in 1488. In 1377 it and its hamlets paid tax for 115 persons.

ONLEY IN BARBY *520715 28 S.E.* This hamlet of Barby has been partly excavated by Mr. Franey in "chapel close".

PAPLEY IN WARMINGTON *106891 19 N.E.* *Bridges*, ii, 483, "depopulated". 54 expelled, 1499, and Star Chamber proceedings in 1539 against John Elmes.

POKESLEY (=PUXLEY) *756426* *61 N.W.* *61 S.W.* Four farms scattered down a long straggling road as if a former street. Depopulated in 1489. Pardon to Sir Nicholas Vaux by Henry VIII.

POTCOTE IN COLD HIGHAM *657527* *51 S.W.* In 1499 30 persons expelled.

PURSTON, LITTLE *c. 510390* *58 S.E.* 43 expelled in 1494. *PN.*, p. 59, equates it with Buston, but there is a Little Purston Farm on the 6-inch O.S. map.

SIBBERSTON (LODGE) IN THORNHAUGH *064998* *7 S.W.* *7 N.W.* *VCH.*, ii, 529. Few traces of village or church. Last record of church, 1389. 13 PT.

SNORSCOMB IN EVERDON. *597561* *50 N.E.* A Knightley depopulation with a string of proceedings against him in the Exchequer (E. 159/298; E. 368/292).

STANFORD ON AVON *590789* *22 S.W.* Now very small. But 131 P.T. in *Down* and *Stanford*, 1377. Bridges suggests it was still substantial in his day. It is eighteenth-century emparking? Mr. Franey says quite extensive earthworks north of the church.

STEANE *555390* *59 S.W.* *Bridges*, i, 196, "Depopulated town". *VCH.*, ii, 418, sketch of earthworks. 1377, 51 people paid poll tax. In 1327 17 paid Lay Subsidy. Few households, 1428.

STONETON *463547* *49 N.W.* *Bridges*, i, 117, "formerly a town", mentioned by Rous *c.* 1490 as enclosed.

STUCHBURY *569441* *59 N.W.* *Bridges*, i, 201, "now stands neither church nor town". A Domesday village. 22 paid Lay Subsidy in 1327. 59 PT. Institutions ceased mid-sixteenth century.

SULBY *660815* *23 N.W.* Bridges says it was 1 m. N.E. Welford. In 1377 89 paid poll tax . Fewer than 10 households in 1428.

THORPE (THRUPP) IN NORTON *600656* *36 S.E.* In 1498 100 persons expelled, and in 1518 *ecclesia in desolacionem*. A Domesday village. Thorpe and Norton taxed together: 1327, 57 pay; 1377 poll tax, 182 pay; 1379, the evaded tax, 136 pay.

THORPE LUBBENHAM *705866* *15 N.E.* *15 S.E.* Hall only on 6-inch O.S. Parish name. Not presented in any sixteenth-century prosecutions for depopulation. PT. 27 in 1377.

THORPE UNDERWOOD IN HARRINGTON *787811* *24 N.W.* 24 persons expelled in 1492 from "the mansion place", which may not indicate a village. PT. with Harrington.

WALTON GROUNDS *506346* *62 S.E.* I have visited this fine site, lying on the Port Way. 80 persons were expelled in 1486, and Bridges says the church was down in Leland's day. In P.R.O. C 47/7/2/3/m2, *tota Villa* is said to be depopulated. In 1327 17 paid the Lay Subsidy including a "William ad Port" and a "Dominus John de le hyle". In 1377 it pays with Aynho (186 people).

WYTHEMAIL (PARK FARM) *840719* *32 S.W.* *VCH.*, iv, 204, "decay . . . late 15th century".

SECOND LIST

This list includes sites for which the evidence is only *prima facie* (*e.g.* a civil parish without a village), and others where the settlement is shrunken to a few houses only.

ACHURCH IN THORPE ACHURCH *022832* *26 N.E.* Church and cottages only. Has village migrated to Thorpe? Achurch is in DB., Thorpe not.

ALTHORPE *682650* *37 S.W.* Bridges suggests there was a village. In 1327 21 paid Lay Subsidy here. 51 poll tax.

ARMSTON *060858* *19 S.W.* Domesday village.

BIGGIN (NOW IN HENFIELD) *010890* *18 N.E.* Some enclosure and depopulation here in 1518.

BOUGHTON IN WEEKLEY *900815* *25 N.E.* Boughton in DB. but Weekley not. In 1377 12 paid poll tax at B. Migration?

BRAUNSTON CLEEVES *see* FAWCLIFF, other list.

BURCOTE NEAR TOWCESTER *695468* or *667508* *56 S.E.* Depopulation here in 1499 but whether Wood Burcote (still there) or Field Burcote (shrunken) I cannot yet say.

CHILCOTES COVERT *PN.*, p. 65, says this is site of Domesday vill.

COTES IN GRETTON *c. 880930* ? *11* *PN.*, p. 166, put this lost village on the Rockingham side of Gretton.

COTTON CAMP IN RAUNDS. *PN.*, p. 194 f.n., makes it sound like a lost village but I cannot see the site on 6-inch O.S. map.

DOWNTOWN *620800* *22 N.E.* *Bridges*, i, 578, "depopulated". PT. with Stanford.

FOXLEY IN BLAKESLEY *640517* *50 S.E.* *Bridges*, i, 235. In one hand by 1535. Hundred meeting place.

GLASSTHORPE HILL IN FLOORE *670607 44 S.W.* Domesday village. *Bridges*: now only a shepherd's house.

HALE IN APETHORPE *027934 13 S.W.* Lost Domesday village. There was enclosure in A. reported in 1517 and 1518, and this may be it?

HEMPLOE *?625787 22 S.E.* ?

HULCOTE *705500 56 N.E.* Depopulation here in 1498 of 30 persons and land included in park, but probably Easton Neston *q.v.*?

KIRBY NEAR DEENE *c. 920920 11 S.E.* 1494 small depopulation here. *PN.*, p. 167, points out that there is no church, but I see that it is on parish bounds which is odd for a village. Bridges says houses remembered here.

KNOSTON NEAR IRCHESTER *c. 930630 39 S.E.* A number of depopulations presented here in 1518, and also possibly at "Chesters" (Chester by the Water C 43/28/6 m. 48).

LILFORD *c. 030840 19 S.W.*

MILTON PARK IN CASTOR *145295 8 S.W.* Is this the site of the many depopulations in Castor presented in 1518?

NORTOFT IN GUILSBOROUGH *677738 30 N.W.* *PN.*, p. 71, Domesday village.

OUNDLE (CHURCHFIELD FM.) *003876 18 N.E.* In 1377 there were people here paying poll tax with Oundle.

PIPEWELL *840858 17 S.W.* Cistercian depopulation? Rebuilt?

SEAWELL IN BLAKESLEY *628522 50 S.E.* Domesday village.

SILSWORTH LODGE *611714 29 S.E.* A site, says Mr. Franey.

TRAFFORD IN CHIPPING WARDEN *527486 54 N.E.* Domesday village.

UPTON *717603 44 S.E.* Shrunken. 50 taxpayers in 1327. Lay Subsidy.

In addition there are one or two other relevant cases:

(i.) EAGLETHORPE IN WARMINGTON *076917 13 S.E.* *Bridges*, ii, 483, says there is a lost village here, but the 6-inch O.S. map would seem to indicate that it has been resettled?

(ii.) HELPSTONE *2 S.E.* 62 evicted from 1491 to 1509, but all there now.

(iii.) MUSCOTT IN NORTON *625633 43 N.E.* Domesday village, now three houses or so.

(iv.) ORTON *806794 24 S.E.* Domesday village, shrunken.

(v.) PLUMPTON *598484* *55 N.E.* Depopulation here in 1515. 9 houses in Bridges' day—shrunken? 60 PT. There are signs of former extent in earthworks behind the church.

(vi.) WARKTON *25 S.E.* 24 evictions reported in 1518. Still there.

(vii.) WARKWORTH *487406* *58 S.W.* Church isolated, but village still there—shrinking?

(viii.) WOLLASTON *46 N.E.* 20 persons evicted 1515. All there now, and in 1591 (DL. 42/115/1).

NORTHUMBERLAND

It might be thought that Northumberland would never have been much concerned with arable farming and would thus be wholly immune from depopulation. In fact, the extents and surveys printed in the *County History* show Northumberland to have been a county largely of nucleated villages and extensive open fields. The old plough-marks on so many fields which have been so long pasture bears this out. The poll tax figures show that the villages here were rather smaller than nucleated villages in the Midlands or the south with an average of fifty-one taxpayers for the villages in Glendale ward, thirty-one in Coquetdale, and twenty-eight in Tyndale. The tax quotas of 1334 average 24*s.* in the south of the county and 15*s.* in the north, compared with averages of 30–70*s.* in the inner Midlands. Many of the townships are smaller in area than those further south, and this would be partly accounted for by the lower fertility of the soil for arable crops. It would partly be accounted for by the use which was made of the commons and the moorland fringes for pastoral husbandry. It was this early combination of arable and pastoral which is most likely to have been the immunising factor for this county; the 1517 Inquiry did not visit it, and no anti-enclosure cases were heard in the Tudor Exchequer from this county.

As has already been explained, there was a short burst of depopulating enclosure towards the end of the reign of Elizabeth when the abolition of border tenure made for less secure conditions. There was also some emparking in the Midlands manner in the seventeenth and eighteenth centuries. The Border warfare could always be counted upon to destroy villages, and there is hardly a village history which does not include at least three or four destructions in the fourteenth and fifteenth centuries. The majority of these were rebuilt, and when we find a village which was not rebuilt this must be interpreted as a reflection on the attractiveness of the site. In a time of retreat from the margin all over England, Northumbrians were being offered unique opportunities. The fact of destruction by the enemy meant that the marginality of a particular site became an immediate practical consideration.

The estates of Tynemouth Abbey show many examples of post-Black Death changes in tenure. At Monkseaton there were fifteen husbandlands (or unit holdings) in the thirteenth century. In 1377 four were in the Prior's hands, tenantless, and six had been reckoned waste ever since the Pestilence. At Middle Chirton (see also West Chirton *infra*) five of the original twelve holdings were tenantless in 1377 and one man farmed the other seven. By the Dissolution this village had been resettled, but with much larger unit holdings, just as at Monkseaton there were again ten holdings in 1538, but the demesne of 500 acres had become pasture.

Many other Tynemouth demesnes were turned over to pasture for lack of tenants, and several townships went wholly over to pastoral activity. At Seaton Delaval about one-third of the present parish was under the plough in 1311. By 1353 there were twenty ruined houses. The complete village was reckoned to maintain twenty-six husbandlands but by the early sixteenth century there were only twelve. The Scots were as destructive as the Plague and their visitations more frequent. Cowpen was burned by the Scots in 1315, and the Prior sought to let out the devastated land on easy terms, finding himself in the same position in which we have seen the Abbot of Fountains later in the century after the raids on Yorkshire.

Among the Elizabethan State Papers (S.P. 15/28 f. 232–274) are surveys of border depopulation made in 1584. There are estimates of how many able-bodied men had been driven away and some attempts made to explain what had caused the decay. In all, some 2,220 men are said to have left the four northern counties, of whom nearly one half were from the eastern marches of Northumberland.

The surveys have a column headed "standing" and a second headed "decayed". By no means all the villages named were totally decayed, and some of those described as totally decayed have been repopulated since 1584. Ford near Wooler was reported to be depopulated, but there is a modern village on the map and the population of the township in 1901 was 1,140.

The cases which concern us are those with zero in the "standing" column, a substantial number of houses in the "decayed" column, and no village visible on the map today.

The year from which the calculations of decay were made was 1535, and individual reasons for decay are not always given. It was exceptional for the surveyor to write, as he did at Langton in Cumberland, "the whole township decaied and converted into pasture" although specific "decaied by Scotts" are rather more frequent. When a general summary of causes is attempted there are two explanations, other than "the steal of the Scotts". Landlords have "converted the tenements to demaines keepinge no men of service"; or, elsewhere, "the tenements are taken by owners and laide to demaine". The use to which the enlarged demesnes were put by the landlords is not stated. Since engrossing of holdings was actively going on elsewhere in England at this time for other purposes than grazing, we cannot assume that all these landlords were would-be sheepmasters seizing an opportunity which their cousins in the south had seized a century earlier, and which came to the Border with the end of official warfare and the changes in tenure of those who had held their land on the "garrison-duty" type of condition.

Details of the more serious decay reported upon in 1584, and of other villages for which we have evidence of depopulation are given in the following list. References in brackets are to the *County History of Northumberland* where manorial and parochial histories will be found, often in illuminating fullness.

PRINCIPAL SITES

WARENMOUTH (=NEWTON FARM). WEST OF BAMBURGH *162355* This new settlement was chartered in 1247, but by 1515 local men did not know of its existence. This points to an early depopulation. [i, 190.]

BURTON BY BAMBURGH *180330* In the tax list of 1296 this village was quite extensive. It is now 1 farm. The enclosure may have been *c.* 1579 [i, 289]. In 1584 18 tenants had left since 1535.

UTCHESTER ALIAS OUTCHESTER *140335* Depopulated just before 1579, "one Thomas Jackson . . . did wholly expell the said xii tenants and put the land thereof to pasture, and so it remains." [ii, 252.] In 1584 it was reported that 12 tenancies decayed.

KEPWICK IN COCKLAW *951714* "one farm, but in a field to the east may be traced foundations of ancient buildings". In 1538 11 armed men were included in the muster here. [iv, 195.]

BUSTON, LOW *228073* LS.: 8*s*. "the site of the village with its garden sloping to the south can be very easily traced in the park-like field to the east of the house, and in four of the grass fields may be seen broad and curved ridges which recall the times when these lands were in tillage and ploughed by oxen . . . there is also the site of the hedge and pallisade which surrounded the 'tun'." [v, 219.]

ACOMB, EAST. *044641* 12 tenements in 1570, but now 2 farms and a cottage. In the 1801 census there were 23 people here. [vi, 118.]

STYFORD *020620* LS.: 13*s*. Possibly by flood in 1771? [vi, 232.]

BLACK HEDLEY. *054518* "An ancient village now a single house." [vi, 294.]

BYWELL *050612* In 1608 there were 25 houses here but the present state is "the two churches situated originally amongst the houses of the village but now almost alone with only the Hall, the vicarage of St. Peter, the old house of the miller and the keep-gateway of the Castle". [vi, 87 and 105.] This seems like emparking. The destruction of the village and the 2 churches in a fire of 1285 does not seem to have been fatal. In 1414 there were at least 25 houses.

CHIRTON, WEST *c. 335680* "Some date between 1377 and 1538 the tenants of West Chirton were evicted and the land annexed to Flatworth (by Tynemouth Abbey). The tillage was converted to cattle pasture in two large closes." In 1559 there were 2,000 sheep here, as well as many cattle. [viii, 335 and 340.]

BACKWORTH, WEST *290725* "Decayed and deserted by 1538." [ix, 39.]

SEATON DELAVAL *320763* LS.: 33*s*. Piecemeal to 1601 when 2 holdings left. In 1628 there were 1300 sheep. [ix, 201.] Since re-occupied by collieries.

NEWSHAM *305790* and BEBSIDE *270810* LS.: 5*s*. "Newsham and Bebside are mining hamlets that have taken their name from vanished villages in adjoining townships." [ix, 303.]

HARTLEY *342757* LS.: 51*s*. Before 1598. See page 172, *supra*. [ix, 124.] 10 "tenancies decaied" by 1584. (S.P. 15/28).

YEAVERING, OLD *923304* PT.: 14 LS.: 10*s*. The farm represents the small medieval community with 6 taxpayers in 1296. By 1541 the 8 husbandlands were in one man's hands. [xi, 241.]

HETTON *040334* PT.: 12 LS.: 20*s*. Temp. James I by a Lincolnshire man, William Carr(e) of Sleaford. [xiv, 229.] It was "good corne soyle". Already decayed 1584.

SHAWDON *095144* PT.: 25 LS: 6*s*. "Swept away by William Hargrave when he built the Hall." [xiv, 554.]

HAUGHTON *920730* Destroyed for emparking, *c*. 1816. [xv, 201.]

WREIGHILL *976019* Local tradition blames the plague of 1665, but this may not be true. [xv, 390.] Already very small in 1377.

BIDDLESTONE *955082* PT.: 24. LS.: 13*s*. "Village and green were displaced by the park" but date not given. [xv, 425.] There are particularly good marks of former ploughlands surrounding this site and running up into the Cheviot fringe. It was still a village in 1410. 9 out of 23 "tenancies decaied" in 1584. (S.P. 15/28.)

CLENNEL *929071* PT.: 23. LS.: 13*s*. One of the "ten towns of Coquetdale". "There is now no village . . . it was cleared away to make room for the very lovely park and gardens surrounding the manor house." [xv, 428.] Good ploughlands are visible here also.

CHIRMUNDESDEN (=PEELS) *942043* Another of the "ten towns". In 1604 Survey it was noted as "sometimes a township". [xv, 444.] I suspect a migration to Newton nearby. The former site is now a "woody tract". [xv, 446.]

RUGLEY *164099* In Mayson's *Survey* (1622), vol. i (Duke of Northumberland's MSS, Alnwick Castle), "there are nowe onely twoe tenants". Plan of "town seite", 1624, by Robert Norton.

SWINELEAS *157067* In 1622 Survey (Alnwick Castle MSS), "since (1377) the seid Swineleage hath been disvillaged and laid waste".

Other and smaller sites

MOUSEN, OLD [i, 210.]

SHORESTON, OLD [i, 306.]

BAVINGTON, LITTLE [iv, 411.]

TOGSTON BY AMBLE [v. 325.]

LEMMINGTON [vii, 163.]

FELTON, OLD AND ACTON [vii, 365–75.]

CLAREWOOD [x, 386.]

FULWELL IN KEARSLEY [xii, 394.]

WOOLSINGTON [xiii, 204.]

EWART [xiv, 181.] Also rebuilt.

NEWHAM BY LUCKER. Depopulated temp. Eliz., empty in 1584 (S.P. 15/28) but resettled later. [i, 275.]

FALLODEN [ii, 110.]

BORTHERWICK BY WARKWORTH [v, 251.] Enclosed by 1624.

MORWICK [v, 343.]

LEARCHILD [vii, 180.]

HETHPOOL [xi, 249.] 10 decayed in 1584 (since 1535).

HUMBLETON BY WOOLER [xiv, 154.] Since rebuilt (20 tenancies decayed, 1584).

PRESTON [viii, 342.]

The list excludes the large number of medieval villages in Tyndale and Inter wards which are now represented only by a small group of farms and cottages, or cases (other than Ewart) where the village (Newtown) has been built outside the park after depopulation.

NOTTINGHAMSHIRE

In 1334 there were 274 villages separately taxed, and fifteen of these are no longer represented by a village. Only two of the lost villages were reported in 1428 as having fewer than ten householders. Six of the lost villages had tax reliefs exceeding 30% in 1434. The number of cases reported in 1517 is considerable, but only a few of these were substantial displacements of depopulation (Wiverton, Thorpe le Glebe and Martin).

In the forest districts it is not possible from tax lists alone to decide whether a church served a compact village which has disappeared or a scatter of houses. The growth of Nottingham has brought the repopulation of several hamlets whose earlier disappearance is recorded.

The list below classifies the villages according to the strength of the evidence.

Villages with separate mention in 1316 and in the tax list of 1334

ANNESLEY *504524* High tax quota and low relief in 1434. An emparking enclosure. I owe this reference to Dr. Chambers.

BURTON, WEST *798855* A high tax quota and a very low relief in 1434. The churchless churchyard has yawning graves, and the village streets can be seen on the Trent bank.

DANETHORPE *841573* Another high tax quota. In 1377 the poll tax receipts named 18 persons. Throsby reports the local legend of a village destroyed by an earthquake.

GRIMSTON *682658* High relief in 1434.

HAUGHTON *692730* Lonely ruins of the church, with no signs of a village on the ground, now ploughed. High relief of 42% in 1434.

KILVINGTON *801429* Fewer than 10 householders in 1428. PT.: 30. High quota in 1334.

KIMBERLEY *500450* A small village with 37% relief in 1434, but since repopulated with collieries.

OSBERTON *624800* High tax quota in 1334, but fewer than 10 households in 1428 and a 33% relief in 1434. Plague casualty?

SUTTON PASSEYS *c. 535390* Now in Wollaton Park. PT.: 19. 1434 relief was 37%. Much topographical detail can be recovered from the Willoughby Cartulary (Wollaton MSS., Univ. of Nottingham Library).

SWAINSTON *c. 810750*? No relief in 1434.

THORPE LE GLEBE *607256* One of the best sites in the Midlands. Reported in 1517. High tax quota, 1334, low relief, 1434. 50 persons expelled.

WHIMPTON *795740* High quota, 1334, low relief, 1434. (See *Trans. Thorton Soc.*, 1907, pp. 139–44.)

WIVERTON *715365* PT.: 46. The history of the village is given, *supra*, p. 310. It was reported in 1517.

Villages now lost, but linked with another village in 1334 tax list

ALGARTHORPE IN BASFORD

HOLBECK IN WESTHORPE *685535*

HORSEPOOL IN THURGARTON *695492*

MARTIN IN HARWORTH *636942*

MEERING IN GIRTON *812655*

MORTON IN BABWORTH *c. 675790* Depopulated in 1504.

NETTLEWORTH IN WARSOP *c. 549658*

NORMANTON IN BOTHAMSTALL *650748*

PLUMTREE AND HESLEY *632923*

RAYTON IN SCOFTON *614793*

WOODCOTES IN FELDBOROUGH *784716*

Forest settlements, absorbed in Parkland

CLUMBER *627746* Tax quota, 6*s*. Relief, 1434, 68%.

THORESBY *639712* Tax quota, 21*s*. Relief, 1434, 85%.

CARBURTON *611733* A flourishing little village in the map of 1615 (P.R.O., S.P. James I, lxxxiii) but now only a church and 3 farms.

Depopulations now within Nottingham

BROXTOWE *not on 1-inch map*. Church stood near Old Hall. Once a wapentake meeting place.

CHILWELL, EAST In or near University Park. See *Thoroton Soc. Trans.*, 1929, pp. 1 seq.

KEIGHTON IN LENTON Similar site. *c.542382* See J. T. Godfrey, *History of Lenton*, pp. 15–16. Excavations, 1953, by Nott. Univ. Arch. Soc. (ex. inf. Mr. M. J. Knight).

MORTON IN LENTON Possibly at Dunkirk Farm, *547373*.

Villages merged or migrated

ADBOLTON *600382* Church down, 1746.

BINGHAM *715398* Noticed by Hadrian Allcroft, *Earthwork of England*, with plan.

COLSTON BASSET *695338* Chapel-of-ease built in present village, 1382. Map of 1600 (T.S.R.S., ix (1941) showed no village near old church by that date.

COLWICK *602390*

FLAWFORD *601331*

HABBLESTHORPE now in North Leverton *785820*

HOLME PIERREPOINT *625393*

KINOULTON *662304*

LANGFORD *821591* See Leake, *History of Collingham*, p. 84.

REMPSTONE *575245* Church once stood half-mile to N.W. with name of St. Peter's in the Rushes.

SERLBY *c. 635895*

STOKE, EAST *748501* Village site by church, near deeply in cised road to river.

WHEATLEY, SOUTH. *766856* Ruined church. South Wheatley was separately taxed from North in 1334.

Early losses

BESTHORPE *730605* A grange of Rufford Abbey.

STEETLEY IN WORKSOP *544788* Land much robbed by quarrying (now in Derbys.).

WARBY IN PLUMTREE *621333* *P.N.*, p. 240. Good small site.

WILLOUGHBY IN NORWELL *687632* *Thoroton*, ii, p. 167. Good small site in Dr. St. Joseph's air photograph.

The lost villages of Nottinghamshire were the subject of an article by W. P. Philimore in *Old Nottinghamshire*, Second Series, pp. 66–87 (ed. Briscoe) in 1884. His information was drawn principally from Thoroton, but he had visited many of the sites. Mr. W. E. Doubleday contributed articles on the subject to the *Notts. Weekly Guardian* in 1942 and 1945. Mr. M. W. Barley is collecting material on the history of the lost villages of the county. I have had assistance from Mr. R. M. Butler in compiling my list which omits some of the very early small depopulations.

OXFORDSHIRE

The 1517 Reports for this county are very full, but (like its neighbour, Berkshire) many of the cases were concerned only with the decay of single houses in a village and the enclosure of a small acreage. There was also sheep depopulation of the Midland type. As in Buckinghamshire, the wooded Chiltern parishes are virtually immune.

ASCOTT IN STADHAMPTON *613981* In 1279 there were 2 freemen, 22 customary tenants and 7 cottars here. Only 1 house was reported in 1517 as having been destroyed, but in 1525 tenants were complaining of victimisation.

ASTERLEIGH *400225* Already having fewer than 10 households in 1428, this village was abandoned by 1466. In 1316 it had been linked with Kiddington, and its subsidy payment was also shared. Mr. E. M. Jope has described the medieval pottery found here in *Oxoniensia*, xiii (1948), p. 67. O.S. map, 6 inch sheet *21 N.W.* has "site of St. Peter's church".

BROOKEND IN CHASTLETON *240310* This was an Eynsham Abbey property. In 1363 there were 15 landholders, but between 1382 and 1462 each court held brought mention of villeins who had left. By 1469 the homage was only 4. Brookend was never separately taxed. In 1316 it was linked with Chastleton.

CASWELL HOUSE *320080* There were 6 tenants at least in 1279. In 1316 Caswell was linked to Witney; only a small area of enclosure was noticed in 1517.

CHALFORD IN CHURCH ENSTONE. *345257* In 1316 linked to Dean. In 1279 it had 2 villeins, 7 cottars and 4 freemen. Mr. R. T. Lattery tells me: "in a field are a mass of banks and dykes and these may be surmised to be either Upper or Lower Chalford". There is a chapel hill farm nearby. Dean is also lost; *sc.* Dean Buildings *335252*.

CHIPPINGHURST *600010* 16 people were evicted in 1512. In 1801 there were only 22 in the township and the settlement is still very small. It was a separate village in 1316.

CLARE *676986* There were 17 tenants in 1279, and lands in the "vill and fields" are mentioned in 1422. There were small enclosures here 1500–16. 11 names in a rental, 1438–9 (Bodleian MSS., Top. Ox. c. 207).

COTE BY CHARLBURY (=? Cotehouse Farm) *c. 352212* This was Eynsham land with 13 virgates in 1279 and at least 5 houses *c.* 1360. Rentals continue 1310–1448. By 1488 Richard Palmer was pasturing 240 sheep.

DORNFORD *450205* 25 names in 1279, 16 in 1377.

DUNTHROP *355285* 16 people reported evicted in 1517.

EASINGTON *662972* A separate township, now only 3 farms.

FULWELL *624348* This former parish of St. Michael had lost its church by 1291 although there is a record of its existence in 1205. It was a grange of Oseney Abbey, who may have depopulated it. 30 acres of enclosure were reported in 1517. Mr. P. J. Parr tells me that the site is visible on the ground.

GATEHAMPTON *610798* 14 people were evicted in 1515. In 1279 there had been 5 *servi* and 6 customary tenants as well as a fulling mill and a fishery. In 1316 it was linked with Goring.

GILTON *47 N.W.* This may be the "Glinton" with fewer than 10 householders in 1428. It lies near to the lost villages. A small eviction was reported in 1517.

GOLDER MANOR *665977* In 1297 it was styled a hamlet with 9 virgates in demesne, 2 villeins and 13 freemen. In 1316 it was linked to Pitton. It had 22 taxpayers in 1377. There was a church here, and in 1517 Magdalen College, Oxford, was accused of destroying 3 houses. There were 7 names in a rental of 1438–39 (Bodleian MSS., Top. Ox. c. 207).

GROVE IN CHASTLETON *243303* 10 people evicted 1502.

GROVE IN GREAT TEW ? *416313* In 1279 17 villagers are listed in this GROVE, between Great Tew and Leadwell.

HAMPSTALL ? With Stanton Harcourt in 1316, but with Leigh in the 1334 Subsidy. It lay west of Eynsham.

HAMPTON GAY *483165* In 1279 there were 9 freemen and 1 villein. Oseney Abbey had land here, and by 1428 there were fewer than 10 householders. The site lies clearly near the church, and Mr. P. J. Parr has visited it for me.

ILBURY *435310* With Nether Worton in 1334 tax list. 9 tenants in 1279.

LANGLEY *302153* 4 tenants only in 1316.

LATCHFORD *660015* Small depopulations reported in 1517. There was once a chapel here, and the 2 remaining farms are surrounded by earthworks of the former hamlet.

LUDWELL FARM. *433224* 26 names in 1279. In poll tax: 16.

MONGWELL *610878* Fewer than 10 householders in 1428. In 1279 there was a church, 2 carucates and 2 virgates in demesne; 16 customary tenants and 7 freemen.

NEWTON MORRELL *610295* Now only a farm. In 1428 it was a parish with fewer than 10 households.

NORTON, COLD *334300* In 1377 there were 10 poll tax payers in this small hamlet by the priory. In 1506 Sir Richard Empson took the priory lands and evicted 20 persons.

PRESCOTE *480485* This hamlet had 8 virgates in demesne in 1279 and 12 villeins' virgates. In 1801 the township had only 22 inhabitants.

PUDLICOTE *312202* In 1279 it had 8 villeins and 9 freemen. It was Eynsham land, linked in 1316 to Sarsden. It appears *cum membris* in 1334.

RADCOT *278000* In 1279 it had 8 freemen and 23 cottars.

ROLLRIGHT, LITTLE *293301* Evictions of 36 persons were reported in 1517. The 1334 tax quota was 26*s*. There is a separate poll tax receipt for this place in 1377, but the amount has been torn off.

RYCOTE *668045* In 1279 there were 11 villeins, 9 freemen and 2 cottars here.

SEWELL *358292* In 1316 this village is explicitly (and, I think, uniquely) described as *parva et paupera* in the *Nomina Villarum*.

SHELSWELL *609307* 11 people evicted here in 1496. The 6-inch O.S. sheet *17 N.E.* has the church site marked. In 1428 there were fewer than 10 households. In 1279 there were 10 villeins named here. In 1316 it was linked with Newton Purcell.

STANDELF IN PYRTON *41 S.W.* This plague depopulation has been described in the text p. 300, *supra*.

TANGLEY HOUSE *234170* Small depopulation here by Bruern Abbey reported in 1517. This may be the lost "Tretona" of Domesday Book (Dugdale: *Monasticon*, v, p. 497) (P.R.O., E 210/o. 8846).

THOMLEY *34 S.E.* 31 paid poll tax in 1377 and the basic tax was 22*s*. In 1279 the village was substantial and confirmatory detail can be found in St. Frideswide's cartulary.

TILGARSLEY ? Depopulated in 1350. In 1370 it was officially described as a former *hamlettus vocatus Tilgerdisle infra bundas de Eynesham* but the exact location is not apparently known. I cannot find anything on the air photographs. Its basic tax of 95*s*. suggests a substantial settlement. 52 names in 1279.

TUSMORE *564306* Fewer than 10 householders in 1428. In 1279 there had been 16 villeins, 4 freemen, and 3 cottars. In 1316 it was linked with Hardwick which was also badly shrunken. In 1355 it had complete tax relief. There was a church here in 1308, to which institutions were still being made in 1434. The village lay on the old Souldern–Coltisford road, diverted outside the park in 1357 when it was "void of inhabitants".

TYTHROP *740070 35 S.E.* In 1279 this was quite a large hamlet. In 1712 there seem still to have been 5 houses, but the map does not show that many today.

WATER EATON *515120* After 1359 Oseney Abbey owned all the village. In a compotus of 1279 both grain and wool being produced. The fields seem still open in 1359. The site here is quite a clear one. Its final destruction is mentioned in the text *supra*, p. 323.

WELD, EAST (=Claywell Farm?) *351052* In a rental of 1360 8 messuages were named. The identification is Salter's.

WHEATFIELD *47 N.W.* 54 people were evicted in 1504. In this very scattered parish there were 89 people in 1801. There were 60 to pay the poll tax. The basic tax quota of 1334 was 58*s*.

WILLESTON FARM *602298* In 1500 John Arden evicted 42 people. In 1377 32 had paid the poll tax, and the tax quota of 1334 was 15*s*. In 1279 the hamlet had included 18 villeins and a cottar.

WRETCHWICK *596214* Now Middle Wretchwick Farm. It is a good clear site. In 1279 there were 24 villeins and 7 cottars here. In 1316 it was a hamlet of Bicester, and it passed into the hands of the Priory. Rentals survive for the fifteenth century, and in 1517 the Prior was accused of evicting 18 people in 1488.

Other sites and suspects

ALBURY, *655051*, had fewer than 10 households in 1428; LITTLE BALDONS, *565980*, had 4 people evicted in 1516; CHILWORTH, *635338*; CLATTERCOTE, *457492*; COGGES, *361095*, was linked with Wilcote in medieval tax lists; COTMORE, *600268*; HARDWICK had fewer than 10 households in 1428 and has clear signs of former houses at *576297*. It had relief for plague in 1437; WIDCOTE, *272118*; WICHELE, by Dornford, *482196*, was a hamlet in 1279, with PT. 33; WILCOTE, *375155*, was linked in 1316 to Cogges; it had 15 names in 1279, and 12 in PT.; WOODPERRY, *575105*, is much shrunken, see *Arch. Journ.*, iii, pp. 116–28; among the villages much shrunken is STEEPLE BARTON, *448250* (ex. inf. Dr. W. G. Hoskins). LEDALL, *PN.* p. 192, had 34 in PT. and 21 houses in 1279; BIGNELL, *559220*, PT. 19; for SAXINTON see *PN.* p. 203.

RUTLAND

This small county has good poll tax and tax quota material, but the number of sites is not large. In this, the county has more affinities with Huntingdon to its east than with Leicestershire to the west. The 1517 Inquiry reported on a small amount of enclosure within the county, but none of it in the depopulated villages. BROOKE has migrated from *844059*.

AILSTHORPE *891124* *5 S.E.* "Chapel Farm." Domesday village. With Burley in tax lists. See *VCH. Rutland.*

BELMESTHORPE *042102* *7 S.W.* The village has shrunken. The church was in ruins by 1636.

GUNTHORPE *869057* *9 S.W.* In 1801 census there were 7 inhabitants of this parish. The chapel was in disuse by 1534. There were 88 poll tax payers and the county average was 99. The tax quota was 23*s.* compared with the average 47*s.* The 1445 relief was 33%.

HARDWICK *968124* *6 S.W.* Blore, *History of Rutland*, p. 142.

HORN *954117* *6 S.W.* The site is within Exton Park near the fishponds. Rectors were instituted by thorn-trees after the church had fallen and the last institution in the Lincoln Registers is 1471–80. In 1445 an extent describes the whole manor as waste. In the Valor the parish was *modo devastata*. Tax quota: 33*s*. with 40% relief in 1445 and 1489.

KILTHORPE *968124 10 S.E. Blore*, p. 147.

MARTINSTHORPE *865046 9 S.W.* In the census of 1921 the population was 1. Old Hall Farm was formerly Martinsthorpe Hall. 39 paid poll tax and the tax quota was 41*s*. The 1445 relief was the high one of 50%, and a similar sum was allowed in 1489. 14 villagers had been wealthy enough to be taxed in 1327. Church ruins. Last institution mid-sixteenth century.

NORMANTON *933063 10 N.W.* Depopulated *c*. 1764 by Sir Gilbert Heathcote. The village stood near the present church. It was already small in 1377 (with 29 paying). Its tax quota of 1334 was 52*s*. of which 26% was allowed in relief in 1489. Some 40% was allowed in 1445.

PICKWORTH *992138 6 N.E.* Said to be empty in 1491. Ruined church, since rebuilt. 99 paid in 1377. Tax quota 100*s*. is higher than average. Low relief in 1445 and 1489.

SCULTHORP *14 N.W. 13 N.E. VCH.* puts the site in a brickyard near Sculthorp Spinney. The local tradition is that the Parliamentary army of 1642 destroyed the village.

SNELSTON *15 N.W.* Domesday village, placed by *VCH.* in Stoke Dry, which has a big empty area in the south of the parish. In tax lists after 1327 with Caldecote.

TOLETHORPE *021105 6 S.E. Blore*, p. 89. In 1327 lined with Little Chesterton.

SHROPSHIRE

This county was visited in 1517, when the eviction of 344 people was presented. This figure is made up of many small depopulations, all of them in villages which are still surviving. The agrarian history of this county does not seem to be very different from Herefordshire or Cheshire, in both of which the depopulations were few. There may have been a village within the outer enclosure of Cause Castle, *337078*. A survey of this borough in 1540–1 shows 9 burgages still occupied and 24 decayed. (*Salop. Arch. Soc. Trans.* liv (1951–2), pp. 45–68.)

SOMERSET

In Collinson's *History* of this county he gives an account of fifteen places where churches had been demolished. Where no village survives today the reference to Collinson is given below by *C.* Villages with fewer than ten households in 1428 have the sign *, and those with † had fewer than fifty inhabitants in the Census of 1801. Poll tax figures from P.R.O. E 179/169/31–5; 238/150–1; and 240/256–9.

Mr. H. S. L. Dewar tells me that a site in Long Sutton parish, *500250*, known as Bineham city has yielded fifteenth/sixteenth-century pottery and substantial limestone walls. The site has erroneously appeared on the Ordnance map as Roman. Bineham is not given as a village name in Collinson. There is an interesting swing in the parish boundary just here. Mr. Dewar also suggests CURRYPOOL, *227385*, where 19 people were assessed in 1327 (E 179/169/5).

BICKLEY *130245* *C.*, iii, p. 16.

*EARNSHILL *385216* "Depopulated" *C.*, i, p. 31.

*EASTHAM IN CREWKERNE *457104* "Depopulated" *C.*, ii, p. 160.

GOOSE BRADON and NORTH BRADON *364200* *C.*, i, p. 16. Goose Bradon had 2 in poll tax, 1377.

HARDINGTON by Frome *742527* "Almost depopulated" *C.*, ii, p. 453.

HORSLEY, with church ruins at *714375*, "depopulated hamlet" *C.*, i, p. 221.

*†SOCK DENNIS *517213* *C.*, iii, p. 308, "an obliterated place". 14 in poll tax, 1377.

†SOUTH BRADON *c. 365187*? *C.*, i, p. 16.

SPARGROVE *671380* Parish joined to Batcombe. *C.*, iii, p. 468.

STANDERWICK *815512* Parish joined to Beckington, 1660. *C.*, ii, p. 228.

†WEST DOWLISH *365135* *C.*, i, p. 38. 5 in poll tax, 1377.

WOODWICK IN FRESHFORD *776604* *C.*, i, p. 125. Joined in 1448 with only "Woodwards Farm" and "Church Field" to mark the spot [ex. inf. Mr. A. T. Wicks].

(The "remarkable depopulation" of the Index to *Collinson*, p. 83, turns out to be Minehead!)

STAFFORDSHIRE

Much of Staffordshire was upland or forest, but there is a suggestive group of sites in the lower Trent valley:

BLITHEFIELD *045240*
BLORE *137495*
CHARTLEY *008285* PT.: 198
CROXALL *196138*
FREEFORD *135075* PT.: 17
HASELOUR *206109* PT.: 30
OKCOVER *158482* PT.: 55
PACKINGTON *164063* PT.: 26
STATFOLD *238071* PT.: 9
THORPE CONSTANTINE *260089* PT.: 66; migrated?
TYNNOR AND FISHERWICK *c. 180100*? Tynnor = Tamhorn? PT. 25.
WYCHNOR *176160* PT.: 57. See Shaw, *Staffs.*, i, p. 125.

All the above are separately taxed in 1334.

SUFFOLK

This county is as diverse as Norfolk in its experience. It was not visited in 1517 and there are no sixteenth-century prosecutions here, but a comparison of the fourteenth-century tax list and the map shows a considerable retreat of settlements in the western half of the county. The position is complicated by the occurrence of the isolated church as a normal feature, with farms scattered or gathered at a Green some distance from the parish church.

ALDHAM *040445* Faint earthworks on valley-side. 23 assessed in 1327.
ASHBY *489990* Common enclosed by John Wentworth who bought out all the tenants, 1599.
BRAISEWORTH *138712* 7 taxpayers assessed in 1327.
CHILTON *890423* Isolated church and Manor House.
DEPDEN *777566*.
EASTON BAVENT *c. 517785* Eroded. Church lost soon after 1568.
ELMHAM, SOUTH, ALL SAINTS *330828* Migration from isolated church and manor to Green?
FLIXTON *518955* Church in ruins by *c.* 1630.

FORDLEY Church down by 1630. It stood in Middleton churchyard, *430678*.

FORNHAM ST. GENEVEVE *840683*. [B.M. Add. MSS. 34689].

ICKWORTH *813611* Emparking depopulation after 1665.

KNETTISHALL *972804*.

LANGHAM *VCH*. says village lay east of church *980690*.

MELLS Ruined church in use till *c.* 1450 *405768*.

NOWTON *863605*.

REDISHAM *402864* Church ruins just inside park; disused by 1450. [B.M., Add. MSS. 23,731].

SAXHAM, GREAT *789628*.

SOTHERTON *442796*.

SOTTERLEY *458854*.

WILLINGHAM *446864* Church of St. Mary completely ruined by *c.* 1530.

This list has been drawn up solely from the 1-inch O.S. map, the printed Lay Subsidy roll of 1327 and the unpublished roll of 1449. The lost ALTEINESTUNA was amalgamated with Trimley in 1362. The church site is said to lie 1½ miles west of Trimley (W. G. Arnott, *Place Names of Debden Valley* (1946), pp. 34–40). It seems likely that a detailed study of the settlement history of the county by a local scholar would repay the effort, and incidentally considerably augment the list above. Professor H. C. Darby has noted (*Domesday Geography of Eastern England* (1952), p. 160) a number of names which are no longer anything more than farms.

SURREY

This county was passed by in 1517, and there are no other signs that depopulation was known here at that period. There has been some emparking. Mr. W. E. Goodchild tells me that ALBURY, *065479* (5 miles S.E. of Guildford), was such.

SUSSEX

There has been some depopulation in the villages at the foot of the South Downs, but nothing was reported in 1517 and everything points to late fourteenth or early fifteenth-century dates. Thirty-four villages were listed in 1428 as having fewer than ten householders, and although most of them still survive they include EXCETE, *522992*, a lost village which was described in 1916 by Mr. W. Bugden. In 1428 there was the unique entry that there is one inhabitant, *et non plus*, and for verisimilitude his name, Henry Chesman, was added. In 1460 the inhabitants of the two remaining houses said that the church was in ruins and the materials carried away. There was still some arable in 1415, in fact more than in 1334, and it may have been a Plague casualty. Local tradition (supported in part by the *Nonarum Inquisitiones*) favours devastation by marauding Frenchmen. (See also *VCH.*, ii, 182.) The Sussex Archaeological Society has erected a stone at the church site which was excavated in 1913.

BROOMHILL *c. 980180* was washed away at the end of the thirteenth century although the church ruins remained until the seventeenth. ALDRINGTON, *c. 270045*, and BRACKLESHAM, *c. 805964*, suffered a similar fate. BINDERTON, *851108*, is probably an emparking loss (*VCH.*, iv, p. 90), while the parishes of LYNCH, *849185*, LORDINGTON, *782098*, and EAST ITCHENOR, *c. 816005*, and the re-settled ALMODINGTON, *826976*, were medieval parishes amalgamated to their neighbours through "fewness and poverty". (*VCH.*, iv, pp. 65, 117, 201 and 203.) BALMER in Falmer, *359100*, was Lewes Priory land, and homesteads were visible under the grass but threatened in 1952 by farm-extensions. HANGLETON church, *267073*, is the sole remains of the village which by 1603 was already no more than a house. Mr. E. W. Holden has made some preliminary excavations here. BALSDEAN, *378060*, is considerably shrunken; as late as 1579 it was reckoned a village. PYECOMBE was revived in the fifteenth century, ¼-mile west of its former site. In PIDDINGHOE, *435030*, "the Lydds" is said to be an early medieval village. OLD ERRINGHAM, *205077*, by Shoreham is suggestive. WISTON and PARHAM, *155124* and *059141*, are excellent examples of the isolated church in the grounds of the great house with no signs of the village community which the medieval church served.

WARWICKSHIRE

Depopulation was severe in this county, with some immunity in the forest areas north of the Avon. The 1517 Inquiry reported many evictions, substantiated by the later proceedings in the court of Exchequer. The Inquiry of 1548, however, produced very few new cases, and the movement seems to have been slowing down before 1517. The evidence of John Rous (*c.* 1490) enables us to say that depopulation had begun here well before 1485. The Hodnell group of sites was probably decayed by 1428, and at Fullbrook we have an early fifteenth-century emparking.

I have published elsewhere a full list of deserted sites in this county, and the small sample below is intended as a guide for visitors.

BILLESLEY TRUSSELL *145568*
CESTERSOVER *504820*
CHESTERTON MAGNA (shrunk) AND PARVA (lost) *348586* and *361575*
HODNELL *424574*
HOPSFORD *425838*
RADBOURN *440570*
SMITE, UPPER AND LOWER *430825*: to S.E. of Mobbs Wood Farm; and *412808*. An early Cistercian depopulation.
STRETTON BASKERVILLE *420910*

See also *Ruined and Desecrated Churches* by P. B. Chatwin (*Tr. Birm. A. S.*, lxviii (1952).

WILTSHIRE

There was no visitation of this county in 1517 and the history of its land-use has nothing to suggest that it would have been particularly susceptible to the attentions of the depopulating sheepmaster in the earlier centuries. In the north of the county there is the scattered settlement which speaks of late enclosure from the forest and its "cheese" nickname speaks of the dairy produce from the stock which it had near the centre of its village economies. In the south, the "chalk" villages depended on sheep for the good heart of its arable fields, and the value of their manure to the husbandman and of the fallow grazing to the sheepmaster meant that there was none of that rivalry between corn and grass so fatal to Midland villages.

The poll tax returns and Lay Subsidy roll of 1334 show a number of hamlets which were no more than a handful of settlers, and the list of parishes with fewer than ten households in 1428 is unusually long. Of those from this list which I have been able to identify with poll tax receipts none had more than twenty souls in 1377 and their 1334 quotas are usually also small.

One lost village in this county has been the subject of a detailed study by Canon J. E. Jackson (*Wiltshire Magazine*, xiii, p. 227) and will also be dealt with in the forthcoming *VCH.* volume for which Mr. Pugh has kindly allowed me to see the proofs. WITTENHAM (alias Rowley) was amalgamated shortly after 1428 with its neighbour, Farleigh Hungerford in Somerset, and the result has been a protruding finger of Somerset into Wiltshire. Canon Jackson did not seem to see the significance of this, but it seems reasonable to take it as the parish area. The site of the church is traditionally at Holy Green in Rowley Lane, midway between Westwood and Farleigh, *c. 810585*, where earthworks can be seen. The deed of union, given in full in the paper cited, states that no priest was willing to occupy the living. By 1585 there were only two houses, and the name is lost from the 1-inch map. Bailiff's accounts for the years 1431–52 are analysed by Canon Jackson.

The motive for the depopulation of WASHERNE, south of Wilton, seems to have been the enlargement of the Park rather than the extension of sheep. The *Pembroke Survey* printed for the Roxburghe Club suggests that its enclosure dates from before 1559. The nearby church of Bulbridge, *085308*, had vicars until 1473 (Hoare, *Modern Wiltshire*, ii, p. 150).

A number of farms, such as PERTWOOD, ASSERTON or NORRIDGE, appear as villages in the *Nomina Villarum* of 1316, but they do not seem to have been more than the daughter hamlets which the villages of the chalk-lands scattered freely up the valleys.

Of the other places which were exceptionally small in 1428 (*Feudal Aids*, v, p. 280), SNAP in Aldbourne, *225762*, is now lost, and it is possible (although I have not visited the site) that the earthworks of the 1-inch O.S. "Ancient Village" may in fact be Snap or Snarpe (which had the low tax of 8*s*. in 1334 and nineteen poll tax payers, 1377). See P.R.O., DL 4/20/21 and MPC. 5. Other suspects, which were separately assessed in 1334 but are now no more than a farm or farms, are:

WALTON in Downtown, 165215; LONGFORD (Castle) in Britford, *172266*; CHILHAMPTON in South Newton, *095330*; HURDCOTT, *040310*; MIDDLETON in Norton Bavant, *905438*, (6-inch map only); BAYCLIFF, *813396*; ANSTYE, *845404*; WHITCLIVE, *859383*; BUPTON, *060760*; ABBOTSTONE (=Addeston in Muddington? site lost); NORTH STANDEN, *310540*; WITCOMB, *025755*; CORTON, *052757*; POLTON (6-inch map only, in Mildenhall *c. 190710*); WEST WIDHILL in Cricklade, ? *c. 128915*; GROUNDWELL, *151890*; THORNHILL in MALMESBURY, *922865*; FRESDEN in Highworth, *226922*; FOXLEY, *896860*; PRESHUTE, *180685* (*Wilts. Arch. Mag.*, liii (1950), pp. 296–9).

Of these, Anstye, Addeston, Corton and Foxley were among those listed as having fewer than ten householders in 1428; all had relatively small quotas in the tax of 1334, but only intensive local study, examination of the sites and excavation would prove whether their earlier size had been greater, and at exactly which point in time they were reduced to one farm. It will be seen that a number of these sites are in the north of the county where the small, scattered settlement is not unusual, even among surviving villages. Since compiling this list, Bupton has been visited and the extent of the field and village earthworks is quite remarkable. LYDIARD TREGOZE has suggestions of the former crossroads of the village at an empty village green, *103848*, and the church stands isolated and splendidly furnished alongside the Manor House.

WORCESTERSHIRE

This county was not visited in 1517. It is a county where champine agriculture never gained a great hold. Its terrain inclined it to the orchard, and the woodland, with many scattered settlements strung out thinly along winding lanes. Tax lists of 1275, 1327, 1332 and 1428 are in print. None of the places mentioned as having fewer than ten in 1428 is now completely deserted, although Huddington and Daylesford are small. Three churches named in 1340 are no longer standing; CLEVELODE in Madresfield; KENSWICK by Knightwick; and WICK EPISCOPI near Powicke Bridge. One or two of the lost villages in the Cotswold hundreds of the county have now been transferred to other counties (*e.g.* DITCHFORD). ELMLEY LOVETT may stand as type of that isolated church site which is so ambiguous in country like this. John Rous' PODEN may be NEDON by Honeybourne, *125435*, where Mr. W. H. Onions tells me that there are earthworks. No township in the county had fewer than fifty inhabitants in 1801.

YORKSHIRE

The great lowland corridor of the Vale of York does not differ radically in its agricultural geography from its southern and northern neighbours, Nottinghamshire and Durham. There are, it is true, areas which in medieval times were marshland or forest, and we shall not expect to find depopulated villages abounding there. If the plain itself resembles the Midlands, the East Riding has affinities with the chalklands of the eastern counties.

Away from the plain, the moorlands and the dales valleys have always had their proportion of pastoral activity, and the incentives to clear away arable cultivators did not operate so strongly here. Although the Inquiry of 1517 did not report very many cases and although no prosecutions followed, the period from 1450 had seen a number of extensive and important depopulations in the East and West Ridings. There are signs that the depopulations of the North Riding included a number of late sixteenth-century cases akin to those in Durham and Northumberland; in the West and North Ridings are a number of Cistercian depopulations—*e.g. Monasticon*, v, p. 530.

Detailed lists of the sites in the three Ridings are in course of publication in the *Yorkshire Archaeological Journal*, that for the East Riding appearing in 1952. The lists here are therefore short and intended as a guide to visitors. Many Yorkshire examples have been quoted in the text *supra*.

WEST RIDING (*Of 544 villages in 1334 LS., 30 have disappeared.*)

WILSTROP *483552* see p. 301, *supra*.

STEETON *532440* Probably enclosed by the Fairfaxes. In the poll tax there were 45 people paying, and the tax quota was 24*s*., the local average being 19*s*. The site has since been partially destroyed by the building of the great pond, now dry.

EAST TANFIELD *290778* "Town gate" on the map marks the street of the village. This was one of those reported upon in 1517.

SLENINGFORD *278774* Lies across the river from East Tanfield and the chapel appears on the air photograph as a crop mark.

CLOTHERHOLME *286722* A small but interesting site near Ripon.

AZERLEY *260749* Possibly an eighteenth-century emparking depopulation.

HUMBURTON This site is neighboured by the lost ELLENTHORPE and the shrunken Milby. (*421685*; *413674*; *403677*.)

NORTH RIDING (*Of 453 villages in 1334 LS., 39 have disappeared.*)

EAST LILLING *665645* This site has been described at page 29, *supra*.

BARFORTH ON TEES *164162* The church ruins and its fine situation overlooking the river make this an attractive site, not a very long walk from the lost ROKEBY and MORTHAM.

SOUTH COWTON *294025* The church here is not ruined, but it stands virtually alone except for the fortified manor house. Depopulation here was reported in 1517 and the site can be seen within two fields of the church.

THORESBY *030900* This village is said to have fathered the Archbishop of York of that name. Its earthworks are quite clear, and near it can be seen the lost WEST BOLTON lying in the park above Castle Bolton.

HINDERSKELFE *716706* This late seventeenth-century depopulation has been mapped in plate 11.

DANBY ON URE *171869* The church stands alone.

EAST RIDING (*Of 366 villages in 1334 LS., 49 have disappeared.*)

WHARRAM PERCY *857642* This site has been dealt with in the text.

COWLAM AND COTTAM *965652 and 993647* These two adjacent sites are excellent examples of preservation in the chalk grasslands.

SUNDERLANDWICK *010550* This is another site of high quality.

SWAYTHORPE *038690*

POCKTHORPE *040634*

TOWTHORPE IN WHARRAM *900630*

EASTBURN *993558*

These sites have been marked on the 1-inch O.S. map.

ESKE *053433* An additional river-side site with good preservation of house-plans.

BURTON CONSTABLE *190370* The village lies in the Capability Brown parkland.

HILDERTHORPE *174655* This clear site is surrounded by the suburbs of Bridlington which have not yet succeeded in destroying it.

ARGAM *113713* There is now no sign of the church, and it is a fine site for a feeling of isolation. Nearby is the lost BARTINDALE, *109731*.

SOUTHORPE BY HORNSEA *195466* Stands on the shores of Hornsea Mere.

APPENDIX I—TABLES

TABLE 13*a*

INFORMATIONS LAID ANNUALLY AGAINST OFFENDERS UNDER THE ACT OF 1533

Year	*Number of cases*	
	Flocks of more than 2,000 sheep	*Acquiring more than one holding*
1542	1	0
1543	0	0
1544	1	17
1545	3	50
1546		10[1]
1547		6
1548		11[2]
1549		8
1550		16
1551		3
1552		0
1553		1
1554		1
1555		4
after 1555		*

1 There is also an Attorney General's information in 1546 for enclosure of 800 acres at Alne, Warws. (E. 159/325/m. 81).

2 One of which was pardoned under the General Act of Pardon of 1 Edward VI.

* The record for 1558 was examined but yielded no case of this kind. The record for 1565 yielded nine; for 1566, one; for 1567, two, and one case (dismissed) against John Spencer of Althorp, Northants., for possessing 12,000 sheep. In the year 1566 there was also one information (under which Act is not specified) for conversion to pasture at Dulverton, Somerset. Since the informer claimed 5*s*. an acre forfeit, it would seem to be under the Act of 1563.

TABLE 13*b*

COUNTIES CONCERNED IN THE OFFENCES INFORMED AGAINST (1542–67) IN TABLE 13*a*

County	*Number of Cases*	*County*	*Number of Cases*
Essex	59	Hunts.	1
Norfolk	18	Oxon.	5
Suffolk	6	Staffs.	1
Kent	5	Salop.	1
Glos.	9	Westmorland	1
Yorks.	7	Warws.	2
Dorset	7	Sussex	5
Devon	1	Herts.	2
Somerset	1	Beds.	1
Bucks.	4	Wilts.	1
Northants.	2	Notts.	2
Lincolnshire	2	Berks.	2
		Derbyshire	1
TOTAL ..	.. ..	.. .. ..	.. 146

TABLE 14

CASES UNDER ACTS OTHER THAN THE ACT OF 1533

In these Tables the date given is the year when a case began. Cases often dragged on for term after term, but subsequent appearances on adjournment are not entered here. Resurrection of a case after the Act of 1536 is counted as a new case. Gay issued a warning against such duplication. He counted 517 enclosure cases by 1558, and I had assumed that he had counted adjourned hearings, but his total is so near to mine (583) that our basis of reckoning must be the same, allowing for possibilities of overlooking a case as we each read some eighty rolls of anything up to 500 membranes each. In Table 14*a* the cases are set out by counties and years, and summarised by years for the whole country in Table 14*b*. In Table 14*c* there is a summary analysis by counties.

TABLE 14*a*

DEPOPULATING ENCLOSURE: CASES IN EXCHEQUER 1518–68 BY YEAR AND COUNTY

Exchequer year	*Exch. Roll no. 159 or 368*	*Bucks.*	*Beds.*	*North.*	*Warws.*	*Oxon.*	*Berks.*	*Leics.*	*Derby*	*Notts*	*Glos.*	*Middx.*	*Unknown*	*Other*	*Total*
Henry VIII															
10	159	0													
(1518-19)	368	1	0	3	1										5
11	159	6	5	5	7	11	7	3	1	2	1				48
	368	2	0	1	1	1	0	2	1	1	0				9
12	159	2	0	2	2	0	5	1	0	0	1				22
	368	0	0	0	1										1
13	159	0	0	1	4	3	2	1	0	0	1				12
	368	0	0	0	0	1	0	2							3
14	159	2	2	1	1	2	0	0	0	0	1				9
	368	3	2	1	2	3	1	3	0	0	0	0	1		16
15	159	2	0												2
	368	3	1	6	3	7	3	3	2	2					30
16	159	0	0												0
	368	3	1	11	6	8	1	0	0	6					36
17	159	1	0	0	0	0	0	1							2
	368	1	0	0	2	7	5	4	0	0	0	1			20
18	159	1	0	0	0	1	0	1							3
	368	1	1	0	1	1	1	1							6
19	159	1	0	0	0	1	0	1							3
	368	4	0	0	1	1	2	0	0	1	0	1			10
20	159	0	0	1	0	0	1	0	0	0	1				3
(1528-29)	368	2	1	1	0	1	0	1	1						7
21	159	0	0	0	0	1	0								1
	368	0	1	4	0	0	0	1	0	1					7
22	159	0													0
	368	2	1	3	1	1	4	0	0	3					15
23	159	0	0	0	0	1									1
	368	0	0	4	2	1	1								8
24	159	0													0
	368	2	0	0	2	1	0	1							6
25	159	0	0	0	0	1									1
	368	0	0	5	0	2									7
26	159	0													0
	368	0	2	0	1	2	0	1	0	0				1	7
27	159	0													0
	368	1	0	0	0	0	0	0	0	1					2
28	159	0													0
	368	0													0
	159	0													

TABLE 14*a*—(*continued*)

Exchequer year	*Exch. Roll no. 159 or 368*	*Bucks.*	*Beds.*	*North.*	*Warws.*	*Oxon.*	*Berks.*	*Leics.*	*Derby*	*Notts.*	*Glos.*	*Middx.*	*Unknown*	*Other*	*Total*
Henry VIII															
29	368	1	1	0	1	0									3
30	159	0	0	1	0										1
(1538–9)	368	3	0	0	2	1	0	1							7
31	159	0													0
	368	2	1	10	3	1	3	1							21
32	159	0													0
	368	13	6	3	7	1	5	3	0	4				3	45
33	159	0													0
	368	0	5	2	3	3	6	1	0	4				1	25
34	159	0	0	1											1
	368	2	0	6	3	0	1	5	3					1	21
35	(All	1	5	5	1	1	4	1							18
36	Roll	0													0
37	368)	3	7	3	1	3	2	3							20
38		2	3	2	1	0	0	2							10
Edward VI															
1		2	0	4	2	0	0	2							10
2		1	0	1	1	0	0	1	1	2					7
3		0	2	1	0	0	0	1						1	5
4		0	0	1	3	2	1	1						4	12
5		3	1	4	2	0	0	0	0	1					11
6		0	2	0	4	0	0	3							9
7		0	2	0	1	0	0	1	0	1					5
Mary															
1		3	0	2	3	2	0	2	0	2				1	15
Philip & Mary															
1 and 2		2	0	1	2	1	0	1	6	2					10
2 and 3		0	2	3	2	1	0	2							10
3 and 4		0	1	2	0	1									4
4 and 5		0	0	1	2	0									3
5 and 6		0													
Eliz. I															
1		—													
8		—													
9		0	0	1											1
10		1	0	0	1										2
TOTALS		79	55	103	83	84	58	58	10	33	5	2	1	12	583

Cases of possessing more than 2,000 sheep and of engrossing houses of husbandry, also occur in the record from 34 Henry VIII (1542) onwards. These are excluded from the above and are summarised in Table 13*a*.

TABLE 14*b*

Summary of Table 14a

EXCHEQUER CASES, ALL COUNTIES, BY YEARS

Exchequer year	*No. of cases*	*Regnal year*	*No. of cases*
Henry VIII		Edward VI	
10 (1518–9)	5	1	10
11	57	2	7
12	23	3	5
13	15	4	12
14	25	5	11
15	32	6	9
16	36	7	5
17	22		
18	9		
19	13	Mary	
20	10	1	15
21	8		
22	15		
23	9	Philip and Mary	
24	6	1 and 2	10
25	8	2 and 3	10
26	7	3 and 4	4
27	2	4 and 5	3
28	0	5 and 6	0
29	3		
30	8		
31	21	Elizabeth I	
32	45	1	0
33	25	8	0
34	21	9	1
35	18	10	2
36	0		
37	20		
38	10		
		TOTAL	583

TABLE 14c

SUMMARY OF DEPOPULATING ENCLOSURE CASES IN THE COURT OF EXCHEQUER 1518–68, BY COUNTIES

	Cases	*% of whole*
Northamptonshire	103	17
Oxfordshire	84	14
Warwickshire	83	14
Buckinghamshire	79	14
Berkshire	58	10
Leicestershire	58	10
Bedfordshire	55	10
Nottinghamshire	33	6
Derbyshire	10	2
Gloucestershire	5	1
Middlesex	2	—
Others and doubtful	13	2
TOTAL	583	

NOTES TO TABLE 14

1 Two parallel but not duplicate rolls were kept by the Remembrancers of the Exchequer. The King's Remembrancer's Memoranda Roll recorded, according to Guiseppi, "occasional debts due to the Crown by seizure, forfeiture, intrusion and trespass" and the Lord Treasurer's Remembrancer's Memoranda Roll, the regular dues. Such a distinction does not illuminate the allocation of enclosure cases to a roll. It will be seen that although the L.T.R. Roll (E 368) has the distinction of recording the first of the cases it quickly loses ground to the K.R. Roll (E. 159), which for the years 1522 to 1544 has a virtual monopoly of cases. In the latter year the record is swollen by the opportunities for the informer, whose information seems always to go in the K.R. Roll. Informations laid by the Attorney General come in this category, although the revival of Crown suits after the Act of 1536 fall to the L.T.R. record.

2 The practice of the Exchequer clerks was to begin any important case on the *recto* side of a membrane (which measures some 10 by 36 inches) and to record all subsequent hearings of the same case on the same membrane, passing over to the *dorse* (and if necessary to a fresh membrane which was unnumbered to avoid disturbing the original numeration of the membranes). I have not counted adjourned hearings in my Table.

TABLE 15

NUMBER OF HOUSES ALLEGED TO BE DESTROYED IN EXCHEQUER CASES 1518–1558

Date of Prosecution. Exchequer Year	*Number of houses alleged*											*More than 11 houses alleged*
	1	*2*	*3*	*4*	*5*	*6*	*7*	*8*	*9*	*10*	*11*	
Henry VIII												
10 (1518–9)	2	1	—	—	—	—	—	—	1	—	1	
11	41	2	8	1	6	—	1	—	2	—	—	2
12	11	0	2	1	—	—	—	—	1			
13	6	2	1	—	—	—	—	—	—	—	—	1
14	15	2	1	—	—	2	1					
15	20	3	2	—	2	—	2	1	—	—	—	3
16	4	5	—	—	—	1	—	1				
17	15	1	2	1	1	—	—	1				
18	1	—	—	—	—	—	—	—	—	—	—	1
19	7	—	1	—	—	—	1					
20	1	—	—	—	1	1						
21	6	1										
22	9	2	—	2	—	—	—	1	1			
23	8											
24												
25	4	1	1									
26	4	—	1									
27	1	—	—	—	—	1						
28												
29	1	1	—	—	—	—	1	1				
30	2	—	1	1	2	—	—	—	—	—	—	2
31	12	2	—	—	2	—	—	1				
32	32	2	4	—	1	1	—	1	2			
33	22	2	—	—	1	—						
34	13	2	—	—	2	1						
35	15	—	1	1								
36												
37	17	2	—	1	—	—	—	1				
38	9	—	—	—	—	—	—	—	1			
Edward VI												
1 (1547–8)	2	1	1									
2	7	—										
3	5	—	—	—	1							
4	6	1										
5	9	1	—	1	—	—	—	1				
6	5	—	—	1	—	—	—	—	1	—	—	2
Mary												
1 (1553–4)	8	—	—	2	—	—	1	—	1	—	—	1
Philip & Mary												
1 and 2	4	—	2	—	1	1						
2 and 3	10											
3 and 4	3	—	—	—	1							
4 and 5	3											
5 and 6	0											
All cases (total: 482)	340	34	28	12	21	7	8	9	10	0	1	12
Percentage of Total	*70*	*7*	*6*	*3*	*5*	*1*	*1*	*2*	*2*	*0*	*0*	*3*

(The total is smaller than that of Table 14 because (*a*) a number of cases are for depopulating enclosure without the exact number of houses stated. (*b*) One or two duplications have been noticed (*e.g.* resurrection of lapsed proceedings) and eliminated from the above Table).

TABLE 15*a*

ANALYSIS OF EXCHEQUER CASES FOR NORTHAMPTONSHIRE BY SIZE OF DEPOPULATION ALLEGED

Year of prosecution	*Place and number of houses destroyed*
Henry VIII	
10	Snorscomb 9 Dogsthorpe 1 Elmington 2
11	Weston Favell 3 Staverton 1 Purston 1 Irchester 1 Islip 1
12	Aston 1 Grafton 6
13	Wyke Hammond 1
14	Kingsthorpe 1
15	Thorpe Mandeville 1 Abington 3 Aldwinkle 1 Bulwick 1 Raundes 1
16	Purston 5 Edgcote 9 Wappenham Fawcote Apethorpe 1 Knuston Pitsord 1
17	nil
18	nil
19	nil
20	nil
21	Broughton 1 Daventry 1
31	Papsley 5 (?10) Grimsbury 2 Horton (?) 7 Charwelton 5 Brington 1 Molton 1 Werrington (?) 1 Everdon 2 Harpole 1
32	Glendon 6 Castor 1 Bradden 1
33	Little Billing 1
34	Stanwick 1
35	Northborough 1 Whittlebur 1 East Haddon 1 Lowick 1
36	nil
37	Barby 1
38	Helpston 1
Edward VI	
1	Wold? Benewith?
2	Doddington 1
3	nil
4	Harrington 1
5	Creaton 1 Caistor 1 Deane 1
6	nil
7	nil
Mary	
1	Titchmarsh 1
Philip & Mary	
1 and 2	Pytchley 1
3 and 4	Newbottle 5

(This list rigidly excludes all re-hearings and resurrected cases. There were thirty-one such repetitions for the county in the years covered by the table. *i.e.*, thirty-one out of eighty-eight cases analysed were duplications. Three more cases of the ninety-one Northants. cases 1518–65 did not involve decay of houses.)

TABLE 15*b*

PRESENTMENTS OF THE 1517–18 INQUIRY (WARWS., BUCKS., BERKS., NORTHANTS.), ANALYSED BY NUMBER OF HOUSES ALLEGED DESTROYED

	Houses alleged															
	None	*1*	*2*	*3*	*4*	*5*	*6*	*7*	*8*	*9*	*10*	*11*	*12*	*13*	*14*	*More than 14*
Warws.	19	74	12	5	2	3	1	2	2	0	2	0	2	0	0	2
Berks.	9	54	16	6	2	0	1	0	0	0	0	0	0	0	0	0
Bucks.	17	19	9	7	3	4	3	2	0	2	0	0	1	0	2	0
Northants	24	48	5	1	5	4	3	1	0	0	1	0	2	0	2	0
TOTAL	69	195	42	19	12	11	8	5	2	2	3	0	5	0	4	2
Percentage of total	*18*	*52*	*11*	*5*	*3*	*3*	*2*	*1*	—	—	—	*0*	*1*	*0*	*1*	—

TABLE 16

THE AINSTY OF YORKSHIRE: EARLY TAX INFORMATION SUMMARISED FOR ALL VILLAGES

Census 1801	*Area in '000 acres*	*Domesday* * *=present*	*Modern names*	*Modern status.* V *=village* NL *=lost* F *=now a farm*	*Kirkby's Quest, 1284 Carucates*
265	1·8	Acastre alia	ACASTER MALBIS	V	4
178	1·5	*	ACASTER SELBY	V	3·375
406	2·9	*	APPLETON ROEBUCK	V	12
295	1·9	*	ASKHAM BRYAN	V	8
170	1·0	*	ASKHAM RICHARD	V	6·5
127	1·1	*	BICKERTON	V	7·5
185	1·4	Milburgh	BILBROUGH	V	7·5
220	1·9	*	BILTON	V	9
218	0·7	Torp	BISHOPTHORPE	V	3
189	2·3	Badetone	BOLTON PERCY	V	8
		Badetorp	BUSTARDTHORPE	NL	3
68	0·7	*	CATTERTON	V	3
155	1·2	*	COLTON	V	4
184	1·6	*	COPMANTHORPE	V	5·5
		*	HAGENBY	NL	3
233	2·7	*	HEALAUGH	V	7
114	1·3	*	HESSAY	V	3
143	1·2	*	HORNINGTON	F	3
143	1·2	*	HUTTON WANDLESLEY	V	6
120	0·9	*	KNAPTON	V	5
		Malchetone	MALCHETONE	NL	no
399	2·8	*	MARSTON, LONG	V	12
47	0·6	Badetorp	MIDDLETHORPE	V	4
256	3·0	*	MOOR MONKTON	V	9
		Ositone	OUSTON	F	3
49	0·7	Ulsitone	OXTON	V	4
		Torp	PALLATHORPE	F	manor
273	2·5	*	RUFFORD	V	4
77		*	SCAGGLETHORPE	F	3
	1·1	*	STEETON	F	5·5
314	1·7	Torp	THORPE ARCH	V	4
390	1·8	*	TOCKWITH	V	7
205	1·4	*	WALTON	V	3
216	2·2	Wicheles i	WIGHILL	V	} 5
		Wicheles ii	WIGHILL ii	F	
92	1·0	*	WILSTROP	F	3
		Not in DB.	FOLIFAIT	F	3
124	0·8	*iuxta civ.?*	DRINGHOUSES	V	4
77	0·5	Not in DB.	ANGRAM	V	no
		*	MULHEDE	NL	no
		*	IUXTA URBEM	NL	no
		*	BITHEN	NL	no

TABLE 16—(*continued*)

Fees 1302 Carucates	*Nom. Vill. 1316 *=present*	*1332 sums* (*Lay subsidy*)	*1334 quota* (*Lay subsidy*)	*1377 poll tax*
4	*	10/3	20/0	90
5	*	22/1	25/0	75
13	*	16/8	23/0	133
8	*	24/9	30/0	97
6·25	*	10/5	15/0	42
7·5	*	12/6	14/0	54
6·5	*	14/11	20/0	60
8	*	6/8	8/0	35
4	*	10/0	13/4	93 including Middlethorpe
8	*	21/6	27/0	90
3	no	no	no	no
3	*	5/0	7/0	22 including Oxton
4·5	*	16/10	18/0	42
5·5	*	30/7	33/4	60
3	* with Wighill	no	no	no
6	*	12/6	15/0	120
2	*	8/8	elsewhere	22
3	* with Bolton	no	no	no
6	*	16/9	20/0	80 including Angram
5	*	11/0	elsewhere	36
no	no	no	no	no
12·5	*	16/0	22/0	80
4·25	*	elsewhere	elsewhere	with Bishopthorpe
9	*	7/2	10/0	48 with Scaggle-thorpe
3	no	no	no	with Catterton 1379
4	*	6/8	8/0	with Catterton 1377 and 1379
3	no	no	no	no
4	*	11/2	18/0	48
3	*	2/0	3/0	with Moor Monkton
6·5	*	20/0	24/0	45
3	*	24/0	28/0	72
8	*	6/8	8/0	90
3	*	12/0	15/0	70
6 }	*	13/0	16/0	53 with Easedike
	* with Wighill	with Wighill		with Wighill
3	*	12/0	17/0	33
3	*	9/6	10/3	13
no	*	6/0	6/8	70
no	no	no	no	with Hutton Wandesley
no	no	no	no	no
no	no	no	no	no
no	no	no	no	no

SUMMARY OF TABLE 16

CATEGORY A. Vills named in 1086, excluding suburbs of York, numbering 37. (These thirty-seven names are given in col. 4 of the Table.)

CATEGORY B. New vills appearing by 1284, numbered 1. (This is Folifait.)

CATEGORY C. Vills first named between 1284 and 1377, numbering 1. (This is Angram.)

TOTAL OF CATEGORIES A, B AND C . . . . . . 39 vills.

CATEGORY D. Vills lost by 1284 (Malchetone & Pallathorpe) . 2

CATEGORY E. Vills lost by 1316 (Bustardthorpe & Ouston) . 2

CATEGORY F. Vills lost by 1332 (Hagenby & Hornington) . 2

CATEGORY G. Vills lost by 1377 (Scagglethorpe)[1] . . . 1?

CATEGORY H. Vills lost since 1377 (Steeton, Easedike,[2] Wilstrop & Folifait) 4

TOTAL OF CATEGORIES D, E, F, G AND H . . . . . 11 vills.

[1] Still named in 1377, but without separate assessment.

[2] Still named in 1377, but linked with Wighill for tax purposes since 1284. (The small site is clear on the ground.)

SOURCES
- Col. 1: Census of 1801.
- Col. 2: *ibid.*
- Col. 3: *Domesday Book*, aided by the identifications made by Mr. I. S. Maxwell in his study for the *Domesday Geography*, edited by Prof. H. C. Darby.
- Col. 6, Col. 7, Col. 8: *Kirkby's Inquest*, ed. R. H. Skaife (Surtees Soc., xlix, 1867).
- Col. 9: P.R.O. E 179/206/47.
- Col. 10: *ibid.*, E 179/206/26.
- Col. 11: *ibid.*, E 179/206/40.

TABLE 17

PROPORTION OF TO-BE-LOST VILLAGES IN VARIOUS SIZE-GROUPS, BY TAX QUOTAS OF 1334

Size of tax quota in shillings	NOTTINGHAM-SHIRE		E.R. YORK-SHIRE		NORFOLK		BUCKINGHAM-SHIRE		WARWICK-SHIRE	
	All vills	*Lost vills*	*All vills*	*Lost vills*	*All vills*	*Lost vills*	*All vills*	*Lost vills*	*All vills*	*Lost vills*
	%	%	%	%	%	%	%	%	%	%
0–10	3	8	1	4	0	0	1	8	1	2
11–20	3	13	17	32	1	4	2	0	13	33
21–30	29	52	17	24	6	24	4	15	15	17
31–40	22	7	21	26	11	21	7	8	18	22
41–50	9	13	7	2	12	13	13	0	17	9
51–60	10	0	9	4	10	13	23	54	13	8
61–70	9	7	9	2	7	13	12	15	7	5
71–80	8		4	2	11	6	6		3	0
81–90	4		4	2	6	0	6		4	2
91–100	1		3	2	4	0	4		3	0
101–110	1		2		4	2	8		1	0
111–120	1		1		4	2	0		0	0
121–130			1		2	0	5		2	0
131–140			1		4	0	0		1	2
141–150			1		2	0	1		0	0
Over 150			2		16	2	8		2	0
	100%		100%		100%		100%		100%	
No. of vills analysed	226	15	366	49	655	47	186	13	286	37

TABLE 17—(*continued*)

PROPORTION OF TO-BE-LOST VILLAGES IN VARIOUS SIZE-GROUPS, BY TAX QUOTAS OF 1334

LEICESTERSHIRE		OXFORDSHIRE		NORTHAMPTONSHIRE		LINCOLNSHIRE		YORKSHIRE WEST RIDING		YORKSHIRE NORTH RIDING	
All vills	*Lost vills*	*All vills*	*Lost vills*	*All vills*	*Lost vills*	*All vills*	*Lost vills*	*All vills*	*Lost vills*	*All vills*	*Lost vills*
%	%	%	%	%	%	%	%	%	%	%	%
2	11	1	2	0	7	6	19	14	30	7	13
10	29	4	13	1	7	20	61	38	44	41	56
18	18	10	18	0	0	27	13	26	20	26	31
22	25	11	21	7	26	17	7	9	3	13	
16	6	12	18	11	7	9		5	3	4	
13	8	11	8	13	13	8		2		3	
6	3	8	2	14	7	4		2		0	
3	0	5	0	11	20	9		2		0	
3		5	5	6	0			0		0	
2		7	11	12	13			0		2	
1		5	0	5				0		0	
2		4	0	6				1		0	
1		3	2	3						2	
1		2	0	3						0	
0		2	0	1						0	
0		10	0	7						2	
100%		100%		100%		100%		100%		100%	
319	37	320	39	227	15	649	29	544	30	453	39

TABLE 18

PROPORTION OF TO-BE-LOST VILLAGES FALLING IN VARIOUS SIZE-GROUPS OF TAXPAYERS, 1377

Number of taxpayers	YORKSHIRE WEST RIDING		YORKSHIRE EAST RIDING		YORKSHIRE NORTH RIDING		LINCOLNSHIRE [1]		NORTHAMPTON-SHIRE		OXFORDSHIRE		LEICESTERSHIRE	
	All vills	*Lost vills*	*All vills*	*Lost vills*	*All vills*	*Lost vills*	*All vills*	*Lost vills*	*All vills*	*Lost vills*	*All vills*	*Lost vills*	*All vills*	*Lost vills*
	%	%	%	%	%	%	%	%	%	%	%	%	%	%
0–10	0	10	0	0	0	5	2	12	0	0	1	0	1	0
11–20	3	32	6	28	6	10			1	12	8	30	0	5
21–30	8	13	0	0	12	24	13	58	1	6	8	12	4	13
31–40	9	13	6	17	15	28			3	0	12	28	5	33
41–50	15	10	4	0	16	28	20	24	3	0	13	9	7	13
51–60	11	4	8	17	12				7	46	10	3	8	0
61–70	11	6	10	17	8		18	6	7	6	6	6	13	15
71–80	10	4	7	11	10				4	0	8	3	10	22
81–90	6	0	4	5	2		12	0	7	6	6	6	13	0
91–100	7	0	10	5	5				7	12	6	0	6	9
101–110	3	0	7		4		12		10	0	3	0	3	
111–120	2	0	9		1				2	6	4	0	3	
121–130	3	4	3		1		5		6	0	2	0	7	
131–140	0		5		1				6	6	1	0	4	
141–150	2		5		1		18		3		3	3	2	
over 150	6		18		6				33		9		14	
	100%		100%		100%		100%		100%		100%		100%	
Total vills analysed	388	30	124	18	226	21	208	17	231	16	280	33	241	22

[1] Excluding parts of Holland (fenland).

A. Translation of the record in the case of Sir Richard Knightley's depopulations.

The Lord King sends his order by this writ under the great Seal to his Treasurer and the Barons of his Exchequer. Henry, by the grace of God etc. . . . to the Treasurer and his Barons of the Exchequer, Greeting.

There has been a plea proceeding before Us in our Court of Chancery between Ourselves and Sir Richard Knightley concerning the half of the income and profits of the seven messuages, two cottages and two hundred and a half acres of arable since the 14th February in the 24th year of the reign of our father the lord Henry the seventh, late King of England. This arose from an Inquisition taken at Northampton in the said county of Northampton on the 11th August 10 Henry VIII before John Vesey Dean of the Chapel Royal (and three others) Commissioners of the said King by virtue of letters patent authorising them to inquire by the oaths of worthy and honest men of the said County, amongst other things, the fuller truth about certain articles of enquiry in the letters patent. The jury were John Moulesworth, gentleman, and thirteen others, who said they were not ready and asked for an adjournment to the 5th of October, which was agreeable to the Commissioners. The jurors swore upon their oath that Sir Richard Knightley was lately possessed in fee among his demesne of 7 messuages 2 cottages and two hundred and a half acres of land (accustomed and fit for sowing and ploughing every year) with each messuage having at least twenty acres laid to it, in the hamlet of SNOTTESCOMBE in EVERTON [Everdon] parish. He was so possessed on the 14th February 24 Henry VII when he threw down these messuages and cottages and laid them waste; he turned these lands which had been used for sowing grain over to pasture for sheep and other animals, and he holds the land still so; by this, seven ploughs have been laid down and fifty people who used to live in the aforesaid houses and cultivate the land until that 14th February have left their homes and have been led into idleness contrary to the Statute of 4 Henry VII.

And the jurors say that Richard Knightley was also possessed etc. of 10 messuages and 260 acres of land, part of Plumpton vill and manor, given to him and his wife, Joan, by Ralph Rodys, clerk. Richard and Joan, on the 11th October 6 Henry VIII had the said 10 messuages and 260 acres of land enclosed with mounds and ditches and turned them over to pasture. On the 1st October 7 Henry VIII they deliberately destroyed the 10 messuages and two other cottages, one where Robert Walcott used to live, and the other where John Reeve used to live. There is no cultivation carried on there and no-one living in eight of the ten houses, contrary to the Statute. On this matter the said Richard appeared before us in Chancery in his own person on the 27th November last. He entered into recognizances to the sum of one hundred pounds, the condition being that he should rebuild or repair all the houses found in the Inquisition to be laid waste, that he should pull down the hedges and turn back the land which had been converted to grass and sow it before the Feast of St. Michael the Archangel next. The said Richard has proved that he has carried out by the appointed day all the conditions required of him in the recognizance. At the same day it was made known to us that the said seven messuages . . . specified in the Inquisition and seven messuages specified in a second Inquisition are the same and not different. The second Inquisition had been taken at Northampton on the 11th of August 10 Henry VIII. The jurors had said that Sir Richard Knightley was possessed of seven messuages, two cottages and 200 acres of Snottescombe of his fee and demesne, viz one messuage called Bodyngtons House, and sixty acres of land belonging to it, of which he was possessed on the 14th February 24 Henry VII when he converted the 60 acres to pasture. This house had been kept in repair and maintained for husbandry since the year 1485. He was also possessed of a second messuage called Clerkes House with 40 acres belonging to it, and another called Everdon House with 70 acres of arable going with it. These two houses were not sufficient to maintain farming there before 1485. At that date Richard let the two houses fall into ruin and he converted all the land belonging to them to grass. The remainder of the said houses and cottages, viz Mychell House, Rysleys House and Alen House have been attached to 20 acres of land and no more.

We, now, are unwilling to burden Richard undeservedly on account of this Inquisition. At the same time it was found by

> the first Inquisition that Richard possessed ten messuages and 260 acres of land, part of the manor and vill of Plumpton. And since on the 24th October (in Michaelmas Term last) Roger Wiggeston informed the Chancellor in the Court of Chancery that Richard had sufficiently repaired all the said messuages in Plumpton and Snottescombe found in the Inquisition to be waste, and had turned the land back to grain, before the Feast of St. Michael. Being unwilling to burden the said Richard, we order you by a writ of supersedeas not to taken anything from the said seven messuages in the first and second inquisitions; nor from half of the income of the eight messuages in Plumpton. Saving only to us, half the profits of the said messuages specified in the second Inquisition and the messuages in Plumpton from the time of their decay until the Feast of St. Michael next. Witness our hand at Westminster 8th November, the eleventh year of our reign.

We also have the writ calling Sir Richard to Chancery in 1518, with his answer. A further document, his plea for benefit of pardon, has been printed in English elsewhere and we need to do no more than summarise it here.

He claimed that Bodyngtons House had had only 100 acres of tillage with it since 1489; that three others had had only sixteen acres with them and not the twenty which would qualify them for statutory protection; that three other cottages had no land going with them; that others were already decayed by 1488;

> as to two other houses of the said seven houses, the said Sir Richard saith that they were greatly in decay before the said statute of anno quarto Henry the seventh and (as now they be) wasted and decayed and seven score acres and ten laid to pasture, parcell of the said two hundred acres and a half specified in the said Inquisition.

In claiming the benefit of the statutory pardon he voluntarily relinquished any right to defend himself at Law.

It will be noticed that the result of the case was a forfeit to the Crown of half the profits of two messuages in Plumpton from 1515 to September 1520, and of two cottages at Snorscomb from 1508 to September 1520. The certificate of rebuilding and the statement that some of the damage had been done before 1488 were sufficient to save Knightley from further action.

B. Translation of part of John Rous' list of villages destroyed in his lifetime, late fifteenth century, as given in Plate 9.

. . . Compton Murdok, Hodnell, Ascote, Radbourn, Over Caldecote, Wolfhamcote, Charlecote (almost wholly emparked), Morton Morrel, Salemorton, Kites Hardwick, Hunscote, Westcote, Compton Scorpion, Stoke, Foxcote (almost entirely), Norton, Weston, Chelmscote, Milcote, Burmington Parva, Brookhampton, Thornton, Goldicote, Rodbrook and Redburn, Idlicote (for the most part), Billesley Trussell, Cawston on Dunsmore, Bickmarsh, Willington, Nedon (Poden) by Honeybourne, Alvescote by Stratford, the three Dishfords, Homburn (which is being mutilated), Alvescote by Stratford [*sic*], Baddesley Clinton (for the most part newly emparked), Church Charwelton on the border of Warwicks. and Northants. where there used to be a well-known and healthy stopping place for travellers from Warwick and other places to London. Now travellers are forced to leave the old road and go down to Lower Charwelton. There is much danger for all these places are now totally or partly destroyed. It arises from avaricious men. All those villages are either destroyed or attacked, and this is great pity. And as I see it so I set it down: how many tenants[1] did these villages have in the 7th and 8th years of the reign of Edward I? (1279) Upper Wodcote had 13 and Lower Wodcote had 14. Compton Murdok—now only a manor and a church—had 27 tenants, bond and free. There was also a small rectory. Kington (or Chesterton Parva as it is sometimes called) had 11 tenants. Compton Scorpion had 60 . . .

C. Translation of tax receipt for Golder, Oxon, shown in Plate 14.

1. This indenture witnesseth that Richard Chamberlain and his colleagues, collectors of the subsidy for the King in the county of Oxford, have received from Richard Carter and John Gater trusty and honest men of the village of Golder, and from Alexander Plot, constable of the same village, seven shillings and fourpence for twenty-two lay persons, men and

[1] The word *tenements* has been added in the margin opposite "tenants".

women exceeding the age of fourteen years and living in the said village; this on their oath, and they have sworn that there are no more persons being lay men and women who dwell in the village aforesaid except true mendicants without fraud. To witness the truth of this Richard and his colleagues on the one part and the said Richard, John and Alexander have set their seals. Given at Watlington, the 25th day of March in the year of the reign of the king Edward the third after the Conquest, the fifty-first.
(P.R.O. E. 179/161 : 41, unnumbered membrane.)

2. *Goldere*

from Robert Carter
Alice his wife
Roger Piper
Cecily his wife
John Gater
Julia his wife
Alice Gater
Joan Gater
Alexander Plot
Matilda his wife
John Plot
John Carter
Lucy his wife
Stephen Freynhe
John Frempler
William Dryver
Richard Carter
Joan his wife
William Halder
John Dryver
William Jolyfe
Joan his wife

Sum of persons: 22

(P.R.O. E 179/161/38/2a.)

APPENDIX III

EXCAVATIONS AT LOST VILLAGE SITES IN GREAT BRITAIN

List compiled by Mr. John Hurst, April 1953

1. BERKSHIRE. SEACOURT. 1938–39. R.L.S. Bruce-Mitford. *Oxon.*, v (1940), pp. 31–40.

   This promising excavation was unfortunately curtailed by the outbreak of the war. A good sequence of pottery was obtained but there was not time to trace the extent of the various structures found.

2. BUCKINGHAMSHIRE. CUBLINGTON. ? Mentioned by Allcroft, *Earthwork of England* (1908), p. 548.

3. CORNWALL. TREWORTHA. 1891–92. Rev. S. Baring Gould. *J.R.I.C.*, xi (1892), pp. 57–70 and 289.

   Seven huts were investigated and a full record produced giving detailed plans.

4. DEVON. GREAT BEERE. 1938. E. M. Jope. Forthcoming, *Arch. Journ.*

   The best scientific excavation that has yet taken place at a deserted village site in England. Two houses, a barn and two corn-drying ovens were excavated.

5. DURHAM. YODEN. 1884. Mrs. R. Burdon. *Arch. Ael.*, N.S., x (1885), p. 186.

6. GLOUCESTERSHIRE. HULLASEY. 1910. W. St. Clair Baddeley. *Trans. Brist. & Glos.*, 33 (1910), pp. 338–54.

   Good plans were produced of three houses and the chapel, but the pottery was not described in any detail.

7. GLOUCESTERSHIRE. SENNINGTON. 1938. Mrs. O'Neil.

8. ISLE OF WIGHT. WOLVERTON. 1952. Major Gordon Fowler.

9. KENT. STONAR. 1936. Dr. W. P. D. Stebbing. *Arch. Cant.*, liii (1940), pp. 62–81; liv (1941), pp. 41–61; and lv (1942), pp. 37–52.

   Excavations at this medieval port have produced a great deal of important pottery evidence, especially in relation to trade, etc., but little information has been obtained of structures.

10. LEICESTERSHIRE. HAMILTON. 1948. Dr. W. G. Hoskins.

11. LEICESTERSHIRE. POTTERS MARSTON. 1945. E. Pochin and Miss J. Haynes. *A.N.L.*, Sept., 1951, Vol. 4, pp. 29–31. *Trans. Leics. Arch. Soc.*, xxviii (1952), pp. 55–62.

A pottery kiln was excavated giving a good series of thirteenth-century pottery.

12. NORTHAMPTONSHIRE. ONLEY BY BARBY. 1949. A. Franey.

13. NORTHUMBERLAND. WEST LILBURN. 1933. E. F. Collingwood. *Arch. Ael.*, 4th Ser., x (1933), pp. 210–33.

The church here was planned.

14. NOTTINGHAMSHIRE. ADBOLTON. 1945. Canon R. F. Wilkinson.

15. NOTTINGHAMSHIRE. THURGARTON. 1948. C. E. Coulthard.

16. NOTTINGHAMSHIRE. WHIMPTON. 1906. T. D. Pryce. *Trans. Thor. Soc.*, xi (1907), pp. 139–44.

17. OXFORDSHIRE. WOODPERRY. Rev. J. Wilson. *Arch. Journ.*, III (1846), i, p. 116.

18. SOMERSET. BINEHAM. 1951. W. A. Seaby. *A.N.L.*, Oct., 1951, Vol. 4, pp. 42–43.

19. SUSSEX. EXCETE. 1913. Rev. W. Budgen. *S.A.C.*, lviii (1916), pp. 138–70.

The church here was planned.

20. SUSSEX. HANGLETON. 1952. E. W. Holden.

21. WARWICKSHIRE. BIGGIN. 1950–51. T. Fawcett. *Rugby School Nat. Hist. Soc.*, 1951, pp. 17–19.

22. WARWICKSHIRE. STRETTON BASKERVILLE. 1947–48. M. W. Beresford. *Tran. Birm. Arch. Soc.*, lvi (1945/6), pp. 69–71.

Important because this sheep depopulated settlement has been placed in its regional setting. Excavation revealed the traditional site of the church with a complicated series of structures.

23. YORKSHIRE. CAWTHORN. 1945–46. R. H. Hayes.

24. YORKSHIRE. EAST LILLING. 1948. M. W. Beresford. *A.N.L.*, April, 1949, p. 16.

25. YORKSHIRE. STEETON. 1951–52. M. W. Beresford.

26. YORKSHIRE. THORNTON RISBOROUGH. 1946. R. H. Hayes.

27. YORKSHIRE. WEAVERTHORPE. 1951. D. Smith, R. H. Hayes.

28. YORKSHIRE. WHARRAM PERCY. 1950. M. W. Beresford. *Y.A.J.*, xxxvii (1951), pp. 479–81; fig. 1*b*, p. 486.

Of all village sites so far excavated in England this is the most promising, for the position of each house is clearly visible, thus precluding the need to trial-trench to find structures. In the first two seasons trial cuts were made on the sites of four houses and the manor house complex. Little result was obtained, but the writer helped to show last summer that the site has a complex history of different periods. The Research Group began to strip a house here during 1953 as a trial of excavation technique.

29. YORKSHIRE. WILSTROP. 1949. M. W. Beresford.

Ireland

1. ANTRIM. GOODLAND. 1949. J. Sidebotham. *U.J.A.*, xii (1950), pp. 44–53; and 1952. H. J. Case. *A.N.L.*, iv (1952), p. 150.

2. LIMERICK. CAHERGUILLAMORE. 1940. Prof. O'Riordain, J. Hunt. *J.R.S. Ant. Irel.*, 72 (1942), pp. 37–63.

3. TIPPERARY. LAITHMORE-MOCHOEMOG. 1940. H. G. Leask, Prof. R. A. S. Macalister. *P.R.I.A.*, li (1945/8), pp. 1–14.

The Irish are much ahead of us in the excavation of deserted medieval sites. Few have been done, but these have produced important evidence of medieval structures in each case.

Scotland

1. PEEBLES. MANOR. 1938. R. V. K. Stevenson. *P.S.A.S.*, lxxv (1940), pp. 92–115.

Few deserted sites are known in Scotland, but valuable evidence of local structures was obtained at this site, though Mr. Stevenson tells me that there are now some doubts as to its exact nature.

Wales

1. CARMARTHENSHIRE. HAWTON. 1948. Prof. J. W. W. Stephens. *A.N.L.*, Dec. 1948, p. 14. See also: *Rep. Hist. Mon. Comm. Wales, Carmarthenshire* (1917), p. 246 and plates.

For a list of abbreviations see p. 11, *supra*.

Chapter One: THE LANDSCAPE OF THE LOST VILLAGE

1. A second copy of the survey, from which the East Lilling page had been excised, came with the papers of Sir Arthur Ingram to Leeds City Library (MS. B 417391). Ingram purchased the manor from the Crown.

Chapter Two: THE FABRIC OF THE VILLAGE

1. *L.P.H.*, ix, no. 1246.
2. *Gray*, frontispiece; *Orwin*, p. 65.
3. *Homans*, p. 13.
4. The account which follows is based largely upon well-known published work by Homans, Orwin and T. A. M. Bishop. Detailed supporting references have not been given.
5. Facing p. 88.
6. C. R. Hansen and Axel Steensberg, *Jordfordeling og Udskiftning* (Copenhagen, 1951), p. 432.
7. *C.L.*, cv (1949), plate 5, p. 474.
8. *Hoskins*, p. 93 f.n.
9. *Ec.H.R.*, 2nd ser., i (1948), p. 34.
10. E. Kerridge, *ibid.*, 2nd ser., iv (1951), p. 14.
11. Padbury: Hovendon maps, All Souls College, Oxford; Laxton: *Orwin*. End-maps.
12. *D.I.*, p. 489.
13. Haterberg in Scalby: L.P.H., xii (i), p. 535; Newton: E 367/1317; E 178/1615; E 134, Easter 4 Jas. I no. 5.
14. Lillingstone, see p. 320. Calceby; Glebe terrier quoted in Miss O. Beaumont, *Lincolnshire Glebe Terriers* (unpublished M.A. thesis, Univ. of Reading (1952)). Cowarne; B.M.Lans. MS. I; in 1517, jurors reported that Thomas Clerke was living at the site of Elmington, Northants., alongside two empty farmhouses, the hall and parlour of a third which had otherwise been pulled down, and the ruins of a fourth which had been accidentally burned: *D.I.*, p. 480; Cestersover, *VCH.*, *Warws.*, vi. p. 177.
15. CPE. UK. 1748/2149.
16. The pond: B.M. Add. Ch. 1785; other detail from Y.A.S., MS. 213.
17. C 43/28/8.
18. *N.C.H.*, ix, p. 124.
19. S.P.D. Chas. I, ccl, no. 68.
20. *D.I.*, p. 432, translated.
21. *C.S.P.D.* Chas. I, 1638: November 3rd., no. 5. There was an Elizabethan inquiry into ruined Kent and Norfolk churches: E 178/7299.
22. D.R.O.(Y.), R. VII H. 4202–5. I am indebted to Dr. Purvis for these and other references.
23. The register is kept at North Grimston vicarage.

24. *T.B.G.A.S.*, xxxiii, p. 338.
25. Quoted in R. L. S. Bruce-Mitford, "Excavations at Seacourt", *Oxon.*, v (1940), p. 31. More recently Professor Hawkes told an audience of archaeologists that the deserted sites of the Lincolnshire wolds were due to the decline [*sic*] of the wool trade: *Arch. J.*, ciii (1946), p. 101. A discussion of archaeological aspects of lost village study began in *A.N.L.*, iv, no. 9 (1952).
26. Mr. Bruce-Mitford kindly examined the pottery recovered from the Midland and Yorkshire excavations and dated the fragments as being from the twelfth to the late fifteenth centuries. I have now passed the collection into the keeping of Mr. J. G. Hurst at the Ministry of Works, for use in his comparative study. For pottery from another Oxfordshire site see E. M. Jope, Oxon, xiii (1948), p. 67.
27. *D.I.*, pp. 432; 340; 272–75; 277; 294; 296; 306; 317.
28. *T.P.*, iii, p. 51.
29. *B.B.T.*, p. 275.
30. *T.P.*, iii, p. 80.
31. *Discourse*, p. 148.
32. *T.P.*, i, p. 89.
33. S.P.(D.), Ch. I., 193, no. 79.

Chapter Three: TRAVELLERS TO THE LOST VILLAGE

1. *Q.J.E.*, xvii (1903), p. 594.
2. *Bradley*, p. 96.
3. *Clapham*, p. 197, modified by his editor in f.n., p. 80.
4. *Foster*; see also a preliminary, and in some cases fuller, list in *L.R.S.* xvii (1920); Hoskins in *T.L.A.S.*, xxii (1948), reprinted with additions in *Hoskins*.
5. *Lipson*, i, p. 180.
6. *Tawney*, p. 261.
7. The text translated here is that of Hearne's edition of 1745 checked with B.M. Cot. Vesp. A. XII and Bodl. MS. Jones 2. A self-portrait of Rous appears in T.D. Kendrick, *British Antiquity* (1950), pl. 2*a*.
8. *Lipson*, i, p. 144.
9. *Discourse*, pp. lii–lxvii. For contested authorship see *Bull. John Rylands Library*, xxi (1937), pp. 167–75.
10. *Ibid.*, p. 15.
11. *Hoskins*, p. 98.
12. *D.I.*, p. 279.
13. *Discourse*, p. 48.
14. B.M. Lans. MS. 238, f. 205.
15. Latimer, *Sermons* (Everyman ed.), p. 85.
16. Quoted *T.P.*, iii, p. 5.
17. *E.E.T.S.*, extra ser., xii (1878), p. lxxvi.
18. More, *Utopia* (Everyman ed.), p. 23.
19. *E.E.T.S.*, extra ser. xxxiii (1871), p. 71.
20. *E.E.T.S.*, extra ser. xiii (1871), pp. 93–102 and xx (1874).
21. *B.B.T.*, p. 275.
22. *T.P.*, iii, pp. 80–81; see also "Nowe A Dayes", *ibid*, p. 18.
23. S.P.D. Chas. I. 362/60.

24. S.P.D. Eliz. 7/58–9.
25. Hovenden maps: I am indebted to the Librarian for permission to examine these beautiful maps and to have them copied for reproduction.
26. *Hoskins*, p. 94; L. A. Parker, *Enclosure in Leicestershire*, unpublished Ph.D. thesis, Univ. of London.
27. Camden, *Britannia* (Gough's translation, 1806 ed.), iii, p. 326.
28. R. Thoroton, *History of Nottinghamshire* (1677 ed.), Preface, unnumbered, p. iv; and p. 38. The 1517 Returns are in *T.S.R.S.*, ii (1904), p. 18; with additional information from C 47/7/2/3 m. 32.
29. W. Stukeley, *Itinerarium Curiosum* (1724); *Dugdale*, p. 90.
30. *A.J.* (1925), p. 30; *Surt. Soc.*, liv (1869), p. 127.
31. G. E. Kendall had drawn attention to the "Town of Hamilton" in 1920: *A.A.S.R.P.*, xxxv, p. 323.
32. *G.J.*, cxvii (1951), p. 148.
33. Dr. Hoskins has shown how the Bosworth Field battle was fought almost over the site of the lost Ambion: *Hoskins*, p. 104; the local tradition about Danethorpe in Langford, Notts., is that it was destroyed by an earthquake; Kelly's *Directory of Lincolnshire* solemnly prints the suggestion that Gainsthorpe village may be "submerged", but it redeems its historical reputation by describing the site of the lost Mere which does not appear in Foster's list. Since the successive editions of Kelly's *Directories* have faithfully reported the names of townships and parishes even where uninhabited, they are useful works of reference for lost village searchers far from sets of 6-inch O.S. maps. At Astwick (Northants.) the traditional site of the "Old Town" was dismissed by the *VCH.* (ii, p. 415) as a mere moated homestead; but the village site lies in the adjacent field, and fiction was truer than history.
34. D.R.O. (Y.), R. VII H. 1885; 1921; Bardney Cartulary: B.M. Cot. Vesp. E. XX; see also *P.N.E.R.*, p. 108.

Chapter Four: THE KING'S PROCEEDINGS

1. *R.P.*, iv, p. 60.
2. Shuckburgh: C1/445/51; Requests 2/8/339; Council of the North: D.R.O.(Y.), R.As. 20/5.
3. Polydore Vergil, ed. D. Hay, Camden Soc., lxxiv (1950), pp. 277–9.
4. 4 Henry VII c. 6 (1488); c. 19 (1489).
5. *L.P.H.*, iv (iii), no. 5750.
6. 6 Henry VIII c. 5; 7 Henry VIII c. 1.
7. The Returns printed in *D.I.* now form part of the file C 47/7/2 together with fresh membranes discovered later. The source of the Returns from other counties printed by Leadam in *T.R.H.S.*, n.s., vi–viii (1892–94), is B.M. Lans. MS. I.
8. *Gay 1517*.
9. *D.I.*, pp. 81–82.
10. Stretton, *ibid.*, p. 431; Wretchwick, p. 340. See also Kennett, *Parochial Antiquities* (Oxford, 1818), ii, pp. 248; 255–57.
11. *D.I.*, p. 417.
12. C 43/28/8 m. 9.
13. File C 43/28.

14. *Gay 1517*; Parker, *op. cit.*
15. Text in H. Hall *Formula Book of Legal Records* (1909), ii, pp. 181, 186, 188–89. Writ and answer: C 43/28/6 mm. 22–24.
16. 27 Henry VIII c. 22.
17. 25 Henry VIII c. 13. For poll tax of 1549, *Ag. Hist. Rev.*, i (1954).
18. E 159/316 Trin. m. 31.
19. E 368/313 Eas. m. 13 (Papley); m. 14 (Grimsbury).
20. The normal end to such a case runs: *visis premissis per Barones habita matura deliberatione inde inter eosdem dictum est per eosdem Barones prefato (Johanne) quod ipse quoad compertum predictum ab eo in forma exactionis ad presens eat sine die pretextu premissorum Salva semper actione regi domino.* Unsuccessful pleas ended with a writ enrolled *inter brevia* on the roll, ordering the sheriff to distrain for the penalty: *e.g.* E 368/320 *inter brevia,* Hil. (Bittesby; Glendon and other depopulated villages).
21. E 159/321 Eas. m. 41.
22. E 159/323 Mich. m. 49.
23. *Gay 1607*, p. 495.
24. Clarendon, *History of the Great Rebellion,* p. 131.
25. *B.B.T.*, p. 273.
26. R. H. Tawney, *The Rise of the Gentry,* in *Ec.H.R.*, xi (1941), p. 1.
27. *Discourse*, p. lix.
28. Proclamation: S.P.D. Henry VIII 231/225; petition: Requests 2/8/256; return: *D.I.*, p. 343.
29. *D.I.*, pp. 656–66.
30. *Discourse*, p. lxiii. 1607 speech: B.M. Lans. MS. 487, f. 218; Cot MS., Titus, F. IV, 320.
31. *D.I.*, pp. 485–87; E 38/344; Requests 3/40/68; E 159/299 Mich. m. 9*d*.
32. E 368/312 Mich. m. 22.
33. At Wollaton Sir Henry Willoughby had moved the evicted tenants into a new house: *T.S.R.S.* ii (1904), p. 39.
34. *E.g.* E 368/319 Trin. m. 84.
35. E 178/424.
36. Twenty years after the Dissolution of the monasteries the Barons of Exchequer were considering the case of the enclosures by the Abbots of Kenilworth at Tachbrook, Warws.: E 368/334 Hil. m. 32. 1573: *Y.A.S., R.S.*, cxv, p. 78; 1609, North Riding Sessions Book, I, f. 73*b*. (N. R. Record Office, Northallerton); Vergil: *loc. cit.*, f.n. 3 *supra.*
37. Bucks: C 43/28/3; Northants.: C 43/28/6 mm. 21; 70; for attempts to blame tenants see C 43/28/6 m. 5 and C1/56/30; the Latin phrase is from C 43/28/6 m. 27; for Claypole's case see *Tawney*, p. 379.
38. C 43/21/8 m. 10; judgment at E 368/299 Mich. m. 38.
39. *D.I.*, pp. 485–87; C 43/28/8.
40. For cases of recognizances in Exchequer see E 159/298 Mich. m. 17*d*; for cancellation see E 159/300 Hil. m. 9*d*; for recognizances on the dorse of the Close Roll we may take as example that of the Prior of Stafford in £40 (1520) and the Earl of Shrewsbury in £200 (1526).
41. *D.I.*, pp. 11–12; schedule: C 47/7/2/3 mm. 6–7.
42. *L.P.H.*, 1539, no. 1350.
43. *D.I.*, p. 11.
44. *Discourse*, p. 49; *T.P.*, i, p. 41.

45. The bishop: C 43/28/7 m. 75. Other pardons from E 368/295–98.
46. *Dugdale*, p. 90; for examples of royal permission to empark at villages subsequently totally depopulated see *Cal. Ch. Roll*, vi, p. 59.
47. Belknap's pardons are all recited in E 368/331 Hil. m. 22, the climax of the litigation involving this family; see also *D.I.*, pp. 426, 478, 656; for Vaux: C1/452/37; for Goodwyn: *Cal. Pat. Rolls, 1553–65*, p. 103; there is a pardon for Glendon (Northants.) in E 368/334 Mich. m. 7. For Belknap, see W. C. Richardson, *Tudor Chamber Administration* (Louisiana, 1952), pp. 201–5.

Chapter Five: THE OCCASIONS OF DESTRUCTION

1. *Supra*, p. 59.
2. Text of the articles of Inquiry in *T.P.*, i, p. 41, where the strong continuity with 1517 will be seen.
3. 1565: E 159/357 Mich. m. 523 ff.; E 178/424. Consequent prosecutions may be represented by E 159/357 Mich. m. 395 and E 159/358 Trin. m. 107.
4. 1607: C 205/5/1–6; Leics. membranes published by L. A. Parker in *T.L.A.S.*, xxiii; for Northants. proceedings at the Assizes of 1609 see E 163/19/8.
5. Warws. returns in *D.I.*, pp. 456–66.
6. For depopulation in Northumberland and Durham at this period see p. 172.
7. *Gay, 1607*; also St. Ch. 8/10/18; 15/12; 15/21. "The Diggers of Warwickshire in haste from Hampton Field to all other Diggers" is B.M. Harl. MS. 787, f. 9*b*.
8. 1607 informations: E 159/431 Mich. m. 202; Hil. m. 113–14; E 159/432 Trin. mm. 69–71, 139, 143–63; E 159/433 Mich. mm. 50, 151, 193, 216–17; Hil. mm. 108–9, 158. For similar insignificant depopulations in 1630–9 see E 159/476–8; SP 16/206/71; 229/112; 189/94; 223/22; 192/93; 192/94; 233/36.
9. Lincs: B.M. Add. MSS. 11574, ff. 66 seq. recently discovered by Mr. J. D. Gould and reported in *E.H.R.*, 1952, pp. 352–55. My cases are taken from a transcript loaned to me by Dr. Joan Thirsk.
10. L. A. Parker, *Enclosure in Leics.* (Unpublished Ph.D. thesis, Univ. of London). The Whatborough map is at All Souls, the Pickwell at the Leicester City Muniment Room.
11. See p. 88.
12. S.P. 12/7/58–59.
13. S.C. 12/176/20; see also *Cal. Cart. Rolls*, vi, p. 8.
14. *VCH., Herts.*, ii, p. 284.
15. *Discourse*, p. lxiii.
16. *D.N.B.*, xlix, p. 319.
17. K.B. 27/1035/East, m. xviii.
18. *Discourse*, p. lxiii.
19. *Tawney*, p. 166.
20. Evidence from *Ledger Book* (Stratford-upon-Avon, Birthplace Library MSS.) f. 9 for Stoneleigh; for Revesby see *Facsimiles of Early Charters*, ed. F. M. Stenton (Northants. Rec. Soc. 1930) pp. 1–7, and Dugdale, *Monasticon*, v, p. 454.

21. Baldersby: T. A. M. Bishop in *E.H.R.*, li (1936), p. 193; for Greenbery, see *Fountains Cartulary* ed. W. A. Lancaster (1915), ii, pp. 329–38; for re-colonisation, *Surt. Soc.*, xlii, p. 203.
22. Dugdale, *op. cit.*, v, p. 351. I owe this reference to Mr. H. M. Colvin in *A.N.L.*, iv, pp. 129–31, where other evidence for monastic depopulation is brought together. For Walter Map see *De Nugis Curialium*, trans. M. A. James, pp. 49–50 (Cymmrodorion Record Series, ix).
23. This information is taken from a leaflet prepared by Dr. Hoskins.
24. Rose Graham in *Journal Arch. Assocn.*, 3rd series, v, p. 173.
25. J. A. Steers, *The Coastline of England and Wales* (1946), map, p. 410.
26. *N.C.H.*, vi, p. 87; 105.
27. W. Bugden, *Excete and its parish church* in *S.A.C.*, lviii (1916), pp. 138–71.
28. For Northumbrian destruction see *N.C.H.*, iv, *passim*; for rapid recovery, *ibid.*, vii, pp. 234, 240, 242. For general destruction in the north in the fourteenth century see *Y.A.J.*, xxv, p. 161 (1919); and for the burning of 140 villages in 1318 see E 359/14 mm. 13–14.
29. *VCH.*, *Yorks. N.R.*, ii, p. 76.
30. 1609 returns: North Riding Sessions Book (MS.) I, f. 73*b*. (County Record Office, Northallerton).
31. F. Baring, *The Making of the New Forest* in *E.H.R.*, xvi, pp. 427–38.
32. Printed in *F.A.* (5 vols.).
33. *Postan*, p. 221.
34. Casthorpe: *Foster*, p. liii; Conesby, *ibid.*, liii; Leics. vills from *Hoskins*, p. 104.
35. K. J. Allison, *Lost Villages of Norfolk* (MS. thesis, Dept. of Geography, Univ. of Leeds, 1952).
36. Instructions to justices: E 163/4/39. *Putnam* has a full account of the redistribution. I have found twenty-eight county lists with reliefs from the years 1352–54. Some of these, although not all, are indicated in the P.R.O. typescript hand-list to the Lay Subsidies.
37. Standelf or Standhill: *Boarstall Cartulary*, ed. H. E. Salter (O.H.S.), p. 53. For Tilgarsley: *Eynsham Cartulary*, ed. H. E. Salter (O.H.S.), ii, p. 69. For very early fourteenth century decline with later recovery see Eversholt, Beds., in *Non. Inq.*, p. 12. Cublington, Bucks., was abandoned and resettled (*Non. Inq.*, p. 339).
38. *Eynsham Cartulary*, p. 19.
39. C 135/164/7.
40. Wykeham: *Foster*, p. lxxii.
41. Dunsthorpe: *ibid.*, p. lv; glebe terrier in Beaumont, *thesis cit.*
42. Fordington: *ibid.*
43. Dexthorpe: *ibid.*
44. North Scarle: *A.A.S.R.P.*, xxiv (1897), p. 428.
45. Whisby: *ibid.*
46. Cublington: *Non. Inq.*, p. 339 and *R.C.H.M. Bucks.*, ii, p. 99.
47. E. 179/202/53.
48. Rubric from the tax roll, *ibid.* Wording from *R.P.*, ii, pp. 238*a*; 234*b*.

49. Both the Towthorpes in the E.R. have been depopulated: this one lay in Londesborough. The writs for the assessment of relief are quite explicit: *dicti collectores denarios inde provenientes inter villatas iuxta necessitatem villarum earundem, per supervisum et dispositionem custodum predictorum distribuant* (E. 179/49/37).
50. 1377: E 179/206/33–40; 1379: E 179/206/49.
51. Printed in *F.A.* by counties.
52. 1433: *R.P.*, iv, p. 425*a* :1439; *ibid.*, v, p. 40; for subsequent years see *Willard and Johnson* and the enrolled subsidies in E. 359. The P.R.O. hand-list does not always indicate whether rolls contain such lists of reliefs. The City of York was still applying this relief among its poorer parishes in 1492: "other some of the said parichez which ar fallen in extreme ruyne and decay to be lestened and abrigged" (*York Civic Records* (Y.A.S., R.S.) ii, p. 84. Lincs. subsidy rolls temp. Eliz. dutifully record the same allowances as in the late fifteenth century, and there are other suggestions that the reliefs became conventionalised in the 1480s or 1490s. (E 179/135/72 and *R.P.*, vi, p. 442.)
53. For example, although there are a number of relief rolls for Devon Dr. Hoskins used only those of 1445 and 1489 in his *Devonshire Studies.*
54. E 179/165/3; 5; 23; 75; 77, for Martinsthorpe. Rokeby and Mortham: 211/87; 89.
55. Rous: *D.N.B.*, xlix (1897), p. 39; Chancellor's speech: *Grants of Edward IV* (Camden Soc. (1854), p. lii); for *depopulatores*: statute, 4 Henry IV c. 2.
56. Notts: *R.P.*, iv, p. 28.
57. Cambs.: *ibid.*, p. 29*b*.
58. Notts. evidence, etc., *D.I.*, pp. 62–9.
59. Printed by Leadam in *T.R.H.S.*, n.s., vi–viii (1892–94).
60. Beresford, *Yorkshire*, part ii (1952).
61. Based on *Foster* and new evidence presented in Chapter Ten.
62. Lincs.: *Foster*, pp. lv; lxxii. *L.A.C.*: Register XIX, f. 26; XX, f. 28*d*. Thorpe: A. H. Thompson, *English Clergy*, p. 112.
63. E 179/135/58.
64. *C.S.P.Dom.Eliz.*, (*1595–97*) p. 347.
65. For Northumberland evidence quoted see *N.C.H.*, i, p. 275; ii, p. 252; xiv, pp. 154, 229; xv, p. 390; xiv, p. 554; xv, p. 201; xv, p. 425; xv, p. 428.
66. The Border depopulations were the subject of a Commission of Inquiry set up by 23 Eliz. c. 4 extended by 2 and 3 Ph. and Mary c.l. In 1555 the Commissions' decrees were to be sent to Chancery, but I have not been able to find them. The returns of 1584 are to be found in S.P. 15/28, no. 26: "tenancies and forces decaied upon the borders since the 27 yere of kinge Henry 8". This is the year named in the Act of 1555.
67. See n. 30 *supra*.

Chapter Six: THE MOTIVES FOR DESTRUCTION

1. C. L. Kingsford, *Prejudice and Promise* (1925); M. Postan, *The Fifteenth Century* in *Ec.H.R.*, ix (1939), p. 160.

2. Tables: *D.I.*, pp. 62–69; taking 15 cases where increased values were specifically mentioned in the returns, Leadam showed that the rental value more than doubled at enclosure and conversion. He thought such cases exceptional, for from a much larger sample he calculated an average increase of 28%: Leics. showed 65% increase but Beds. and Berks. had much lower values for enclosed pasture. This squares with what we know of the slight degree of enclosure at this time in these two counties.
3. *E.g.* E 179/213/209 (N.R. Yorks.); 203/251 (E.R.); 208/211 (W.R.); 99/315 (Devon).
4. *D.I.*, pp. 403–4; 485; *Dugdale*, p. 378.
5. Ed. R. Pauli, p. 22.
6. Charge to jury: *T.P.*, i, p. 43; *Discourse*, p. liv; pp. 49–57; 121–22.
7. *Bradley*, p. 96.
8. J. E. T. Rogers, *History of Agriculture and Prices* (1866–1902). Rogers himself was well aware of the defects of his statistics, and the fault lies in those who have leaned too heavily upon them. "I regret nothing so much as the poverty of my information about wool" (*ibid.*, iv, p. 215); "I do not myself feel justified in drawing general averages from such scanty materials" (iv, p. 328). Rogers hoped that wool prices might be inferred from his cloth prices, but these prices had other important determinants than the price of the raw wool. For other comment on the use of Rogers' prices in this connection see *Lipson*, i, p. 147 f.n.; E. V. Morgan, *The Study of Prices and the Value of Money* (1950), p. 19.
9. That is, in 1951.
10. In Dr. Bowden's index, wool prices from various districts were weighted for varying quality, and an average price for both wool and corn calculated over the period 1490–1610. With this average as 100, the actual prices have been plotted as a three-year moving average. Until 1572 the differential in favour of wool was maintained except in the years: 1501–2; 1527–29; 1553–56 and 1562; after 1572 wheat prices steadily gain and hold their ground. P. J. Bowden, unpublished thesis, Ph. D., University of Leeds (1952). Price indices in *Yorkshire Bull. of Econ. and Social Research*, iv (1952), pp. 109–24.
11. 1607: B.M. Lans. MS. 487, f. 218. *Treatise*: *T.P.*, iii, p. 97.
12. *Power*, p. 37.
13. J. C. Russell, *British Medieval Population* (1948), c. 5.
14. *Postan*, p. 245.
15. *Ibid.*, p. 232.
16. *Ibid.*, pp. 233–35.
17. 1515: 7 Henry VIII c. 1; 1514: *L.P.H.*, iv, pt. 3, no. 5750; 1533: 25 Henry VIII c. 13; 1489: 4 Henry VII c. 19.
18. *Power*, p. 40.
19. *D.N.B.*, liii, p. 367.
20. Details from the files of E 159 and E 368 examined for Chapter Four.
21. *Hoskins*, pp. 75–81; 92.
22. Detail from *D.N.B. sub nominibus*; with additional evidence from *VCH.*, Warws., vi, p. 177 (Cestersover); *T.R.H.S.*, n.s. vii, p. 238 (Fairfax); the list of wool growers at S.P. 1/238, ff. 264–68 was pointed out to me by Dr. Bowden.

23. Knightley: C 142/57/2; Tyringham: C 142/46/43 (1); Vaux: C 143/41/60 and 43/10; Verney wills: Birmingham Reference Library, MSS.
24. *Op. cit.*, p. 99.
25. 27 Henry VIII c. 22; the phrase was often used in the 1517 Returns.
26. *C.S.P.D.* 1566–79 pp. 249–51; 2nd and 10th March 1570.
27. S.P. 16/342/47.
28. *Tawney*, p. 114.
29. *Postan*, p. 238.
30. Russell, *loc. cit.*
31. These figures come from E 179/136/293 (tax quotas); and E 179/135/70; 196/40; 237/74 (poll tax).
32. Even a casual study of the extents among the inquisitions *post mortem* of the early fourteenth century shows many examples of land lying uncultivated. The *Nonarum Inquisitiones* of 1340 have many such entries in all counties: an extreme case is that at Eversholt, Beds. (*ibid.*, p. 12), *septies viginti acrae terrae iacuerunt eodem anno incultae et friscæ, et multae mansiones infra eandem parochiam exstrepuntur ubi magnus numerus bidentium nutriebantur et loca his mansionibus rediguntur in pasturam*; see also n. 39 *infra*.
33. Pendley: S.C. 12/176/20; *Cal. Ch. Rolls*, vi, p. 8; *VCH., Herts.*, ii, p. 285. Fulbrook: *Beresford, Warwickshire*, p. 91; Wiverton: *Cal. Ch. Rolls*, vi, p. 59 and C 47/7/2/3 mm. 25–27.
34. J. D. Chambers, *Nottinghamshire in the Eighteenth Century*, pp. 166–72.
35. An examination of the numbers of freeholders in to-be-lost villages in the Hundred Rolls of 1279 does not show any significantly low proportion of freeholders: but 1279 is far from 1479.
36. *Hoskins*, p. 91.
37. *L.R.S.*, xxiii (1926), p. 225.
38. Filgrave: C 1/536/15; Shuckburgh: C 1/445/51; Grimston: Castle Howard MSS. Survey Book of 1562; Givendale then had three tenants, but extents like that in C 135/220/14 describe the land as waste and uncultivatable before the Black Death; Longborough: C 1/739/17; Sezincote: listed in Rous; Brook End and Grove: *Eynsham Cartulary*, ed. Salter (O.H.S., xlix–l (1906–8), ii, p. xxvii).
39. For extents which link stoniness with lack of cultivation after the Plague see Givendale, C 135/220/14; Wyville, C 135/164/7; 10 bovates at the lost Kiplingcotes had been worth nothing "for many years" before 1349 (C 135/106/23). When Lincolnshire parishes were amalgamated, both plague and infertility were blamed for their emptiness: *sterilitate quarum terrarum et defectu culturæ.* (*L.A.C.*, Register XIX, f. 26.) At Azerley (W.R.) there were 80 acres in 1362 which had "lain waste up to now, and are worth nothing as grassground or as anything else on account of the large quantity of grassground that there is in these parts" (C 135/168/21). At Settrington in the same year two reasons were given for there being 4 waste carucates: "the poorness of the land and the want of tenants" (C 135/168/13).
40. Bray: C 43/28/6 m. 21; Willington: C 43/28/8 m. 10; Bittesby: E 368/314 Eas. m. 15.
41. See n. 37 *supra*, and E 179/159/31 (poll tax).
42. See n. 31 *supra*.

43. *B.B.T.*, p. 275. The same sentiments occur in the Acts of 1489 and 1597.
44. 1597 debate: *ibid*, p. 272; Bacon: *History of Henry VII* (ed. 1858), p. 94.
45. *York Civic Records* (Y.A.S.R.S.), i–vii, *passim*.
46. Coarse-woolled sheep from Wales and other "outward parts" were used for stocking new pastures: *T.P.*, iii, p. 101.
47. F. J. Fisher, *Ec.H.R.*, x, p. 105.
48. *D.I.*, pp. 485–9.

Chapter Seven: *THE LOCALE OF DESTRUCTION*

1. 1517 Returns in *T.R.H.S.*, n.s., vi (1892).
2. *Ibid.*
3. p. 114 *supra*.
4. p. 234 *infra*.
5. It should be emphasised that this use of the word "margin" refers to the geographical situation of the counties concerned in relation to the inner core of Midland counties. It has no implication that they were economically on the margin.
6. *Discourse*, p. 49; at p. 51 the Doctor argues from the analogy of breeding rabbits: to breed rabbits is a "commodity to the Realm", but to devote all resources to breeding rabbits "were a great folly".
7. Ed. Pauli, p. 26; *Rous*, ed. Hearne, p. 116.
8. S.P. 16/206/69.
9. *T.P.*, p. 53.
10. *B.B.T.*, p. 247.
11. 39 Eliz. c. 2.
12. *G.J.*, cxviii (1951), p. 148.
13. *D.I.*, pp. 426, 429; Crimscote open field map: Tithe Awards, Shire Hall, Warwick.
14. J. B. Black, *The Reign of Elizabeth* (1936), p. 449; Gay's complex map first appeared in *Q.J.E.*, xvii (1903), p. 576.
15. E. C. K. Gonner; *Common Land and Inclosure* (1912), end maps.
16. F. Hull, *Agriculture and Rural Society in Essex*, 1560–1640 (unpub. Ph.D. thesis, Univ. of London), pp. 47 and 527.
17. R. H. Kinvig, *The Birmingham District in Domesday Times* (reprinted from British Association, *Birmingham and its Regional Setting* (1950)), pp. 11, 17, 21.
18. R. H. Hilton, *Social Structure of Rural Warwickshire in the Middle Ages* (Dugdale Society Occasional Papers, no. 9 (1950)), pp. 15–17 and Appendix.
19. *Lot Acres*, in *Ec.H.R.*, xvii (1943), p. 74.
20. *Beresford*, *Warwickshire*, p. 80 and plate xiii.
21. The tax quotas of the Cambridgeshire fen villages in 1334 averaged 292*s*. each; those of the fens of Lincolnshire, 416*s*. These sums can be compared with the average sums for champine villages in Table 7, p. 251.
22. R. A. L. Smith, *Ec.H.R.*, x, p. 37.
23. The figures are calculated from information in the Subsidy Rolls and Poll Tax receipts in Class E. 179 at the P.R.O.
24. John Leland, *Itinerary*, quoted in H. C. Darby ed., *Historical Geography of England before 1800* (1936), p. 346.

25. W. Burton, *Description of Leicestershire* (1622), p. 2.
26. 27 Henry VIII *c.* 22.
27. *E.g.* E 368/319 Mich. 25 m. 85: *iuxta naturam soli et cursum iconomie.*
28. S.P. 16/206/69; the lost Hetton was on "good corne soyle" in Northumberland: *N.C.H.*, xiv, p. 229.
29. L. D. Stamp, *The Land of Britain, its use and misuse* (1948), p. 67.
30. The memorial tablet in West Heslerton church is quoted in S. E. J. Best, *East Yorkshire* (1930), c. 4: "witness the country around Sledmere transformed from an open, sandy, barren, extensive sheepwalk [of] several thousand acres into well-cultivated farms".
31. *E.J.*, lxi (1951), p. 864. Compare *Hoskins*, p. 106, where the plague factor is minimised.
32. In four adjacent West Riding villages, for example, the 1379 figures were respectively 18%, 7%, 0% and 25% less than the 1377 figures.
33. 1332: E 179/206/47; 1334: E 179/206/75.
34. *R.P.*, ii, p. 184.
35. *Cal. Inq. Misc.*, iii, no. 75.
36. If the 1334 and 1377 figures were inter-comparable (which we cannot certainly assume) the lost villages were losing some ground between these two years. This was most marked in Lindsey, W.R., and least in Northants.
37. *The Lost Villages of Norfolk*, unpublished dissertation, Dept. of Geography, University of Leeds, 1952.
38. The average tax quota in 1334 of Westmorland villages was 25*s.*; for four Hundreds in Devon it was 20*s.*; for Carhampton Hundred in Somerset, 26*s.*; in North Lancashire it was 23*s.* These sums may be compared with Warwickshire's 54*s.*, and the 96*s.* and 98*s.* from Huntingdonshire (excluding its fens) and Northamptonshire. (Figures calculated from E 164/7.)

Chapter Eight: THE FINAL JOURNEY

(No footnotes)

Chapter Nine: THE SEARCH FOR THE LOST VILLAGE

1. *Cartulary of St. Frideswide's* (O.H.S., 1896), p. 195.
2. *Surt. Soc.*, xlix (1866), ed. R. H. Skaife.
3. *F.A.*, i–v.
4. *Discourse*, p. lxiii.
5. *R.H.*, ii, p. 350; p. 778; p. 812. The Warws. Rolls are E 164/15; for some relevant figures given me by Dr. Hilton see *Beresford, Warws.*, pp. 105–6.
6. This account up to 1334 is based on *Willard*; and after 1334 on *Willard and Johnson*. I have also drawn upon my own examination of the collector's accounts in E 179.
7. E 179/211/7a.
8. E 179/206/3.
9. E 179/211/2.
10. *Willard and Johnson*: Introduction to Part B.

11. E 179/211/32.
12. E 179/192/24.
13. *F.A.*, i, p. iii, has an account of the 1428 tax.
14. *Ibid.*, i, p. 193.
15. *R.H.*, ii, p. 559; E 179/242/76; 242/6; 81/65.
16. For details see Chapter Ten.
17. The excision of the East Lilling page from Ingram's copy of the Survey may have been due to such a fear during the revival of anti-enclosure prosecutions in the 1630s.
18. S.C. 11/569.
19. *Ibid.*
20. S.C. 11/567; see also the extent of 1262: C 132/29/2 m. 12.
21. 1323: E 142/32; 1517: *D.I.*, p. 164.
22. S.C. 12/13/29.
23. 1367: C 135/198/12; 1436: C 139/80/22; 1457: C 139/168/26; see also C 143/149/7 for a mill-pond in 1321.
24. C 135/47/16; C 135/98/5; *Y.A.S.*, *R.S.* xxiii, p. 160.
25. E 179/202/60. CPE. UK. 1748/2149.
26. E 315/408, f. 78*d*.
27. *D.I.*, p. 340.
28. LR 2/210, f. 40.
29. *VCH.*, *Bucks*, iii, p. 337.
30. S.P. 12/51/5.
31. LR 2/160 f. 40.
32. *Yorkshire Deeds* (*Y.A.S.*, *R.S.*), i, p. 58; iii, p. 150; ix, p. 54. The rental of 1569 is E 164/38, f. 26. The 1446 tax is E 179/211/87.
33. B.M. Eg. Roll 2108.
34. B.M. Cot. Vit. C. 6., ff. 201–35.
35. S.C. 6/1087/11. Rentals, Cartwright Hall, Bradford.
36. Leadam, *T.R.H.S.*, n.s., vii (1893).
37. Bodl. MS. Rawl. B. 450, f. 200; E 179/211/28; 87.
38. L.A.C.: Ancaster Deeds IIa/2/2.
39. The following paragraphs are based on detail from *Boarstall Cartulary*, ed. H. E. Salter (O.H.S. lxxxviii, 1930). This editor's feeling for local topography led him to the identification of a number of Oxfordshire lost villages in the course of his life-time of work for the O.H.S.
40. Star Chamber cases: *Y.A.S.*, *R.S.*, xli, pp. 15 and 166; the poll tax of 1377 is E 179/206/39, and the names from 1379 are in E 179/206/49 m. 53*d*; the 1332 tax list is E 179/206/47; the 1306 extent in *Y.A.S.*, *R.S.*, xliv, p. 123; cartulary: Rylands Library MS. 251.
41. *Supra*, p. 99.
42. Details of institutions and amalgamations are taken from *Foster*, supplemented by search in the Registers (*e.g.* Fordington, Reg. XIX, f. 26; Beesby and Hawerdby, *ibid.*; Maidenwell, f. 159).
43. *Lincs. Notes and Queries*, ix, p. 233 (1906).
44. W. M. Palmer *History of Clopton* (reprinted from *P.C.A.S.*, xxxiii (1933)).
45. *L.R.S.*, xxxiii (1939), p. 44.
46. *D.I.*, p. 171.
47. Leadam, *T.R.H.S.*, n.s., vii (1893), pp. 163, 168, 212.
48. *L.R.S.*, xxiii (1926), pp. 225 ff.

49. *Tax. Ecc.*, pp. 297; 320. The *Valor* is generally too late to report depopulation. A church like Hodnell, Warws., which was already in ruins at that date might be silently entered if the living was being enjoyed. Thorpe le Glebe (*Val. Ecc.*, v, p. 166) has a unique entry, recording a depopulation: *fuit quondam villa, sed modo convertitur in pasturam animalium . . . et rector habet diversas clausuras in recompensacionem glebae suae.* For Norfolk there are the inventories of church goods taken in 1368, another useful guide to the state of the fabric (*Norf. Rec. Soc.*, xix, (1947–8)).
50. *Tax. Ecc.*, *loc. cit.* Institutions can be traced in episcopal registers, but as we saw at Argam and Stretton could be continued long after a depopulation, so that taken by themselves institutions are not a source for dating depopulation.
51. *Non. Inq.*, p. 1.
52. *Ibid.*, p. 340; Rokeby and Mortham (N.R.) show the effect of the Scots raids: *ibid.*, p. 233; Farforth, Lincs., was not taxed *propter debilitatem*: *ibid.*, p. 261; from the unpublished inquisition from Argam (E.R.) we find that there were still parishioners to muster a jury: E 179/202/41 m. 127; at Eversholt, Beds., 140 acres had gone over to grass and many houses ruined and their site turned to pasture, but the village has recovered: *Non. Inq.*, p. 12. There are many accounts of land being waste or agriculture decayed, but they are usually in terms of a bad winter or the recent murrain, and not, as above, in general terms. For Lincs. lost villages not yet impoverished, see unprinted *Non. Inq.* in E 179/135/29.
53. St. Ch. 8/285/18.
54. See n. 47.
55. C 1/445/51.
56. Requests 2/8/339; *D.I.*, p. 410.
57. *Hoskins*, p. 88; C 1/356/70.
58. C 1/536/15.
59. C 47/7/2/3 mm. 7; 32.
60. C 47/7/2.
61. C 43/28.
62. Hall, *op. cit.*, p. 187 (from C 43/28/6 mm. 22–23).
63. *E.g.* K.B. 27/1035 Eas. mm. 16; 16*d*; 17; 18; K.B. 27/1037 Mich. mm. 19; 25.
64. E 164/10/7.
65. 1517: *D.I.*, p. 197; C 43/28/3 m. 55; for 1540 hearings: E 368/314 Mich. m. 40.
66. Terrier, 1601: Bodl. MS. O.A.P. Bucks.; 1625: L.A.C. "terriers".
67. B. Stapleton, *Three Oxfordshire Parishes* (O.H.S., xxiv (1893)), pp. 61; 105; *Cartulary of Oseney Abbey*, ed. H. E. Salter (O.H.S., ci), pp. 196–98; 230; 261.
68. W. Kennett, *Parochial Antiquities* (1818), p. 224. The Prior was sole lord from 1272; see also p. 295.
69. Palmer, *op. cit.*, quoting C 1/446/22.
70. D.R.O. (Y.), R.As. 26.
71. *Y.A.S.*, *R.S.*, xxxvii p. 64; lix, p. 17. In 1377 there were 69 poll tax payers: E 179/202/59.
72. *Beresford, Warwickshire*, p. 64.
73. N.R. Sessions Book, I, f. 73*b*.

74. Arras: C 1/925/30; C 2/5/33; photograph: S 541/1819/3015–5; 4015; also CPE. UK. 1748/6197; Skaife, *Surt. Soc.*, xlix (1866), p. 80.
75. Skaife, *op. cit.*, pp. 80; 241.
76. I am indebted to the Hon. Geoffrey Howard for permission to see the maps, surveys and estate papers at Castle Howard.
77. S.C. 12/22/41.
78. Y.A.S. MS. 282, f. 107*d* is Dodsworth's note on the prebendal estate; another virtually identical note by Torre in York, Dean and Chapter MS. 34, which I saw by the kindness of Canon Harrison; the text of a late thirteenth-century survey of the manor is printed in *Y.A.S., R.S.*, xciv, p. 26, but Mr. Bishop wrongly identified it as Holme on the Wolds.
79. Cestersover: *VCH., Warws.*, vi, p. 177; Rowley: *Y.A.S., R.S.*, xlix, p. 122; *T.E.R.A.S.*, xxv, p. 91; Cleaving: Selden Society, *Rolls of the Justices in Eyre, 1218–19* (lvi (1937)), case 317; Gainsthorpe: *L.R.S.*, xxii, p. 122 (Lincoln Assize Roll, 1202); Weedley; *Records of the Templars in England*, ed. B.A. Lees (1935), p. 131: *apud Withele Nicholavus filius predicti tenet molendinum venti pro viii solidis pro omni servicio* (1185); Compton Verney: E 212/RS 382.

Chapter Ten: LOST VILLAGES, COUNTY LISTS

(No footnotes)

Index One

COUNTY INDEX TO LOST VILLAGE SITES mentioned in the text. The annotated gazetteer in Chapter Ten is self-indexed by counties.

28

NOTTINGHAMSHIRE

OXFORDSHIRE

RUTLAND

SOMERSET

SUFFOLK

SUSSEX

WARWICKSHIRE

WILTSHIRE

YORKSHIRE, WEST RIDING

YORKSHIRE, NORTH RIDING

YORKSHIRE, EAST RIDING

IRELAND

SCOTLAND

WALES

Index Two

GENERAL INDEX